THE ANCIENT MAYA

THE YOUNG CORN GOD, COPAN, HONDURAS

THE ANCIENT MAYA

SYLVANUS GRISWOLD MORLEY

Revised by GEORGE W. BRAINERD

THIRD EDITION

STANFORD UNIVERSITY PRESS

STANFORD, CALIFORNIA

Stanford University Press
Stanford, California
Copyright © 1946, 1947, 1956 by the Board of Trustees
of the Leland Stanford Junior University
Printed in the United States of America
First published 1946
Second edition 1947
Third edition 1956
Last figure below indicates year of this printing:
78 77 76 75 74 73 72 71 70 69

PUBLISHER'S NOTE

Since the second edition of *The Ancient Maya* was published in 1947, much new material has come to light. To preserve the late Dr. Morley's signal contributions and, at the same time, to serve the present-day reader's needs, it was found necessary to revise the work and to take into account such recent discoveries as the wall paintings at Bonampak and the Palenque tomb. Late in 1954 Dr. George W. Brainerd, Associate Professor of Anthropology at the University of California at Los Angeles, began the preparation of a third edition.

Dr. Brainerd rewrote some material entirely; many sections, however, were left intact, and others were abridged in order to permit the addition of new material. He had corrected the galley proofs of the work and was planning to write a new, concluding chapter, "Appraisal of the Maya Civilization," when his work was cut short by his death in February 1956. The final chapter was written by Betty Bell, who had served as editorial assistant to Dr. Brainerd and was well acquainted with his intentions. Mrs. Bell also prepared the Notes, revised the Bibliography, and helped in innumerable other ways to bring the work to its completion.

Professor Norman A. McQuown, of the University of Chicago, gave his time and advice on the presentation of the linguistic material; Dr. Joseph Hester, of the University of California at Los Angeles, contributed his knowledge of Maya population and agricultural methods; Professor Gordon Willey, of Harvard University, made helpful suggestions on the Index: to them we owe our thanks and appreciation. We also wish to thank Giles Healey, for material on and photographs of the Bonampak paintings, and Alberto Ruz, for photographs of the Palenque tomb.

Stanford, California
July 1956

PREFACE TO THE FIRST EDITION

THE STORY of the Maya has been "in the writing" for more than sixteen hundred years; in fact, ever since the early part of the fourth century of the Christian Era, when the ancient Maya themselves began to carve their earliest known records on stone monuments.

This purely Maya contribution to their history covers about twelve centuries (A.D. 320–1541), and while very little of historical detail as we understand it has survived, the Maya hieroglyphic inscriptions, nevertheless, furnish us with a more accurate chronological background than that found anywhere else in aboriginal America.

During the century (1550–1650) following the Spanish conquest, a number of native as well as Spanish writers carry on the story for us. Educated Maya who had been taught by the early Catholic missionaries to write their language in the characters of the Spanish alphabet in order to facilitate their instruction in the Catholic faith set down brief summaries of their own ancient history, probably copied directly from their then still surviving historical manuscripts in the Maya hieroglyphic writing.

In addition to the foregoing native sources, several of the early Franciscan Fathers have left admirable accounts of the Maya as they were in the middle-sixteenth century, by far the most important being the contemporary narrative by Fray Diego de Landa, the second Bishop of Yucatan. His *Relación de las cosas de Yucatán*, written in 1566 and extensively quoted in the following pages, is unquestionably our leading authority on the ancient Maya.

During the next two centuries (1650–1840) very little new was added to the Maya story, but in 1839–1841 John Lloyd Stephens, the American traveler, diplomat, and amateur archaeologist, accompanied by Frederick Catherwood, an English artist, visited the Maya area twice and embodied his impressions thereupon in two outstanding works: *Incidents of Travel in Central*

America, Chiapas, and Yucatan (1841) and *Incidents of Travel in Yucatan* (1843). Both were illustrated by Catherwood's superb drawings; today, more than a hundred years later, they still remain the most delightful books ever written about the Maya area.

Stephens' writings were chiefly responsible for bringing the great cities of the Maya civilization to the attention of the outside world. Before the publication of his two books, the very existence of these cities was unknown outside of Yucatan and northern Central America, but, after their appearance, knowledge of the Maya, who developed our greatest native American civilization, became general on both sides of the Atlantic. With Stephens also begins the period of the modern exploration of this region.

Since Stephens' time many scientific institutions as well as individual students have been engaged in piecing together different parts of the Maya picture-puzzle. To mention all would expand this preface beyond reasonable limits, but the three most important should be noted: (1) the English archaeologist, Sir Alfred P. Maudslay, the results of whose fifteen years of exploration in the Maya region (1881-1894) were published in the magnificent section on Archaeology of the *Biologia Centrali-Americana*, the first scientific publication about the Maya civilization; (2) the Peabody Museum of Archaeology and Ethnology of Harvard University, which, between 1888 and 1915, sent many expeditions to the Maya area under able leaders who have made many important contributions to our knowledge of the ancient Maya; (3) the Carnegie Institution of Washington, which has been carrying on intensive studies in the Maya field for the past three decades. No fewer than twenty-five annual expeditions under trained archaeologists have been sent to different parts of the Maya area and a vast amount of new material in many fields—archaeology, ethnology, anthropometry, history, linguistics, agriculture, botany, zoology, geography, medicine, and epidemiology—has been obtained.

It will be seen from the foregoing that many different cooks have had a hand in brewing the Maya broth as we have it today, but especially I wish to express here my deep gratitude to my colleagues in the Division of Historical Research of the Carnegie

Institution of Washington, without whose untiring and unselfish studies in many phases of the Maya problem, often carried on under most trying, even perilous, conditions, this book could not have been written.

The Maya story as related here may be divided thus:

1. A description of the region where the Maya lived, the several branches into which they were divided, and their physical and psychological characteristics . . .*

2. Maya history—the origin of their civilization, its rise, first florescence, and first decline . . .

3. Ancient and modern Maya manners and customs—agriculture, government, social organization, life of the common people, religion, deities, hieroglyphic writing, arithmetic, chronology, astronomy, cities, architecture, sculpture, modeling, ceramics, textiles, basketry, matting, painting, lapidary art, mosaics, feather and metalwork, and flint chipping . . .

4. An appraisal of the Maya civilization and its comparison with other aboriginal American cultures . . .

Finally, if we are to grasp the real significance of the Maya story, and its essential meaning, we must realize that primarily it was one of the world's most notable experiments in agriculture; in a word, that it was based exclusively upon and conditioned by the cultivation of maize, or Indian corn, than which nothing was of greater importance in ancient Maya life, nor indeed still is even today.

SYLVANUS GRISWOLD MORLEY

HACIENDA CHENKU
MÉRIDA, YUCATAN, MEXICO
June 7, 1946

* The omitted material, of page references and dates, is not relevant to the present edition.

TABLE OF CONTENTS

I. THE COUNTRY 3
II. THE PEOPLE 17
III. THE ORIGIN OF THE MAYA CIVILIZATION . . . 40
IV. THE CLASSIC STAGE 57
V. THE POSTCLASSIC STAGE 79
VI. THE SPANISH CONQUEST OF YUCATAN . . . 100
VII. THE SPANISH CONQUEST OF PETEN 114
VIII. AGRICULTURE 128
IX. GOVERNMENT AND SOCIAL ORGANIZATION . . . 143
X. LIFE OF THE COMMON PEOPLE 163
XI. RELIGION AND DEITIES 183
XII. HIEROGLYPHIC WRITING, ARITHMETIC,
AND ASTRONOMY 227
XIII. ARCHITECTURE 261
XIV. SCULPTURE AND MODELING 330
XV. CERAMICS 367
XVI. MISCELLANEOUS ARTS AND CRAFTS 380
XVII. AN APPRAISAL OF THE MAYA CIVILIZATION,
by Betty Bell 424
APPENDIX: Correlation of Maya and Christian
Chronologies 443
NOTES, by Betty Bell 449
BIBLIOGRAPHY 467
INDEX 483
LIST OF TABLES 495
LIST OF FIGURES 496
LIST OF PLATES 499

ACKNOWLEDGMENT OF SOURCES
OF PHOTOGRAPHS

Plates: 2, (a) Bertha P. Dutton, (b) R. Eichenberger; 3, CIW; 4, (a) C. Longworth Lundell, (b) unknown; 5, (a) CIW, (b) Richard A. Hedlund; 6, (a) Enrique Palma Losa, (b) EC; 8–9, GH; 10–11, FRM; 12, (a) FRM, (b, c) BR; 13, BR; 14, (a) U.S. National Museum, (b) CIW, (c) National Geographic Society; 15–17, CIW; 18, (a) CIW, (b) PM, (c) MUP; 20, GH; 21, TU; 22, PM; 23–24, CIW; 26, (a, b) Alberto Galindo, (c, d) CIW; 27, S. Greco; 30, (a) CIW, (b) GH; 31, SD; 33, (a) Museum für Völkerkunde, Basle, (b) MN; 35, CIW; 36, PM; 37, (a) Bob Edgerton, (b) MUP; 38, MUP and Fairchild Aerial Surveys; 40, (a) CIW, (b) FG; 41, (a) FG, (b) EC; 42, (a) CIW, (b) EC; 43, CIW; 44, (a) FG, (b) IN; 45, SD; 46, (a) FRM, (b) FG; 47–48, CIW; 51, CIW; 52, (a) T. Proskouriakoff, (b) Buffalo Museum of Science; 53, PM; 54, (a) MN, (b) CIW, (c) MUP; 55, CIW; 56–57, EC; 58, CIW; 59, (a) CIW, (b) PM; 60, (a, b) Daniel F. Wagner, (c) FRM; 61, (a) IN, (b) EC; 62, CIW; 63, (a, d) PM, (b, c) CIW; 66, (a, c, d) MUP, (b) MN; 67, (a, b, c) CIW, (d) BCA; 68, CIW; 69, MUP; 70, (a) MUP, (b) AM; 71, BCA; 72, School of American Research, Santa Fe; 73 (a, e) IN, (b, c) EC, (d, f) FG; 74, (a, b) CIW, (c, d) IN; 75, (a, b) CIW, (c, d) MC; 76, CIW; 77, BCA; 78, TU; 79, PM; 8ᴄ, CIW; 81, (a, b) CIW, (c, d) PM; 82, MC; 83–84, CIW; 85, (a) PM, (b) CIW; 86, PM; 87–90, GH; 95, (a) Stanley Stubbs, (b) CIW, (c, d) TU, (e, f) PM; 96, (a) Secretaría de Agricultura y Fomento, Mexico, (b, c) CIW; 97, (a) EC, (b, c) MM; 98–100, ARL; 101, (a, b) MN, (c) PM; 102, CIW.

Key: ARL, Alberto Ruz Lhuillier; AM, American Museum of Natural History, New York; BCA, *Biologia Centrali-Americana*; BR, Bernardo Reyes; CIW, Carnegie Institution of Washington, Washington, D.C.; EC, Estudio Cámara, Mérida; FG, Fotografía Guerra, Mérida; FRM, Frances Rhoads Morley; GH, Giles Healey; IN, Instituto Nacional de Antropología e Historia, Mexico, D.F.; MC, Museo Arqueológico, Etnográfico e Histórico, Campeche; MM, Museo de Arqueología e Historia, Mérida; MN, Museo Nacional de Antropología e Historia, Mexico, D.F.; MUP, Museum of the University of Pennsylvania, Philadelphia; PM, Peabody Museum of Archaeology and Ethnology, Harvard University, Cambridge; SD, San Diego Museum; TU, Middle American Research Institute, Tulane University, New Orleans.

THE ANCIENT MAYA

"If one looks closely he will find that everything [these Indians] did and talked about had to do with maize; in truth, they fell little short of making a god of it. And so much is the delight and gratification they got and still get out of their corn fields, that because of them they forget wife and children and every other pleasure, as if their corn fields were their final goal and ultimate happiness."— CHRONICA DE LA SANTA PROVINCIA DEL SANTISSIMO NOMBRE DE JESUS DE GUATTE- MALA, Cap. VII (XVIth century MS).

THE COUNTRY

LOCATION

PROJECTING NORTHWARD into the Gulf of Mexico lies the Peninsula of Yucatan, where, during the fourth to sixteenth centuries of the Christian Era, flourished the most brilliant civilization of the New World. This area, humid and tropical for the most part, presents a contrast to the climates where our civilization centers. The sparse and backward modern population of the Yucatan Peninsula underscores the changes which have taken place since this area was in the cultural vanguard of the Americas.

The region in which the Maya civilization developed includes the present states of Yucatan, Campeche, Tabasco, the eastern half of Chiapas and the territory of Quintana Roo, in the Republic of Mexico; the Department of Peten and the adjacent highlands to the south in Guatemala; the western section of the Republic of Honduras and all of British Honduras—a total of some 125,000 square miles. This is an area roughly equal to the six New England states, New York, New Jersey, and a quarter of Pennsylvania combined, or to the State of New Mexico.

THREE NATURAL SUBDIVISIONS

This region (Plate 1) divides naturally into three general sections, the second and third merging without a clear-cut line of demarcation. These sections are: (1) the southern Maya area: the mountain ranges and intermediate plateaus—the Cordillera of Central America—which border the region to the south; (2) the central area: the interior drainage basin of the Department of Peten, Guatemala, and its adjacent exterior valleys, which together comprise the southern half of the Yucatan Peninsula; and (3) the northern area: the low limestone plain which is the northern half

3

of the peninsula. The distinctive physiographic characteristics of these regions limited, and perhaps even to a degree directed, the course of Maya culture, and should be studied for its understanding.

THE HIGHLANDS OF GUATEMALA, WESTERN HONDURAS, AND EASTERN CHIAPAS, MEXICO

Somewhere in the highland region, probably in western Guatemala, during the third or second millennium before Christ, was developed the agricultural system upon which the Maya civilization depended. This region is a high plateau with mountain ranges of volcanic origin separating the upland valleys, the highest peaks reaching elevations of more than 13,000 feet. Two principal river systems drain this region: (1) the Motagua River, rising in the Department of El Quiché, Guatemala, flowing progressively east, northeast, and north, empties into the Gulf of Honduras on the Caribbean coast; (2) the Usumacinta River (Plate 3a), which is composed of three tributaries—the Pasión, the Salinas or Chixoy, and the Lacantun—forms the western boundary of the Department of Peten and empties into the Gulf of Mexico through several channels. The Usumacinta River with its tributaries was the principal water highway of the central Maya area.

Human settlements in the Guatemala highlands are concentrated in valleys at an altitude of 4,000 feet and more. The winters are dry and cool to cold, ice forming in the higher mountains. The summers are cooler than in the Peten and Yucatan lowlands to the north, and the rainy season—May through November—is somewhat shorter than in the Department of Peten. The upland plateaus and valleys are not so heavily forested as the lowlands. There are open grasslands in the valleys, while a variety of evergreens and some deciduous trees clothe the mountain slopes. True forests disappear at about 10,000 feet, though massive conifers and other trees grow at still higher levels. The land is not cultivated above 10,000 feet, but on the upper slopes there are grassy areas now used for grazing.

There are two large lakes in the highlands, Lake Amatitlan in

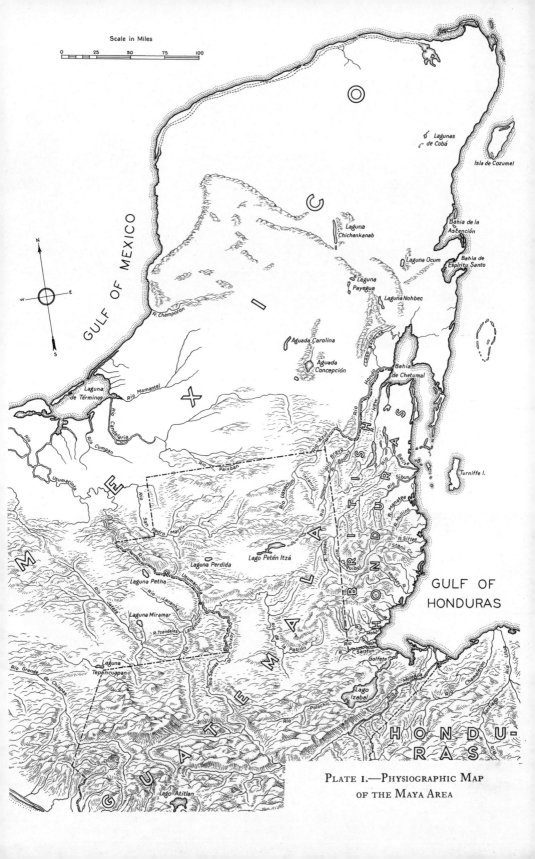

PLATE I.—PHYSIOGRAPHIC MAP
OF THE MAYA AREA

↑ *a*) Cuchumatanes Mountains, Guatemala.

PLATE 2.—VIEWS OF THE SOUTHERN HIGHLANDS

↓ *b*) Volcán de Agua, Guatemala, with Antigua in the foreground.

the Department of Guatemala, and Lake Atitlan in the Department of Solola. The latter, surrounded by sharply rising mountains of volcanic origin, is one of the most spectacular lakes in the New World. Near the eastern end of the mountain chain is Lake Izabal, 30 miles long and 12 miles wide, which is connected with the Gulf of Honduras by the *golfete* and the Rio Dulce (Plate 1). The latter enters the Gulf of Honduras at the modern town of Livingston, Guatemala.

Although the fauna of the highlands is by no means as abundant as that of the Peten and northern Yucatan, jaguars, pumas, deer, and small mammals are numerous. The gorgeous quetzal, the national bird of the Republic of Guatemala, is almost exclusively confined to the highlands of Guatemala and Honduras and the adjacent mountains of Chiapas, though found to a lesser extent as far south as Panama.

Somewhere in the upland valleys of western Guatemala, Indian corn or maize, the great food staple of ancient America, may have originated, perhaps sometime during the third millennium before Christ.

THE LOWLANDS OF PETEN AND THE SURROUNDING VALLEYS

The interior drainage basin of central Peten and its surrounding valleys form the second main division of the Maya area. The average elevation of the central Peten savanna is about 500 feet above sea level, while the generally east-and-west-running ranges of hills enclosing the interior drainage basin rise perhaps another 500 feet. This basin is about 60 miles long east and west, though never more than 20 miles wide. At the base of the range of hills forming the northern side of the drainage basin is a chain of thirteen or fourteen lakes, several of which are connected in the rainy season. The largest of these is Lake Peten Itza, the ancient name of which was Chaltuna (Plate 4*b*), located about midway of the basin east and west; this lake is 20 miles long by 3 miles wide.

South of the range of hills on the southern side of the basin lies the great irregularly shaped savanna of central Peten. Few trees grow on this grassy plain (Plate 4*a*). The soil is a close, red

↑ *a*) Usumacinta River near Yaxchilan, Chiapas.

PLATE 3.—VIEWS
OF THE SOUTHERN
LOWLANDS

b) Rain forest from the Acropolis
at Uaxactun, Guatemala.   →

clay, not suited to the cultivation of maize. This fact, coupled with the almost complete absence of the remains of human habitation, indicates that the savannas were largely unoccupied in ancient times.

The few streams rising in the central savanna find their way south and west into the Pasión River. East of this central Peten savanna, in extreme southeastern Peten and southern British Honduras, rise the jagged Maya Mountains of relatively recent origin, the highest point of which, Cockscomb Peak, has an elevation of 3,700 feet. The narrow coast plain east of the Maya Mountains is watered by a number of short streams which flow into the Caribbean Sea. The largest, the Sarstún River, forms part of the present boundary between British Honduras and Guatemala.

In the low ranges to the northwest, north, and northeast of the interior drainage basin, six rivers of medium size have their origin; the first three, the San Pedro Mártir, the Candelaria, and the Mamantel, flowing generally west and north, empty into the Gulf of Mexico on the west side of the Yucatan Peninsula. The remaining three, the Hondo, the New, and the Belize or Old River, flow generally northeast and empty into the Caribbean Sea on the east side of the peninsula.

The ranges of hills north of the central basin and the valleys between bear generally east and west; the southern slopes of the hills are sharp, the northern slopes dropping almost imperceptibly from each crest to the next watercourse. Both hills and valleys are covered with a dense tropical forest (Plate 3b) in which grow mahogany, sapodilla, rubber, mamey, Spanish cedar, ceiba or *yaxche*, the *copó* or wild fig, breadnut, aguacate, allspice, cohune palm, *escoba* palm, and many others. The forest averages from 125 to 150 feet in height (Plate 5a), but the undergrowth, except in the occasional swamps (Maya *akalche*) which dot the valley floors, remains relatively sparse, owing to the dense shade afforded by the higher trees.

It was in the valleys and on the northern slopes of the ridges—in fact, wherever there was high forest—that the ancient Maya built their ceremonial centers.

↑ *a*) Central savanna, Guatemala.

PLATE 4.—VIEWS OF THE SOUTHERN LOWLANDS

↓ *b*) Lake Peten Itza and the island town of Flores, Guatemala.

In addition to Indian corn, other vegetables, fruits, and edible plants were cultivated: black and red beans, two kinds of squash, *chayote*, tomatoes, breadnut, cacao, and a variety of tubers—sweet potato, *jicama*, cassava, and several kinds of yams. Other economic plants raised were chili pepper, vanilla, and allspice for flavoring; and cotton, tobacco, fibers, and gourds. The forest itself yielded many useful materials—poles and withes for the framework of the houses, palm leaf for the thatching of roofs, resin of the copal tree (Maya *pom*) for incense in religious ceremonies.

Animal life is much more abundant in this region than in the highlands to the south. The forests of Peten teem with jaguar, deer, brocket, peccary, tapir, monkeys, and smaller mammals such as armadillos, vampire bats, and agoutis. There are parrots, macaws, toucans, herons, hummingbirds; many game birds—partridges, quail, curassows, *cojolites*, doves, and the famous ocellated turkey, found only in Yucatan; vultures, hawks, and eagles. There are many reptiles, both poisonous and nonpoisonous: the python, the tropical rattler, the fer-de-lance or *nahuyaca*, the tropical moccasin and other equally deadly pit vipers, the coral snake, and crocodiles.

Most abundant of all is the insect life: ants of all kinds, termites, hornets, the stingless bee (which makes the wild honey of the Yucatan Peninsula), butterflies, gnats, bloodsuckers, fleas, flies of all kinds and sizes, ticks, chiggers, and numerous other pests. At night there are hordes of mosquitoes and countless enormous fireflies.

The climate of Peten is warmer than that of the southern highlands, and more humid than that of northern Yucatan. The rainy season is longer, extending from May through January, and showers are not infrequent during the so-called dry months of February, March, April, and May. The rainfall is high, increasing from about 70 inches in northern Peten to about 150 inches in the south as the Cordillera of Guatemala is approached. Water never freezes, though cold "northers" in the winter frequently drive the temperatures down into the 50's Fahrenheit. The hottest months are April and May, just before the rains break, when the temperatures rise above 100° F.

a) Rain forest, Guatemala. →

PLATE 5
VIEWS OF THE SOUTHERN AND
NORTHERN LOWLANDS

b) Low forest and bush of north-
↓   ern Yucatan.

Although this is today one of the most difficult New World areas in which to live, it must have seemed an ideal environment to the ancient Maya. Extensive areas were available for agriculture. Rich plant and animal resources supplied food, clothing, and medicine in great abundance. The local limestone made a fine building material; not only was it easily quarried with tools of stone and wood (the only ones at the disposal of the ancient Maya builders), but it also hardens on exposure to the elements; on burning, it reduces to lime. Finally, throughout the region there are beds of friable granular limestone, which the Maya used, as we use sand and gravel, in making lime mortar.

The earliest stone architecture and sculptured stone monuments are found at Uaxactun (Plate 19), forty miles north of the eastern end of Lake Peten Itza. Here are found the oldest dates in the Maya hieroglyphic writing, going back to the first quarter of the fourth century after Christ.

From this northern central section of Peten, Maya culture spread during the next two centuries until it had covered the entire peninsula of Yucatan and the adjacent valleys and northern slopes of the Cordillera to the south—the area of the Classic Maya culture, which reached its golden age during the eighth century of the Christian Era.

THE PLAIN OF THE NORTHERN YUCATAN PENINSULA

The high Peten forest changes into the bush of the northern half of the peninsula almost imperceptibly. As one goes from south to north, the trees become lower; the giant mahoganies, sapodillas, Spanish cedars, and ceibas give place to lower trees and a much thicker undergrowth (Plate 5b).

Palmetto grows in abundance along the east coast of the peninsula. Some distance inland there is a long, finger-like extension of the southern rain forest which contains mahogany, Spanish cedar, sapodilla, and other hardwoods. This stand of high forest extends into the northeastern corner of Yucatan.

The northern half of the peninsula is low and flat; the humus is usually not more than a few inches in depth, as contrasted with

↑ *a*) Sierra or low range of hills, northern Yucatan.

PLATE 6.—VIEWS OF THE NORTHERN LOWLANDS

↓ *b*) *Cenote* or natural cavern, Valladolid, northern Yucatan.

the Peten soil, which is two to three feet deep. There are extensive outcroppings of the porous native limestone (Tertiary and Recent), and owing to the immediate underground drainage of rainfall there are almost no surface streams.

A low range, not exceeding 300 feet in height, begins at Champoton on the west coast of the peninsula, runs as far north as the city of Campeche, turns northeast to the town of Maxcanu and then extends southeastward to beyond Tzuccacab in central northern Yucatan (Plate 1). These hills are known locally as the *serrania* or *puuc* (Plate 6*a*).

Only a few lakes and rivers are found, the latter little more than creeks. The largest body of water in the northern half of the peninsula is Lake Bacalar in southeastern Quintana Roo, which is 35 miles long and only 6 or 7 miles wide. There are several smaller lakes and three small rivers which are little more than shallow arms of the sea.

There are two large bays on the east coast—Ascension and Espíritu Santo—both relatively shallow. As one approaches the Guatemala border in southern Campeche and Quintana Roo, swamps become more frequent, but these are usually dry in the spring months. The ranges of east- and west-running hills grow progressively higher toward the south, until elevations of 1,000 feet or more are reached in northern Peten.

The northern half of the peninsula is unusually dry, owing to low rainfall and the extensive underground drainage. The only surface water, barring the few lakes and small brackish streams near the coast, is that afforded by the *cenotes*, or large natural wells. Fortunately they are fairly numerous, especially in the extreme north. The cenotes are natural formations, places where the surface limestone has collapsed and exposed the subterranean water table. Some of these natural wells are 200 feet or more in diameter. Their depth varies according to the level of the water table where they are located (Plate 6*b*). Near the north coast this subterranean water table is less than 15 feet below the ground level, but as one proceeds southward the depth of the cenotes increases to more than 100 feet.

In a country as devoid of surface water as northern Yucatan, cenotes were the principal factor in determining the location of the ancient centers of population. Where there was a cenote, there a settlement grew up. The cenotes were the principal source of water supply in former times, even as they are today. They were the most important single factor governing the distribution of the ancient population in northern Yucatan.

It has been pointed out that the physical characteristics of the southern and northern halves of the Yucatan Peninsula merge imperceptibly. The high rain forest in the south gradually gives way to lower trees and impenetrable thickets in the north. Most of the economic plants characteristic of the southern half of the peninsula are with but few exceptions also found in the north; the same is true of most of the animal life.

The Maya lowland area is unique among the geographic environments in which the great early civilizations of the world developed, but although the Yucatan Peninsula is unsuited to advanced agriculture and to concentrated human settlement, the intellectual heights attained by the Maya priesthood do not seem to have depended upon rich economic support. Perhaps the isolation of the area—off main intercontinental routes of travel, and hemmed by dense bush and swamps—allowed freedom from the competition of aggressive neighbors. The insularity of the area may also have fostered the growth of closely knit traditions of behavior among the Maya, sufficiently at least to allow for the necessary body of common knowledge and belief which must underlie the development of any great philosophical or artistic tradition.

•   •

THE PEOPLE

NUMBER AND DISTRIBUTION OF MAYA-SPEAKING PEOPLES

THE DIFFERENT TRIBES of Maya-speaking Indians number altogether a little less than two million people. Over a million are found in Guatemala alone, but they are also distributed through Honduras and British Honduras, and the Mexican states of Yucatan, Campeche, Chiapas, Tabasco, Veracruz, San Luis Potosí, and Quintana Roo.

The Maya linguistic stock has been likened to the Romance languages of the Old World, which are known to have developed their present-day differences from a common tongue, Latin, within approximately the past two thousand years. In the case of the Maya, however, we have no clear indication of what the original Maya language was. Nor are students of the problem in agreement, either as to the number of families into which the Maya linguistic stock should be divided, or their present distribution.

Among the various theories on Maya linguistics, there is some opinion in favor of an original threefold division: (1) the proto-Guatemala-Yucatan family in the southern highlands (Guatemala) and in the northern lowlands (the northern half of the Yucatan Peninsula); (2) the proto-Chiapas family in the highlands of Chiapas with extensions in Tabasco, Mexico, and across southern Peten, Guatemala, as far as western Honduras; and (3) the Huastecan in the lowlands of northern Veracruz and the adjacent foothills of eastern San Luis Potosí.

This threefold division of the Maya-speaking peoples and their present distribution is shown in Table I, which lists the groups of languages composing each family, and the region where each language is spoken. The same information is shown graphically in the linguistic map in Plate 7. The number of Maya-speakers

17

TABLE I

Classification and Distribution of People in the Maya Linguistic Stock

Family	Group	Language	Country	Province
		Yucatec	Mexico	Yucatan, Campeche, Quintana Roo
	Maya proper		British Honduras	Corozal, Orange Walk, El Cayo
			Guatemala	Peten
		Lacandon	Mexico	Chiapas
		Kekchi	Mexico	Chiapas
			Guatemala	Alta Vera Paz, Baja Vera Paz, Peten, Izabal, Zacapa
	Kekchian		British Honduras	Toledo
		Pokonchi	Guatemala	Alta Vera Paz, Baja Vera Paz
		Pokomam	Guatemala	Guatemala, Jalapa, Chiquimula
		Rabinal	Guatemala	Baja Vera Paz
		Uspantec	Guatemala	El Quiché
Proto-Guatemala-Yucatan		Quiche	Guatemala	Huehuetenango, Chimaltenango, Quetzaltenango, Totonicapan, El Quiché, Baja Vera Paz, Retalhuleu, Suchitepéquez, Sololá, Escuintla
	Quichean	Cakchiquel	Guatemala	Chimaltenango, El Quiché, Guatemala, Sololá, Escuintla, Sacatepéquez
		Tzutuhil	Guatemala	Sololá
	Motozintlec		Mexico	Chiapas
		Mam	Mexico	Chiapas
			Guatemala	Huehuetenango, Quetzaltenango, San Marcos
	Mamean	Aguacatec	Guatemala	Huehuetenango
		Ixil	Guatemala	Huehuetenango, El Quiché
		Jacaltec	Guatemala	Huehuetenango
		Kanhobol	Guatemala	Huehuetenango
		Solomec	Guatemala	Huehuetenango
	Chuh		Guatemala	Huehuetenango
Proto-Chiapas-Tabasco	Tzeltalan	Tzeltal	Mexico	Chiapas
		Tzotzil	Mexico	Chiapas
		Toholabal	Mexico	Chiapas
	Cholan	Chontal	Mexico	Tabasco, Chiapas
		Chol	Mexico	Chiapas
		Chorti	Guatemala	Chiquimula
			Honduras	Copan
Huastecan	Huastec	Veracruzano	Mexico	Veracruz
		Potosino	Mexico	San Luis Potosí, Tamaulipas

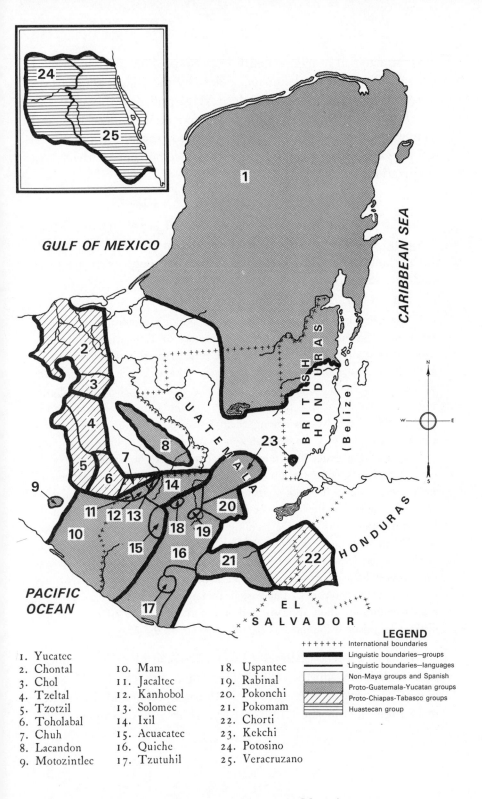

GULF OF MEXICO

CARIBBEAN SEA

PACIFIC OCEAN

1. Yucatec
2. Chontal
3. Chol
4. Tzeltal
5. Tzotzil
6. Toholabal
7. Chuh
8. Lacandon
9. Motozintlec
10. Mam
11. Jacaltec
12. Kanhobol
13. Solomec
14. Ixil
15. Acuacatec
16. Quiche
17. Tzutuhil
18. Uspantec
19. Rabinal
20. Pokonchi
21. Pokomam
22. Chorti
23. Kekchi
24. Potosino
25. Veracruzano

LEGEND

+ + + + + + International boundaries
━━━━━━ Linguistic boundaries—groups
─────── Linguistic boundaries—languages
Non-Maya groups and Spanish
Proto-Guatemala-Yucatan groups
Proto-Chiapas-Tabasco groups
Huastecan group

PLATE 7.—LINGUISTIC MAP OF THE MAYA AREA

was estimated at nearly two million in 1940. The map and Table 1 also indicate that the language spoken by the Classic-stage Maya was some progenitor of the modern Maya proper.

Both archaeological and linguistic evidence have been advanced suggesting that the Huasteca had separated from the original mass of Maya-speaking people before the development of the Maya civilization.

NATURE OF THE MAYA LANGUAGE

It is probable that since Classic times (317–889) one Maya language has been spoken from the southern highlands northward throughout the entire Yucatan Peninsula, although there are local dialectic variations.

Says A. M. Tozzer in this connection:

The geographical unity of the Maya speaking peoples is remarkable when one takes into consideration the colonies of Nahuatl speaking peoples scattered along the Pacific coast of Central America even as far south as the Isthmus of Panama. The Mayas seem to have been content to remain very much in one place and it is evident that it was not their general custom to send out colonies to distant parts of the country. Moreover the wandering of the Mayas among themselves in the comparatively small territory occupied by them is not shown by investigation to have been great.

Most of the dialects of the Maya seem to have been identified with certain localities from the time of the earliest Spanish records down to the present. There does not seem to have been that shifting of population which one might naturally expect. The geographical conditions may have had something to do with the seeming lack of mingling of the people of one dialect with those of another. The peninsula of Yucatan is comparatively isolated from the rest of the Maya territory and the dialect spoken there is very little changed as far as can be made out from the earliest times of which we have records. The various mountain ranges in the south often render communication difficult and a mountain system often separates distinct linguistic differences as regards dialects of the Maya.

During Postclassic times (889–1540) considerable modification took place in the Maya language, due to the Mexican (Nahuatl-speaking) invaders of northern Yucatan and the Guatemala highlands in the tenth century. These modifications probably influenced the Maya vocabulary more extensively than its syntax and morphology.

Tozzer in describing the Maya language writes:

Maya is a polysynthetic or incorporating language where a pronominal subject of the verb is always expressed. Maya follows, in general, the same methods of expression as those found in the greater number of American languages. From the point of view of lexicography it is distinct from any of the other languages spoken in Mexico or Central America, . . . [and] has no affiliation, as far as can be made out, with any other language of Mexico or Central America. Some authorities claim that the Zapotec is nearer akin to Maya than it is to Nahuatl. Maya [however] is morphologically distinct from the latter.

William Gates, in describing the Maya language, has the following to say:

There are practically no changes of form in its meaningful elements of word development, from the basic neutral roots to their most involved forms of incorporation; the same union of form and value persists from first to last, and the methods of employment are regular and consistent, always recognizable—once the primary classification of the natural major elements has been reached; the natural nouns, adjectives, intransitive and then transitive (effect-producing) words of action, with their needed connecting particles and prepositions. The final language has all the type of "classicity."

Alfredo Barrera Vásquez, a leading authority on the Maya language, states that during the four centuries Maya has been in contact with Spanish in Yucatan, it has strongly influenced not only the Spanish vocabulary in use there but also its lexicography, morphology, phonetics, and syntax. The Spanish spoken in Yucatan has affected the Maya vocabulary chiefly by the addition of words for objects previously unknown among the Maya.

PHYSICAL CHARACTERISTICS OF THE YUCATAN MAYA

In attempting to describe the appearance and physical characteristics of the ancient Maya, we have four lines of evidence upon which to draw: (1) the modern descendants of the ancient Maya, especially in the northern half of the Yucatan Peninsula; (2)

TABLE II

Average Heights, Cephalic Indices, and Some Weights for Males and Females of Certain Maya Tribes, Plains and Pueblo Indians, American Whites, and Negroes

Group	Average Height		Average Weight		Average Cephalic Index	
	Male	Female	Male	Female	Male	Female
Yucatan Maya	5 ft. 0.87 in.	4 ft. 8.16 in.	116.3 lbs.	110 lbs.	85.8	86.8
Chontal	5 ft. 2.88 in.	4 ft. 10.32 in.	—	—	83.2	82.0
Chol	5 ft. 1.32 in.	4 ft. 7.68 in.	—	—	80.8	80.0
Tzental	5 ft. 1.32 in.	4 ft. 8.64 in.	—	—	76.8	75.9
Tzotzil	5 ft. 1.32 in.	4 ft. 8.76 in.	—	—	76.9	76.8
Huasteca	5 ft. 1.80 in.	4 ft. 9.96 in.	—	—	84.4	86.2
Pueblo Indians	5 ft. 4.68 in.	4 ft. 11.40 in.	126.8 lbs.	123.3 lbs.	82.5	82.5
Plains Indians	5 ft. 7.68 in.	5 ft. 2.40 in.	136.2 lbs.	128.2 lbs.	80.8	80.8
American Caucasians, Amherst and Smith Colleges	5 ft. 8.28 in.	5 ft. 3.84 in.	154.1 lbs.	122.3 lbs.	79.3	80.06
American Negroes, Tuskegee Institute	5 ft. 7.20 in.	5 ft. 2.28 in.	154.1 lbs.	122.8 lbs.	77.38	78.32

representations of the ancient Maya, from their pictorial art; (3) a few contemporary descriptions by Spanish writers of the sixteenth century; and (4) a relatively small amount of skeletal material recovered from excavations. Of these sources, the first is the most important. Many of the modern Maya of Yucatan so closely resemble the figures on the monuments and in the paintings that they could have served as models for them (Plates 8, 9, 10, and 11, *a* and *b*).

The Yucatan Maya are fairly short in stature and relatively thick-bodied. They have rather long arms and small hands and feet. The average height of the men is 5 feet 1 inch and of the women, 4 feet 8 inches. They are one of the broadest-headed peoples in the world. Their cephalic index averages 85.8 for Maya men and 86.8 for Maya women, as compared with 79 for American men and 80 for American women.

Among the modern Maya of Yucatan more than 50 per cent of the individuals are entirely free from dental decay in their permanent teeth until after they are twenty, while among white Americans more than half have dental decay in their permanent teeth before they are nine and more than 90 per cent before they are fourteen. The basal metabolism of the modern Maya is from 5 to 8 per cent higher than that of the average American. Their pulse rate is 20 points lower, 52 as compared with our own average pulse rate of 72. Measurements on Maya are given in Table II, with measurements of other groups for comparison.

In color the Maya are copper-brown. The hair is straight, black to dark brown in color, and rather coarse. The Maya are not a hairy people. The men either have no beards and moustaches, or only very sparse ones, while other parts of the body have less hair than in the case of American whites. Beards and moustaches were held in such little esteem by the ancient Maya that mothers burned the faces of their young sons with hot cloths to keep their beards from growing, or plucked out the hairs. However, there is evidence both from the sculptures and the painted pottery of the Classic stage that beards were occasionally worn; it has been suggested that they were confined to the upper classes.

Two other physical characteristics of the modern Maya suggest the northeastern Asiatic origin which they share with other American Indian groups: (1) the epicanthic eye fold, and (2) the Mongolian spot. The epicanthic fold is a fold at the inner corner of the eye which is characteristic of eastern Asiatics; it is also common among the modern Yucatan Maya (Plate 9c). Judging by its frequency in representations of the face in sculptures and paintings, it must also have been a prevalent characteristic in ancient times.

The Mongolian spot is an almost universal physical characteristic of the peoples of eastern Asia, and is also very common among Maya babies of northern Yucatan. It is a small, irregular-shaped spot at the base of the spine, which is present at birth but generally disappears before the tenth year. It is bluish to purple in color, which gradually fades to slate.

Infant mortality is high among the Maya, about 70 per cent of all children born alive dying before they reach the age of five, but their birth rate is correspondingly high. The average birth rate in the United States for 1935 was 16.9 births per thousand, while in Yucatan for the same year three representative Indian villages had an average birth rate of 57.4 per thousand. In a study of the deaths of 605 Indians in northern Yucatan, 68.8 per cent died before they were 5 years old; 7.9 per cent died between 5 and 15; and the average age at death of the remaining 22.3 per cent was only 38½ years. In another Indian village the 1933 census showed that 36 per cent of the population died under 10 years of age, 70 per cent under 25, and 90 per cent before the age of 40.

The people of the native villages of Yucatan present a relatively youthful appearance due to this high adult mortality. Three Indian villages between 1933 and 1937 showed adult death rates of 26.4, 27.5, and 34.2 per thousand, as compared with a death rate in the United States of less than half that number.

Maya girls marry at the average age of 16⅔ years and Maya youths at the average age of 21, though Bishop Diego de Landa says, "In olden times they married when they were twenty years old; but now they marry at twelve or fourteen." The average

a) Man in front of Stela 1, Bonampak. →

PLATE 8
LACANDON MAYA, CHIAPAS

↓ *b*) Man of Petha.

↓ *c*) Girl of El Cedro.

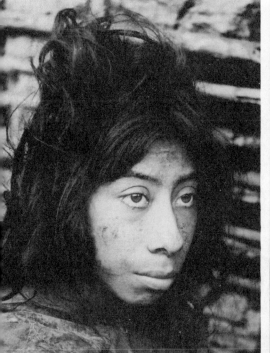

↑ *a*) Delousing a child's hair with cigar smoke.

↑ *b*) Girl holding a peccary she has tamed.

PLATE 9.—LACANDON MAYA, CHIAPAS

↓ *c*) Family of El Cedro at North Laguna.

↑ *a*) Woman.

↑ *b*) Wife of the head chief.

PLATE 10.—YUCATAN MAYA, TIXCACAL GROUP, QUINTANA ROO

↓ *c*) Young girl.

d) Juan Bautista Poot, minor Tixcacal
↓   chief.

↑ *a*) Young boy.

↑ *b*) Young girl.

PLATE 11.—(*a, b*) YUCATAN MAYA, CHICHEN ITZA, AND
(*c, d*) QUICHE MAYA, GUATEMALA

↓ *c*) Man.

↓ *d*) Young man.

a) Yucatan family. →

b) Huasteca, young wife with baby carried
   hetzmek or straddled on hip.

↓ *c*) Huasteco, young husband.

↑ *b*) Young girl, Iztapa.

↓ *d*) Old man, Zinacantan.

↑ *a*) Youth, Chamula.

PLATE 13.—TZOTZIL MAYA, CHIAPAS

↓ *c*) Young man, Chamula.

Maya girl has her first child when she has been married a little over a year and she continues bearing for about 18½ years thereafter, her last child being born when she is about 36½ years old. The average Maya woman bears 8 children, but succeeds in raising fewer than half of them.

Marriage, or at least a fairly durable conjugal relationship, is the practice in modern Indian villages in Yucatan. In one Indian settlement where an eight-year record was kept of the civil status of 70 adult women, only 4 were found to have remained unmarried. In the same village there was not one man over 25 who was not either married or a widower living with a woman.

Although no such close studies of other Maya groups have been made as those undertaken among the Maya of northern Yucatan by Dr. Morris Steggerda, all Maya-speaking groups seem to have sprung from a common ancestral stock.

PSYCHOLOGICAL CHARACTERISTICS OF THE YUCATAN MAYA

The Maya of Yucatan are active, energetic, and hard-working—all on a diet extremely low in proteins. The average Maya's protein intake is only one-sixth of a pound per day. Of everything he eats, 75 to 85 per cent is carbohydrates—maize in one form or another, mostly as tortillas, and to a lesser extent as two beverages called *pozole* and *atole*. The average daily Maya diet contains only 2,565 calories, as compared with our own average caloric intake of 3,500. On this diet the ancient Maya found energy to build the pyramids, temples, and palaces which characterize their great ceremonial centers.

As to cleanliness and neatness, the Maya present a curious contradiction. Their persons and clothing are scrupulously clean, everyone bathing at least once a day and sometimes oftener. When the man of the family returns home from work in the cornfield, his wife has a hot bath ready for him; under Spanish colonial law, failure to do so gave her husband the right to beat her. None of the houses outside the towns has running water or pumps of any kind, and all water has to be carried from the nearest well or cenote, where it is raised by the old-fashioned bucket-and-rope method, sometimes for as much as a hundred feet. Yet the Maya devotion to personal cleanliness is almost fanatical.

Their thatch-roofed, single-roomed houses are far less clean and orderly, although the Maya housewife cleans house daily and even sweeps the dirt street in front of her home. Chickens, turkeys, dogs, goats, and pigs roam the house at will. In the yard, refuse lies about for years, lending an air of untidiness and disorder.

Some foreigners who have visited Yucatan have thought the Maya cruel, especially toward animals. Perhaps they are not so deliberately cruel as they are insensitive to suffering, not only in others but in themselves; they are stoical under pain, and when they see it in others they are correspondingly indifferent. They will let their dogs slowly starve to death, but they would not think of killing them outright.

The Maya are fundamentally conservative. They have even succeeded in preserving their own language in the face of four centuries of Spanish domination, so that today the affairs of everyday life in the smaller towns and villages throughout Yucatan are conducted in the Maya language and not in Spanish.

Maya dress, especially that of the women, has not changed appreciably in hundreds of years. Their pottery, weaving, and cross-stitch embroidery have remained much the same throughout Maya history. In recent years, under the impact of the machine age, Maya conservatism has at last begun to give ground, at least in the matter of mechanical conveniences. The automobile and the bicycle appear in the larger towns, and hand-operated corn grinders are everywhere replacing the old stone metates. Even in the smaller villages, motor-driven mills are now in general use for grinding corn. Radios are beginning to appear, sewing machines and phonographs are common, and there are even a few electric lights in the homes of the well-to-do of the smaller towns. Most villages now have a weekly or semiweekly movie.

They are a happy, sociable people. They love to laugh, joke, and talk; they are good-natured, trusting, unselfish, and have a strong sense of justice. They are courteous and friendly to strangers, bearing out Bishop Landa's estimate of them nearly four hundred years ago:

The Yucatecans are very generous and hospitable; since no one may enter their houses without being offered food and drink, of what they may have had during the day, or in the evening. And if they have none, they seek it from a neighbor; and if they come together on the roads, all join in sharing, even if little remains for themselves.

The Maya of today show little inclination toward leadership and are generally disinclined to assume administrative responsibility. This seems strange in view of the organized activity of ancient times, as indicated by the great ceremonial centers of both the Classic and Postclassic periods. It is probable, however, that when the Maya civilization was at its peak, leadership and administrative functions were confined to the nobility and the priesthood. The common people were essentially a peasant-artisan laboring class, whose industry and toil built the pyramids, temples, and palaces, but always under the direction of the civil and religious authorities. It was upon these groups that the greatest impact of the Spanish Conquest fell. The Spanish stripped the native authorities of effective political power and the Catholic clergy replaced the native priesthood, so that there were few Maya leaders left. And yet one finds an occasional leader among the modern Maya. Don Eustaquio Ceme of Chan Kom, for example, is an Indian leader of outstanding ability. Chan Kom is a little Indian village of only four or five hundred people, and were it not for the personal qualities of Don Eustaquio it would be like scores of other similar Indian villages. But the energy, administrative ability, and civic pride of this one man have made Chan Kom the most progressive community of its size in the state of Yucatan. In ancient times he would have been an outstanding figure, playing his role on a much larger stage.

The modern Maya are pronounced individualists and extremely independent. Children early learn to make their own decisions, and their parents respect their individual rights. In making annual series of anthropometric measurements of Maya children in Yucatan the scientists of the Carnegie Institution found it necessary to seek each child's permission anew each year. Each child was paid the equivalent of ten cents in American money for permitting himself to be measured; but in spite of their poverty, their sense of individual independence demanded that they not grant the request too readily.

Competition is not strongly developed among the modern Maya. Even as children their games are noncompetitive, and as adults they seem to be without desire to excel. They are content to be small corn farmers, raising sufficient food for their families and a little more to trade for the few articles they cannot produce themselves. They work in the hemp plantations for little more than subsistence wages. Some of the more able accumulate a few domestic animals and even rise to the higher status of being small storekeepers in their villages, but not many go beyond this.

The Maya have a strong respect for law and a keen sense of justice. Among the semi-independent native groups of Quintana Roo there is an unusually high reliance placed upon community responsibility. The characteristic punishment among these Indians is the *azote* or bastinado. In the case of a heavy sentence, say of a hundred lashes, the culprit receives twenty-five on each of four consecutive mornings. The sentenced man, however, is not kept in prison between successive lashings; he is allowed at large, but the responsibility of presenting himself for punishment each morning rests solely with him. If he is not present at the appointed time, the whole community regards him as an outlaw; any member may kill him at sight without being punished. It is quite conceivable that this sort of group solidarity may have played a part in the remarkable cultural accomplishments of the Classic Maya.

The Maya are not quarrelsome, but if they have been wronged they harbor resentment. Disputes among the Maya of today are chiefly due to domestic troubles and to damage to crops by livestock. In rare cases a husband may kill his wife's paramour, but often he pardons her or allows her to go off with the other man. Injury to crops by livestock is a more serious matter, and the owner of the animals is obliged to pay for the damage.

As a people the Maya are unusually honest. Petty thieving is almost unknown, and houses are left unlocked most of the time. Rarely does one Indian steal corn from another, in spite of the fact that opportunities to steal are ever present, since the unguarded cornfields are often several miles from the village. One writer says in this connection, "Men who steal from cornfields are killed by the guardian-spirits of the fields and these beliefs are the real locks on the open granaries in the distant bush."

Nor are the Maya given to begging. During the seventeen years the Carnegie Institution carried on archaeological investigations at Chichen Itza, a free medical clinic was maintained for Indians of the surrounding region. Although the Indians came to know that this service was free, after receiving treatment and medicines they invariably offered to pay for them. When payment was refused, the next time they visited Chichen Itza they would bring gifts of food and native embroideries. There was a deep-felt need to repay an obligation.

Foreigners agree that the Maya have a rough sense of humor, practical jokes being considered the most amusing. A boy will strike another an unexpected blow behind the knee, causing him to fall. During the archaeological excavations at Chichen Itza, an absent-minded wheelbarrow boy would find his barrow quickly overloaded by the other Indians. Maya family ties are strong, although among adults outward demonstrations of affection are rare. Affection between man and wife is shown by each carrying out his duties in the home. With their children, however, they are much more demonstrative. Mothers fondle their babies, talk affectionately to them, and rarely punish them physically. Children are trained more by their own desire to conform to established social practices than by disciplinary measures. When physical punishment has to be administered, however, it is the mother who does it. The older children take care of their younger brothers and sisters and have authority over them. Respect for older members of the family is deeply ingrained. The father is the undisputed head of his family and nothing is done without his approval, though respect for the mother is also strong. This respect for elders goes back to ancient times, for Bishop Landa in writing of the six-teenth-century Maya says:

> The young men respected the elders highly, and took their counsels, and tried to pass as mature themselves. The elders said to the younger ones that since they had seen more, what they said should be believed, so that if the youths heeded their counsels, the elders would credit them more. So much respect was given to the elders that the youths did not mingle with them, except in cases of necessity such as when they were married; and with married men they mingled very little.

Bishop Landa remarks upon the extreme modesty of the Maya women at the time of the Conquest: "The women were accustomed to turn their shoulders to the men in passing them, and of turning aside that they might pass; and the same, when they gave them to drink, until they had finished." Landa also says that in his day men and women did not eat together: "The men are not accustomed to eat with the women but by themselves upon the ground, or at most upon a mat which takes the place of a table." This custom persists even to the present day. The men eat first, being served by the women, and later the women of the family eat together by themselves. Modesty in small children is confined exclusively to the little girls, who have to wear huipiles (the Maya woman's dress) from birth. Their little brothers up to the age of six and older are allowed to play about the house and yard naked.

Sexual promiscuity among married women, and even among unmarried girls, is not uncommon. The former is not regarded with particular disapproval, except by the jealous husband, while the unmarried girl with one or more illegitimate children has no more difficulty in finding a mate than have her more continent sisters. Prostitution, however, is uncommon. Most boys are introduced to sex by older women, while young girls have their first sex experience with their youthful lovers. Incest, though rare, occurs from time to time, usually between father and daughter.

The Maya are not particularly religious. At present Christian worship is carried on almost exclusively by the women, though in ancient times religion was largely an affair of the men. Practically all children are baptized, but few receive additional instruction in the tenets of the Church because of the present scarcity of priests in the smaller villages. Hence the majority know little about the real meaning and significance of Christianity.

If they are not religious, however, all Maya are intensely superstitious. There are countless superstitions, many of them fragmentary survivals of the ancient Maya religion, mixed with Spanish medieval folklore and even perhaps with West African importations. Certain dreams and omens are regarded as sure fore-runners of death. If one dreams that he is floating on air, or that he is having a tooth pulled and is suffering intense pain, a member of his immediate family will die; if, in the dream, the suffering is slight, a less close relative will die. To dream of red tomatoes means a baby will die; to dream that a black bull is trying to push its way into one's home or to dream of breaking a water jug indi-cates that a member of the family will die.

The Maya are fatalistic. What will come, will come. Old people have been known to announce that their time had come and, though not even ill, have lain down in their hammocks and quietly died.

Sickness is caused by dwarfs, for whom gourds of food are placed in the doorway of the house in order to prevent an epidemic. If one gives away embers of burning wood, one's turkeys will die. Eggs set on Fridays will not hatch. This latter belief is suggestive of the bad luck attending Fridays throughout Christian countries.

There are many weather superstitions. Thin cornhusks indi-cate a mild winter; thick ones, a cold winter. If a swallow flies low, it will rain; if high, it will be clear. Cicadas are honored weather prophets among the Maya, and the time for burning the cornfields is often determined by their chirping. Evil winds take the form of animals, and individuals struck by them will die. If a match drops on the floor and continues to burn, it is a sign of good luck; if it burns to the end, the person who dropped it will have a long life.

The hunter has many difficulties to contend with. If he sells the head, liver, or stomach of a deer he has killed, he will have bad luck in future hunting; should he sell the paunch, he will never be able to kill another deer. To bring bad luck to a hunter, one has only to buy meat from him and throw the bones into a cenote. The Maya believe there is a king deer in the bush, with a wasp's nest between his horns; if a hunter kills this deer, he will die immediately.

The following signs indicate that visitors are coming: an oriole singing, a dragonfly coming into the house, a butterfly flying high, a cat washing its face, or a fire hissing.

From ancient times, the Maya have lived under the influence of lucky and unlucky days. The modern Maya continue to follow this practice, with one difference: the seven days of the Christian week have now replaced the 260 days of the ancient *tzolkin* or sacred divinatory year. Tuesdays and Fridays are considered unlucky, Mondays and Saturdays lucky. Marriages are usually celebrated on Mondays; Saturdays are considered lucky days on which to buy lottery tickets.

The Maya have always venerated numbers. Nine has always been especially lucky, perhaps because of its association with the nine steps leading to the ancient Maya heaven, or perhaps because of its having been the number of the Nine Gods of the Underworld. If a centipede is found on Tuesday it must be cut into nine pieces in order to bring good luck. If a green snake is seen, it will cause one's death within the year, unless it is caught and cut into nine pieces. Whooping cough may be cured by hanging gourds of fresh *atole* in the doorway for nine successive days, and on the morning of the ninth day it must be shared with one's friends. Nine kernels of ground corn applied to granulated eyelids will cure them; skin troubles may be relieved with a brew of nine pieces of fish skin, nine pieces of corncob, and nine small pebbles.

Thirteen is another lucky Maya number, perhaps because of its important function in the ancient Maya calendar, or perhaps because it was the number of the Thirteen Gods of the Upper World. The use of thirteen as a lucky number seems to be confined chiefly to religious ceremonies, for which offerings of thirteen loaves of bread, thirteen bowls of food, and thirteen cakes made of thirteen layers each are prepared.

Most Maya superstitions have unpleasant connotations. Many
more things are thought to bring bad luck rather than good luck.
The Maya have a fatalistic strain, perhaps the heritage of their past,
where death by sacrifice was common and more of their gods were
hostile than friendly.

Opinions differ as to the general intelligence of the Maya.
Some American observers have believed them to be very bright;
many have classified them as fairly bright; others as average and
a few only as rather dull. No one regarded them as downright
stupid. They are not inventive, however, but are content to follow
the same pattern of living as did their ancestors. Their memory
is considered very good and their powers of observation, especially
in the bush, are excellent. They are rather imaginative and have
a fair sense of beauty, which was probably more highly developed in ancient times than it is today.

THE ORIGINS OF THE MAYA CIVILIZATION

A SUMMARY of Maya history will be found in Table III, with corresponding dates in the Maya and Christian chronologies, and the accompanying ceramic and architectural phases. Maya history may be divided into three stages: (1) Preclassic, extending from about 1500 B.C. to A.D. 317; (2) Classic, from A.D. 317 to 889; and (3) Postclassic, from 889 until 1697, when the last organized Maya were conquered.

Maya civilization, as the term is used in this book, refers only to the culture of the Classic stage, which begins with the earliest decipherable Maya dates so far discovered in the central Peten lowlands. The word "civilization" is generally employed to describe a culture which has developed to the point of centralized government, craft specialization, and formalized religion. Although the appearance of Maya dated inscriptions is at best but an arbitrary marker for these developments, it is a long-accepted one, and will be followed here. These earliest dates, inscribed on stone stelae, are associated in the Peten with corbel-vaulted masonry buildings and polychrome pottery. There is reason to believe these three archaeologically diagnostic traits may have come into use at roughly the same time there, and that all three lasted through the Classic stage in that area. There is also evidence that the practice of erecting Maya-style dated stelae gradually spread outward from the Peten region and, at least in the Usumacinta Valley to the west, was accompanied by the use of masonry corbel vaults. At Copan, to the extreme southeast of the Maya area, the erection of stelae, of fine masonry architecture, and the making of polychrome pottery seem also to have arrived together, brought presumably by priests who were devotees of the Classic Maya religious cult. Thus there is archaeological evidence that Maya civilization, as here defined, had a relatively restricted area of origin and spread as a unified complex through the central Maya area.

40

There is also evidence that as Maya civilization spread to the east
and the west, this area of its origin had already begun a cultural decline.

In the Guatemala highlands there is no archaeological evidence of such a spread. Diagnostics such as datable stelae and corbel-vaulted buildings do not appear there, and Maya-style polychrome pottery seems to have arrived only as a luxury import. This area shows both archaeological and documentary evidence of repeated contact with the Mexican highlands, dating from as early as Preclassic times. There are also groups of Aztec-speakers here. Thus the Guatemalan highlands and the south coastal plain did not participate in the cultural florescence which we here call the Maya civilization.

The cultural ties between the northern and central Maya areas were much closer than those to the southern highlands, a situation which parallels their geographic relationships; the two lowland areas are relatively homogeneous as compared to the highland area. Yucatan archaeological remains dating from Preclassic times show striking similarities to those of the Peten, and a comparable cultural advancement, although evidence from the central area is slim, owing to the difficulties of archaeological excavation there. In early Classic times, northern Yucatan seems to have been culturally provincial to the civilized central Maya area. In late Classic times, a distinctive culture developed and expanded there; it was in its way as advanced as that of the central Maya area and incorporated various of its components, but with a somewhat different emphasis. This culture was finally displaced by foreign invaders at the end of the Classic stage. The northern Maya culture reached its height contemporaneously with the full development of the ceremonial centers at the eastern and western extremities of the central Maya area but after the beginnings of cultural decline in the original Peten center.

SEARCHING FOR ORIGINS

The Maya economy was based upon maize agriculture. Although no archaeological information on the period of agricultural

TABLE III

The Principal Epochs of Maya History

Stage	Dates According to 11.16.0.0.0 Correlation		Highlands: Southern Maya	Lowlands	
	Christian	Maya		Central Maya	Northern Maya
Preclassic (Formative)	1500 B.C.	Maya calendar probably invented about 7.0.0.0.0 (353 B.C.)	High developments in pottery, lapidary work, etc. Elaborate tombs, with gifts and sacrificial victims, dug into mounds which later bore temples. Custom lasted till Spanish Conquest.	House foundations, *chultuns*, Mamom pottery. Chicanel pottery. Small, elaborate, stuccoed substructure E-VII-sub at Uaxactun.	Simple, early pottery. Large, masonry temple substructures. Nearly all the larger religious centers were begun in Formative times. Yucatan Regional stage: shows strong connections with the Central area. Dated stelae, vaults, lime-mortar masonry.
Classic (Initial Series)	A.D. 300 ——— A.D. 500	8.14.0.0.0 ——— 9.0.0.0.0 ——— 9.10.0.0.0	Strong ties with Teotihuacan. Trade with Peten. No lime-mortared masonry, stelae, or vaulting.	Vault I—crude lime-mortared masonry and vaults. Initial series stelae. Fine polychrome pottery (Tzakol) and stone carving. Geographical spread of stela cult from Peten. Vault II—finer masonry. The height of stone carving, most elaborate and numerous stelae, naturalistic art styles, Tepeu pottery.	Yucatan Florescent: Distinctive culture develops in Puuc-Chenes-Rio Bec area and spreads over the northern area.

			Final decadence and abandonment of area.	Fine veneer masonry, mosaic stone façades, slateware pottery, no stelae.
Classic (Initial Series)	10.0.0.0.0	Late Classic shows cultural regression save along northern mountain flanks.		
	A.D. 1000			
	10.10.0.0.0	Toltec conquest. Effigy Plumbate pottery made.		Toltec Conquest. Great governmental center at Chichen Itza. Kukulcan worship. X Fine Orange and Plumbate pottery imported. Puuc area abandoned.
Postclassic (Mexican)	11.0.0.0.0	Fortified hilltop sites. Rulers here and in Yucatan boasted of Toltec descent.		Chichen Itza abandoned. Capital moved to Mayapan, a walled town. Dissension; Mexican mercenaries imported. Mayapan falls. Local governments.
	11.10.0.0.0		Peten area nearly deserted, until today. No more religious centers built.	
	A.D. 1500			
	12.0.0.0.0			Spanish Conquest (1527).
Colonial			Spanish Conquest (1697).	

beginnings is yet available, there is good botanical evidence that the
Guatemala highlands were a center from which maize agriculture
later spread to the central and northern Maya areas. However, the
richness of Preclassic archaeological remains from the highlands
bolsters the botanical evidence that this region was an early cultural
center; the Preclassic ceramics recently recovered from the west
Guatemala coastal region and from the vicinity of Guatemala City
are among the most elaborate of early Mesoamerican potteries, and
fine Preclassic lapidary work and stone carvings, some of them
monolithic stelae, have recently been discovered in this area.

The exact origins of the central Maya civilization are hard
to trace at present, but should become progressively clearer with
archaeological advances in Mesoamerica. The Preclassic-stage
archaeological sites from such widely separated areas as Honduras,
northern Veracruz, and the Valley of Mexico show sufficient similarities in their pottery to indicate continuing relations among them.

The areas known to show advanced culture during this period
are surprisingly widespread. In northern Veracruz well-made pottery is found, and the existence of circular mud temples is suspected. In the Valley of Mexico the elaborately furnished graves
at Tlatilco show handsome pottery vessels, exquisite clay figurines,
and occasional lapidary work which was probably imported from
the south. In Oaxaca the famed *dansantes,* sculptured on stone
slabs, show the development of a distinctive art style which probably symbolizes an elaborate formal religion. The carving of stone
monolithic monuments bearing simple calendric dates attests the
early presence of priestly specialists in astronomy; the anthropomorphic religious figurines found in tombs bear the symbolic accouterments of gods which were still worshiped at the time of the
Spanish Conquest. The most elaborate tombs of this period, which
bear amazingly intricate pottery and lapidary work, are found in
the Guatemala highlands.

Preclassic-stage artifacts show distinct regional variation
throughout Mesoamerica, but share more characteristics than do
those of the Classic stage. The presence of several culturally insignificant but complex gadgets such as whistling jars, stirrup

spouts, and cylindrical stamps in both Peru and Mesoamerica indicate that the people of the two areas knew of each other and
profited by technical advances at a level common to both. The millennium following the development of agriculture in the New
World must have been a progressive one, with rapid technological
advance and open-mindedness to foreign ideas. During this period
the subsistence pattern of the common people was established, and
the formalized ritualistic religions which characterize the following Classic stage gradually developed. The formalized masks of
Pyramid E-VII-sub at Uaxactun (Plate 58), the *dansantes* of
Monte Alban, and probably the stylized human and tiger heads of
the Olmec area mark the development of religious iconographies.
The large earthen mortuary platforms of highland Guatemala,
the huge temple substructures at Cuicuilco and Teotihuacan in the
Valley of Mexico, and the lesser but still impressive substructures
in Yucatan demonstrate the levies of manpower which could successfully be demanded by the priests. Evidence of simple calendrics in Oaxaca, carved stelae in the Guatemala highlands, and
inferred evidence of early astronomic observations and records in
the central Maya area suggest that cycles of religious ritual had
already become geared to calendric counts.

The growing power of the priestly classes over the farming
population is not easy to explain by forthright economic necessity.
There seem to have been few material advantages which could
have been promised by the priests to compensate for hard labor.
Weather predictions even by modern meteorologists are of little
importance to Mexican farmers, so the priests cannot have gained
power by developing this specialty. It is argued that in the Old
World the necessity of community labor on irrigation canals allowed the priests to control large groups, but no evidence for such
a situation has been found in Mesoamerica. There is also no evidence of warfare as a nationalizing force in those times. We know,
however, that among nearly all American Indian corn farmers,
calendrically regulated ceremonies and sacrifices are considered
necessary to the production of crops. How this firm conviction
originated and attained general credence is hard to say, but its ac-

ceptance among modern Maya argues that it may have allowed priestly control in ancient times.

The Maya farmers in their relative isolation must have grown into a closely integrated group, in which priestly sanctity had few questioners. We may picture them coming in to their ceremonial centers from their scattered milpas, drawn by religious devotion rather than by material compulsion.

The Maya of the central area, it may be seen, were but one of several regional groups in Mesoamerica which reached a high stage of development in early Classic times. Among these groups, they were pre-eminent in several types of activity and strikingly retarded in others. It is this peculiar orientation, this distinctive cultural patterning, which gives our best clues to the genius of Maya culture; it evidences the underlying world view which allowed the notable intellectual progress of the Maya.

1. The Maya show a marked homogeneity in their writing, calendrics, architecture, and art over a large area. The area of Classic Maya culture constituted nearly 100,000 square miles, a major segment of Mesoamerica, and far greater than that of any other Classic-stage culture. Over this region there is evidence of the rapid spread of calendric innovations and an identity of religious symbolism, as well as a series of concurrent changes in such homely fashions as pottery shapes. This argues for much travel and exchange of ideas among the ruling priests, and among certain of the commoners as well. It also argues for a close religious communion: the gods must have been pan-Maya, with few if any local deities, and with arrangements for the exchange and common training of priests and probably of artisans throughout the whole area.

This remarkably widespread homogeneity in an area notable nowadays for its nearly impassable terrain offers a paradox most easily explained by the wide gulf between the Maya culture and ours. The Maya traveled afoot and with dugout canoes, both excellent for such country, and they occupied an area doubtless unattractive and unrewarding in natural resources to the surrounding groups who were unadapted to it. There seems little doubt that the Maya achieved a high degree of cultural solidarity, the sort of

unanimity of outlook which encourages the growth of formality
in religion and art.

2. There is a marked contrast between the luxuriance of all objects connected with religious ritual and the stark simplicity of utilitarian objects. The masonry buildings are magnificent, but completely nonfunctional. It is questionable if the priests lived in them, for more uncomfortable quarters would be hard to imagine. Diligent searching has produced scanty domestic architecture in the Maya area, and the excavation of house sites characteristically produces few and simple artifacts. Domestic construction seems to have been limited to wood and thatch structures, despite the fine masonry temples.

3. There is no evidence that the lowland Maya area ever bore a heavy population; an estimate of 30 people per square mile, about that of modern Yucatan, seems a likely maximum. There is also no archaeological evidence of the concentration of the Classic Maya into large residential settlements. Modern agricultural practices, which are probably aboriginal, necessitate a scattered population during much of the year. In Old World archaeological theory urbanization is nearly synonymous with civilization, but not among the Maya.

4. There is comparatively little evidence of massive conscription of labor. Maya public works, the largest of which are the acropolis-like platforms of the major religious centers, probably never exceeded one-twentieth the volume of the famous Pyramid of the Sun at Teotihuacan, which in turn is about a quarter the volume of the Pyramid of Cheops in Egypt. The renown of Maya architecture does not rest upon its mass or size. On the other hand, the proportion of skilled labor to total labor expended is much higher than in the architecture of other American civilizations, and the quantity of outstanding stone sculpture bears favorable comparison with any area. This suggests that the Maya stonemasons were full-time specialists, and that levies on the farming populace were largely in food rather than in unskilled labor.

A more penetrating hypothesis concerning the Classic Maya scale of values can be drawn from Maya architecture. The emphasis is on skilled workmanship rather than size; on quality rather than quantity. Only thus could a thinly spread, economically poor population achieve intellectual and artistic superiority over contemporaries of the far richer Mexican highland area.

The early civilizations of the Old World are believed to have centered about the flood plain of the Tigris and Euphrates rivers. Here large, concentrated populations arose, supported by the development of highly organized canal irrigation on rich flood plains. It is argued that city life, urbanization, was closely related to craft specialization, the development of a religious hierarchy, and the invention of writing; that irrigation agriculture allowed a close governmental control over the population and their taxation and conscription for public work. It has recently been suggested that many of these traits may be assumed to be universal necessities in the development of civilization. To such a theory the Maya area presents an intractable exception.

At Uaxactun in the central Peten, where the earliest associated dates, corbel vaults, and polychrome pottery have been found, there is a hiatus in the ceramic record. Following the monochrome pottery of late Preclassic times come well-developed polychrome vessels of new forms and design. This developmental gap has been bridged in the northern Maya area, and suggestions of a similar transitional period from monochrome to polychrome pottery come from several other areas in Mesoamerica. Uaxactun, a small religious center, cannot be taken as an adequate sample of the Peten area. More excavations there will certainly fill this gap, but until more evidence becomes available the central Peten should not be claimed as a center where vaults, dates, and pottery originated simultaneously.

The early carved calendric inscriptions of Oaxaca have been mentioned. Bar and dot numerals similar to those used by the Maya have been found in Preclassic deposits in Veracruz and in undatable context at other sites throughout a zone from the Guatemala west coast to the Gulf of Mexico, just south of the Isthmus of Tehuantepec. The Tuxtla statuette, which was probably carved in this area, bears the Maya-style date of A.D. 162, and a carved

↑ *b*) Stela 1, El Baul, Guatemala.

PLATE 14.—EARLY MONUMENTS

↑ *a*) Tuxtla Statuette, San Andres Tuxtla
       Veracruz.

↑ *c*) Stela C, Tres Zapotes, Veracruz; back view.

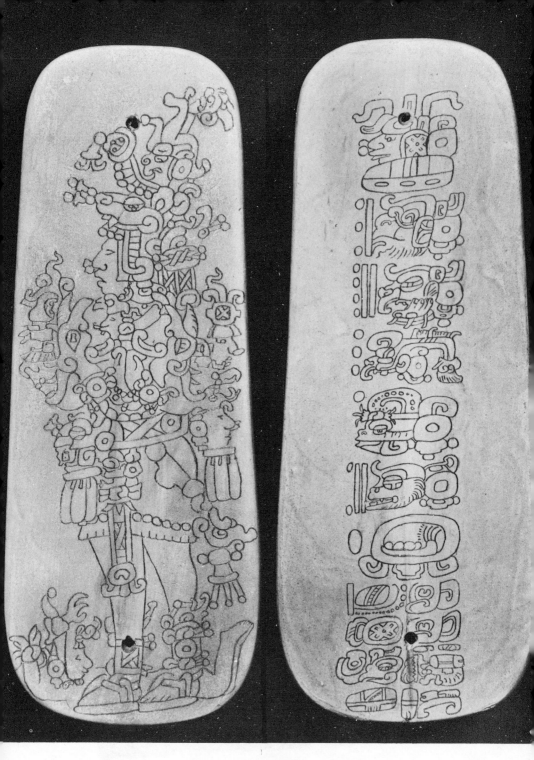

PLATE 15.—THE LEYDEN PLATE

stela has been found in the Guatemala highlands in a Preclassic
association. Although these indications all point away from the
Peten as the area of origin for the Maya system of dated stelae,
it should be pointed out that the Peten is less accessible and thus
less explored than other areas, and may in the future produce new
and earlier inscriptions. Although there is even less information
on the origin of corbel vaulting and polychrome pottery, this is
of but slight importance. The significance of Classic Maya culture
rests on the complex religious and social structure of which this
combination of traits is but the archaeological diagnostic.

The distribution of peoples and cultures during Preclassic times
is pertinent in reconstructing the origins of Maya civilization.
Evidence from physical types sheds little light on this problem;
both the modern peoples and the archaeological skeletal materials
from Mesoamerica are similar enough so that regional differences
are unclear. Archaeology of Preclassic cultures has not reached
a stage where regional differences are well described; the general
picture thus far is one of surprising similarity over all areas sampled. The wide regional extent of lowland Maya Preclassic culture is suggested by evidence from the Huastec area, where archaeological excavations at Panuco and Tampico show Preclassic pottery
bearing notable similarity to that of the lowland Maya, followed
by Classic influences from the Mexican highlands. The Huastec
Maya linguistic island (see Plate 7) suggests that the area between
it and the Chiapas lowlands must at one time have been Maya-
speaking, later eliminated by incursion of languages from the west.
It would thus seem that the Huastec area has been isolated since
Preclassic times.

THE OLDEST SURELY DATED OBJECTS IN THE MAYA AREA

The earliest surely contemporaneous date in Maya hieroglyphic
writing is that engraved on the back of the Leyden Plate, a small
celt-like object of jade, 8½ inches long by 3 inches wide, found
near Puerto Barrios, Guatemala, in 1864. This records the Maya
date 8.14.3.1.12, corresponding to 320 of the Christian Era (Plate
15b). By contemporaneous date is meant the date the Leyden

Plate was actually engraved; a few Maya dates have been demonstrated to record past events.

On the Leyden Plate the detail of the captive figure closely resembles figures on the monuments at Tikal, in north central Peten. At the same time, it is so different from all other representations of this motif elsewhere among the Classic Maya that there is little doubt the Leyden Plate was executed at Tikal, although it was not found there. If so, Tikal is the oldest Maya city now known on the basis of the dated remains. It is also the largest Classic Maya ceremonial center.

The oldest large stone monument or stela now known is Stela 9 at Uaxactun (Plate 16*b*), which has carved upon its back the Maya date 8.14.10.13.15 (A.D. 328). This is only seven and two-thirds years later than the date of the Leyden Plate, which was probably executed at Tikal, only eleven miles south. We may therefore conclude that Maya calendrics were well under way by the beginning of the fourth century of the Christian Era in this region at the very center of the Yucatan Peninsula (Plate 1).

PRECLASSIC MAYA-SPEAKING PEOPLES IN PETEN

Prior to Preclassic times it is probable that the Yucatan Peninsula was occupied by nomadic peoples who lived on the natural products of the forest and by hunting and fishing, long before the knowledge of maize agriculture reached them from the Guatemala highlands to the south.

We do not know whether agriculture was introduced to the Maya lowlands by immigration of new people or through adoption by the older inhabitants. It is likely, however, that corn was cultivated there for a thousand years or so before the beginning of the Maya civilization during the fourth century of the Christian Era.

BEGINNINGS OF THE MAYA HIEROGLYPHIC WRITING

The earliest Maya dates which may be regarded as surely contemporaneous fall in the first third of the fourth century of the Christian Era (320 and 328) and at the close of the third quarter

↑ *a*) Front.

↑ *b*) Back.

PLATE 16.—STELA 9, UAXACTUN

↑ *a)* E-VII before excavation.

Plate 17.—Pyramids E-VII and E-VII-sub, Uaxactun

↓ *b)* E-VII-sub after excavation.

of Baktun 8 of the Maya Era—8.14.3.1.12 and 8.14.10.13.15.
Both the Leyden Plate and Stela 9 at Uaxactun, in addition to presenting the two earliest contemporaneous dates, have another significant characteristic in common. The calendric data presented on each show the complex structuring which is standard for all classic Maya inscriptions. These inscriptions do not document the steps which must have been made in developing the calendar.

It has been suggested that the earlier stages in the development of Maya hieroglyphic writing and chronology must have been recorded on some medium other than stone. No evidences of such material have been discovered, possibly owing to the destruction of perishable materials in the moist, hot climate of the Peten.

Centuries must have elapsed while the early Maya astronomers were making and preserving observations on the sun to determine the exact length of the tropical year (365.24+ days). They probably observed the moon as well, to determine the exact length of a single lunation (29.52+ days). Once the true lengths of these two periods had been determined—and the ancient Maya had measured both with extraordinary accuracy—the development of the Maya calendar and chronological system could have followed in a very short time.

There is internal evidence in the Maya chronological system that it was first devised either at the end of Baktun 7—7.0.0.0.0 of the Maya Era (353 B.C.)—or shortly after—7.6.0.0.0 (235 B.C.). It seems probable that the Maya priests developed their unique hieroglyphic writing in order to record their newly devised chronological system. If this is true, writing must have developed during the six or seven centuries preceding the earliest carved dates.

MAYA ART, ARCHITECTURE, AND CERAMICS IN AGREEMENT WITH THE EPIGRAPHY

In addition to Stela 9 at Uaxactun there are at least ten other monuments in this city, four actually dated and six approximately dated by means of their stylistic characteristics, which date from the last quarter of Baktun 8 of the Maya Era (337–435). The human figures on these monuments are poorly proportioned and crudely executed. They are usually shown in modified left profile (Plate 16a), though an occasional figure appears in modified right profile (Plate 63c). The feet are in tandem position, the toe of the left foot touching the heel of the right foot (Plate 16a). The arms and torso are portrayed in full front, the head being in left or right profile. This awkward posture is typical of the figures on all the earliest known Maya stone sculptures.

The architectural evidence as to the antiquity of Uaxactun is impressive. The earliest pyramid found there is E-VII-sub (Plate 17b), which was buried inside the later pyramid, E-VII (Plate 17a). The style of the stucco masks (Plate 58) on the sides of this pyramid suggests that at the time they were executed the Maya art style was just beginning to crystallize. E-VII-sub had never supported a masonry building on its summit, though four stucco-filled postholes in the lime-plaster flooring on top of this pyramid indicate that it had originally supported a superstructure of some perishable material, probably of poles and thatch. This suggests that Maya stone buildings with their typical corbeled stone roof vaulting may not have been invented when E-VII-sub was built.

The ceramics of the Classic stage have not been studied sufficiently to permit general conclusions on such points as priority of origin and centers of distribution of pottery types. Excavations in refuse heaps and below plaza floor levels at Uaxactun have brought to light the best sample of Preclassic pottery and clay figurines yet found in Peten. Some types, especially among the figurines, strongly resemble objects from the earliest agricultural horizons in the highlands of Mexico, Guatemala, and El Salvador.

Although the finds from Uaxactun cannot be taken as evidence that the Classic-stage Maya archaeological diagnostics all originated simultaneously in this area, their presence there at an early date and the evidence of their subsequent spread as a complex well demonstrate the cultural unity which so characterizes the Maya civilization.

THE CLASSIC STAGE

CENTRAL MAYA AREA

THE DIRECTION of development of the Maya civilization was fixed by early Classic times in central Peten, and held with remarkable conservatism during its 570 years. This fixity of outlook or cultural conservatism is documented in the priestly monopolies of writing, calendrics, and religious art and architecture. Lay styles such as those of the pottery, and such artisan-controlled procedures as masonry techniques and sculptural detailing, show a normal rate of stylistic change. The Maya preoccupation with religious panoply may account for the paucity of technical advances during Classic times.

The type of formal governmental organization was an unusually successful one in comparison with that of other areas of Mesoamerica, judged by the area and time span of its control; the method of its enforcement, however, presents a problem. The priests cannot have offered their subjects rich material rewards; the Maya economy was simple and quite self-sufficient. A major deterrent from the use of repressive governmental methods was the scattered nature of the population, living near their widely separated cornfields, for not over a fifth of the land was in cultivation at any one time. Nor do the priests seem to have held an economically valuable monopoly of knowledge; weather forecasting, for example, is unreliable even now in the Maya area. Moreover, there are no archaeological indications of the strong ruler or tyrant. The inscriptions are impersonal; they record the ends of major time periods, which in turn were thought to signalize changes in the reigns of gods, not men. In the Bonampak murals, our most detailed scenes of Maya life, no individual stands alone in power (Plates 88 and 89). Although a single figure on a throne dominates the famous wall panel from Piedras Negras (Plate 69), the accompanying figures, like those from Bonampak, are grouped in a most unregimented fashion. The big stick does not seem to have been wielded frequently by Maya rulers. A near absence of warfare and evidence of wide trade in religious and luxury items, probably used in ceremonies, also argue against repressive tendencies in government. This remarkably smooth-running yet informal style of government must have depended upon a placid and well-adjusted citizenry, who held a remarkably unanimous opinion as to proper behavior. Lest this give an impression of timid conformity, Lord Moulton may be quoted, that "the measure of civilization is the extent of man's obedience to the unenforceable." In this criterion, the Maya must have measured high.

The uniform religious control suggested by the evidence for calendric and iconographic unity throughout the Maya area must have influenced political matters to some degree, although in the absence of warfare and of widespread trade in utilitarian objects, co-operative political endeavors may be assumed to have been limited. Proof of some co-operation between cities is given by the causeways, which stretch in carefully engineered straight lines between them. Such works required political agreement between at least the religious centers concerned, implemented by considerable labor forces, which presumably were recruited from both sites.

There are evidences of occasional raiding between centers, suggested in the Bonampak murals, by the nude fettered captives common on Maya stelae, and by the widespread Conquest-period custom of obtaining slaves for sacrifice by raiding. Such raiding would hardly have occurred had all the centers been on amicable terms with each other. There is evidence of at least one and probably several rather sharply drawn cultural frontiers in the Yucatan Peninsula during the second half of the Classic stage, and there seems every reason to believe that political boundaries coincided with them. These suggestions of Maya turmoil do not, however, negate the picture of surprising homogeneity and comparative tranquility in the central Maya area during Classic times.

In attempting to reconstruct the history of the Classic-stage Maya we must depend almost exclusively on archaeological evidence, since the Classic Maya were overcome by a foreign group, the Toltecs, over a half millennium before the European Conquest.

The archaeological data for the reconstruction of Classic-stage history have been developed by excavation and from close study of the Classic sites themselves—their epigraphy, art, and architecture. The evidence supplied by the dated monuments provides a reliable chronological framework in the areas where such monuments are found. The sculpture and architecture can be analyzed stylistically to indicate the boundaries and distribution of archaeologic subprovinces and to reflect the interplay of the forces which brought about the development, florescence, and decline of the Classic Maya. Because of its universal utility, pottery closely reflects the domestic habits of its makers, and changes due to outside influences appear quickly. The position of different wares in stratified refuse heaps shows the order in which such influences have made themselves felt. The presence of occasional pottery trade pieces permits time relations with other cultures to be established. If we interpret the archaeological evidence in the light of conditions obtaining among the Conquest-period and modern Maya, we shall come as near as possible to a reconstruction of the major trends of Classic history.

The Classic stage in the central Maya area may be divided into two major periods: Early and Late. The Early period is thought to have begun a little before the earliest Maya date, at about 8.14.0.0.0 (A.D. 317), and it ended at 9.8.0.0.0. (A.D. 593). (See chapter xii for an explanation of Maya dates.) This period of a little more than three centuries saw the spread of Maya-style dated stelae, and the accompanying vaulted architecture from restricted origins in the Peten region to almost their greatest extent. Although the architecture shows consistent refinement and improvement through this period, the sculpture of stelae cannot be so characterized; the sculpture of the Early period, although less ornate and complex than that of later times, is vigorous and naturalistic. The Tzakol pottery which accompanies this period is the earliest polychrome painted ware of the Maya area; it is decorated in a bold, handsome manner in motifs ranging from geometric figures to Maya-style masks.

The Late period lasted from 9.8.0.0.0 (A.D. 593) to at least the end of the Maya Initial Series inscriptions at 10.3.0.0.0 (A.D. 889). This period saw first an accelerated activity, and an increasing refinement in architecture and the arts, coupled with extensive religious construction in the eastern and western regions of the central Maya area. Both the architecture and sculpture of the central area reached their heights during the century preceding 9.18.0.0.0 (A.D. 790) in such eastern and western Maya centers as Copan, Piedras Negras, Yaxchilan, and Palenque. From this time on, the decline was rapid, with the Peten region in its van, until, by A.D. 900, Long Count inscriptions were no longer written, and organized religious activities ceased. In the western part of the central area there is some evidence of the intentional defacement of religious sculpture; over all the central area the religious centers fell to ruin.

The architecture of the Late period at Uaxactun follows a course in accord with the above-described general developments. There is a gradual refinement in masonry techniques and architectural form until sometime later than 9.14.0.0.0, after which architectural construction shows little change. Classic Maya sculpture, according to Proskouriakoff's analysis, also follows a course consistent with the general sequence of change. She divides the Late period into four sequent phases named Formative, Ornate, Dynamic, and Decadent. The first three show progress to a peak extending from 9.16.0.0.0 to 9.19.0.0.0. From here the sculpture deteriorates.

In the northern Maya area the course of events was distinctively different in cultural content and emphasis and later in time of florescence. This sequence will be discussed later in the chapter.

a) Lintel 1, Oxkintok, Yucatan.

←

PLATE 18.—SCULPTURES OF THE CLASSIC STAGE

←

b) Stela 11 (back), Yaxchilan, Chiapas.

c) Stela 12 (front), Piedras Negras, Guatemala.

→

GULF OF MEXICO

GULF OF
HONDURAS

PACIFIC
OCEAN

Dzilam

Dzibilchaltun
T'Ho   Izamal   Ichmul
Acanceh
Mayapan   Ikil   Chichén Itzá
Oxkintok   Sotuta   Causeway   Cobá
Yaxuná
Nohpat Mani
Uxmal Tabí I
Jaina   Tzocchen Kabah   Cave of Loltún
Holactun Xculoc Sayil Labná
Huntichmul I
Keuic

Tulum

Santa Rosa Xtampak
Laguna
Chichankanab

Etzná   Dzibilnocac
El Tabasqueño
Chunchintok
Hochob

Ppustunich

Pechal

Civiltuk

Laguna de
Términos

Becan   Tzibanche
Pasión del Cristo   Santa Rita Corosal
Oxpemul Xamantun   Río Bec
Calakmul   El Palmar
Comalcalco
Jonuta   Uxul Balakbal
Alta Mira   La Milpa
Naachtun
Chochkitam
El Tortuguero   Kaxuinic
Xultun La Honradez
Xmakabatun
Palenque Chinikiha   Uaxactun
Tila Chuctiepa   El Encanto   Holmul
Tikal Nakum Chunhuitz
Uolantun Yaxhá Naranjo
La Florida   San Clemente Benque Viejo
Pestac Quexil Piedras Negras   Petén-Itzá Ixlu
Santo Ton   Motul de San José
Toniná El Cayo Laguna Perdida   Ucanal Yaltitud
La Mar Yaxchilan Itsimté   Tzimin Kax
Laguna Tayasal
Bonampac Perdida Polol
El Amparo Poco Uinic   Ixkun
Laguna
Aguas Calientes   Lubantun
Miramar La Amelia El Caribe
Comitán   Altar de Sacrificios Seibal Pusilhá
Tenam
Chinkultic   Tzendales   Cancuen
Quen Santo   Pasión

Chama
Lago
Izabal   Quiriguá
Lago de   Los Higos
Atitlán   Río Amarillo
Copan
Lago
Yohoa

Bahía de la
Ascención

Bahía de
Espíritu Santo

Turneffe I.

PLATE 19
ARCHAEOLOGICAL MAP OF
THE MAYA AREA

At the beginning of the fourth century of the Christian Era, sculptured stone monuments, corbeled roof vaulting, and Tzakol pottery had made their first appearance at Uaxactun, where there are six dated monuments, three of which are surely and three probably referable to Baktun 8. In addition to these stelae, there are at least four other monuments at Uaxactun which on stylistic grounds are probably referable to Baktun 8. Two other Baktun 8 monuments are known, one each at Uolantun and Balakbal, the former twelve miles south of Uaxactun, the latter thirty-five miles north (Plate 19).

Figure 1 summarizes the history of the erection of Maya stelae. The names of the centers appear in the column at the left. The vertical lines represent time periods during the Classic stage; above each line is given the corresponding date in both Maya and Christian chronology. The solid, horizontal lines indicate the length of time between the earliest and the latest known dates at each site listed. The beginning or end of any horizontal line shown as broken indicates that at such sites there are monuments which, on stylistic grounds, may be considered either earlier or later than the surely dated monuments there. At first, the ends of katuns (19.71 years) were chosen for the dedication of stelae. Shortly, as their resources grew, the ceremonial centers were able to erect period markers more frequently. The ends of lahuntuns or half-katuns were next chosen, in addition to the katun endings, for this important ceremony. In fact this ten-year period was the interval most commonly selected during Classic times.

In the early part of the Late Period a monument was erected at Piedras Negras in western Peten at the end of a hotun or quarter-katun. However, the practice of marking the five-year period endings must have proved too costly for the Maya, and only two sites—Piedras Negras and Quirigua—regularly followed this practice. A few others, notably Copan and Naranjo, occasionally erected hotun period markers.

The century embraced by the first quarter of Baktun 9 (435–

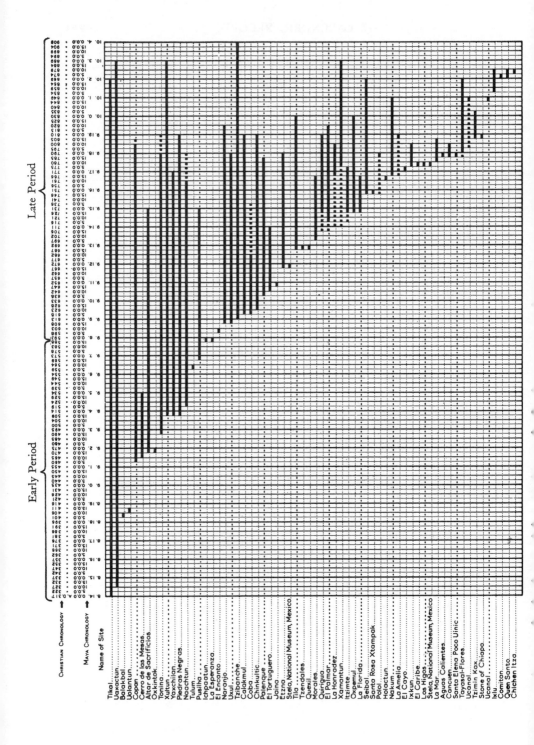

534) witnessed an expansion of the sculptured-stela complex. The custom of erecting such monuments had probably spread to Copan on the extreme southeastern frontier of the Maya area as early as 465 (Plate 19). Other cities erecting monuments during the first quarter of Baktun 9 (435–534) were Cerro de las Mesas (467); Oxkintok and Altar de Sacrificios (475); Tonina (495); Xultun, Piedras Negras, Yaxchilan, Palenque, and Calakmul (514); and Naachtun (524).

The map of the Maya area in Plate 19 shows that by 9.5.0.0.0 stelae were erected in all parts of the Yucatan Peninsula. They are also found in the Usumacinta Valley in the west, at Altar de Sacrificios, Yaxchilan, Piedras Negras, and Palenque; in the southeastern area at Copan; in the southwestern highlands at Tonina; and in the state of Yucatan at Oxkintok.

A rather surprising hiatus occurred in the erection of monuments between 9.5.0.0.0 and 9.8.0.0.0, the beginning of the Late Classic Period. Then nine centers burst into activity. Five of these new centers were in the nuclear region—El Encanto, Yaxha, Naranjo, Pusilha, and Uxul; one in the southwestern highlands—Chinkultic; and three in northeastern Yucatan—Tzibanche, Ichpaatun, and Coba.

Late in the second quarter of Baktun 9 at least fourteen new ceremonial centers began to erect stelae. Only two of these centers, Quirigua and Etzna, became important, the former because of its series of fine sculptured monuments and the latter because of its extensive architecture.

From 9.15.0.0.0 to 9.18.0.0.0 (731–790) the Classic Maya continued to expand, but chiefly in the outlands. Only two new large centers, Seibal and Nakum, both in Peten (Plate 19), began to erect monuments during this period. However, there are eight smaller centers, also in Peten or in the adjoining region to the east; at least twelve other small sites, six of them in the Usumacinta Valley immediately to the west; two in the southeastern highlands; one in the southeast; and three in the far north, all of which erected monuments for the first time during the Late Period.

At the end of Katun 18 (790) the Maya were at their esthetic

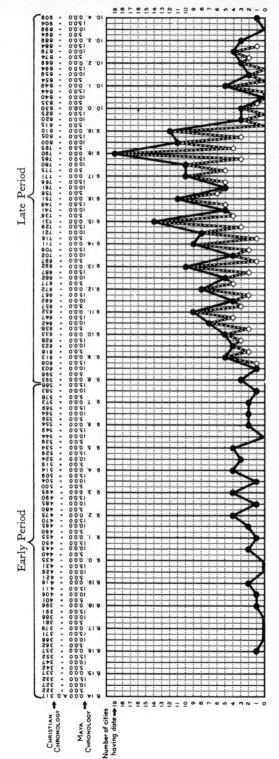

Fig. 2.—Diagram showing frequency of dated monuments during the Classic stage. The black line shows monuments erected at *katun*-ending (20-year) dates; the dotted line shows monuments marking *hotuns* and *lahuntuns* (5- and 10-year periods).

peak. A century and a half earlier, Palenque had begun to produce masterpieces of low-relief sculpture in its temple tablets. This highly specialized art form is found only at this site and at one or two near-by centers. The most notable example is the tablet of the Temple of the Cross at Palenque (Plate 32*b*). The latest known example of the low-relief tablet is the beautiful hieroglyphic slab found at the foot of the tower in the adjoining court of the Palace group at Palenque, which was dedicated in 783. Yaxchilan began producing beautiful reliefs as early as 692 but did not reach its sculptural zenith until 726 with the fine Lintels 24 (Plate 71*b*), 25 (Plate 71*a*), and 26 in Structure 23. Thirty-five years later magnificent stelae were still being erected there.

Piedras Negras reached a high artistic plane in 731, and continued at this level until 795. It reached its peak of sculptural brilliance in 761 in the Lintel, or Wall Panel, 3 from Structure O-13, one of the finest sculptures produced in ancient America (Plate 69*a*).

At the end of Katun 18 (790), the stela cult reached its widest extension. Nineteen cities erected period markers to commemorate this one katun ending: twelve in Peten; Piedras Negras in the Usumacinta Valley; Copan and Quirigua in the southeast; Tonina, Santa Elena Poco Uinic, and Chinkultic in the southwestern Chiapas highlands; and Etzna in the northern half of the Yucatan Peninsula. The diagram in Figure 2 shows graphically this all-time high of monumental activity in 9.18.0.0.0 (790), and the sharp decline in the practice of erecting period markers after Katun 18.

At the end of Katun 19 (810), twelve cities erected period markers: six in the central area; Piedras Negras; Quirigua; and four in the Chiapas highlands, at Chinkultic and Chiapa. By the end of the next katun, 10.0.0.0.0 (830), the number of sites which erected period markers had dropped to three: Uaxactun and Oxpemul in the central area, and Tila in the Chiapas highlands.

At the next katun ending, in 10.1.0.0.0 (849), five centers erected period markers, all in the central Peten area. The lahuntun ending in 859 was marked by the erection of monuments at two cities, both in central Peten. The katun ending 10.2.0.0.0 (869) was celebrated by the erection of monuments at three cities: Tikal, Tayasal-Flores, and Seibal, again all in Peten. On the following lahuntun ending, 879, four sites erected stelae: Ixlu and Xamantun in the central region; Quen Santo in the western Guatemala highlands; and Chichen Itza in northeastern Yucatan.

The last katun of the Classic stage to be commemorated by the dedication of a monument was 10.3.0.0.0 (889). Only three cities erected monuments on this date: Uaxactun, Xultun, and Xamantun, all in the central area. The katun ending 10.4.0.0.0 (909) is found engraved on a jade gorget from Tzibanche in southern Quintana Roo, Mexico. This is the latest certain Long Count date.

It cannot be presumed that the cities of the central Maya area were abandoned immediately after each had erected its last known monument. Undoubtedly many people lingered on after the centers had ceased to erect monuments; but it is doubtful that the sites long retained their importance as ceremonial centers, or as cultural foci. The old pattern of living, which had depended upon elaborate social organization, was gone. The remnants of the central area Maya dwindled in numbers. When Cortez crossed Peten from northwest to southeast in 1524–25, all the centers were entirely abandoned. The first Spaniards saw Yaxchilan and Tikal in 1696; at that time both these sites were completely overgrown with tropical forest.

It must be cautioned that this section presents only a history of dated stelae. This restriction eliminates large areas and certain time periods from consideration. The story told here is likely, however, to present an accurate account of the spread and activities of the central Maya priestly hierarchy.

CAUSES OF THE DECLINE AND FALL OF THE CLASSIC CULTURE

A number of causes have been suggested as responsible for the decline and fall of the Classic Maya—earthquakes, climatic changes, epidemics, foreign conquest, civil war, intellectual and esthetic exhaustion, social decay, governmental disorganization, and economic collapse due to the failure of the Maya agricultural system to meet the needs of the increasing population. Each of these suggestions should be examined more closely before attempting to decide among them.

The first cause, earthquake activity, seems the least likely. It rests primarily upon two factors: (1) the present ruined condition of the Classic-stage cities and (2) the prevalence of severe earthquakes in the highlands of Guatemala immediately south of Peten. However, the following objections may be raised. Although the Guatemala and Chiapas highlands are sometimes violently shaken by earthquakes, the Peten lowlands, owing to their distance from the principal earthquake belt, do not experience the heavy shocks of the highlands. Earthquakes there are much less severe, although it may be noted that in 1936 the whole Maya area was shaken severely enough to damage certain monuments. However, most of the destruction seen in the Maya sites can be accounted for by the irresistible tropical growth which levels all before it. No other region, either in the Old World or the New, is known to have been permanently abandoned because of earthquake activity. Individual cities, it is true, have been permanently abandoned on account of earthquake and volcanic activity—Pompeii and Herculaneum, for example—but never whole countries. Thus the earthquake hypothesis may be rejected.

The idea that climatic changes brought about the destruction and abandonment of the Classic Maya sites is based upon the assumption that the Peten lowlands had a much lower annual rainfall at that time than they have today, owing to a supposed southward shift of general climatic zones in the Western Hemisphere. This assumed lower rainfall in Peten is supposed to have allowed better living conditions there, with a less luxuriant vegetation which was easier for the Maya farmer to clear. Later, toward the end of the Classic stage, the general climatic zones are hypothesized to have shifted northward again, bringing back an increased rainfall to the Peten lowlands. The dry seasons are assumed to have become so short that the bush could no longer be effectively burned, and agriculture, as practiced by the ancient Maya, had to be given up.

The data upon which this hypothesis is based are derived from evidence concerning past rainfall in central and northern California, as established by the varying thicknesses of the tree rings in the redwoods there. While these tree rings present an accurate record of rainfall in the northern half of California for a long period, it has since been demonstrated that it is unlikely that changes in California were accompanied by corresponding changes in the Yucatan Peninsula.

According to supporters of the malaria and yellow fever hypothesis, recurring epidemics of these diseases so decimated the Maya that they were forced to abandon their cities in the Peten lowlands and seek more healthful surroundings elsewhere. Neither of these diseases, however, is known to have existed in the New World prior to the Conquest. Malaria is known from before this time in Europe, and the high resistance to yellow fever shown by Negroes is living evidence of an African origin of this disease. The devastating effect of the earliest yellow fever epidemic recorded in the Americas, in 1648, indicates further that it was an imported disease.

There is no archaeological evidence that foreign conquest brought about the depopulation of the central Maya area, although there is possible evidence of an anticlerical revolt at Piedras Negras, where various religious sculptures were defaced. Central Classic sculpture is conspicuously lacking in the representation of warlike scenes. Bound captives are occasionally portrayed, but the context in which they appear suggests religious ceremonies, and warfare is almost certainly not implied.

It has been suggested that the tendency toward flamboyance in Maya art, which became more pronounced as the Late Period neared its end, must indicate a corresponding cultural decadence among the late Classic Maya, and that this was sufficient to have brought about the downfall and abandonment of their centers. Although this explanation seems plausible, it leaves unexplored the ultimate causes of the collapse of the Maya priesthood, and does not adequately explain the depopulation of the sites in the central Maya area.

Another possible explanation may be sought in agricultural exhaustion. If the Maya system of agriculture was followed uninterruptedly for a long time in any one region, it might finally have ceased to yield sufficient crops to support the resident population, owing to soil exhaustion. When the Maya civilization first developed in the lowlands of northern Peten, this region was densely forested. However, the repeated clearing and burning of areas to serve as corn lands may have gradually converted the original forests into man-made grasslands. Since the ancient Maya had no implements for breaking the sod, such areas would have become useless for agriculture.

Savanna areas are common in some parts of the Peten but, as Eric Thompson has pointed out, ruins are not usually found near them, and grass areas such as town plazas characteristically revert immediately to forest if untended. It is unlikely that the savannas in the Peten and elsewhere are man-made. Kidder has pointed out the inadequacy of the agricultural failure theory to explain the abandonment of Copan, which is situated in a river valley so fertile and well watered that exhaustion of its agricultural resources seems impossible.

The fall as well as the rise of the central Maya civilization is difficult to explain by environmental factors or known historical events. The causal element for the Maya decline may be restricted and defined if we assume that the contemporaneous decline of other Classic New World civilizations were influenced by historically related causes. These cultures are widely enough separated to preclude the action of similar environmental factors or of directly related political events. Trade communications did not unite them. Just as peoples in widely spaced areas of aboriginal America developed similar formal governments ruled by priests, they may have tired simultaneously of this way of life. The lower classes must have revolted, and word must have traveled. Such a drastic change may well have been caused by the formation of an organ-

TABLE IV

Surely Dated Monuments and Buildings in Yucatan, Northern Campeche, and Quintana Roo, Mexico

City	Location in the Northern Half of the Peninsula	Class	Name of Monument	Date Maya Era	Date Christian Era
Oxkintok	West coast region	3	Lintel 1	9. 2. 0. 0. 0	A.D. 475
Tulum	East coast region	3	Stela 1	9. 6.10. 0. 0	A.D. 564
Ichpaatun	East coast region	4	Stela 1	9. 8. 0. 0. 0	A.D. 593
Tzibanche	East coast region	3	Wooden door lintel	9. 9. 5. 0. 0	A.D. 618
Coba	East coast region	2	Stelae 4 and 6	9. 9.10. 0. 0	A.D. 623
Coba	East coast region	2	Stela 3	9.10. 0. 0. 0	A.D. 633
Coba	East coast region	2	Stela 2	9.10.10. 0. 0	A.D. 642
Coba	East coast region	2	Stela 21	9.11. 0. 0. 0	A.D. 652
Island of Jaina	West coast region	4	Stela 1	9.11. 0. 0. 0	A.D. 652
Coba	East coast region	2	Stela 5	9.11.10. 0. 0	A.D. 662
Etzna	West coast region	2	Stela 18	9.12. 0. 0. 0	A.D. 672
Coba	East coast region	2	Stela 1	9.12.10. 5.12	A.D. 682
Coba	East coast region	2	Stela 20	9.12.12. 0. 5	A.D. 684
Etzna	West coast region	2	Stela 19	9.13. 0. 0. 0	A.D. 692
Etzna	West coast region	2	Stela 2	9.15. 0. 0. 0	A.D. 731
Coba	East coast region	2	Stela 16	9.15. 1. 2. 8	A.D. 732
Santa Rosa Xtampak	West coast region	2	Stela 5	9.15.19. 0. 0	A.D. 750
Santa Rosa Xtampak	West coast region	2	Stela 7	9.15.19.17.14	A.D. 751
Holactun	West coast region	3	Temple of the Initial Series	9.16.13. 0. 0	A.D. 764
Etzna	West coast region	2	Hieroglyphic Stairway	9.17.12. ?. ?	A.D. 782
Chichen Itza	East coast region	1	Temple of the Initial Series	10. 2.10. 0. 0	A.D. 879
Tzibanche	East coast region	3	Jade gorget	10. 4. 0. 0. 0	A.D. 909

ized set of new ideas as to the purpose of existence—a new philosophy.

Whatever caused the fall of the Maya priests it was amazingly complete. The central Peten is virtually uninhabited at the present time save for a sparse, seasonal scattering of chicle gatherers. Although it is possible that the commoners survived the collapse of the priestly hierarchy for a while, there is little archaeological evidence of population of any sort after the erection of monuments ceased.

CLASSIC-STAGE OCCUPATION OF THE NORTHERN AREA

At least parts of the Mexican states of Campeche, Yucatan, and Quintana Roo were a part of the widespread lowland tradition in Preclassic times and became provincial to the Peten during the early Classic stage. Late in the Classic stage this area saw the florescence of an indigenous culture, influenced by, but not born of, the central Classic Maya civilization. This culture expanded to cover the whole northern area by the end of the Classic stage, and was invaded, seemingly at the height of its development, by Toltecs from the Mexican mainland.

A total of twenty-one surely dated monuments and buildings at ten sites are now known in northern and central Yucatan, Campeche, and Quintana Roo; these will be found listed in Table IV. This table shows that there are ten dated sites represented here: five sites in the east coast region—Tzibanche, Ichpaatun, Tulum, Coba, and Chichen Itza (Plate 19)—and five in the west coast region—Santa Rosa Xtampak, Etzna, Holactun, Oxkintok, and the Island of Jaina. More than twenty stelae at Dzibilchaltun, and one at Dzilam, none of them datable, show that stelae were erected over most of the northern area, but that many of them were not of central Maya type.

The dates in Table IV indicate that the ten sites were contemporaneous with the last four and a quarter centuries of the Classic stage—475–909. It will also be noted from Table IV that the earliest certain date in the northern half of the peninsula,

9.2.0.0.0 of the Maya Era, or 475, is inscribed on a lintel at Oxkintok in the northwestern corner (Plate 18a).

Unfortunately for an accurate chronological background, the Maya Long Count did not survive in any of the peripheral areas after the collapse of civilization in the central region. In the north, during late Classic times, an abbreviated form of the Long Count was used in its place, but this is neither so accurate nor so well understood as the older Initial Series dating (see chapter xii). For this reason later Yucatecan history lacks the solid chronological framework offered by the dated monuments of the Classic stage.

Ceramic studies over the northern Yucatan Peninsula show an extensive Formative occupation in which three successive periods can be recognized. Twelve sites have so far produced Formative ceramics. A considerable part of this area was provincial to the Peten until about 9.12.0.0.0 (A.D. 672). The architecture as well as the inscriptions at Coba compare closely and favorably with those of contemporaneous Peten sites. At Yaxuna, although the architecture has been razed for later construction, the pottery is Peten-like, of the Tzakol and Tepeu phases. At Acanceh in central Yucatan a similar picture emerges, although Peten resemblances are not so striking. The famous stucco façade (Plate 79) is of early Classic date. There is further evidence, as yet not fully investigated, that the early Classic architecture of northern Yucatan is similar to that of the Peten.

At Oxkintok the picture is different. Although the early Classic architecture is in general similar to that of the Peten, the pottery is distinctive and highly developed. It is mainly monochrome, some of it showing mottled firing effects; the forms are delicate and handsome and many pieces are highly burnished. A little pottery of this type has been found at Campeche and a few similarities to Tabasco pottery are recognizable. There are also suggestions that some characteristics of the Puuc-style pottery, which overlies the early Classic occupation at Oxkintok, may have been inspired by these early Classic wares. Although the Tabasco lowlands are generally considered a part of the central Maya area because of architectural and sculptural similarities, their ceramics are nearly unknown and may prove distinctive enough to set that area apart. It is quite possible that Oxkintok is an outlier of that culture zone. Peten trade wares are rare in the Oxkintok collections, but are sufficient to date them.

At Etzna, farther south in Campeche, there are evidences of Peten-like early Tepeu polychromes, but the architecture contemporaneous with them is uncertain. The architecture at Holactun and Santa Rosa Xtampak, and the overlying architecture at Acanceh, Oxkintok, Holactun, and Etzna is of Puuc-Chenes style, and is associated at all these sites with slateware pottery. Thus there is evidence at several points throughout northern Yucatan of cultural similarities to the early Classic central Maya area in both architecture and ceramics, followed by even stronger cultural ties with the Puuc region in late Classic times. The exception is Oxkintok, which shows an early Classic-stage culture of unknown affiliations.

Directly north of Peten there are three regions showing distinctive architecture and pottery, and almost lacking in stelae. These are, from south to north, the Rio Bec, Chenes, and Puuc regions. The sites of all three regions show a somewhat looser plan than do the Peten sites. There are fewer temples on tall pyramids and more palace-type buildings, which are often placed about closed quadrangles. In all these areas the predominant pottery is slateware, a handsome, finely formed and finished, but plain pottery, which contrasts with the softer, thinner monochromes and polychromes of the Peten and northern Yucatan.

The buildings of the Chenes and Rio Bec areas have much in common: doors in the form of dragon mouths, with elaborate, heavily stuccoed mask forms surrounding them, are characteristic. Towers in the form of dummy temples on the tops of pyramids ornament building corners; masonry is of block form, with well-finished faces. Puuc architecture is distinguished by finely cut stone mosaic in the upper zones of building façades, and by the use of circular columns dividing doorways. Puuc masonry is faced with thin stone slabs having beveled edges. It is likely that the Chenes and Rio Bec sites belong to a single large culture area, the center of which is still nearly unexplored. The Puuc area is much smaller. Many sites in the Chenes and Puuc areas bear buildings in the style of both. In such sites, the Puuc-style buildings are stratigraphically later than the Chenes.

The border region between the Rio Bec and Peten seems to show a marked lack of the cultural overlap so characteristic of the Chenes and Puuc regions. Peten- and Rio Bec-style sites, even when separated by only a few miles, are distinct architecturally, in their plans, and in the absence of stelae in the Rio Bec sites. Although the ceramics of these two types of sites have not been thoroughly investigated as yet, preliminary checks suggest that they will prove to be at least partially contemporaneous as well as quite distinctive. This must mean that a sharp cultural boundary existed for a time between the Rio Bec and the Peten. Since these regions form a continuous physiographic area with imperceptible change in rainfall and vegetation, and since there is no evidence of a former linguistic boundary, some sort of a political division seems likely to have caused the culture boundary. It also seems probable that the center of the Chenes–Rio Bec culture area lay well to the north of the boundary zone, perhaps in east central Campeche.

This archaeological evidence is considerably at variance with the earlier reconstructions of northern Maya history, based on Conquest-period native accounts. The concept that the Puuc sites represent a renaissance of activity of the central Maya which followed a northward migration subsequent to the abandonment of their home area is not borne out. It is significant that both ceramic influence and trade from the central area into the northern part of the peninsula declines sharply after Tepeu 1 times, indicating the growth of a strong indigenous culture in the north, contemporaneous with the height of central Maya development.

The late Classic cultural florescence in the Puuc area has left the most spectacular concentration of architectural remains in the Americas. In addition to the several larger sites—Uxmal, Labna, Sayil, and Kabah—many square miles of country are studded with standing corbel-vaulted buildings and numerous remains of house platforms and cisterns. There is ceramic evidence that Puuc culture finally extended over the northern Yucatan plain, succeeding the Peten-affiliated early Classic culture. The increasing use of Puuc-style slateware in northern sites while the early Classic-stage monochromes were still in use also documents a gradual spread of influence from the Puuc. The brilliant spurt of architectural activity in the Puuc must have depended upon the development of underground cisterns which drained the paved plaza areas surrounding their mouths. It has been estimated that the drainage area of the major plazas of Uxmal alone could supply five thousand people with water throughout the year. The Puuc Maya did not live at their religious centers, although they must have visited and worked at them frequently. Cisterns with collecting platforms and house foundations are scattered throughout the open country. The Puuc is almost uninhabited at present, and seems to have been at all times save during its cultural heyday. Although it is agriculturally rich, there is no available water there for six months of the year.

The dearth of Postclassic cultural remains in the Puuc is startling, following such a heavy occupation. The Toltec invaders who overwhelmed Chichen Itza at the start of the Postclassic stage must have forcibly removed the inhabitants of the Puuc. The Yucatan plain, with its abundance of cenotes, would have allowed the concentration of people into easily controlled large settlements, and the Toltecs may well have done this.

The historical accounts current among the Yucatan Maya at the time of the Spanish Conquest bear but uncertain resemblances to the archaeological reconstruction given above. Fray Lizana in his *Historia de Yucatán* describes the tradition as follows:

The early fathers who first emplanted the faith of Christ in Yucatan knew that the people here came, some from the west and some from the east, and thus in their ancient language they call the east in another way than today. Today they call the east Likin which is the same as when the sun rises, as with us. And the west they call Chikin which is the same as the setting or end of the sun or when it hides itself, as with us. And anciently they called the east Cenial and the west Nohenial cenial which is to say the small descent, and nohenial the great descent. And the reason they say this is because from the part of the east there came down to this land few people, and that of the west, many, and with this word they understand few or many, the east and the west; and the few people from one part and the many from the other.

The eastern of the two "descents" described by Lizana may correspond to certain passages in the Chilam Balams, a series of documents which probably are copies of pre-Conquest Maya codices (see chapter xii). The Chilam Balam of Mani gives the following account of the "discovery" of Chichen Itza:

> Then took place the discovery of the province of Ziyancaan, or Bakhalal; Katun 4 Ahau, Katun 2 Ahau, Katun 13 Ahau [specific 20-year periods], three-score years they ruled Ziyancaan when they descended here; in these years that they ruled Bakhalal it occurred then that Chichen Itza was discovered. 60 years.

The first chronicle from the Book of Chilam Balam of Chumayel is much more brief:

> In Katun 6 Ahau took place the discovery of Chichen Itza.

The Tizimin chronicle says:

> Katun 8 Ahau; it occurred that Chichen Itza was learned about; the discovery of the province of Ziyancaan took place.

The province of Ziyancaan Bakhalal is the area surrounding Lake Bacalar in southeastern Quintana Roo. In addition to the discrepancies in dates shown in the three passages, all the Chilam Balam dates repeat cyclically every 256 years, and thus cannot be fixed in time. As may be seen, Yucatan Conquest-period documents are of little service in writing Classic-stage history.

THE POSTCLASSIC STAGE

WITH THE FLOWERING of the Puuc culture during late Classic times, the center of Maya activity had shifted from the Peten to Yucatan. There is evidence that during this period—about A.D. 800 to 900—Puuc culture spread throughout the northern half of the peninsula, and that architectural achievement reached a final peak of elegance.

The ceremonial centers of the central area were in decline from Copan to Palenque, and in the Valley of Mexico Teotihuacan had long since been burned. Kaminaljuyu, near Guatemala City, seems to have lost its ceremonial splendor. Only at Tajin in central Veracruz, and at Xochicalco, southwest of Mexico City, do we suspect that major ceremonial centers were functioning. The reasons for the decline of the central Maya area have been discussed in chapter iv. If these causes were social and political rather than factors in the natural environment, their wide geographic spread is more easily explained.

The Puuc sites, as well as those of the Chenes and Rio Bec, are less formal in plan and less effort was spent on the monumental aspects of architecture. The ceramics show handsome form and unusual technical competence but are less elaborate and were made with less meticulous care than Peten ceramics. Population in these sites was probably heavier and social organization may even have been more complex, but class structuring must have been less sharply marked than in the Peten. Similar interpretations may with some reason be made for Tajin, Xochicalco, and the sites of this period in the Valley of Mexico, but our data for such inferences are as yet scanty.

Into this rather easygoing milieu came the Toltecs, with such catalytic effect over Mesoamerica that stories concerning them were almost universally encountered by the Spanish five hundred years later. In Yucatan the Toltec conquest changed the Maya way of life considerably more than did the Spanish.

Various accounts—from Guatemala, Yucatan, and the Mexican mainland—chronicle the coming of the Toltecs to the Maya area. They are described as leaving Tula, their capital northwest of Mexico City, and proceeding to Veracruz. From there they went south and split into two groups in extreme southern Veracruz. One group went to the Guatemala highlands, the other eastward along the shore of the Gulf of Campeche to Yucatan.

Archaeological remains of Toltec influence are found in the Guatemala highlands and in Yucatan. The most impressive Toltec site in the Maya area is Chichen Itza, Yucatan. The most coherent account of Chichen Itza and of the later site of Mayapan was given by Bishop Diego de Landa in his *Relación de las cosas de Yucatán*, written about 1566:

Chichen Itza is a very fine site, ten leagues from Izamal and eleven from Valladolid. It is said that it was ruled by three lords who were brothers who came into that country from the west, who were very devout, and so they built very beautiful temples and they lived very chastely without wives, and one of them died or went away, upon which the others acted unjustly and indecently and for this they were put to death. . . . It is believed among the Indians that with the Itzas who occupied Chichen Itza there reigned a great lord, named Kukulcan, and that the principal building, which is called Kukulcan, shows this to be true. They say that he arrived from the west; but they differ among themselves as to whether he arrived before or after the Itzas or with them. They say that he was favorably disposed, and had no wife or children, and that after his return he was regarded in Mexico as one of their gods and called Quetzalcoatl; and they also considered him a god in Yucatan on account of his being a just statesman; and this is seen in the order which he imposed on Yucatan after the death of the lords, in order to calm the dissensions which their deaths had caused in the country.

This Kukulcan established another city after arranging with the native lords of the country that he and they should live there and that all their affairs and business should be brought there; and for this purpose they chose a very good situation, eight leagues further in the interior than Mérida is now, and fifteen or sixteen leagues from the sea. They sur-

rounded it with a very broad stone wall, laid dry, of about an eighth of a
league, leaving in it only two narrow gates. The wall was not very high
and in the midst of this enclosure they built their temples, and the largest,
which is like that of Chichen Itza, they called Kukulcan, and they built
another building of a round form, with four doors, entirely different from
all the others in that land, as well as a great number of others round about
joined together. In this enclosure they built houses for the lords only,
dividing all the land among them, giving towns to each one, according
to the antiquity of his lineage and his personal value. And Kukulcan gave
a name to this city—not his own as the Ah Itzas had done in Chichen Itza,
which means the well of Ah Itzas, but he called it Mayapan, which means
"the standard of the Maya," because they called the language of the country
Maya, and the Indians [say] *"Ichpa"* which means "within the enclosure."
This Kukulcan lived with the lords in that city for several years; and leaving them in great peace and friendship, he returned by the same way to
Mexico, and on the way he stopped at Champoton, and, in memory of him
and of his departure, he erected a fine building in the sea like that of
Chichen Itza, a long stone's throw from the shore. And thus Kukulcan
left a perpetual remembrance in Yucatan.

Kukulcan, the Feathered Serpent, was the Toltec culture hero
(Quetzalcoatl in the Nahua language) and was an exiled king
of Tula, notable for his widespread conquest. The Itzas are characterized in the Yucatecan sources as foreigners. Although their
relation to the Toltecs is not completely certain, they were the ruling
house at Chichen Itza, and are in most accounts identified as the
followers of Kukulcan. At the fall of that city they migrated south
with their followers to Lake Peten Itza, where they formed the
last organized group of Maya to be conquered by the Spanish.

The relationship of Mayapan to Chichen Itza has been clarified
archaeologically during the last few years. Mayapan was built
after the fall of Chichen Itza and, according to sixteenth-century
documents, was abandoned before the Spanish Conquest, about
A.D. 1450. Bishop Landa in another passage describes the rule of
Mayapan as follows:

After the departure of Kukulcan, the nobles agreed, in order that the
government should endure, that the house of the Cocoms should have the
chief power because it was the most ancient or the richest family, or because

he who was at the head of it was a man of greatest worth. This being done since within the enclosure there were only temples and houses for the lords and the high priests, they ordered that other houses should be constructed outside, where each one of them could keep servants, and to which the people from their towns could repair, when they came to the city on business. Each one then established in these houses his major domo, who bore for his badge of office a short and thick stick, and they called him *caluac*. He kept account with the towns and with those who ruled them; and to them was sent notice of what was needed in the house of their lord, such as birds, maize, honey, salt, fish, game, cloth and other things, and the *caluac* always went to the house of his lord, in order to see what was wanted and provided it immediately, since his house was, as it were, the office of his lord.

We have indications from other accounts that several local Yucatecan kings in addition to the Cocoms participated in the rule of Yucatan from Mayapan. The government thus would seem to have been a confederation, centered in a capital where local rulers could spend part or all of their time, supported by feudal retainers.

The circumstances under which Mayapan replaced Chichen Itza as the capital are confused in the account. There are stories of political intrigue, and of the kidnaping of the wife of the ruler of Chichen Itza by the ruler of Izamal. In the ensuing war Hunac Ceel, ruler of Mayapan, conquered Chichen Itza. There is definite archaeological evidence that the Toltec-introduced religion of Chichen Itza was continued at Mayapan; temples and religious art at Mayapan copy the earlier style of Chichen Itza slavishly. There is both archaeological and documentary evidence of continuous pressure from Mexico on political affairs in Yucatan. Hunac Ceel is said to have employed Mexican mercenaries against Chichen Itza, and twice later Cocom rulers of Mayapan brought in Mexican soldiers from garrisons in Tabasco. The second time the Mexicans were defeated but were allowed to stay as colonists in northwest Yucatan.

The above accounts suggest that the Postclassic stage in Yucatan divides naturally into two main periods, first that of Chichen Itza, then Mayapan, and that these were followed by a period of political

collapse. The order of the first two periods, and in fact their dis-
tinctiveness in time, has been determined archaeologically. With
this order determined, the length of the periods can be hypothesized with some degree of likelihood from the katun-round dates
assigned to historical events in the various Chilam Balams. These
may be checked against datings arrived at independently in the
Valley of Mexico. Table III shows the time sequence of Postclassic
Yucatecan history.

The archaeological evidences of Toltec influence at Chichen
Itza are amazingly exact and definitive when the distance to the
Toltec area is considered. Tula, the Toltec capital, has been excavated and restored during the last fifteen years, allowing a whole
series of close comparisons in sculpture and architecture with Chichen Itza. The Mexican characteristics at Chichen Itza nearly all
appear as Postclassic innovations in Yucatan; many of them are
duplicated or nearly duplicated at Tula, and the rest occur at other
sites in central Mexico. Among such innovations are:

1. Colonnades either within or adjacent to buildings. These
colonnades are formed either of square or round columns, often
sculptured in low relief, which are built of a series of stone drums.
The form of the colonnades varies widely. A large interior room
may be roofed on rows of columns (Temple of the Warriors,
Plate 40). A colonnade or series of colonnades, often multiple-
ranged, may be found at the base of a pyramid which bears a temple
on its summit (Temple of the Warriors, Temple of the Wall
Panels). Colonnades also stand alone, backed by a solid wall and
sometimes with end walls (South Temple of Great Ball Court,
Plate 41a). Such a colonnade may be backed by a square or rectangular courtyard surrounded interiorly by another colonnade,
and communicating by means of a doorway with the colonnade in
front (Mercado). Colonnades with backing walls often have ac-
cessory structures such as benches and a dais attached to the rear
wall. Roofing on the colonnades may be either beam and mortar
roofing (Warriors), thatch roofing (Mercado), or Maya corbel
vaulting (many structures). The vaulted roofs are supported on

exceedingly long wooden lintels, the column-lintel arrangement being substituted for the continuous masonry walls of Classic-stage Maya buildings.

2. Round temples occur from early times on the Mexican mainland, but first appear in the Maya area at this period (Caracol, Plate 42*a*).

3. Wide doorways contain two stone columns in the form of feathered serpents; the head is on the ground, the body is vertical, and the tail runs forward and up and bears a wooden lintel (Plate 41*b*).

4. General use of feathered serpents as ornaments on balustrades, panels, etc.

5. A battered basal zone on the exterior faces of most pyramids and building walls. This zone usually stands at an angle of about 75 degrees, to a height of about 3 feet, and contrasts with the characteristically vertical Maya walls.

6. Prowling jaguars, full-faced Tlaloc figures, vultures in profile holding a human heart in their talons, and a reclining human figure holding a long, diagonally placed spear. These motifs are nearly identical at Tula and Chichen Itza as bas-relief carvings.

7. *Tzompantli* or skull rack. This is a low platform, walled in stone and covered with human skulls sculptured in relief. Although no tzompantli has been found at Tula, they have been found at other sites in central Mexico.

8. Atlantean figures, men with hands upraised to support a dais or door lintel, sculptured in full round.

9. Warrior figures in a variety of sculptural treatments, but wearing characteristic clothing, ornaments, and insignia. They are found in processions on altars, singly on square columns, as caryatids sculptured in full round at Tula. Insignia include butterfly-shaped gorgets and headdress ornaments, various styles of headgear including headdresses identifiable as related to those of the Aztec military orders of Eagles and Jaguars. Many figures carry spear throwers.

10. Chac Mools, figures of men lying on their backs with the knees and head raised, and with the hands surrounding a bowl-

shaped depression carved at about the position of the navel. These
are sculptured in full round.

11. Standard bearers, sculptured standing figures with hands
held in front of the body and a perforation between the hands,
seemingly designed to hold a pole which likely bore a flag at its top.

12. Paintings showing human sacrifice by removal of the heart
of a man stretched supine over an altar. This is known as an Aztec
custom and was doubtless older on the Mexican mainland.

13. The carving of bas-relief sculpture on a previously constructed masonry wall is extremely rare in late Classic Yucatan
sites, but is common on Toltec buildings at Tula and Chichen Itza.

It will be noted that the above listed Toltec innovations at
Chichen Itza are concerned with the form of objects and of buildings which were connected with warfare and religion. There are
also several representations of the military conquest of the Maya by
Toltec warriors, whose spear throwers and characteristic shields and
insignia contrast with Maya-style weapons and costume. Most of
the sculptured figures which ornament the temples are elements of
Toltec religious and civil iconography, and the plans of Toltec
religious and governmental architecture must also be related to
Toltec formal ceremony.

In contrast to such foreign forms, the craftsmanship of all the
carving and of much of the painting and the constructional details
of the buildings clearly belong to the native craft traditions of
Yucatan. Comparison of Chichen Itza with Tula sculpture shows
basic differences in the handling of the subject matter, as well as
in many details of form. This is clear despite a near identity of
subject matter and iconographic detail. Tula figures are simpli-
fied and squarish when compared with the curvilinear elaboration
of the Maya work; Chichen Itza veneer masonry and corbeled
vaulting have no counterparts at Tula.

From these archaeological indications we can safely conclude
that the Toltecs conquered the native Maya, and that they brought
priests who used the iconography of their religion and the para-
phernalia necessary for its ritual. A major change in religious
buildings, for example, was the creation of large areas covered by

beamed roofs supported by spaced columns. The Toltec priests must have sketched and talked and the Maya produced sculpture and architecture to order, but their products were both technically and esthetically more refined than those of Tula. On the other hand, the foreign nature of the Toltec religious symbolism to the Maya craftsmen doubtless explains the lifelessness of many of the Toltec symbols in comparison to various livelier and probably less rigidly specified carvings and paintings.

The Conquest-period Maya documents, although often historically confused, add a wealth of enlightening details. There are frequent references to the Mexicans as lewd tricksters. There are prophecies of their downfall by internal dissension and there are laments for the happier, earlier days.

In due measure did they recite the good prayers, in due measure they sought the lucky days, until they saw the good stars enter into their reign. Then they kept watch while the reign of the good stars began. Then everything was good. Then they adhered to the dictates of their reason; in the holy faith their lives were passed. . . . The foreigners made it otherwise when they arrived here. They brought shameful things when they came. They lost their innocence in carnal sin. . . . No lucky days were then displayed to us. This was the cause of our sickness also. There were no more lucky days for us; we had no sound judgment. At the end of our loss of vision and of our shame everything shall be revealed. There was no great teacher, no great speaker, no supreme priest when the change of rulers occurred at their arrival. Lewd were the priests when they came to be settled here by the foreigners. Furthermore they left their descendants here at Mayapan. These then received the misfortunes, after the affliction of these foreigners. These, they say, were the Itza. Three times it was, they say, that the foreigners arrived.

Landa's characterization in the *Relación de las cosas de Yucatán* is at variance with the uncomplimentary characterization above. The rulers of Chichen Itza are described as "three lords who were brothers who came into that country from the west, who were very devout and so built very beautiful temples and lived very chastely without wives, and one of them died or went away, upon which the other two acted unjustly and indecently, and for this they were put to death." The Chilam Balam of Mani describes the Itzas as "holy men." From other passages we gather that the brother who went away to Mexico was Kukulcan, whereas another passage says that Kukulcan founded Mayapan after the building of Chichen Itza. It must be remembered that all these stories come from a common source; they are the Yucatecans' concept of their history. There is evidence in them of considerable garbling through the misplacement of the order of events in time, and a frequent tele- scoping of the time scale to make successive events contempora- neous.

The Maya respect for the piety of Kukulcan, and the luxuriance of religious construction at Chichen Itza suggest that the Maya may have lent their talents and labor willingly to the furtherance of a new religion. Perhaps the Toltec conquest of Yucatan was ac- complished as much by religious evangelization as by military force. The abandonment of Chichen Itza for the new political center of Mayapan may reflect discontentment with dissolute and arbitrary Mexican successors to the revered Kukulcan. At any rate, the close copying of religious architecture at Mayapan suggests that the prestige of the imported religion survived political and moral dissolution.

The religious innovations made by the Toltecs must not have displaced the Maya faith entirely at any time. At present they form no part of the numerous vestiges of Maya religion still held by the Yucatecan farmer. In the sixteenth century Landa reports the cele- bration of a ritual in honor of Kukulcan, but only as part of a pre- dominantly Maya religious calendar. Human sacrifice, a part of Toltec ritual, was still prominent at the Conquest, but probably as an adjunct to Maya ceremonies.

There was also a high priest over all of Yucatan, who received no assignment of servants from the political lords but was sup- ported by gifts. He held himself apart from things political, and from most sacrifices. He appointed all priests, and his advice on matters of learning was much respected by the lords. The office was hereditary and it seems possible that this man was the head of the old Maya priestly hierarchy, shorn of direct political power but still influential and respected. The second sons of lords were trained in priestly learning, which included the calendar and related ceremonies, divinations and prophecies, Maya writing, and cures for diseases.

The relative strength of the various types of Maya institutions may be gauged by the results of the Toltec impact: although a number of important Toltec additions were made, the essential framework of Maya religion survived. In contrast, Toltec political rule was supreme, and Maya learning was used only as an adjunct.

The ruling political groups at the time of the Spanish Conquest prided themselves on their Mexican ancestry, and their leaders periodically conducted a curious sort of interrogation of officials to ensure that no Maya impostors had crept into their ranks. This series of riddles, quite nonsensical in form, was called the language of Zuyua, and survives in the Chilam Balam of Chumayel. Zuyua is a mythical place, associated with Aztec origins and also considered the birthplace of Kukulcan. This "language" must have been taught by father to son among the rulers, and presumably was unknown to those not of Mexican descent. Question 2 of the interrogation may be cited as an example: "Let them go and get the brains of the sky, so that the head-chief may see how large they are.—This is what the brains of the sky are: it is copal gum." Despite its claim as esoteric Mexican lore, the language of Zuyua is studded with Maya calendric and religious references, presumably added during the five-hundred-year stay of the Mexican rulers in Yucatan.

The buildings and sculpture at Chichen Itza are finer and on a grander scale than those at Tula, and compare favorably with those at Uxmal, which it displaced as the most magnificent center in Yucatan. The grandeur of Chichen Itza is more easily understandable if sixteenth-century traditions are true, that Chichen Itza ruled over areas in Guatemala and the Mexican mainland as well as over Yucatan. Uxmal and the other sites of the Puuc area show no signs of a gradual decadence; the finest buildings as well as the most refined pottery were the latest made. The sudden abandonment of the flourishing Puuc area must have been forcibly accomplished. A plausible explanation may be that the Toltecs, accustomed to governing towns rather than scattered farmers, seized the Puuc centers and herded the Maya into settlements around the cenotes of the northern Yucatan plain. These natural wells provide an inexhaustible water source during the dry season, whereas the Puuc area is almost uninhabitable without the carefully dug cisterns or *chultuns* which the Maya had developed. It should have been fairly simple for the Toltecs to have rendered chultuns useless by systematic sabotage. No chultuns have been made in Yucatan since the Toltecs, and the Puuc has remained uninhabited for nearly a thousand years.

There is no evidence of a town around the religious center of Chichen Itza, although there have been reports of fragments of a wall which may have surrounded the site. The massive construction of Chichen Itza and the huge amount of sculpture suggest a considerable labor force, which may have consisted of friendly Maya, perhaps led by a group pacified earlier in Tabasco and Campeche to the west. However, it seems evident from the accuracy of the Toltec iconography reproduced at Chichen Itza that the priestly rulers, artists, and architects were from Tula. There is also evidence of continued trade with the Mexican mainland. Fine Orange pottery, which was manufactured in central Veracruz, has been found in quantity at Chichen Itza—a dozen or more whole vessels and over a thousand fragments. This pottery is the best made of any in Mesoamerica. It must have been shipped in dugouts along the coast, a distance of 650 miles, plus perhaps another 75 miles by land. The dugouts were paddled; no sails are described in this area by the early explorers. A month's trip must have been the minimum for such a haul, and either an unusually peaceful coastline or considerable Toltec authority must have been needed to assure its passage in quantity.

Smaller quantities of other Mexican mainland pottery were found at Chichen Itza. A long, fragile clay pipe seems to have been brought from far west of Mexico City, and vessels of Plumbate pottery came from the Guatemala highlands. This was all trade in luxury goods; gold in some quantity came from Panama, turquoise and jade from various highland areas. The effects on the local craftsmen of the importation of Fine Orange pottery are clearly evident. Native pottery of all sorts save the cooking pots shows copying of Veracruz shapes, but it is usually not accurate because of the retention of the old Yucatecan forming techniques. The designs are also copied, but have little of the verve and precision of the imported pieces. The incised designs are done before application of the slip, a native Yucatecan practice not found in the Veracruz pottery.

The absence of pottery *comales* at Chichen Itza suggests that the Toltecs brought no women with them. Comales form a major constituent in Valley of Mexico archaeological collections of the Toltec period. They are used to roast tortillas, an exclusively feminine task. It is difficult to imagine that if women who knew how to make tortillas lived at Chichen Itza, they would not have been provided with comales.

Archaeological excavations in Yucatan have provided a chronological sequence to which the documentary accounts cited earlier add substance (see Table V). Two sequent architectural periods, the earlier at Toltec Chichen Itza, the later at Mayapan, are well understood. Associated with the Toltec buildings at Chichen Itza is the Early Mexican ceramic substage. Almost entirely postdating these structures is found pottery of the Middle Mexican substage; such pottery is also found in the lower levels at Mayapan, mixed with the Late Mexican pottery characteristic of that site. Since Mayapan is known to have been abandoned about A.D. 1440, a hiatus exists between this site and the Conquest, unexplored archaeologically unless the east coast sites of Tulum and Santa Rita Corozal bridge this gap.

Shortly before the abandonment of Toltec Chichen Itza (about A.D. 1200) a new tempering material was introduced in the pottery-making craft and spread rapidly over the peninsula. Shortly after the establishment of Mayapan a new slip color appeared, and has lasted in Yucatan popularity until now. Using these changes as time markers we know that Chichen Itza, in contrast to the earlier Puuc sites, was depopulated gradually, and its abandonment was preceded by a period of decadence. There is also ceramic evidence of a time lapse of unknown duration between the abandonment of Chichen Itza and the founding of Mayapan. The religious importance of Chichen Itza, however, lasted until the Spanish Conquest, and there is abundant evidence, both archaeological and documentary, of pilgrimages to the site.

The Mayapan buildings, in distinction to those of Toltec Chichen Itza, are made of crudely shaped blocks, set in mud or plaster mortar. Not a vaulted roof of this period remains standing at Mayapan, and the sculpture is equally slipshod. How great was this loss to the Maya tradition will be realized by anyone who has seen the delicately worked veneer walls of Chichen Itza and Uxmal.

The pottery of Mayapan is undistinguished, though competent enough. The influence of Veracruz shapes continued, and the sizes and forms of vessels are reminiscent of the Aztec, with a few identical details. Another style of Fine Orange ware was imported in some quantity from the near-by Campeche coast, but it was of a poorer quality. Two new vessel forms of particular interest were introduced at some time late in the history of Mayapan. Since both seem to have had western origins, they may have come with the Mexicans who were introduced as mercenary soldiers to fight for Cocom supremacy in the confederacy of Mayapan. A new cooking pot, the cauldron, was introduced, suggesting that women came with the mercenaries. The figurine incensarios, which also appear at this time, must stem from early roots in the Oaxacan highlands, where such vessels were made from Preclassic times on. These Mayapan incensarios are similar in detail to those of a very wide area, stretching from southern Veracruz through British Honduras. Over this whole area figurine incensarios are found on the surfaces of more ancient Maya ruins, as well as near temples of their own time period, and the early Spaniards destroyed such "idols" in large numbers during the first years of their stay in Yucatan.

At Santa Rita Corozal a remarkable series of murals has been found, dating from shortly before the Conquest. Their style and

TABLE V

A SUMMARY OF THE LEADING EVENTS OF MAYA HISTORY FOR FOURTEEN CENTURIES—A.D. 317–1717

Name of Period	The Long Count (The Initial Series)		Gregorian Equivalents (A.D.)	Events
	8.14. 0. 0. 0	7 Ahau 3 Xul	317, September 1	Leyden Plate engraved at Tikal. Earliest dated object in the Maya hieroglyphic writing.
	8.14. 3. 1.12	12 Eb 0 Yaxkin	320, September 17	
	8.14.10.13.15	8 Men 8 Kayab	328, April 11	Stela 9, Uaxactun. Earliest dated monument in the Maya hieroglyphic writing.
	8.16. 0. 0. 0	3 Ahau 8 Kankin	357, February 3	Stelae 18 and 19, Uaxactun. First monuments to be erected at the ends of katuns of the Maya chronological era.
Classic (Early Period)	8.18.10. 0. 0	11 Ahau 18 Pop	406, May 17	Stela 5, Balakbal, first monument to be erected at the end of a half-katun of the Maya chronological era.
	8.19. 0. 0. 0	10 Ahau 13 Kayab	416, March 25	Stela 18, Tikal. Earliest known monument at this city.
	9. 0. 0. 0. 0	8 Ahau 13 Ceh	435, December 11	The first Katun 8 Ahau.
	9. 2. 0. 0. 0	4 Ahau 13 Uo	475, May 15	Earliest date in the north. Lintel at Oxkintok, Yucatan, Mexico.
	9. 4. 0. 0. 0	13 Ahau 18 Yax	514, October 18	Chichen Itza occupied by the Itza; the new land divided.
	9. 6.10. 0. 0	8 Ahau 13 Pax	564, January 29	Stela 1, Tulum, Quintana Roo.
	9. 8. 0. 0. 0	5 Ahau 3 Chen	593, August 24	Stela 1, Ichpaatun, Quintana Roo.
	9. 9. 0. 0. 0	3 Ahau 3 Zotz	613, May 12	Stela 1, Island of Jaina, Campeche.
	9.11. 0. 0. 0	12 Ahau 8 Ceh	652, October 14	Stela 18, Etzna, Campeche.
	9.12. 0. 0. 0	10 Ahau 8 Yaxkin	672, July 1	Stela 1, Coba, Quintana Roo.
	9.12.10. 0. 0	9 Ahau 18 Zotz	682, May 10	Chichen Itza abandoned; the Itza moved to Chakanputun.
	9.13. 0. 0. 0	8 Ahau 8 Uo	692, March 18	Stelae 5 and 7, Santa Rosa Xtampak, Campeche.
Classic (Late Period)	9.16. 0. 0. 0	2 Ahau 13 Tzec	751, May 9	Temple of the Initial Series, Holactun, Campeche.
	9.16.13. 0. 0	2 Ahau 8 Uo	764, March 1	Xiu history begins with their arrival at Nonoualco.
	10. 2. 0. 0. 0	3 Ahau 3 Ceh	869, August 17	Temple of the Initial Series, Chichen Itza, Yucatan.
	10. 2.10. 0. 0	2 Ahau 13 Chen	879, June 26	Last stelae of the Classic stage: Stela 12, Uaxactun; Stela 10, Xultun, both in Peten; and Stela 1, Xamantun, Campeche.
	10. 3. 0. 0. 0	1 Ahau 3 Yaxkin	889, May 4	
	10. 4. 0. 0. 0	12 Ahau 3 Uo	909, January 20	Latest certain Long Count date of the Classic stage: jadeite gorget, Tzibanche, Quintana Roo.
	10. 6. 0. 0. 0	8 Ahau 8 Yax	948, June 24	Chakanputun abandoned. The Itza entered northern Yucatan from the southwest. Xiu left Nonoualco, moving eastward.
	10. 8. 0. 0. 0	4 Ahau 13 Cumhu	987, November 27	Chichen Itza reoccupied by the Itza. Mayapan founded by Kukulcan.

Period	Long Count	Calendar Round	Date	Event
Postclassic (Puuc Period)	10.9.0.0.0	2 Ahau 13 Mac	1007, August 15	Uxmal founded by Ah Zuitok Tutul Xiu. League of Mayapan began.
	10.10.0.0.0	13 Ahau 13 Mol	1027, May 2	
	10.12.0.0.0	9 Ahau 18 Pax	1066, October 4	
	10.16.0.0.0	1 Ahau 3 Muan	1145, August 11	
	10.18.0.0.0	10 Ahau 3 Tzec	1185, January 13	
	10.18.10.0.0	9 Ahau 13 Uo	1194, November 22	Plot of Hunac Ceel. The Itza driven from Chichen Itza by the Cocom of Mayapan. League of Mayapan ended.
Postclassic (Mexican Period)	10.19.0.0.0	8 Ahau 8 Cumhu	1204, September 30	
	11.1.0.0.0	4 Ahau 8 Mol	1244, March 4	
	11.3.0.0.0	13 Ahau 13 Pax	1283, August 7	The Ascendancy of Mayapan.
	11.7.0.0.0	5 Ahau 18 Kankin	1362, June 14	
	11.9.0.0.0	1 Ahau 18 Zotz	1401, November 17	
	11.11.0.0.0	10 Ahau 3 Mac	1441, April 21	
Postclassic (Period of Disintegration)	11.12.0.0.0	8 Ahau 3 Mol	1461, January 6	Destruction of Mayapan. All large cities abandoned; end of centralized authority (1441).
	11.13.0.0.0	6 Ahau 3 Zip	1480, September 23	Hurricane (1464). Pestilence (end of 1480); mortality due to the wars (1496). Spaniards first seen (1511); Smallpox (?), *Mayacimil* or "the easy death" (1515 or 1516).
	11.14.0.0.0	4 Ahau 8 Pax	1500, June 11	
	11.15.0.0.0	2 Ahau 8 Zac	1520, February 27	Spaniards arrived; Mérida founded (1542, January 6, O.S.); conquest completed (1546).
	11.17.0.0.0	11 Ahau 8 Pop	1559, August 1	
	12.1.0.0.0	3 Ahau 18 Kayab	1638, June 7	Fathers Fuensalida and Orbita visited Tayasal (1618, October).
	12.4.0.0.0	10 Ahau 18 Uo	1697, July 27	Tayasal, last capital of the Itza, destroyed by Martin de Ursua.
	12.5.0.0.0	8 Ahau 3 Pax	1717, April 14	

subject matter is very close to that of the codices of the Mixtec area southeast of the Valley of Mexico, but only a few scattered similarities have been noted between the figurine incensarios of the northern Maya area and Mixtec art. As can be seen, both the incensarios and the frescoes document strong western religious influences at a very late date in the Yucatan Peninsula, but it is uncertain whether both document the same religion.

A widespread tradition in Colonial Yucatan relates that Kukulcan introduced idolatry and human sacrifice. Archaeologically the introduction of human sacrifice in the Mexican manner by removing the heart is documented for the Toltec period. The making of clay idols came later, and probably from Campeche rather than from the Valley of Mexico. Thus it is probable that two waves of religious evangelization from the west may be evidenced by the archaeological finds, although the picture is far from clear as yet.

Intensive archaeological excavations have been conducted by the Carnegie Institution at Mayapan over some five years, producing a variety of information on settlement plan and domestic and religious architecture. Mayapan was a walled settlement, covering an area of 1.6 square miles. Its gateways show careful planning against military attack. There is documentary evidence that the bow and arrow as well as quilted cotton armor were introduced from Campeche during the occupation of Mayapan, supplementing the spear thrower, which the Toltecs had already introduced. Within the wall was a religious precinct, as described by Landa, although the low, secondary wall said to have surrounded it has not been located archaeologically. Around the temples of the major center were grouped colonnaded rectangular buildings with solid rear walls, which probably represent the official quarters of the regional kings. These buildings face upon a series of paved plazas. Thirty-five hundred buildings have been counted within the wall of Mayapan, and the population must have totaled over fifteen thousand.

Throughout the town are irregularly spaced houses, most of which were at least partially of masonry construction. When available, slightly elevated ground was chosen for their location, presumably for reasons of drainage, which is always a problem in Yucatan during heavy rains. Low, dry-stone property walls surround these houses, enclosing irregularly shaped dooryards which average perhaps 0.25 of an acre in area. Meandering among the haphazardly placed houses are lanes or passages of a sort, their irregular boundaries fixed by whatever property walls chance to be adjacent. This house arrangement varies strikingly from that in the Valley of Mexico, where houses were built in contiguous lines or masses. It seems reasonable to speculate that the Maya, when brought into town by the Mexicans, kept the plans of their rural farmsteads, and probably continued to keep bees and raise fruit and garden vegetables as they still do in Yucatecan villages. Although Mayapan is described as dependent on tribute from other parts of the country for subsistence and thus may not be a typical settlement, it fits the description of native towns given by the early Spaniards. As Landa put it:

Before the Spaniards had conquered that country, the natives lived together in towns in a very civilized fashion. They kept the land well cleared and free from weeds, and planted very good trees. Their dwelling place was as follows: in the middle of the town were their temples with beautiful plazas, and all around the temples stood the houses of the lords and the priests, and then of the most important people. Thus came the houses of the richest and of those who were held in the highest estimation nearest to these, and at the outskirts of the town were the houses of the lower class. And the wells, if there were but few of them, were near the houses of the lords; and they had their improved lands planted with wine trees and they sowed cotton, pepper and maize, and they lived thus close together for fear of their enemies, who took them captive, and it was owing to the wars of the Spaniards that they scattered in the woods.

The best-preserved architectural remains of the period of Mayapan are those at Tulum on the east coast of Yucatan; others are on the Isla de Mujeres and Cozumel Island off the east coast, and small shrines of this period have been identified at Coba. The architecture of these ruins is distinctive, and unlike that known from

Mayapan. The fine group of murals from Santa Rita farther down the east coast shows close similarities to less well-preserved paintings on the Tulum temples. Both show striking similarities to the design of pre-Conquest Mixtec codices from the Mexican highlands, and to murals from the same area at Mitla. Figurine incensarios and pottery of the same style as that of Mayapan come from these east coast ruins.

The documentary sources are unsatisfactory concerning the east coast of Yucatan. Tulum, the most spectacular archaeological site of the area, is still a landmark to mariners in the Cozumel Channel. It was occupied nearly until Conquest times but is not certainly identified in any of the early accounts of Spanish voyages. The Chilam Balams, although they mention the names of eastern towns and give an impression of friendly relations with them, do not give data on their political affiliations.

The Mexican connections suggested by the Santa Rita and Tulum murals are roughly equivalent in degree to those of Toltec Chichen Itza—they suggest that men reared in the Mixtec religion were their designers. Although the similarity between Mayapan and east coast figurine incensarios is close enough to suggest that the same religion was introduced into the two areas, the east coast gives the most exact Mixtec parallels, and also shows fewer of the copied Toltec features of Mayapan. It is as though a new religion was introduced over the whole area and was accepted wholeheartedly along the east coast, but formed only an overlay to the existing Quetzalcoatl cult at Mayapan. Perhaps the ease of coastal dugout traffic, abetted by a lack of Maya political organization on the east coast, allowed a more complete religious conversion there. We have no evidence as to whether military and political power accompanied religious conversion, but at Mayapan there is a suggestion of political pressure in the use of Mexican mercenaries by the local rulers.

The collapse of the central government at Mayapan began a final phase of decadence. Discord among the petty kings was a contributing factor to the success of the Spanish Conquest.

Bishop Landa, in describing the calamities that befell Yucatan during the century between the fall of Mayapan and the Spanish Conquest, definitely fixes the former event as having taken place in the year A.D. 1441. Four of the five native chronicles, as well as the two leading early Spanish authorities—Cogolludo, writing in 1656, and Villagutierre Soto-Mayor in 1700—corroborate this dating.

Taking the year of his writing, 1566, as his point of departure, Landa says:

> Since the last plague, more than fifty years have now passed, the mortality of the wars was twenty years prior, the pestilence of the swelling was sixteen years before the wars, and the hurricane another sixteen years before that, and twenty-two or twenty-three years after the destruction of the city of Mayapan. Thus according to this count it has been 125 years since its overthrow, within which the people of this country have passed through the calamities described.

This fixes the date of the plague as 1516 or 1515, the date of the mortality due to the wars as 1496, the date of the pestilence as 1480, the date of the hurricane as 1464, and the date of the destruction of Mayapan as 1441. The chronicle from the Book of Chilam Balam of Tizimin and the first and second chronicles from the Chilam Balam of Chumayel record that there was a pestilence in Katun 4 Ahau (1480–1500), which, according to Landa, occurred at the very beginning of this katun. The first chronicle from the Book of Chilam Balam of Chumayel describes an epidemic of smallpox as having taken place in Katun 2 Ahau (1500–1520). This is doubtless Landa's pestilence "with great pustules that rotted the body," which occurred according to his reckoning in 1515 or 1516. Small though these two items of confirmation may be, they suggest a high degree of reliability for at least this time span in the native chronicles.

After the fall of Mayapan, all the larger cities were abandoned. The Chels, a prominent noble family of Mayapan, left after the fall of the city and established their principal settlement at Tecoh. The only surviving son of the slain Cocom ruler, gathering the remnants of his people about him, established his rule at Tibolon, near Sotuta. The victors, the Tutul Xiu, founded a new capital which they called Mani, meaning in Maya "it is passed."

The last important event in the pre-Conquest history of Yucatan was the ill-fated pilgrimage of the Xiu ruler and his court to offer human sacrifice in the Well of Sacrifice at Chichen Itza in 1536. In this year, not a Spaniard remained in Yucatan. After two unsuccessful attempts to subjugate the Maya in 1527–28 and again in 1531–35, the Spaniards had withdrawn completely from the peninsula.

Ah Dzun Xiu, ruler of the Tutul Xiu at their new capital of Mani, thought the moment auspicious for undertaking a pilgrimage to appease the Maya gods, who for so many years had afflicted the land with calamities. He applied for a safe-conduct from Nachi Cocom, the ruler of Sotuta, through whose province the pilgrims had to pass. The Xiu ruler no doubt feared reprisals on the part of Nachi Cocom, because of the leading part his great-grandfather, Ah Xupan Xiu, had played in the slaying of Nachi Cocom's great-grandfather, the last ruler of Mayapan.

Nachi Cocom, however, had not forgotten the death of his great-grandfather, for which he held Xiu treachery responsible, and he welcomed the Xiu request as an opportunity for revenge. The request for a safe-conduct was promptly granted, and a pilgrimage headed by Ah Dzun Xiu, his son Ah Ziyah Xiu, and forty other leaders of the Xiu nation set out for Chichen Itza via the province of Sotuta. Nachi Cocom, with a large delegation of his people, met them at Otzmal, five miles southeast of the Cocom capital.

The Xiu pilgrims were royally entertained for four days, but at a banquet on the evening of the fourth day the Cocom fell upon their guests and killed them all. This act of treachery split the warring Maya anew, and pitted the two most powerful houses in the northern peninsula against each other. Even before 1536,

the Xiu had offered their submission to the Spaniards, in the second
phase of the Conquest (1531–35), but the Cocom had resisted.
This probably added fuel to ancient Cocom hatred of the Xiu and
was an additional motive for the Otzmal slaughter.

This massacre, coming so shortly before the third and final
phase of the Spanish Conquest, sealed the fate of the Maya. It
revived old hatreds and effectively prevented a united stand against
the Spaniards when they returned to Yucatan in 1540 in their successful attempt to subdue the country. Exhausted by civil war,
betrayed by some of their own leading native houses, and decimated by calamities, the Maya were unable to resist the better-
armed Spaniards and finally succumbed to their superior might
(Table V).

THE SPANISH CONQUEST OF YUCATAN

THE FIRST ENDURING MAYA CONTACT WITH
THE WHITE MAN IN 1511

THE FIRST white men reached Yucatan in 1511. In that year a Spanish official named Valdivia set out from Darien in a caravel for the island of Santo Domingo to report to the governor of that island concerning the quarrels between Diego de Nicuesa and Vasco Nuñez de Balboa. Near Jamaica the caravel foundered and sank, but Valdivia and eighteen sailors escaped in a small boat, without sails and without food. The Yucatan Current carried the survivors westward for fourteen days, during which time seven men died. The survivors were cast upon the east coast of Yucatan, probably somewhere in the Province of Ekab. On land, further misfortunes were in store for them. They were seized by an unfriendly Maya lord, who sacrificed Valdivia and four companions and gave their bodies to his people for a feast. Gerónimo de Aguilar, Gonzalo de Guerrero, and five others were spared for the moment as being too thin for this cannibalistic orgy. Says Aguilar, in describing their situation, "I together with six others remained in a coop, in order that for another festival that was approaching, being fatter, we might solemnize their banquet with our flesh."

Aguilar and his companions escaped and fled to the country of another lord, an enemy of the first chieftain. This second lord enslaved the Spaniards, and soon all of them died except Aguilar and Guerrero. Aguilar was serving still another Maya chieftain when Cortez reached Yucatan in 1519. Gonzalo de Guerrero in the meantime had drifted farther south and entered the service of Nachan Can, Lord of Chetumal, whose daughter he married. He rose to a powerful position in that province. When Cortez' messengers offered to take Guerrero back to the Spaniards he declined, choosing to spend his life with his Maya family. Aguilar suggests that Guerrero was ashamed to rejoin his countrymen "because he has his nostrils, lips, and ears pierced and his face painted, and his hands tattooed . . . and on account of the vice he had committed with the woman and his love for his children."

This was the first contact between the Maya and members of the white race. It is probable that the pestilence of 1515 or 1516, the *mayacimil* or "easy death," which was characterized by great pustules that "rotted their bodies with a great stench so that the limbs fell to pieces in four or five days," may have been smallpox, perhaps introduced among the Maya by survivors of the Valdivia expedition or transmitted overland from Darien by Indian traders.

THE FRANCISCO HERNÁNDEZ DE CÓRDOBA EXPEDITION, 1517

Early in 1517, Francisco Hernández de Córdoba sailed westward from Santiago de Cuba in search of slaves. It is not clear exactly where he first sighted the Yucatan mainland, but it is believed that he first landed at the Isla de Mujeres on the northeast coast. After leaving this island, Córdoba turned northwest to Cape Catoche and then, skirting along the north coast of the peninsula, sailed southward as far as the Bay of Campeche, where he landed on February 23, 1517. At Campeche the Spaniards heard of a large town called Champoton, farther south along the coast, where they next landed. The Lord of Champoton received the Spaniards with open hostility, and a fight ensued. In spite of the gunfire, which the Maya encountered for the first time in this battle, the Indians fought bravely, inflicting heavy losses on the better-armed Spaniards. Córdoba himself received thirty-three wounds and "sadly returned to Cuba" to report the new land as very rich, because of the gold trinkets he had found. He died of his wounds shortly after his return.

THE JUAN DE GRIJALVA EXPEDITION IN 1518

Diego de Velásquez, governor of Cuba, was greatly excited by the reports of gold, and fitted out another expedition of four ships and two hundred men under command of his nephew, Juan de

Grijalva. Francisco de Montejo, the future conqueror of Yucatan, was also a member of this second expedition, which left Cuba in April 1518.

Grijalva's pilot was Anton de Alaminos, who had piloted the Córdoba expedition. The first landing was made at the Island of Cozumel off the east coast, where the Maya fled at sight of the Spaniards. Grijalva continued southward along the coast, passing three large sites, one of which is described as follows:

We followed the shore day and night, and the next day toward sunset we perceived a city or town so large, that Seville would not have seemed more considerable nor better; one saw there a very large tower; on the shore was a great throng of Indians, who bore two standards which they raised and lowered to signal us to approach them; the commander [Grijalva] did not wish it. The same day we came to a beach near which was the highest tower we had seen. . . . We discovered a wide entrance lined with wooden piles set up by fishermen.

The largest of the sites seen by Grijalva was probably the ancient town of Zama (perhaps the archaeological site of Tulum), and the "highest tower" was almost certainly the Castillo of Tulum. The large bay was Ascension Bay, so named because it was discovered on Ascension Thursday, 1518.

This was the southernmost point reached. From here Grijalva sailed north again and around the peninsula to Campeche on the west coast. Continuing southward from Campeche, he discovered the Laguna de Términos, named the San Pablo and San Pedro River, and entered the Rio Tabasco. In this region considerable treasure was obtained, including the first Aztec turquoise mosaic work the Spaniards had seen. Following the gulf coast northward, Grijalva first heard of the Aztec nation, presumably at some place on the Veracruz coast, and finally reached as far north as the Pánuco River. On the return voyage to Cuba, the armada put in at Champoton to avenge the defeat of Córdoba, the year before. Here the Maya again attacked the Spaniards fiercely, killing one and wounding fifty others, including Grijalva. From Champoton, Grijalva returned to Havana, having been gone for five months.

The voyage of Grijalva caused tremendous excitement in Cuba. Yucatan was thougnt to be a land of gold and plenty, awaiting only the adventurous to seize its riches. A third expedition was fitted out, consisting of eleven ships, five hundred men, and some horses. Hernando Cortez was put in command of the armada, and with him went a number of other captains: Francisco de Montejo, Pedro de Alvarado, Diego de Ordaz, Gonzalo de Sandoval, Cristóbal de Olid, and Bernal Díaz del Castillo, most of them destined to win fame in the conquest of Mexico.

The armada first anchored off the Island of Cozumel, where Cortez spent some days. Idols in the temples were destroyed, and a cross was erected in one of them. While here, Cortez learned of the presence of "bearded men" on the mainland. These seemed to be white men and Cortez sent messengers to summon them. In this manner Gerónimo de Aguilar was rescued, and later served Cortez well as interpreter.

Leaving Cozumel, the armada sailed around the north coast of the peninsula and continued on to the Tabasco River, which was renamed Grijalva in honor of its discoverer. In Tabasco, Cortez was given a beautiful young Indian girl named Marina, who was to play a vital role in the conquest of Mexico. Her father, who was a chief, seems to have died when she was young. She was given by her mother to people in Xicalanco, who later gave her to others in Tabasco, and these gave her to Cortez. Marina spoke both Maya and Nahautl and Gerónimo de Aguilar spoke Maya and Spanish, so the two of them supplied Cortez with a means of communicating in Nahuatl with the Aztecs. They played roles of great importance in the conquest of Mexico.

THE CONQUEST OF YUCATAN BY FRANCISCO DE MONTEJO

The conquest of Yucatan lasted for twenty years (1527–46), and may be divided into three active phases, separated by two quiescent periods:

First phase (1527–28). Conquest of Yucatan attempted from the east

First interval (1528–31)

Second phase (1531–35). Conquest of Yucatan attempted from
the west

Second interval (1535–40)

Third phase (1540–46). Conquest of Yucatan completed from
the west

Francisco de Montejo was a member of both the Grijalva
and the Cortez expeditions. He did not take part in the conquest
of Mexico, however, having been sent to Spain in 1519 by Cortez
in charge of the King's share of the treasure which had been collected. At the same time Montejo was to plead Cortez' cause at
the Spanish Court, because irregularities in connection with Cortez'
departure from Cuba had brought him into open rupture with
Diego de Velásquez, the Governor of Cuba.

During the seven years Montejo was at Court, he applied to the
King of Spain on his own behalf for permission to conquer Yucatan. In a royal decree, dated December 8, 1526, Montejo was
granted the hereditary title of Adelantado, and he was authorized
to raise an army for the conquest and colonization of Yucatan.

FIRST PHASE: CONQUEST ATTEMPTED FROM THE EAST
(1527–28)

The Montejo armada, consisting of three ships and four hundred men, set sail from Spain in 1527, with Alonso d'Avila as
second in command. A stop was made at Santo Domingo to pick
up supplies and horses, and one ship was left behind to bring additional supplies later. The two other ships made the Island of
Cozumel toward the end of September, where Ah Naum Pat, the
Lord of Cozumel, received them peaceably. After a brief stop,
the ships sailed for the mainland, where Montejo took possession
of the land in the name of God and the King of Castile, somewhere near the town of Xelha in the Province of Ekab.

To quell a mutiny among his troops, Montejo set fire to his
two ships. Leaving forty men at Xelha under command of

d'Avila, and another twenty at the near-by town of Pole, he set
out with one hundred twenty-five men on a tour of the towns and
villages in the northeastern corner of the peninsula. None of the
towns visited survives today, and even the location of most of
them is unknown: Xamanha, Mochis, and Belma; the last may
perhaps be identified with the modern settlement of El Meco.
Here the chiefs of the surrounding towns were called together to
swear allegiance to the Spanish Crown.

From Belma the little army proceeded to Conil in the Province of Ekab, a settlement which is said to have been composed of
five thousand houses; here the Spaniards rested for two months.
They left Conil in the spring of 1528 for the capital of the Province
of Chauaca. Here the first serious encounter with the Indians took
place. The Maya, abandoning the town in the night, attacked
vigorously the next morning, but were defeated.

From Chauaca the army moved to Ake, ten miles north of the
modern town of Tizimin. There a great battle took place, in which
more than twelve hundred Maya were killed. In this action

the Indians appeared with all the arms which they use in the wars: quivers
of arrows, poles with their tips hardened by fire, lances with points of sharp
flints, two-handed swords of very strong woods inset with obsidian blades,
whistles, and beating the shells of great turtles with deer horns, trumpets
of large conch-shells of the sea; naked except for the shameful parts
which were covered with a cloth, [their bodies] daubed with earth of divers
colors, so they appeared as most ferocious devils; their noses and ears pierced
with nose- and ear-plugs of bone and stones of varied colors.

As a result of this battle all the neighboring Maya chiefs surrendered.

From Ake, the Spaniards went to Sisia and Loche, and then
returned to Xelha by an inland route. At Xelha, Montejo found
his first settlement in desperate straits. Of the forty Spaniards
he had left there, only twelve remained, while all twenty of those
stationed at Pole had been massacred. Of the one hundred twenty-
five Spaniards who had accompanied him on his journey, only sixty

returned. The entire force must now have numbered fewer than one hundred men.

The third vessel of the flotilla having arrived from Santo Domingo, Montejo decided to continue exploration of the coast to the south. D'Avila was sent overland, and Montejo sailed southward. He discovered a settlement called Chetumal on a good bay and learned that Gonzalo de Guerrero, a Valdivia survivor, was in the vicinity. Although Montejo sent messengers to persuade him to rejoin his countrymen, Guerrero again refused. The Adelantado and d'Avila failed to meet in the Province of Chetumal as the Maya purposely kept them apart by false reports. D'Avila, after waiting some time, made his way back to Xelha and moved the Spanish settlement from this location to the near-by town of Xamanha.

After waiting in vain for d'Avila to appear at Chetumal, Montejo continued southward to the Ulua River in Honduras and then turned back, rejoining his lieutenant at Xamanha. Late in 1528, leaving d'Avila at Xamanha as Lieutenant Governor, Montejo sailed around the northern coast of the peninsula and returned to New Spain (Mexico), ending the first attempt to conquer Yucatan.

FIRST INTERVAL (1528–31)

Montejo, having secured an appointment as *Alcalde Mayor* of Tabasco, left Mexico City for that province in 1529, taking with him his son, also named Francisco de Montejo. They succeeded in pacifying the province and founded the town of Salamanca at Xicalanco near the north coast of Tabasco.

D'Avila was brought back from the east coast of Yucatan and sent to reduce the Province of Acalan south and east of the Laguna de Términos. Montejo did not long enjoy his new position in Tabasco, however; the former governor, regaining power there, threw Montejo into prison. Later the Adelantado was allowed to rejoin his son at Xicalanco and both father and son moved over to Champoton in southwestern Yucatan, where d'Avila had already preceded them.

From Champoton the Adelantado moved to Campeche. With this as a base of operations, the second attempt to reduce Yucatan was launched. D'Avila was sent to the Province of Chauaca in the east. On his way there he passed through the Province of Mani, where the Xiu gave him a friendly reception; finally he reached the Province of Chetumal in the far southeast, where he founded a *Villa Real*, or Royal Town. The natives here resisted so stubbornly that d'Avila found himself obliged to abandon the newly founded Royal Town and to embark in canoes for Honduras. He got as far as Trujillo before turning back, after an absence of two years.

After the departure of d'Avila for the east in 1531, the Montejos withstood a strong attack at Campeche in which the elder Montejo nearly lost his life. The Spaniards, however, won the battle, which resulted in the surrender of the Province of Ah Canul, north of Campeche.

Montejo next sent his son to conquer the northern provinces, instructing him to divide among his followers the services of the Indians encountered. The younger Montejo first went to the Province of the Cupules, to the site of the former Itza capital at Chichen Itza, where he was received somewhat reluctantly by the Cupul ruler, Naabon Cupul. Montejo, finding the population submissive, founded the first *Ciudad Real* or Royal City at Chichen Itza, and divided the towns and villages of the region among his soldiers, each Spaniard being allotted the services of two or three thousand Indians.

The Cupules soon became dissatisfied under Spanish rule. After six months of the foreign yoke, Naabon Cupul tried to kill Montejo but lost his own life in the attempt. The death of their ruler increased the hatred of the Cupules for the Spaniards, and about the middle of 1533 they blockaded the small Spanish garrison at Chichen Itza. Fortunately for the invaders, however, the Xiu, Chel, and Pech tribes in the western peninsula remained faithful.

The younger Montejo, seeing that the countryside was roused against him, decided to abandon the Royal City, which was probably no more than a small military camp, and to rejoin his father in the west. To accomplish this maneuver, according to an early chronicler, he resorted to the following ruse.

. . . finally one night they abandoned the town, leaving a dog attached to the clapper of a bell, and a little bread placed at one side so that he could not reach it; and the same day they wearied the Indians with skirmishes, so that they should not follow them. The dog rang the bell in his efforts to reach the bread, which greatly astonished the Indians, who thought the Spaniards wished to attack them; later when they learned how they had been tricked they resolved to look for the Spaniards in all directions, as they did not know which road they had taken. And those who had taken the same road overtook the Spaniards, shouting loudly as at people who were running away, because of which six horsemen awaited them in an open place and speared many. One of the Indians seized a horse by the leg and felled it as though it were a sheep.

Young Montejo finally reached Dzilam in the Province of the Chels, where the young lord, Namux Chel, received him with friendship. Later in the spring of 1534 Montejo rejoined his father at Dzibikal in the Province of Chakan near T'ho (the present Mérida).

Meanwhile, the Adelantado had advanced inland as far as the Province of Mani and visited the Xiu ruler there. Throughout the conquest the Xiu repeatedly showed their friendship for the Spaniards, and it was largely owing to their aid that Spanish authority was established permanently. The Montejos met at Dzibikal and shortly afterward the Adelantado founded the second Royal City at Dzilam, where the Spaniards are said to have "suffered many privations and dangers."

When the Adelantado determined to return to Campeche, the friendly Namux Chel offered to conduct him there, accompanied by two of his cousins. The cousins were taken in chains, perhaps as hostages, though Namux Chel was provided with a horse for the long overland journey. Montejo left his son at Dzilam to carry on the work of conquest and pacification as best he might. The Adelantado was well received by the Indians around Campeche,

where he was presently joined by d'Avila and shortly afterward
by his son, who found his position at Dzilam no longer tenable.

At this point the conquest of Yucatan received a setback. News of the conquest of Peru and of the riches to be had there reached the disheartened followers of Montejo at Campeche. The Spaniards had been fighting through northern Yucatan for seven years, and had found no more gold than would fill a few helmets. They had begun to realize that there would be no rich rewards such as the soldiers of Cortez had reaped in Mexico, and such as the companions of Pizarro were now gaining in Peru. The Adelantado could no longer hold together his already depleted forces. The little army dwindled until it became necessary to abandon the conquest of Yucatan a second time. Late in 1534 or early in 1535, the Adelantado withdrew from Campeche to Veracruz with the remnant of his army.

SECOND INTERVAL (1535–40)

Since he had first visited Honduras in 1528, the Adelantado had been petitioning the Spanish King for the governorship of that province. Combined with the *Adelantazgo* of Yucatan and certain administrative rights in Tabasco and Chiapas, this would have given him jurisdiction over all of what is now southern Mexico and northern Central America. In answer to his petitions, Montejo was named Governor and Captain General of the province of Honduras-Hibüeras in 1535, although notice of the appointment did not reach him until after he had left Yucatan for Mexico City. He did not actually return to Honduras until 1537.

The Honduras episode was unsuccessful from the outset. Montejo found himself seriously involved with another Adelantado, Pedro de Alvarado, who had been named Governor and Captain General of Guatemala by royal appointment. But Alvarado also claimed jurisdictional rights over Honduras as well as Guatemala, and in August 1539 Montejo was obliged to give up his interests in Honduras-Hibüeras to Alvarado. Montejo returned to Tabasco, where his son was acting as Lieutenant Governor and Captain General during his father's absence.

In 1535 a Franciscan named Fray Jacobo de Testera had gone

to Champoton to subdue Yucatan by peaceful means. The Crown had promised him that all Spanish soldiers would be excluded from the country until he had first made an attempt to subjugate it by preaching. He was having some success at this when Captain Lorenzo de Godoy appeared at Champoton with Spanish soldiers sent by Montejo the Younger to reduce the region. Trouble between Testera and Godoy broke out, and the priest returned to Mexico.

Under Godoy, affairs at Champoton went from bad to worse. The Couohs of the surrounding region were becoming more warlike until, in 1537, Montejo the Younger was obliged to send his cousin from Tabasco to take charge of the situation. The new Spanish leader was more politic than Godoy and persuaded the Indians to be less hostile, but want and misery continued and this last Spanish toe hold in Yucatan became more and more precarious.

THIRD PHASE: CONQUEST COMPLETED FROM THE WEST
BY FRANCISCO DE MONTEJO THE YOUNGER
(1540–46)

The Adelantado was now about sixty-seven years old and had been trying unsuccessfully for thirteen years to conquer Yucatan. He was weary, disillusioned, impoverished, and resolved to entrust the active prosecution of the conquest to his son.

In 1540 the Adelantado drew up a formal document turning over the conquest of Yucatan to his son and giving him elaborate instructions. Early in 1541 Montejo the Younger left Tabasco for Champoton, where his cousin had already been stationed for more than two years. Shortly after his arrival, Montejo moved his headquarters to Campeche, which was the first permanent Spanish *cabildo* or town government to be set up in the northern Maya area. The army again numbered between three and four hundred soldier-colonists under the command of Montejo, the son, with his cousin as second in charge.

Early in 1541 Montejo summoned the Maya lords to Campeche to render submission to the Spanish Crown. The Xiu ruler and a number of neighboring caciques obeyed the summons, but the Province of Ah Canul refused. Montejo dispatched his cousin to subdue the Ah Canules, while he remained behind to await the arrival of new recruits. His cousin met the Ah Canules in the Province of Chakan, near T'ho (the modern Mérida), and defeated them. In the late summer of 1541 Montejo the Younger, on his way from Campeche to T'ho, met more of the Xiu chieftains at Tuchicaan and received their submission. In the early fall of 1541 he reached the site of T'ho, and on the following January 6, 1542 he founded "The Very Noble and Very Loyal City of Mérida," setting up the second Spanish *cabildo* in the northern Maya area.

Seventeen days after the founding of Mérida, Spanish sentries stationed at the base of the pyramid where Montejo's army was encamped sighted a throng of Indians escorting a young Maya lord, seated in a palanquin. From the deference shown him it was obvious that he was a person of high degree. The Spaniards were terrified, fearing an immediate attack in force, but the Indian lord made signs that he came in peace, bringing with him food, which the Spaniards direly needed.

Through an interpreter, this Indian indicated that he was the Lord Tutul Xiu, supreme ruler of the Province of Mani, that he admired the bravery of the white men, and that he wanted to know them and see some of their religious ceremonies. Montejo ordered the chaplain of the army to celebrate "a solemn Adoration of the Holy Cross," in which all the Spanish soldiers took part. The Xiu ruler was deeply impressed, and said that he wished to become a Christian. He stayed at the Spanish camp for two months, during which time he was instructed in the Catholic faith and baptized Melchor.

The results of this visit were far-reaching. Since the fall of Mayapan a century earlier, the Xiu Province of Mani had been the most powerful political unit in northern Yucatan and its peaceful submission to the Spaniards was followed by that of other western provinces. Before leaving T'ho, Melchor promised to send ambassadors to the other Maya lords, urging them to give obedience to Montejo, and the pacification of the west was accomplished without further fighting. However, the east still remained unconquered.

After the submission of the western provinces, Montejo the Younger sent his cousin to the Province of Chauaca. All the eastern lords received him peacefully except the Cochua chieftains. After a brief though bitterly contested campaign against the Cochua lords, Montejo defeated them.

Next the Cupules, incited by their priests, revolted and were subdued. Montejo finally reached the east coast at Pole in the Province of Ekab and tried to cross to the Island of Cozumel, but was prevented from so doing by stormy weather. In the attempt, however, nine Spaniards were drowned and a tenth was killed by the Maya. Exaggerated reports of these losses encouraged both the Cupules and the Cochuas to revolt again.

Landa describes the unrest among the eastern Maya as follows:

The Indians received with sorrow the yoke of slavery, but the Spaniards had the towns of the country well divided into *repartimientos* [individual holdings].

The eastern provinces, Cupul, Cochua, Sotuta, and Chetumal, and to a lesser degree that of the Tazes, managed to retain their independence, and it was obvious that further military action against them would be necessary.

The conquest of Yucatan was drawing to a close, but one more revolt was to occur before final Spanish victory. This revolt involved a conspiracy of almost all of the eastern provinces, and the night of November 8, 1546, was chosen for the uprising. Through information from friendly natives, Mérida and Campeche had word of the impending revolt, but in the east the surprise was complete. Says a contemporary Spanish writer:

Late in the year of '46 the natives of all these provinces, of the Cupules, Tazes, and Chikin Cheles rose and rebelled against His Majesty, making a great massacre of the Spanish *encomenderos* [those among whom the Indians had been divided] of whom they killed eighteen Spaniards who were in their towns, where they sacrificed them . . . and besides more than four hundred Indian free-men who served the Spaniards as servants, without leaving anything alive, if it was a thing that savoured of the Spanish, including the herds and other things, until help came from the city of Mérida in the same year and the natives became peaceful again, the culprits being punished.

When the revolt began, both the younger Montejos were in Campeche, awaiting the arrival of the Adelantado from Chiapas. The Adelantado reached Mérida in December, raised additional troops in his plantations at Champoton and Campeche, and placed them under the command of the nephew. After losing twenty Spaniards and several hundred of the contingent of friendly Indians, the coalition of the eastern Maya chieftains was defeated in a single engagement. With these victories the conquest of Yucatan was brought to a successful conclusion.

∴ ∴

THE SPANISH CONQUEST OF PETEN

THE HERNANDO CORTEZ EXPEDITION TO
HONDURAS-HIBÜERAS, 1524–25

CORTEZ WAS THE FIRST white man to enter the region
occupied by the central Maya, when in 1524–25 he crossed the
Department of Peten, Guatemala, on his march from Mexico to
Honduras.

In 1524, Cortez sent one of his captains, Cristóbal de Olid, to
subdue Honduras. Olid seized the opportunity to rebel against
his leader and to set himself up independently. When news of this
defection reached Mexico, Cortez set out from Tenochtitlan on
October 12, 1525, to march to Honduras, a trip which took six
months.

This formidable undertaking constitutes one of the most sus-
tained efforts in military history. Because of the difficult character
of the terrain, the attendant hardships and privations were almost
beyond endurance and the army was always just one step ahead
of actual starvation.

Cortez was accompanied by about 140 Spanish soldiers, 93 of
them mounted, and by more than 3,000 Indians from Mexico,
with 150 horses, a herd of pigs, artillery, munitions, and supplies.
Because he dared not leave them behind, he also took Cuauhtemoc,
Cohuanacox, and Tetlepanquetzal, the deposed rulers of Tenochtitlan, Texcoco, and Tlacopan. To transport such a large body of
men across this wilderness would tax the strength and endurance
of a well-organized modern army. When it is remembered that
this expedition was undertaken in the early years of the sixteenth
century, Cortez' outstanding qualities of leadership are magnified
to almost unbelievable proportions.

Cortez entered the Maya area in what is now central Tabasco

114

and crossed the Usumacinta River just below the modern town
of Tenosique. Pushing eastward, he reached the Province of Acalan, ruled by a Chontal-Maya lord named Paxbolon Acha, toward
the close of February 1525. Somewhere near the western frontier
of this province occurred the blackest deed of Cortez' brilliant
career—the summary execution of the last Aztec emperor, Cuauhtemoc, and his fellow ruler, Tetlepanquetzal, Lord of Tlacopan.

When these princes had surrendered at Tenochtitlan, Cortez
had promised them their lives, but here in the wilds of Acalan this
promise was broken. The two eyewitnesses of this tragedy who
have left accounts of it are Cortez himself and one of his captains,
Bernal Díaz del Castillo; both agree that there was a conspiracy
among the Aztec lords to fall upon the Spaniards and slay them.
That this was no idle fear is confirmed by a recently discovered
document in the files of the Archives of the Indies at Seville. This
document, dated in 1612, is a petition of the Chontal ruler of that
day, a grandson of the Paxbolon Acha who was Lord of the Province of Acalan when Cortez passed through. It appeals to the
Crown of Spain for a pension for himself, because of his grand-
father's services nearly a century earlier.

The petitioner relates that Cuauhtemoc approached his grand-
father and urged him to join the conspiracy against the Spaniards,
pointing out how Cortez was abusing and robbing the Chontal.
According to the testimony of his grandson, Paxbolon Acha was
wary of these counsels and betrayed the conspiracy to the Spanish
leader.

The danger was obviously great. The Spaniards were tremen-
dously outnumbered by their Indian troops, and immediate action
was imperative. Cortez arrested the two leaders and hanged them
without delay. Pablo Paxbolon, however, says in his account of
the affair that the lords were beheaded. An Aztec hieroglyphic
manuscript dating from the middle sixteenth century seems to
indicate that both accounts may be correct. This manuscript portrays Cuauhtemoc's headless body hanging by its feet (Fig. 3).
Above appears the body of the dead Aztec ruler swathed in bandages—the Aztec symbol denoting death; his name glyph, an eagle,

is attached to his head, and below appears his headless body hanging by its feet from a tree.

Cortez, with six hundred Chontal Indians as carriers, left the Province of Acalan on March 5, 1525, and reached the shores of Lake Peten Itza eight days later. Here Canek, the Itza ruler, met Cortez on the northern shore of the lake. Cortez had the Catholic priests with the expedition celebrate Mass, which so impressed

FIG. 3.—Death of the Aztec Emperor, Cuauhtemoc, in the Province of Acalan in 1525, according to the Mapa de Tepechpan.

Canek that he promised to destroy his idols and replace them with the worship of the Cross. He invited Cortez to visit Tayasal, the Itza capital, and the invitation was accepted. Cortez took with him twenty Spanish soldiers, while the rest of the army proceeded around the lake and met him on the southern shore.

The army next entered a terrible terrain, the rugged country on the western flanks of the Maya Mountains (Plate 1). Here they encountered a pass so tortuous it took the tired army twelve days to travel twenty miles. During this time more than two-thirds of the horses were lost.

Emerging from this pass, they reached a large river swollen by the torrential rains, which had never ceased falling. Turning upstream, they encountered a series of "terrifying and impetuous

rapids." Today these same rapids are ironically known as "Gracias
a Dios." It took the army two days to find its way over the rapids,
and more horses were lost in the crossing. Beyond lay the village
of Tenciz, which the crippled force reached on April 15, the Satur-
day before Easter, in 1525.

After leaving Tenciz, the army became lost in a wilderness of
hills north of Lake Izabal (Plate 1). The Indian guides deserted
here, and had it not been for the capture of an Indian boy, who
finally led them out, they would all have died of starvation.

Just beyond this point, Cortez heard definite news of the Spaniards he was seeking. To the delight of the exhausted army, it was
learned that Nito, the objective of their wanderings, lay only two
days' journey ahead.

The final lap of this odyssey took the Spaniards three days
before they finally emerged on the northwestern bank of the Rio
Dulce opposite Nito; here Cortez was met by Diego Nieto representing the authorities of the settlement. Cortez and ten or twelve
companions crossed immediately to the other side of the river and
the rest of the army straggled in during the next five or six days.

On his march across the Maya area, Cortez visited the site of
only one important Maya center, Tayasal, though he must have
passed within a few miles of several others, notably Palenque,
Laguna Perdida, Itsimte, Polol, Motul de San José, Ixkun, and
Pusilha, and ended his journey at Nito, not far from Quirigua
(Plate 19).

THE PERIOD FOLLOWING THE EXPEDITION
OF CORTEZ, 1525–1696

With the conquest of Yucatan completed (1546), there remained only one independent Maya group—the powerful Itza
nation, centering around the western end of Lake Peten Itza. The
Itzas were able to resist the Spaniards and to maintain their political
independence for another century and three quarters.

Tayasal, the Itza capital, was a long distance both from Mérida
in northern Yucatan and from St. James of the Gentlemen of
Guatemala, the Spanish capital in the southern highlands. For

nearly a century after Cortez had visited Tayasal in 1525, neither Yucatan nor Guatemala attempted to reduce the remote and hostile Province of the Itza. Between 1550 and 1556 Franciscan missionaries had made evangelizing expeditions from Campeche into the Province of Acalan and had persuaded the Chontal Maya of that region to move nearer to Campeche, where they could be instructed in the Catholic faith, but the warlike Itza, farther to the southeast, were left alone.

In 1618 two Franciscans, Fathers Bartolomé de Fuensalida and Juan de Orbita, having secured permission to attempt to Christianize the Itza peaceably, set out from Mérida for Tayasal. They left Mérida in the spring of 1618, traveling by way of Lake Bacalar, and were accompanied by the alcalde of Bacalar and a number of Indian converts. With the delays incident to travel, the fathers did not reach Tayasal until nearly six months later. Canek, the Itza ruler, received them with friendliness.

They remained at Tayasal for some days, attempting to Christianize the Itza, but Canek, though interested in the services held by the missionaries, refused to renounce his own religion. He believed that the time had not yet arrived when, according to their ancient prophecies, the Itza were to accept a new faith.

The fathers were shown a large idol in the form of a horse, called Tzimin Chac or the "Thunder Horse." When Cortez had visited Tayasal, he left a lame horse with the Canek of that day, promising to return for it himself or to send for it. After Cortez' departure, the Itza treated the horse as a god, offering it fowl, other meats, and flowers, on which diet the horse died. The Itza, terrified at the death of a god on their hands, made a stone idol of the horse, which they worshiped in order to prove they were not responsible for its death. When Father Orbita saw this image, he became so infuriated at the idolatry that he smashed the image into bits. The Itza, outraged at such a sacrilege, tried to kill the missionaries, but Father Fuensalida seized the occasion to preach a sermon of such eloquence that the tumult subsided and the missionaries' lives were spared. When the fathers saw that they were making no progress in Christianizing the Itza, they took friendly farewell of Canek, who seems to have borne them no ill will for destroying the idol. Father Fuensalida reached Mérida on December 8, 1618, but Father Orbita remained at Tipu, a small settlement near Lake Bacalar.

The fathers set out from Tipu for Tayasal a second time in September of the following year, accompanied by some Tipu Indians as guides and servants. They reached the Itza capital at the beginning of October and remained there for eighteen days. Although Canek was at first friendly, the Tipu Indians were suspicious of the Itza and deserted in a body; later, however, three of them came back to serve the fathers. The Itza priests were becoming jealous of the influence of the Catholic missionaries and persuaded Canek's wife to urge her husband to expel them. The fathers' house was surrounded by armed Indians; the fathers themselves were hustled into a canoe with their Tipu servants and told never to return, as the Itza wanted no more of their religion. Father Orbita made some resistance, but a young Itza warrior seized the collar of his habit and twisted it so violently that Orbita fell to the ground senseless. The party was shoved off in a canoe without food or drink, the Itza hoping they would die of hunger on the long trip back to Tipu.

The Tipu Indians, however, had managed to secrete a little food, and the five subsisted on this until they reached Tipu. The fathers rested here for a few days, but, seeing that the time was not opportune for further attempts to convert the Itza, they left Tipu and returned to Mérida.

Three years later, in 1622, the governor of Yucatan authorized Captain Francisco de Mirones to conduct a military expedition against the Itza. On March 30 of that year, Mirones with 20 Spaniards and 140 Indians left Hopelchen in Campeche for the Itza country. A Franciscan missionary, Father Diego Delgado, joined the army later. The force marched to Sacalum, where Mirones' treatment of the Indians was such that Father Delgado decided to leave the soldiers and go on without them. He left camp secretly and proceeded to Tayasal by way of Tipu, taking with him eighty converted Tipu Indians. Father Delgado and his Indians were escorted to Tayasal by the Itza with a great show of friendship. On reaching the town, however, all were seized and sacrificed to the Itza idols.

News of the death of Father Delgado reached Mérida slowly, but as soon as the authorities at the capital heard of it they sent word to Captain Mirones at Sacalum to be on his guard. However, the news came too late. On February 2, 1624, the Spaniards at Sacalum were all in the village church, without arms, when the Indians fell upon them and slaughtered them.

These two massacres put a stop to all attempts either to Christianize or to conquer the Itza. When, about twelve years later, the Tipu Indians began to apostatize, returning to their former idolatry, the last link of friendly Indian contact between northern Yucatan and the province of the Itza was severed. And thus affairs remained for nearly three-quarters of a century. The Spanish continued to consolidate their positions in Yucatan and in Guatemala, but the territory lying between remained unconquered and un-Christianized, a continual irritation to both the military and ecclesiastical authorities of the two provinces.

In June 1695, Martin de Ursua, governor of Yucatan, sent a contingent of Spanish soldiers and Indians to the village of Cauich in northern Campeche, to start building a road to the shores of Lake Peten Itza. Toward the end of the month, the road builders reached a village called Nohthub in southern Campeche, where three Franciscans headed by Father Andres de Avendaño joined them. The priests soon became disgusted with the way the Spanish captain treated the Indians, and they returned to Mérida.

On December 15, 1695, Father Avendaño again left Mérida for the province of the Itza, accompanied by two other Franciscans, four Indian singers from Yucatan, and three Indian guides. Instead of going around by way of Tipu, Father Avendaño followed the new road as far south as it had been built and then pushed on through the forests with his Indian guides to Lake Peten Itza.

They reached the lake on January 13, 1696, and were given a boisterous reception by the Chakan Itza living at the western end. The next day Canek met them at the village of the Chakan Itza, having crossed from Tayasal with an escort of eighty canoes. The fathers remained at Tayasal for three and a half days, and baptized more than three hundred Indian children. Father Avendaño urged Canek and his councilors to surrender to the Crown of Spain and accept Christianity. The Itza council took this proposal under consideration, but their final decision was that the time had not yet arrived when their prophecies had foretold that they should give up the worship of their old gods. They promised that if Governor Ursua would send the fathers back in another four months, the Itza would become vassals of the Spanish King and embrace Christianity.

Canek, learning of a plot among the Chakan Itza to waylay and kill the fathers on their return trip, persuaded Avendaño to return to Mérida by the longer though safer route through Tipu. On the night of January 17, 1696, the three fathers with their Indians from Yucatan, after taking an affectionate farewell of Canek and his family, embarked in a canoe.

From this point on, bad luck and increasing hardships beset the fathers. The promised guides to Tipu were not forthcoming, and after waiting two days the fathers set out on January 20 on the long, dangerous return journey to northern Yucatan. At the end of five days the party came to a large stream, probably the Holmul River, which they followed for another five days, becoming hopelessly lost. At this point they determined to strike west, hoping to reach the road which Ursua was having built from Cauich to the shores of the lake. They pushed on in this direction for fifteen days more, living on a meager diet of wild honey, green mamey, and palm nuts. On the fourth day of this exhausting trek Avendaño became so weak that the two other Franciscans, taking one of the four Indians as a guide, pushed on in hope of locating some frontier settlement and bringing back help and supplies.

After six days of terrible hardships, Father Avendaño came upon the ruins of an ancient city, which he describes as follows:

With so few comforts and so many hardships my strength was failing rapidly, which brought home to me the truth of the adage that the Biscayans, my countrymen, have, namely, that "the belly supports, or carries the legs, and not the legs, the belly."

Among these high mountains which we passed there are a number of ancient buildings; among them I recognized some as living places, and although they were very high and my strength very little, I climbed them, but with difficulty. They are in the form of a convent with small cloisters and many rooms for living, all roofed, surrounded by a terrace and whitened with lime inside, which latter abounds in these parts, because all the hills are of limestone; and these said buildings are of such form that they did not appear like those of this province [Yucatan] which latter are entirely of dressed stone put together without mortar, especially as to their arches, but these [in Peten] are of stone masonry plastered over with lime.

The only archaeological site answering this description which he could possibly have reached is Tikal. He was therefore the first European to see this greatest of all ancient Maya cities.

A month later, a Spanish expedition under Jacobo de Alcayaga, coming down the Lacantun and Usumacinta rivers, discovered the site of another large ancient city, which from its description must have been Yaxchilan:

In another landing that some soldiers made, they came upon a site, which, because of its many stone foundations and most ancient ruined buildings, had the appearance of having been a very old settlement; this site was about a league in circumference.

Thus two of the largest central Maya cities were seen for the first time by Europeans within a month of each other.

After leaving Tikal with his Indians, Father Avendaño traveled westward and northward for another three days until his strength gave out altogether. He ordered the Indians to leave him propped against a tree with a lighted fire and a gourd of water, and to push on for help. The next morning his Indians returned with ten carriers. After leaving Avendaño the day before, they had come out on a trail which led them to Chuntuqui on the new road from Cauich to Lake Peten Itza. Here they found some Indian carriers and took them back to rescue the father. The Indians carried him in a hammock to Chuntuqui, where they arrived on

February 19, 1696, after being lost for thirty-one days. At Chuntuqui he found the two other Franciscans who had left him eighteen days before in search of help. After resting at Chuntuqui for a few days, Avendaño and his companions continued to Mérida, where they reported on their mission.

THE CONQUEST OF THE ITZA, 1696–97

Although the road from Cauich to Lake Peten Itza had been opened for fifty miles beyond Chuntuqui by September of 1695, heavy rains prevented supplies being brought forward. Road gangs were obliged to return to Zucthok, north of the present boundary between Mexico and Guatemala, until the rainy season was over.

As the result of an embassy from Canek, which reached Mérida in December 1695, Ursua became convinced that the Itza were at last ready to submit to Spanish rule. He ordered Captain Paredes, who was still at work on the road, to proceed to Tayasal. Paredes, unable to comply with the order in person, sent Captain Pedro de Zubiaur with sixty Spanish soldiers, some Indian warriors, and Father San Buenaventura, to take possession of the province.

By this time the road had advanced to within twenty miles of the lake, and Zubiaur's command reached the shore on January 18, 1696. Zubiaur had expected a peaceful reception by the Itza, but as the Spaniards approached the lake, they saw a flotilla of canoes filled with armed Indians advancing toward them. Leaping ashore, the Itza attacked vigorously, seizing some of the Indians from Yucatan as prisoners. Father San Buenaventura, a lay Franciscan brother, and a Spanish soldier were also made prisoners, and a fourth Spaniard was killed in the fight. The Itza numbered about two thousand.

Battle having been forced upon them, the Spaniards defended themselves bravely, but finding his force outnumbered, Zubiaur withdrew to the main camp of Captain Paredes. A second and larger Spanish force was dispatched to the lake a day or so later. When it met with a similar hostile reception, further attempts to press the attack were discontinued.

The news of the Chakan Itza's hostility to Father Avendaño and of Zubiaur's defeat reached Ursua at the same time, and made it evident that the Itza were to be reduced only by military force. One hundred extra soldiers, shipwrights, and carpenters were needed to build a pirogue and a galley to navigate the lake, in order to dominate Tayasal and the other villages. The men were recruited in Mérida and sent to Paredes with instructions to press forward the work of opening the road the remaining twenty miles. However, Ursua at this time became engaged in a lawsuit with a political rival; he ordered Captain Paredes to retire to Campeche to await his coming with larger forces the next year.

The close of 1696 and the beginning of 1697 were spent in reassembling the army at Campeche. This army consisted of 235 Spanish soldiers, 120 Indian muleteers and road workers, and a number of Indian carriers. The infantry, artillery, and supply trains were sent ahead under Paredes, with orders to Zubiaur to proceed to within five miles of the lake with the ship carpenters and calkers. There they were to cut and trim sufficient timber for a galley and a pirogue, and to await the arrival of the rest of the army. Ursua followed shortly with the cavalry, his personal suite, and the rest of the supplies. He left Campeche on January 24, 1697. On March 1, timber for the galley and the pirogue being ready, the whole army moved forward to the shore of the lake, where a fortified camp was built.

For the next twelve days the Itza made hostile demonstrations against the Spanish camp. Flotillas of canoes maneuvered in front of the camp daily. Companies of painted warriors surrounded it on the land side, beating their war drums and threatening the Spaniards with death and sacrifice. On March 10, a number of canoes were seen approaching the camp from the direction of Tayasal, the first canoe carrying a white flag. It was an embassy from Canek, consisting of the Itza high priest and other chiefs, who came to offer peace. Ursua received them in a friendly manner, and through them invited Canek to visit the Spanish camp the third day hence. The embassy was dismissed after being given a number

of gifts, and the camp settled down to await the arrival of the Itza
ruler.

On the appointed day, the Itza ruler did not appear. Instead,
a great flotilla of canoes was seen moving across the lake toward
the camp, while on shore companies of warriors threatened to attack. However, as night fell, both canoes and land forces withdrew. Ursua called a council of war of all his officers and requested
each to give his opinion as to what should be done. They agreed
that further efforts to reduce the Itza by peaceable means were
useless and that the only course was to conquer them by force of
arms. A decree was read to the army ordering the attack on Tayasal
the following morning.

On March 13, before dawn, Mass was celebrated, breakfast was
eaten, and the soldiers selected for the attack embarked on the
galley. Ursua took with him 108 Spanish soldiers, the vicar-general of the army, and a nephew of Canek, who had shown himself
friendly to the Spanish cause. He left behind, as a garrison, 127
Spaniards and all the Indian bowmen, road workers, and servants.

The galley swept toward Tayasal at dawn. The order of the
preceding day was read again aboard ship; the vicar-general urged
all who had sinned to ask forgiveness and granted a general abso-
lution.

Soon those on the galley saw canoes putting out from the shore
in two flanking squadrons, the occupants shouting and threatening
with their weapons. Ursua ordered the oarsmen to row with all
speed toward the town itself, which was now clear in the morning
light. The number of canoes grew so rapidly that, as the galley
neared shore, they formed a crescent around it, cutting it off from
the lake. The Spaniards were now close enough to see the forti-
fications that had been built against them and the multitude already
under arms waiting to defend the town.

Having come within bowshot of the galley, the Itza began to
discharge a hail of arrows. In spite of this attack, Ursua still held
back, shouting above the tumult, "No one fire, for God is on our
side and there is no cause for fear." The Itza pressed closer, the

arrows fell more thickly, and still Ursua held fire, shouting that no one was to discharge a shot, under pain of death. The Itza, mistaking this restraint for cowardice, mocked the Spaniards as not only already vanquished but killed and eaten.

Finally the Spanish general made one last appeal. The galley was slowed down and through an interpreter he told the Itza that the Spaniards came in peace and friendship. Unless the Itza laid down their arms, he said, they alone would be responsible for the slaughter which would follow. Although the Itza heard Ursua's plea, they again mistook his forbearance for weakness. Jeering at the Spaniards, they let fly more arrows. In spite of the congestion on the galley, only two Spaniards were wounded—Sergeant Juan González and a soldier named Bartolomé Durán.

Durán, infuriated, ignored Ursua's orders not to begin fighting, and discharged his arquebus at the Itza. The others followed his example until firing from the galley became general. The Spaniards, not waiting for the galley to ground, leaped into the water, firing their arquebuses. Even here Ursua showed mercy, for he prevented his men from discharging the artillery. Had this been brought into action, the slaughter would have been frightful, as the enemy were so numerous and so closely packed.

Having gained the shore, the Spaniards continued firing with such effect that the Itza were soon in full flight, not only from the town but also from the rest of the Tayasal peninsula. Everyone who could took to the lake, swimming frantically for the opposite shore. The stretch of water which separates Tayasal from the mainland is so long and was by this time so thick with people that swimming was almost impossible and many perished.

Ursua and the victorious Spaniards pressed up the hill, while the galley was rowed back and forth, with the men shooting from its deck. The Itza in the canoes sought to escape by hurling themselves into the lake and swimming for the mainland, so that soon the entire population of Tayasal was in the water and the peninsula was completely deserted.

Upon reaching the highest point of the hill, which was crowned by a large temple, Ursua planted the royal standard. From this

temple, Ursua with his principal captains and the two Catholic
priests gave thanks to God for their victory and for having preserved them from any loss of life. On every side there were con-
gratulations; Ursua thanked his officers and men for their bravery
and constancy, which had made possible the whole undertaking.
The amenities being concluded, and finding themselves masters of
the town, Ursua formally renamed Tayasal "Nuestra Señora de
los Remedios y San Pablo de los Itzaes."

Ursua and the vicar-general made a tour of the temples, breaking the idols found in them as well as in the dwellings of the Itza.
So vast was the number of idols that their destruction took the
entire Spanish force from nine in the morning to half past five in
the afternoon. As the final act of the day, Ursua selected the principal temple, where human sacrifice had recently been offered to
the Itza deities, to be the sanctuary of the Christian God. Thus, in
the morning of a single day the power of the Itza was crushed, and
the last independent Maya political entity was brought under the
domination of the Spanish Crown.

··· ═══

AGRICULTURE

THE ORIGIN OF AGRICULTURE IN THE NEW WORLD

ALL PLANT BIOLOGISTS agree that high civilization in the New World was first developed in connection with the cultivation of maize or Indian corn (*Zea mays*), the staff of life of the American Indian in pre-Columbian times, just as it is today. As to where corn originated in the Americas there is no unanimity of opinion. One school of thought believes that agriculture developed in South America, in the highlands of Peru, while another holds that it developed somewhere in Mesoamerica, perhaps in the highlands of western Guatemala.

Although recently discovered sites on the west coast of Peru show that corn was introduced there well after other plants had been domesticated, the basic importance of corn as the staple food of New World peoples makes its origin of major importance to the historical reconstruction of civilization in the Americas.

The two areas at present favored by plant geneticists as the locale of the origins of cultivated corn are the east slopes of the Andes and the highlands of Mesoamerica; decision between the two is not yet possible. The date of domestication is also uncertain, although recent radiocarbon dates from northern Mexico and New Mexico suggest that corn was cultivated in Mesoamerica as early as 2500 B.C.

MAYA MAIZE AGRICULTURE

Modern Maya agricultural practices are the same as they were three thousand years ago or more—a simple process of felling the forest, burning the dried trees and bush, planting, and changing the location of the cornfields every few years. This is the system of agricultural practices in the American wet tropics even today,

and is the only method available to a primitive people living in a
heavily wooded, rocky, shallow-soiled country like that of the
northern Yucatan Peninsula, where a plow cannot be used and
where draft animals are not obtainable.

This system is known as milpa agriculture, from the Aztec word
for cornfield. It was so named because the Spaniards first came in
contact with this method of raising corn in Mexico and, since the
sixteenth century, the use of this word to denote a cornfield has
spread to all other parts of Mexico and Central America. The
Yucatan Maya word for cornfield is *col*, and all the Maya languages
have similar words for it. Making the cornfield is the most important single activity of Maya men today, as it was in ancient times.

Nor, so far as we now can judge, has milpa agriculture changed
materially since Classic times, and even before. In those days the
chief agricultural tools were the fire-hardened, pointed planting
stick (Maya *xul*), the stone axe (*baat*), and the fiber bag for carrying the seed corn (*chim*). The most important modern additions
to these implements are the steel machete, a heavy, single-bladed
knife about two feet long, the steel axe, and the iron point which
has been added to the planting stick. Modern agricultural implements are of little avail in the Maya area, particularly in northern
Yucatan, where the thin, rocky soil makes their use impossible.

Because maize forms a preponderant part of the modern Maya
diet—from 75 to 85 per cent is corn in one form or another—it is
necessary to understand Maya milpa agriculture and its several
steps. Maya milpa agriculture can be divided into eleven successive
stages of work: (1) locating the field; (2) felling the forest and
bush; (3) burning the dried bush; (4) fencing the field; (5) planting the field; (6) weeding the field; (7) bending the cornstalks;
(8) harvesting the corn; (9) storing the corn; (10) shelling the
corn; (11) hauling the corn to the village.

1. *Locating the field.*—The selection of a plot of ground for
the new cornfield is an important step. The *milpero* or corn
farmer, working alone, spends at least one day carefully looking
for the proper kind of soil, which he determines by the height and
thickness of the forest and bush growing on it; the higher the trees

and the thicker the bush, the richer the soil. Another desirable factor is proximity to water. Yucatan is a parched land with very little surface water, and the farmer tries to locate his milpa as near water, either in cenotes or shallow water holes, as possible. The distance of the cornfield from the village where the farmer lives varies. In a survey of five villages in northern Yucatan, 162 cornfields were found to vary from 2⅛ to 15⅛ miles from the nearest village. The average distance in northern Yucatan today between house and cornfield is 3½ miles, but an extreme case is reported from the highlands of Guatemala—the Indians of a certain village have to go 50 miles in order to find suitable lands.

When the field has been selected, the farmer divides it into *mecates,* or squares measuring 65 feet (20 meters) on each side, making piles of stones as markers at the corners of each mecate. In measuring his land, the Maya farmer uses a rope which is a little longer than the regulation 20 meters; in northern Yucatan these measuring ropes average 21.5 meters, or 70 feet. The Maya say the mecates have to be measured a little larger "because of what the birds take."

2. *Felling the forest and bush.*—Today the bush is felled with a steel axe or machete. When the trees are very large, they are ringed and allowed to die. The milpero begins to fell the bush soon after sunrise and continues until early afternoon. Usually two mecates are cut a day, or about one-fifth of an acre. As cornfields in Yucatan average about 100 mecates in size (10 to 12 acres) it takes 50 days to cut the average cornfield. High bush is usually cut in August at the height of the rainy season. The trees are full of moisture at this time and are easier to fell. The low trees, vines, and bushes are cut first, and later the higher trees. The fallen trees and bushes are sometimes dragged into piles to facilitate burning. Fields that have already had one year's corn crop grown upon them are not bushed until a few weeks before burning.

In ancient times this step in milpa making must have taken a longer time and been more laborious than today. Clearing Maya cornfields has been enormously facilitated by the introduction of the steel axe and machete (Plate 20).

PLATE 20.—LACANDON FELLING A TREE

The use of the platform is necessary to get above the thick base of the tree.

3. *Burning the dried bush.*—The felled bush is burned in March or April, after the blazing suns of February and March have thoroughly dried it. The cornfield is fired on a day when the wind is blowing strongly in order to secure a good "burn." A torch made from a frayed branch of the *catzim* tree is used, and fires are started at a number of places on the side from which the wind is blowing. The gods of the winds are summoned by constant whistling, for nothing is more fatal to a good "burn" than to have the wind die down before the bush is entirely consumed.

There is archaeological and documentary evidence indicating that the day upon which the cornfields were to be burned was chosen carefully by the priests. At Copan, for example, there are two monuments—Stelae 10 and 12—standing on ranges of hills that enclose the western and eastern sides of the Copan Valley at this point. These monuments are 4⅛ miles apart in an air line, the true bearing of Stela 10 as observed from Stela 12 being N. 81° 09′ W. (Fig. 4). As observed from Stela 12, the sun sets directly behind Stela 10 on April 12 and again on September 7. It has been suggested that April 12, falling at about the time the corn-fields are burned in the Copan region, was the official date chosen by the priests to begin burning the milpas. The purpose of erecting monuments in these two positions may have been to define a line of sight to determine the date upon which the Copan cornfields should be burned.

There is evidence in documentary sources to indicate that in Postclassic times also the day for burning the cornfields was of ceremonial importance. In the Codex Perez (post-Conquest) the days of a sacred year are given which deal especially with the ritual of burning the cornfields. In it, such expressions are used as, "On this day 'the burner' [Maya *ah tooc*] takes the fire; on this day 'the burner' applies the fire," etc.

Cornfield fires do not start forest fires in the Yucatan Peninsula. Even in the dry season, the forest and bush are too green to burn. The flames sweeping against the standing trees kill those on the edges of the milpas, but the fire does not penetrate far and gradu-ally dies out. In Mexico today there are laws which require fire

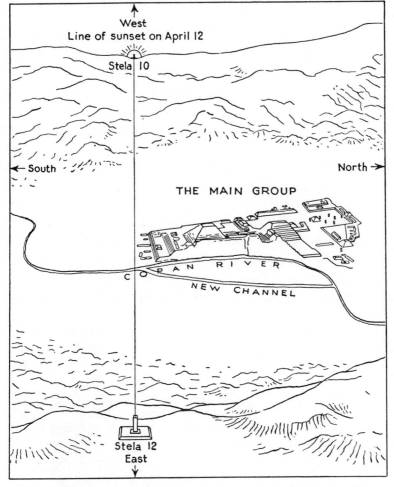

Fig. 4.—The "sundial" composed of Stelae 10 and 12, Copan, Honduras.

lanes to be cleared around the edges of the fields, but the individual Maya in his cornfield, remote from the nearest town or village, pays little attention to these regulations.

4. *Fencing the field.* — This operation was not necessary in early times, since the ancient Maya had no domesticated animals, which today make fencing necessary. These fences are temporary affairs made of brush, hastily thrown together and lasting only two or three years, but since the cornfields are almost never planted

for more than two years in succession, the fences last as long as they are needed.

5. *Planting the field.*—Planting is begun immediately after the first rains, which all Maya believe will fall on the Day of the Holy Cross (May 3), but which may come any time between April and July. Sowing the milpa is usually completed before the end of May. It takes two days to shell sufficient corn to plant a 10- to 12-acre cornfield (100 mecates) and the actual planting of such a tract requires 12 days. The Maya use about 9½ pounds of seed corn per acre, while the practice in the United States is to use about 8 pounds per acre. The corn is planted in holes made with the iron-pointed planting stick (Fig. 5); the holes are 4 to 5 inches deep and are roughly laid out in lines, as nearly as the terrain will permit. From three to six kernels of corn are dropped into each hole, the holes being about 4 feet apart, and two or three stalks of corn grow on each hill. In the usual 10- to 12-acre milpa there are about 5,000 hills of corn. Bean and squash seeds are occasion-

Fig. 5.—Planting corn with the planting stick. Page 36, Codex Tro-Cortesianus.

ally planted in the same hole, which is then closed by a brush of the foot.

Bishop Landa described this process nearly four centuries ago.

They plant in many places, so that if one fails the others will suffice. In cultivating the land they do nothing more than clear the brush, and burn it in order to sow it afterward, and from the middle of January to April they work it and then when the rains come they plant it, which they do by carrying a small sack on the shoulders, and with a pointed stick, they make a hole in the ground, dropping in it five or six grains, covering them with the same stick. And when it rains, it is marvelous to see how it grows.

There seems to have been little change in the Maya method of planting corn since ancient times.

6. *Weeding the field.*—The number of times a cornfield is weeded during the growing season (May to September) varies considerably. A new milpa, made in high bush, is weeded only once, when the corn is about 2 feet high. A second-year milpa, however, has to be weeded more frequently—two or three times before the corn matures. When one realizes that it takes more time to weed a mecate of low bush than to fell a mecate of high bush, one wonders why the modern Maya ever plants the same field for two years in succession.

A second-year milpa has more weeds and vines in it than the high bush. This is due principally to the modern method of weeding with a machete. In ancient times, weeds must have been pulled out by the roots, and the consequent scattering of seeds thus held to a minimum. Today, however, weeds are cut with a sweep of the machete and the seeds are scattered in every direction. This difference may be of great importance in its influence upon the length of time a cornfield may be successively cultivated. When weeds were pulled out by their roots, weed competition may have been eliminated sufficiently to permit the cultivation of the milpas for up to five successive years before they had to be abandoned. In Yucatan today the yield from a second-year milpa has decreased to from 10 to 20 per cent less than that of the first year.

That soil exhaustion is not the chief factor responsible for this decrease is suggested by results from the Carnegie Institution's experimental milpa at Chichen Itza. After the harvest each successive year, specimens of soil were taken from this cornfield. Over a ten-year period the annual analyses of these specimens showed no appreciable decrease in the amount of necessary nitrogenous salts, nor sufficient deterioration in the chemical composition of the soil to account for the diminishing yearly yield. Therefore it seems probable that increasing weed competition and not decreasing soil fertility is responsible for the diminishing yield from Maya milpas today.

7. *Bending the cornstalks.*—When the corn is ripe, the stalks are bent over. This practice is general throughout Mesoamerica and is done after the ears have matured in September or October. This practice has no counterpart in American corn farming. The Maya have one kind of corn which matures in two and a half months, another which ripens in four months, and still another which ripens in six months. Corn grows very tall in Yucatan, the average stalk being 12 or 13 feet high. The stalks are bent just below the ears, and in this position the corn is left to harden. The Maya say the purpose of bending the stalks is to keep rain from entering the ears, which causes them to mold.

8. *Harvesting the corn.*—About a month after bending the stalks, perhaps in November, the Maya corn farmer begins to gather in his crops. Harvesting is at its height in January and February and continues through March into April, the corn being harvested as needed. Husking is done with a pin made of wood, bone, or deerhorn; only the outside of the husk is removed in this preliminary operation. A man can harvest an acre in about three days, and the average yield is 17 or 18 bushels of shelled corn per acre, or about 35 bushels on the ear.

9. *Storing the corn.*—Storing practices vary. In northeastern Yucatan raised rectangular cribs are built at the cornfields, the corn being stored without shelling. The crib is made of saplings and the roof of thatch, materials found in abundance in the near-by forest. The ears are stored vertically, as close together as possible. The final husking is usually done just before planting the new crop in May. In northern central Yucatan the ears are shelled at the milpa, and the corn is hauled to the village, where it is stored in a circular bin lined with palm leaves.

10. *Shelling the corn.*—The corn may be shelled in several ways: (*a*) by hand; (*b*) by putting the ears in a hammock which holds from ten to fifteen baskets of ears; the hammock is beaten vigorously with a club and the kernels fall through the meshes to the ground; and (*c*) by putting the ears in a pole rack and then

beating them with long poles, the kernels falling through to the
ground as in the second method. Shelling is usually done at night,
because the chaff is thought to cause less itching than in the daytime.
The corn is finally stored in hemp bags, each containing 2 *cargas*
or 190 pounds per bag.

11. *Hauling the corn to the village.*—Corn is hauled from the
milpa to the village on the backs of men or horses, or, where there
are highways, by trucks. A man can carry one carga (95 lbs.) and
a horse, two. As highways increase in number, horse- and man-
transport are slowly disappearing.

THE YIELD OF CORN

The foregoing steps are those followed today in raising corn
in Yucatan. With the exceptions of fencing the milpa and hauling
the corn to the village on the backs of draft animals or by motor
trucks, they are the same as those followed by the ancient Maya.

The average size of milpas in the Chichen Itza area of northeastern Yucatan is 10 to 12 acres. This estimate is based upon a
survey of 638 milpas, which were planted over a period of five
years in three villages near Chichen Itza. In northern Yucatan the
same cornfield is not planted for more than two years in succession.
The third year a new site is selected, and the old milpa is allowed
to lie fallow for about ten years until sufficient bush has come back
to warrant its being felled again. If the average cornfield is 12
acres in size and each field is in corn for only two years and has
to lie fallow for ten, it will take 72 acres of land to maintain the
average family permanently. To support a village of 500 people
(100 families) 7,200 acres, or about 11.2 square miles, are necessary. In the highlands of Guatemala, in forested regions with only
occasional fertile valleys, 100 to 200 acres are required to support
the average Indian family. In partially denuded or impoverished
areas, 500 or even 1,000 acres may be necessary to sustain the average family permanently.

The general practice in Yucatan is to replant 5 or 6 acres of
first-year cornfield and to fell another 5 or 6 acres of forest to put
into new milpa, bringing the total area up to 10 or 12 acres of milpa

each year. Milpas are rarely planted a third consecutive year. Experience has shown that the yield of a third-year milpa is less than
half that of a new milpa, and that by the third year the brush fences
are so broken down that they offer little protection against cattle.

The average yield for a first-year milpa in the Chichen Itza
area is nearly 1⅔ cargas per mecate, or about 25 bushels of corn
per acre. Although the Maya say the second year's crop amounts
to only half the first year's crop, reliable figures show that the second year's crop is, at worst, only about 20 per cent less than the first
year's yield.

If continuously planted year after year, a milpa will produce
less and less corn. An experimental milpa near Chichen Itza which
was planted for eight consecutive years (1933–40) showed the following results:

Year	Yield per acre	
Machete-weeded	Pounds	Bushels
1933	708.4	13
1934	609.4	11
1935	358.6	6
1936	149.6	3
Hand-weeded		
1937	748.0	13
1938	330.0	6
1939	459.8	8
1940	5.5	0.1

For the first four years the annual yield of corn rapidly decreased under the modern method of weeding. The fifth year the
experimental milpa was weeded the ancient way, by completely
pulling up the weeds. Under this more thorough method of weeding, the yield slightly exceeded even the first year's crop, but lost
more than half the next year (the sixth year). It gained again in
the seventh year, dropping to almost nothing for the eighth year
because of a three-year plague of locusts which began in 1940.

These figures suggest that the ancient method of weeding prolonged the life of the average cornfield to perhaps seven or eight years before it had to be abandoned. If the ancient Maya milpa was cultivated continuously for four times as long as the modern Maya milpa, only about half as much land would have been necessary to maintain the average family permanently.

It is thus quite possible that during the height of the Maya civilization land may have produced double its present yield, allowing a doubled population in the lowland area. A limiting factor to the indefinitely continued use of a plot of land through hand weeding may have been the incursion of grass, a difficult plant to weed by hand. At the experimental milpa of the Carnegie Institution, in the last three or four years it was planted, grass invaded the tract until it became covered with a thick mat through which not even weeds could push their way.

In general the Maya of the Chichen Itza area expect 1 to 1½ cargas of shelled corn per mecate; this is from 1.7 to 2.5 bushels per mecate, or 17 to 25 bushels per acre. But Chichen Itza is one of the best corn-producing regions in the northern peninsula. A more accurate average for the northern peninsula as a whole would probably be not more than 1 carga per mecate, or 10 cargas per acre (17 bushels per acre). Based upon a survey of a number of villages in northern Yucatan, it may be estimated that the corn-growing regions there produce from 10 to 12 cargas per person, or from 17 to 20 bushels per individual per year.

The agricultural survey of Yucatan undertaken by Dr. Morris Steggerda, formerly of the Carnegie Institution of Washington, has developed another fact of historical significance. Assuming that his cornfield is the average size for northern Yucatan, 100 mecates or 10 acres, the Maya farmer will have worked only 190 days out of the year, leaving 175 days for activities other than the production of his principal food. But even this does not tell the whole story. During the 190 days spent on the milpa, the Maya farmer raises more than twice as much corn as he and his family actually consume, and feeds some livestock, which he did not own before the Spanish Conquest.

The average Maya family is composed of five persons. This

figure is based upon a survey of 265 households, distributed among four Indian villages in northern Yucatan. The average daily consumption of corn per individual was found to be 1.31 pounds—for the average family of five, 6.55 pounds daily. But the modern Maya, unlike his ancestors, has a few animals. He feeds his livestock another 3.25 pounds a day, making the average daily corn consumption of himself, his family, and his stock 9.8 pounds, or a total of 64 bushels per year. Since the average cornfield produces 168 bushels of shelled corn per year, there is a surplus of 104 bushels per year. It is this surplus of corn which, turned into cash, buys the few outside necessities and luxuries which the Maya family cannot produce. Their wants are simple and the corn surplus is usually sufficient to satisfy them all.

If the Maya farmer and his wife are content to do without store-bought extras and if they keep only a few pigs and chickens, he can produce enough corn for his family and limited livestock in only 76 workdays. If he has no livestock at all he can raise enough corn for himself and his family in 48 days. In short, he has between 293 and 317 days out of the year for non-food-producing activities.

Here is the surplus time—roughly nine to ten months—during which the ancient Maya ceremonial centers were built; during which, in the Spanish colonial period, the great churches and other public buildings were erected; and during which today the hemp fields of northwestern Yucatan are cultivated. With so much free time, the Maya Indian for the last two thousand years has been exploited—first by his native rulers and priests, next by his Spanish conquerors, and more recently by private owners in the hemp fields.

OTHER CULTIVATED AND WILD, EDIBLE AND
USEFUL PLANTS

The second most important food crop of the Maya is beans (*buul*), which are often planted in the same holes as the corn and grow up around the cornstalks. There are two varieties, the small

black bean and the red bean, the black bean being the overwhelming favorite. In addition to being planted with the corn, they are
raised in separate patches, and in ancient times must have contributed a large part of the protein intake.

Numerous varieties of squash and pumpkin are grown, sometimes in the milpas among the corn. Sweet potatoes, tomatoes, and
cassava also are raised. Other common food plants of the Maya
are: *chayote*, a herbaceous vine bearing a tender fruit not unlike
summer squash; *chaya*, the leaves of which are boiled and served
as a vegetable; *jicama*, a root which looks like a turnip and is eaten
raw. There are many fruits: the mamey, a sweet, red-meated fruit
that grows wild throughout the Yucatan Peninsula; avocado, a rich
and important item in the Maya dietary; the chicle sapote—a
tree whose sap makes chewing gum, and the timber of which was
used as lintels in temples; the papaya; several species of annonas,
cashews, oranges, bananas, plantains, granadilla, guava, *ciricote*,
nanze; and many others.

Another tree which grows in the Yucatan Peninsula is the
breadnut (*Brosimum alicastrum*, Maya *ox*). It, like the sapote,
is common in the high forests near the ruins of ancient settlements.
This greater frequency of the breadnut and sapote near archaeological sites suggests that the ancient Maya may have planted these
trees in the vicinity of their settlements, as their descendants do
today. The leaves of the breadnut are the chief fodder of mules
and horses in the Yucatan Peninsula. The outer covering of the
fruit is sweet and edible. The seeds, when boiled, are also eaten
as a vegetable, or are dried and ground into flour.

Plants raised for seasoning and flavoring are chili pepper,
vanilla, allspice, oregano, *apazote* (chenopodium), *culantro* (cori-
ander), and other herbs, roots, and leaves. A number of plants
are raised for their fibers. Although today the Maya buy machine-
made cotton textiles, this is a recent development. Formerly cotton
was extensively planted, since Maya clothing was made almost
entirely of hand-woven cotton textiles. Another important fiber is
henequen, hemp, or sisal, as it is variously called. Today this con-

stitutes almost the only exportable product of Yucatan. The fiber of the *bayal* palm is used in making baskets and the young leaves of the *guano* palm in making hats and mats.

Maya colors are for the most part of vegetable origin. The annatto tree, known locally as *achiote*, is raised for its fruit, which yields a rich orange-red color and is extensively used in flavoring. Logwood is common in the swamps of the middle part of the peninsula and, until the appearance of aniline dyes, was exported in tremendous quantities. The *mora* tree yields the fustic wood of commerce, which gives green and also a yellow-brown color.

The Yucatan forests afford an abundance of the materials required for construction of the thatched houses of the common people: sapodilla for the house timbers and posts; mahogany and Spanish cedar for the doors, windows, and frames; *guano* and corozo palms for thatching. From the forests come the vines which are used in tying together the wooden framework of the house; nails are never used in making the Maya thatched house even today.

Other useful nonedible plants and trees are gourd plants for water bottles and food containers, tobacco, rubber, and the copal and gumbo-limbo trees, the resin of which is used as incense. There is fat pine for torches, and the soapberry tree bears fruit which gives a pulp that lathers. The wood of lignum vitae and *maha* trees makes the containers and swizzle sticks used in the preparation of chocolate.

Ancient Maya life depended upon a similar variety of native products. There was stone, lime, and gravel for their ceremonial buildings, and timber and thatch for the houses of the common people. A rich and varied flora supplied vegetables, seasonings, kitchen utensils, medicines, and fibers for textiles and basketry. The forest supplied game of all kinds; the jaguar and deer were especially hunted, their pelts being made into cloaks and sandals for the rulers and priests. There were also many birds of beautiful plumage.

With all this abundance, nature's richest gift was maize, without which the Maya could not have developed their distinctive culture, the most brilliant aboriginal civilization of the New World.

····

GOVERNMENT AND SOCIAL ORGANIZATION

DOCUMENTARY SOURCES FOR CLASSIC-STAGE HISTORY LACKING

WE HAVE NO DIRECT evidence as to the governmental and social organization of the Classic Maya, since no contemporary evidence on these points has survived. What little may be said of the governmental and social organization of the Classic stage depends upon (1) the indirect evidence furnished by what is known of such organization in Postclassic times, and (2) the direct evidence supplied by Classic-stage pictorial art. If we may draw from what is known of Postclassic governmental and social organization, and abstract from it certain known importations from mainland Mexico, it may be possible partially to reconstruct the Classic pattern. Since Maya culture is known to have been continuous in many ways, the Classic and Postclassic stages will be treated together, though most of the material on these subjects has been drawn from Postclassic northern Yucatan.

POLITICAL AND SOCIAL ORGANIZATION

In Yucatan during the Postclassic stage, the country is said to have been governed by a confederation among the rulers of Mayapan, Uxmal, and Chichen Itza. These three sites have been shown archaeologically to have been built during successive time periods rather than contemporaneously. Still, the durable quality of Maya architecture makes it possible that Chichen Itza and Uxmal may have remained as political capitals long after their major building periods, and Mayapan is known to have been occupied until less than a hundred years before the Spanish Conquest.

The governments of these three states must have controlled

143

most of Yucatan, each with a region considerably larger than the agricultural area directly surrounding it. Thus, in Postclassic times the governmental units must have included a considerable number of religious centers.

Political organization in Classic times is hard to reconstruct. The Postclassic organization resembles that known from central Mexico and may have been introduced in the tenth century by the Toltecs, or at some time thereafter. It can safely be said that the Classic Maya culture was much more homogeneous than that of its period on the Mexican mainland, and this might suggest a measure of political hegemony over the Maya area.

An important factor to consider in reconstructing the government of the Classic Maya is the lack of warfare among them. This may be considered an indication of the overwhelming importance of religion in government, and there is every reason to believe that the priests of a highly organized and dogmatically inflexible religious cult ruled the central Maya area. As to how far religion penetrated into political affairs, it is difficult to say; but perhaps the cultural homogeneity and isolation of the Maya area minimized the need for political control.

Relying upon archaeological evidence for the Classic stage, which indicates a number of subprovinces, we may hazard the guess that each of these archaeological subprovinces corresponded roughly to a political unit of some sort. In the central area during the Classic stage there may have been at least four: (1) central and northern Peten, Guatemala, and British Honduras; (2) the Usumacinta Valley; (3) the southeastern subprovince; and (4) the southwestern subprovince. In the northern area eastern Campeche and southern Yucatan formed a region apart. In the late Postclassic there were three principal political entities—Chichen Itza, Uxmal, and Mayapan.

THE TERRITORIAL RULER

The head of the Yucatecan area at the time of the Conquest was the *halach uinic* (Maya for "True Man") or territorial ruler.

This position was hereditary in a single family. Bishop Landa,
describing conditions in late Postclassic times, states that the lords were succeeded by their oldest sons:

If the lord died, although his oldest son succeeded him, the other children were always very much respected and assisted and regarded as lords themselves; . . . if, when the lord died, there were no sons [old enough] to reign, and he [the deceased lord] had brothers, the oldest of the brothers, or the best qualified, reigned, and they taught the heir their customs and feasts against the time he should become a man; and these brothers [paternal uncles of the heir], although the heir was [ready] to reign, commanded all their lives; and if he [the deceased lord] had no brothers, the priests and principal people elected a man proper for the position.

The halach uinic was also called *ahau*, a word the sixteenth-century Maya manuscript-dictionaries define as "king, emperor, monarch, prince, or great lord." This was the title used by the Maya of the colonial period in referring to the King of Spain. The powers enjoyed by the halach uinic were broad. He probably formulated foreign and domestic policies with the aid of a council composed of the leading chiefs, priests, and special councilors (*ah cuch cabob*). He appointed the town and village chiefs (*batabob*), who stood in a sort of feudal relation to him, and the most important of whom were no doubt his close blood relatives.

In addition to being the highest administrative and executive officer of the state, it is likely that the halach uinic was the highest ecclesiastical authority as well. It has been suggested that the Classic-stage government may have been a theocracy, the highest civil and religious powers being combined in the person of one individual who perhaps even then was called the halach uinic.

Judging from the Classic-stage sculptures, the insignia of the halach uinic varied, depending upon whether his civil, religious, or military function was represented. As administrative head of state he carried in his right hand the Manikin Scepter, and in his left a round shield. The Manikin Scepter is a small anthropomorphic figure with a long curling nose, and one of the legs terminates in the head of a serpent (Fig. 6, *a*, *b*, and *c*). In a fresco in the Temple of the Warriors at Chichen Itza the seated figure of a halach uinic holds in his right hand what is probably a Postclassic version of this same type of scepter (Fig. 6*c*), and in his left hand he grasps the usual Postclassic round shield.

As head of the religious hierarchy, the halach uinic holds the Double-Headed Ceremonial Bar (Fig. 6*h*). This is usually carried horizontally across the breast, though occasionally it is held diagonally, one end resting on the shoulder (Plate 67*b*). The ends of this emblem terminate in heads which are sometimes serpent-formed, sometimes human. On the back of Stela 11 at Yaxchilan (Plate 18*b*), a halach uinic is shown impersonating a deity with a mask of the god's head held in front of his face. As the highest military officer of the state, he carries a weapon, usually a spear (Fig. 6*d*), occasionally a throwing stick, *hulche* (Fig. 6*e*), or a club (Fig. 6*f*), but never the bow and arrow, which were unknown in Classic times and do not appear in Maya history until late in the Postclassic.

The magnificent Classic-stage murals found at Bonampak, Chiapas, give a far more intimate view of social structure among the ruling class than do Landa's accounts. They take the observer through the course of a Maya ceremony, with scenes so naturalistically presented that the viewer can observe as though he were there. There are many clues to the organization of Maya religious procedure in these murals, and the protocol of the ceremonies will be long discussed by experts. The over-all impression, however, is clear. There is an informality, an anecdotal air to these paintings which departs far from the stiffer panoply of Old World ceremonies as recorded in Egyptian and Mesopotamian art. The participants show a refreshing lack of self-conscious dignity, an individuality and lack of servility which supports the suggestion, made elsewhere in this text, that the Maya staged ceremonies, not because they were forced to participate, but because they enjoyed doing so. And although the religious centers were abandoned less than a hundred years after the Bonampak murals were painted, one suspects that the priests rather than the religion were in dis-

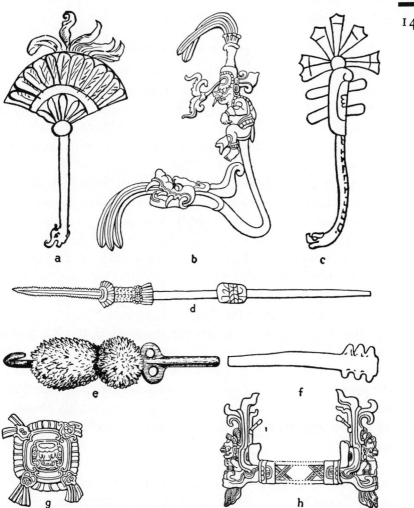

Fig. 6.—Classic and Postclassic ceremonial insignia, and weapons: (*a*) Probably a late Postclassic example of the Manikin Scepter, from the Xiu genealogical tree; (*b*) the Classic Manikin Scepter, from Zoömorph P at Quirigua; (*c*) a Postclassic example of the Manikin Scepter, from a fresco in the Temple of the Warriors at Chichen Itza; (*d*) a spear, symbol of military rank from Classic times on; (*e*) a throwing stick, symbol of military rank; (*f*) a war club, symbol of military rank; (*g*) a small, round ceremonial shield (Classic); (*h*) a Double-Headed Ceremonial Bar, symbol of highest religious rank during Classic times.

favor, and that the process of abandonment of the centers was in the main a quiet one.

RULING HOUSES OF LATE POSTCLASSIC TIMES

At the time of the Spanish Conquest, the five leading families of the peninsula were: (1) the Xiu, or Tutul Xiu, with their capital at Mani; (2) the Cocom, with their capital at Sotuta; (3) the Canek, with their capital at Tayasal in central Peten; (4) the Chel, with their capital at Tecoh; and (5) the Pech, with their capital at Motul.

The foremost of these was the Xiu, perhaps because this family had taken the leading part in the successful revolt against Mayapan in 1441. In the Peabody Museum of Archaeology and Ethnology at Harvard University there is a portfolio of 145 documents, the proofs of nobility of the Xiu family, which were accumulated during the Spanish colonial period. The three earliest— a map, a land treaty, and a genealogical tree—date from 1557, only fifteen years after the Spanish Conquest.

The map (Plate 21) shows the Province of the Xiu with its capital, Mani, at the center. The symbol for each town and village is a Catholic church with a tower surmounted by a cross; in the cases of the smaller villages there are only crosses. The symbol for Uxmal, the former Xiu capital, which was entirely abandoned by the middle fifteenth century, is the representation of a Maya temple.

The treaty of the Maya lords, which accompanies the map and bears the same date, is the earliest known document to be written in Spanish script in the Maya language. It describes the boundaries between the Xiu state and the adjoining provinces.

The genealogical tree (Plate 22) shows Hun Uitzil Chac Tutul Xiu, the founder of Uxmal, seated at its base, holding a fan. The foundation of this city, according to the fragmentary hieroglyph to the left of the fan, took place in a Katun 2 Ahau. The handle of this fan terminates in the head of a serpent, and the fan is thus probably a late Postclassic form of the Manikin Scepter. At Hun

Uitzil Chac's right side kneels his wife Yx . . . of Ticul; she points
to their joint achievement—the spreading Xiu family tree. It is
to be noted, however, that the tree rises from *his* loins and not from
hers, a graphic insistence upon patrilineal descent. The object of
the tree was to prove to the Spanish Crown the descent of the Conquest-period Xiu from the former royal house of Uxmal. For
this reason the founder of Uxmal, Hun Uitzil Chac, appears as
the progenitor of the family. The papers in the portfolio carry
the Xiu story down to the time of Mexican Independence in 1821,
and from living members of the family it has been possible to continue their history to the present day. The present members of the
family live at Ticul in northern Yucatan.

How far the Xiu have fallen since the days when they ruled
in northern Yucatan is reflected in the changes of residences of
the heads of the family. Plate 24*a* shows the Palace of the Governor at Uxmal, which may well have been the official residence
of the Xiu when they were halach uinicil. Plate 24*b* shows their
residence at Mani in the early Colonial Period, when the Xiu had
been created Spanish hidalgos; this is the house of Francisco de
Montejo Xiu, who aided Francisco de Montejo the Younger in the
conquest of Yucatan. Plate 24*c* is a picture of the simple thatched
house of Don Nemesio Xiu on the outskirts of Ticul.

SOCIAL CLASSES

Ancient Maya society seems to have been divided into four
general classes: the nobility (Maya *almehenob*); the priesthood
(*ahkinob*); the common people (*ah chembal uinicob*); and the
slaves (*ppencatob*).

The nobility.—Below the halach uinic stood the *batabs* or lesser
chiefs. They were the local magistrates and executives, who administered the affairs of the towns and villages. In the Postclassic and
probably in the Classic stage as well, although appointed by the
halach uinic, they were members of a hereditary nobility, the almehenob. They exercised executive and judicial authority in their
communities, and, although in times of war all served under one

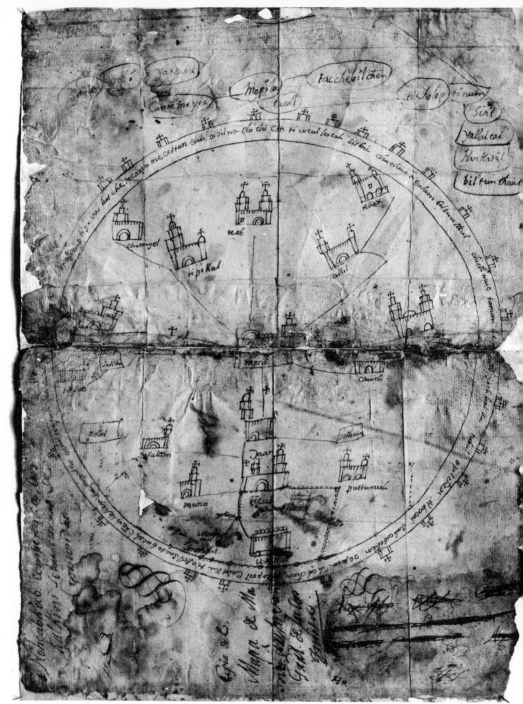

PLATE 21.—ANCIENT MAP OF THE PROVINCE OF MANI, YUCATAN

PLATE 22.—GENEALOGICAL TREE OF THE XIU FAMILY OF MANI,
THE FORMER RULING HOUSE OF UXMAL

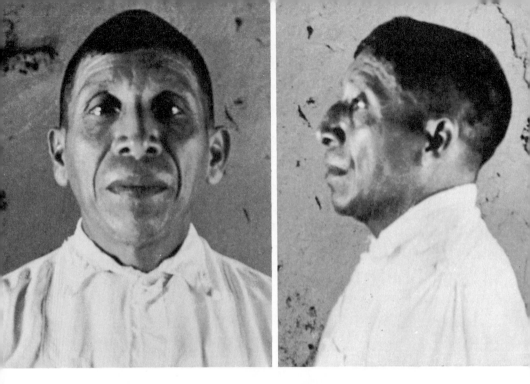

a) Don Nemesio Xiu.

PLATE 23.—THE PRESENT HEAD OF THE XIU FAMILY AND HIS OLDEST
SON, TICUL, YUCATAN

b) Don Dionisio Xiu.

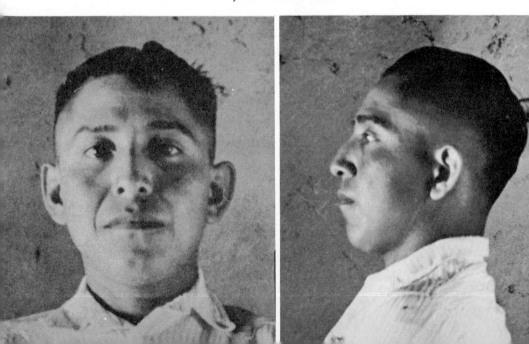

↑ *a*) Palace of the Governor, Uxmal, Yucatan; the Xiu as Maya rulers.

↑ *b*) House of Francisco de Montejo Xiu, Mani, Yucatan; the Xiu as Spanish nobles.

↑ *c*) House of Don Nemesio Xiu, Ticul, Yucatan; the Xiu as Mexican corn farmers.

PLATE 24.—RESIDENCES OF THE HEADS OF THE XIU FAMILY UNDER
THE NATIVE MAYA, SPAIN, AND MEXICO

supreme military chief, each batab personally commanded his own soldiers. He presided over the local council and saw to it that the houses were kept in repair and that the people cut and burned their fields at the times indicated by the priests. In his capacity as judge he sentenced criminals and decided civil suits. If these were of unusual importance he consulted the halach uinic before passing judgment. No tribute was paid directly to the batab, being rendered only to the halach uinic, but he was supported by the people. One of the batab's principal duties was to see that his town or village paid its tribute promptly to the halach uinic.

There were two kinds of war captains: one hereditary, presumably the batab; the other, of greater importance, was elected for a period of three years and given the title of *nacom*.

This one, called the *nacom*, could not, during these three years, have relations with any woman, even his own wife, nor eat red meat. They held him in great veneration and gave him fish and iguanas, which are like lizards, to eat. In this time [his tenure of office] he did not get drunk, and he kept separate in his house the utensils and other objects which he used, and no women served him and he had but little communication with the people. At the end of these three years [all was] as before. These two captains [the *nacom* and *batab*] discussed the affairs of war and put them in order . . .

[And again] They bore him [the *nacom*] in great pomp, perfuming him as if he were an idol, to the temple where they seated him and burned incense to him as to an idol.

It would seem that the elected nacom formulated the strategy of war, while the batabs, the hereditary chiefs, led their respective contingents into battle.

Next below the batab were the town councilors, the *ah cuch cabob*, two or three in number. Each had a vote in the town government and without their assent nothing could be done. Each stood at the head of a subdivision of the town, and they were likened by Spanish writers of the sixteenth century to the *regidores* in Spanish town governments.

The *ah kulelob*, or deputies, accompanied the batab wherever he went and were the assistants who carried out his orders; there were usually two or three of them.

The duties of the *ah holpopob*, meaning in Maya "those at the head of the mat," are not so clear. They are said to have assisted the lords in the government of their towns, and through them the townspeople approached the lords. They were the advisers of the lords on matters of foreign policy, and are said to have been masters of the *popolna* or house where the men met to discuss public affairs and to learn the dances for the town festivals. The ah holpopob were also the chief singers and chanters in charge of the dances and musical instruments in each town.

The *tupiles*, or town constables, stood at the bottom of the law-enforcement structure.

The priesthood.—Bishop Landa, describing conditions in the late Postclassic, says that both chiefs' and priests' offices were hereditary and were derived from the nobility:

> They taught the sons of the other priests and the second sons of the lords who [were] brought them from their infancy, if they saw that they had an inclination for this profession; . . . and his [the high priest's] sons or his nearest relatives succeeded him in office.

Herrera, another early Spanish historian, writes:

> For the matters concerning the worship of their gods they had one who was the high-priest, whose sons succeeded him in the priesthood.

There is little doubt that both the highest civil and religious offices were hereditary, being filled from the members of one family in each state.

Landa says that the high priest in late Postclassic times was called *Ahaucan* Mai. This, however, seems to be a combination of the title *ahaucan* and the family name Mai, which is common in Yucatan. The high priest may have been called simply the ahaucan, since this word in Maya means "the Lord Serpent." In combining the surname Mai with it, Landa was doubtless referring to a specific family in which the office seems to have been hereditary. Landa says further that

> He was very much respected by the lords and had no *repartimiento* of Indians [no Indians specially set aside for his personal service], but besides the offerings, the lords made him presents and all the priests of the town

brought contributions to him. . . . In him was the key of their learning and it was to these matters that they [the high priests] mostly dedicated themselves; and they gave advice to the lords and replied to their questions. They seldom dealt with matters pertaining to the sacrifices except at the time of the principal feasts, or very important matters of business. They provided priests for the towns when they were needed, examining them in the sciences and ceremonies and committed to them the duties of their office, and set good example to people and provided them with books and sent them forth. And they employed themselves in the duties of the temples and in teaching their sciences as well as writing books about them. . . .

The sciences which they taught were the computation of the years, months and days, the festivals and ceremonies, the administration of the sacraments, the fateful days and seasons, their methods of divination and their prophecies, events and the cures for diseases and their antiquities [history] and how to read and write with their letters and characters [hieroglyphics] with which they wrote, and [to make] drawings which illustrate the meaning of the writings.

The direction of the manifold activities of the great temple establishments of Classic and Postclassic times must have been as complex as the governing of a political state. The high priests had to be not only able administrators but also outstanding scholars, astronomers, and mathematicians, and this in addition to their religious duties. If they were not the actual rulers in Classic times, they must have been councilors of state, advising the halach uinic on political matters. Being of the ruling house themselves, their interest in the state was as great as his.

Another class of priests were the *chilanes* or diviners, whose duty it was to give the replies of the gods to the people. The chilanes were held in such high respect that the people carried them on their shoulders when they appeared in public.

Another priest was the *nacom* (not to be confused with the war chief of the same title), who was elected for life. According to Landa, he was held in little esteem since he was the functionary who slit open the breasts of the sacrificial victims and plucked out their hearts:

At this time came the executioner, the *nacom*, with a knife of stone, and with much skill and cruelty struck him [the sacrificial victim] with

the knife between the ribs of his left side under the nipple, and at once
plunged his hand in there [the opening in the breast] and seized the heart like a raging tiger, tearing it out alive, and having placed it on a plate, he gave it to the priest, who went quickly and anointed the face of the idols with that fresh blood.

The nacom was assisted in the ceremony of human sacrifice by four aides called *chacs,* respectable old men chosen anew on each occasion.

The *chacs* seized the poor man whom they were going to sacrifice and with great haste, placed him on his back upon that stone and all four held him by the legs and arms so that they divided him in the middle.

Other duties of the chacs were to assist at the puberty ceremony, to kindle the new fire at the beginning of the Maya New Year, and to fast and anoint idols with blood in the month of Mol, which was dedicated to making new idols.

Ahkin was the general name for "priest" in Maya. The word means literally "he of the sun." Some of the ahkins had specialized duties, for example as prophets of the thirteen Maya ages, or thirteen differently numbered katuns. At a sanctuary of the Island of Cozumel and at the Sacred Cenote at Chichen Itza, an ahkin served as the oracle. It was also an ahkin who received the hearts of the sacrificial victims from the hands of the nacom and offered them to the idols of the Maya gods.

The modern Maya of northern Yucatan, when they practice the few ancient ceremonies which have survived among them, employ the service of an *ahmen* or medicine man—in Maya, "he who understands." The ahmen is a prophet and, at the same time, the inflicter as well as the healer of diseases.

The priesthood was probably the most powerful group in the state. Their knowledge of astronomy, their ability to predict eclipses, their penetration into every phase of life, made them feared and respected and gave them a hold on the superstitions of the people equaled by that of no other class. The lack of a class struggle between the Maya nobility and priesthood may be explained by the fact that among the ancient Maya the members of each group were probably quite closely related.

The common people.—The great mass of the people in both Classic and Postclassic times were humble corn farmers, whose toil supported not only themselves but also their supreme ruler, their local lords, and the priesthood. In addition, they were the builders of the great complex ceremonial centers and the raised stone highways (Maya *sacbeob*) which connected the principal cities.

Other obligations of the lower class were to pay tribute to the halach uinic, to give presents to their local lords, and to make offerings to the gods through the priests. The tribute and offerings consisted of all kinds of vegetable produce, a kind of woven cotton cloth called *pati*, domesticated fowls, salt, dried fish, and all kinds of game and birds. It also included cacao, *pom* (copal) for incense, honey and wax, strings of jade and coral beads, and shells. Their lands were held as community property and were tilled in common. Bishop Landa says:

The common people at their own expense made the houses of the lords. . . . Beyond the house, all the people did their sowing for the lord, cared for his fields and harvested what was necessary for him and his household; and when there was hunting or fishing, or when it was time to get their salt, they always gave the lord his share, since these things they always did as a community. . . . They also joined together for hunting in companies of fifty, more or less, and they roast the flesh of the deer on grills, so that it shall not be wasted [spoil] and having reached the town, they make presents to their lord and distribute [them] as among friends. And they do the same in their fishing.

The common people lived on the outskirts of the towns and villages, and the distance of a man's house from the central plaza depended upon his position in the social scale.

We do not know what term was used to describe the common people in ancient times, though sixteenth-century Maya dictionaries give *ah chembal, uinicob, memba uinicob,* and *yalba uinicob* as meaning "the common people, the plebeians"; these terms in Maya mean "the inferior or lower men." At the time of the Spanish Conquest the common people were called *mazehualob,* a Nahua word which means the lower classes, as compared with the nobility.

It is still used in northern Yucatan, but it now carries a distinct connotation of social inferiority.

Slaves.—At the bottom of the social scale were the slaves, called *ppentacob* in Maya. Slavery seems to have been practiced in both the Classic and Postclassic stages, despite Bishop Landa's assertion that it was introduced in late Postclassic times by one of the Cocom rulers of Mayapan. This is difficult to believe in view of the frequent representations of the so-called "captive figures" on Classic Maya monuments. These "captive figures" are very likely representations of enslaved prisoners of war, though they may represent the people of a whole town rather than any specific individual. Sometimes their faces are of a different type from those of the principal figures, a distinction which may indicate that the lords belonged to a special hereditary class.

In Postclassic times, when we have documentary evidence for slavery, the condition would seem to have arisen in one of five different ways: (1) by having been born a slave; (2) by having been made a slave in punishment for stealing; (3) by having been made a prisoner of war; (4) by having become an orphan; and (5) by having been acquired by purchase or trade. Provision was made by law and custom for the redemption of children born into slavery. If a person were caught stealing, he was bound over to the person he had robbed and remained a slave for life, or until he was able to repay the value of the stolen articles. Prisoners of war were always enslaved. Those of high degree were sacrificed immediately, but those of lower rank became the property of the soldier who had captured them. Slaves of this kind are represented in a mural painting from the Temple of the Warriors at Chichen Itza, where they are portrayed as naked, their bodies being painted with black and white stripes (Plate 25).

Orphans were acquired for sacrifice either by purchase or by kidnaping. If purchased, the price of a small boy varied from five to ten stone beads. Orphans who had been brought up by rich lords were frequently sacrificed, especially if they were the children of slave women. Finally, slaves were acquired by purchase or in trade. Landa, in enumerating the vices of the Maya, mentions

PLATE 25.—BATTLE SCENE FROM A WALL PAINTING IN THE TEMPLE OF THE WARRIORS, CHICHEN ITZA

idolatries and repudiation of their wives and orgies of public drunkenness and buying and selling slaves. .... The occupation to which they are most inclined was trade, carrying cloth and salt and slaves to the lands of Tabasco and Ulua [the present Ulua Valley in Honduras], exchanging all of it for cacao and stone-beads which were their money; and with this they were accustomed to buy slaves or other beads because they were fine and good, which their chiefs wore as jewels at their feasts.

One early authority writing of Nicaragua says that "a slave costs one hundred almonds [cacao beans], more or less, according to his condition and the agreement between the buyer and seller." If this is true, the value of cacao beans must have been extremely high in ancient times or the price of slaves correspondingly low.

TRACES OF FORMER CLAN ORGANIZATION

By the time of the Spanish Conquest few traces of clan organization among the ancient Maya remained, but there are suggestions that originally such a system had prevailed. For example, Bishop Landa says:

They always called their sons and daughters by the name of the father and the mother, that of the father as the proper name, and that of the mother as the appellative name as follows. The son of Chel [patronymic] and Chan [matronymic] is called Na Chan Chel, which means the son of such and such people [using the mother's family name, here Chan, as a middle name]. And this is the reason the Indians say that those bearing the same name are all of one family, and that they are treated as such. And on this account when one comes to a place which is not known to him and he is in need, he at once makes use of his name, and if there are any of the same name there, they receive him at once and treat him with the greatest kindness. And thus no woman or man was ever married to another of the same name, for that was in their opinion a great infamy.

This is in reference to the prevalence of an exogamous marriage restriction which may have been based originally upon the clan system of claiming descent from a common ancestor.

This ancient Maya taboo against marriages between persons of the same family name has survived to the present day among the

Tzeltal and Lacandon Maya. In a number of Tzeltal villages in the highlands of Chiapas, marriage between persons having the same Indian family name is either forbidden outright or strongly discouraged. This taboo operates so strongly in some villages that it extends even to Tzeltal families who have lost their Indian surnames and have adopted Spanish surnames. If even these Spanish names are the same, marriages are forbidden.

Among the Lacandon Maya of the Chiapas lowlands, now reduced to around two hundred people, everyone was found to belong to one clan or another, the membership being determined by the father's. The clan names among the Lacandon all derive from animals or birds and suggest a former totemic significance. Although not common, marriages do occur between Lacandones of the same surname and clan name. If exogamy ever existed among them, it has disappeared before the necessity of finding mates of any surname and clan at all, for the total number of the group has dwindled almost to the vanishing point.

Superimposed on the clan organization of the Lacandon, there is evidence of larger social groups composed of several clans each, but these are not so clearly understood. These larger groups may be the remains of a more elaborate social organization of groups of families originally supposed to have had a common ancestor.

LIFE OF THE COMMON PEOPLE

BIRTH, NAMES, AND THE *HETZMEK* CEREMONY

THE ENTIRE LIFE of the common people was dominated by their religious beliefs as interpreted by the priesthood. The ceremonial pattern of everyone's life was predetermined for him according to the day of the *tzolkin*, or sacred year of 260 days, upon which he was born. Among the Cakchiquel of the highlands of Guatemala there was the belief that the day of one's birth even controlled one's temperament and destiny. This fact determined for the ancient Maya the gods who were friendly to him and those who were hostile. Among the Cakchiquel, for example, the given name of every person was fixed automatically, since his name had to be that of the day upon which he was born. This practice, if ever present among the Maya of northern Yucatan, had disappeared before the time of the Spanish Conquest.

The ancient Maya loved their children deeply. Children were greatly desired and the women even "asked them of the idols with gifts and prayers." In order to induce pregnancy, a woman placed under her bed an image of Ixchel, goddess of pregnancy and childbirth.

Depressed foreheads were considered a mark of beauty among the ancient Maya, and this deformation was achieved by binding the heads of the babies between a pair of flat boards, one at the back of the head, the other against the forehead. These boards were left in place for several days, and, after they were removed, the head remained flattened for life. Maya representations of the human head in profile show that this practice must have been almost universal, at least among the upper class.

Another mark of distinction was to be cross-eyed, and mothers tried to bring about this condition by hanging little balls of resin to the hairs falling between their children's eyes. These pellets of resin dangling between the eyes made the children look at them and thus tended to cross their eyes. The ears, lips, and septum of the nose were pierced to hold ornaments.

A ceremony performed among the modern Maya of Yucatan which may be a survival from ancient times is that of the *hetzmek*, when the baby is carried astride the hip for the first time. Maya babies are carried astride the left hip and the child is held in place by the left arm of the person carrying it (Plates 10*b* and 12*c*). This is done the first time for a girl when she is three months old, and for a boy when he is four months old. The difference in time is said to be because the Maya hearth, symbolic of woman's activities in the home, has three stones; and the cornfield, symbolic of man's activities in the field, has four corners.

There are usually two godparents for this ceremony—a husband and wife. If there is only one, it is a man for a boy and a woman for a girl. Nine objects, symbolic of what the child will use in later life, are placed on a table. The father hands the baby to the godfather, who sets the child astride his left hip and makes nine circuits of the table, each time selecting one of the nine objects and putting it into the child's hand, instructing him at the same time as to the object's use. He then turns the child over to the godmother, who repeats the procedure. The child is then given back to the godfather, who returns it to the father saying, "We have made the hetzmek for your child." The parents kneel before the godparents in sign of gratitude and an assistant distributes food, rum, boiled fowls, and tortillas to those present.

In ancient times the young child was carried to a priest, who forecast its horoscope and gave the child the name it was to bear during childhood. The ancient Maya had three or four different names: (1) his *paal kaba* or given name; (2) his father's family name; (3) his *naal kaba* or father's and mother's family names combined; and (4) his *coco kaba* or nickname.

Until the age of three or four, children were brought up by their mothers. When a boy was about four or five a small white bead was fastened to the hair on the top of his head. When a girl

reached the same age a string was tied around her waist, from
which hung a red shell as a symbol of virginity. To remove either
of these before the puberty ceremony was thought to be highly
dishonorable.

PUBERTY

According to Bishop Landa, the day for the puberty ceremony
was carefully selected; pains were taken to ascertain that it would
not be an unlucky day. A principal man of the town was chosen
as sponsor for the children participating; his duty was to assist
the priest during the ceremony and to furnish the feast. Four
honorable old men were selected as *chacs*, to assist the priest and
sponsor in conducting the ceremony. On the appointed day, all
assembled in the court of the sponsor's house, which had been
newly swept and strewn with fresh leaves. An old man was assigned to act as godfather for the boys, and an old woman as godmother for the girls. When this was done the priest purified the
dwelling and conducted a ceremony to expel the evil spirit.

When the spirit had been expelled, the court was swept out
again, fresh leaves were strewn about, and mats were spread on
the floor. The priest changed his vestments to a handsome jacket
and a miter-like headdress of colored feathers, taking in his hand
an aspergillum for sprinkling holy water. This latter consisted of
a finely worked short stick with rattlesnake tails hanging from it.
The chacs approached the children and placed on their heads pieces
of white cloth, which their mothers had brought for this purpose.
The older children were asked if they had committed any sin or
obscene act. If they had, they were separated from the others
(Landa does not say whether they were refused permission to participate further in the rite). This concluded, the priest ordered
everyone to be seated and to preserve absolute silence, and after
pronouncing a benediction on the children, he sat down. The sponsor of the ceremony, with a bone given him by the priest, tapped
each child nine times on the forehead, moistening the forehead,
the face, and the spaces between the fingers and toes with water.

After this anointing, the priest removed the white cloths from the children's heads. The children then gave the chacs some feathers and cacao beans which they had brought as gifts. The priest next cut the white beads from the boys' heads. The attendants carried pipes which they smoked from time to time, giving each child a puff of smoke. Gifts of food, brought by the mothers, were distributed to the children, and a wine offering was made to the gods; this wine had to be drunk at one draught by a specially appointed official.

The young girls were then dismissed, each mother removing from her daughter the red shell which had been worn as a symbol of purity. With this, the girl was considered to have reached a marriageable age. The boys were dismissed next. When the children had withdrawn from the court, their parents distributed among the spectators and officials pieces of cotton cloth which they had brought as gifts. The ceremony closed with feasting and heavy drinking. This ceremony was called "the descent of the gods," and it will be seen that it is much more likely to have been a puberty ceremony than a baptismal rite, which Landa mistakenly calls it.

As the boys grew older they began to live in a house set apart for the young unmarried men of the community. They came together here for their diversions and usually slept together in this house until marriage. They painted themselves black until they were married, but were not supposed to tattoo themselves before that time. The youths were constantly with their fathers and at an early age accompanied them to work in the family cornfield. Says Landa: "In all other things they always accompanied their fathers, and thus they became as great idolators as they, and served them very well in their labors."

After the puberty ceremony the girls were considered ready for marriage. They were taught to be modest: whenever they met a man they turned their backs to him, stepping aside to allow him to pass; when giving a man a drink of water they lowered their eyes. Mothers taught their daughters how to make tortillas, an occupation which consumed a great part of every woman's time. The women were the housekeepers, cooks, weavers, and spinners. They raised fowl and went to market to buy and sell the articles which they produced. When need arose, they carried burdens alongside their menfolk and assisted them in sowing and cultivating.

MARRIAGE

Bishop Landa says that formerly the Maya married when they were twenty years old but that in his time they married when they were twelve or fourteen. In the eighteenth and early nineteenth centuries Maya boys of Yucatan married at about seventeen or eighteen and girls at about fourteen or fifteen. Today in the Indian villages of the northern peninsula the average age of the boys at marriage is twenty-one years, and that of the girls nearly seventeen.

The fathers took great care to find suitable wives for their sons, preferably girls of the same social class and of the same village. Certain relationship taboos existed. It was considered wicked to marry a girl who had the same surname, or for a widower to marry the widow of his brother, his stepmother, the sister of his deceased wife, or his maternal aunt, though first-cousin marriages were not forbidden.

It was thought to be mean-spirited if a man sought a mate for himself or for his children personally, instead of employing the services of a professional matchmaker (*ah atanzahob*). This custom has survived in rural districts in northern Yucatan to the present time. The matchmaker having been selected, the ceremony was discussed and the amount of the dowry agreed upon. This usually consisted of dresses and other articles of little value, for which the boy's father paid the girl's father. The boy's mother at the same time made ready clothing for her son and daughter-in-law to be. Today, in northern Yucatan, the groom or his family defrays all expenses of the wedding, even including the bride's trousseau. This is true of all classes of society from the most aristocratic *hacendado* (plantation owner) to the humblest Indian laborer.

When the day of the ceremony arrived, the relatives and guests assembled at the house of the bride's father. As soon as the priest entered the house, the fathers of the couple presented the young people to him. The priest made a speech setting forth the details of the marriage agreement, after which he perfumed the house and blessed the bridal pair, and the company sat down to a feast which concluded the ceremony. From this time forward the young couple were allowed to live together, and the son-in-law lived and worked in the house of his wife's parents for six or seven years. His mother-in-law saw to it that her daughter gave the young husband food and drink as a token of their recognition of the marriage, but if the young man failed to work for the appointed time, he could be put out of the house.

Marriages were often arranged between families when the boy and girl were still very young, and after they had come of age the arrangement was carried out. Widows and widowers remarried without ceremony; the man simply went to the house of the woman of his choice, and, if she accepted him, she gave him something to eat. Custom decreed that widowers and widows should remain single for at least a year after the death of their previous mates.

Although the Maya were monogamous, divorce was easy, and consisted of little more than simple repudiation. It was of common occurrence, as an early Spanish witness indicates:

> They did not have marital relations with more than one woman [at a time], but they left her for trifling reasons, and married another, and there were men who married ten and twelve times; and the women had the same liberty to leave their husbands and take another, but the first time they got married it was by a priest.

Landa says:

> And on this account they repudiate more easily, since they marry without love and ignorant of married life and of the duties of married people.

This is probably often true of the present-day Maya, who marry without love in the modern American sense. It seems rather a matter of routine. The boy wants a home and children of his own, and either his parents or the matchmaker simply arranges for his marriage with a suitable girl.

The principal garment of the men was the breechclout, called *ex* in Maya. It was a band of cotton cloth, five fingers wide and long enough to be wound around the waist several times and passed between the legs. These breechclouts were woven on hand looms, the two ends often being elaborately embroidered with feathers:

> They wore the *mastil* [probably a corruption of *maxtli*, the Aztec word for the same garment] between their legs, which was a large strip of woven *manta*, which, tying it on the abdomen and giving it a turn below, covered their private parts, the two long points having on them much plumage hanging before and behind.

The *ex* is represented everywhere in Maya graphic arts, from the gorgeously decorated breechclouts worn by the rulers, priests, and nobles to the simple, unadorned loincloths of the lower classes (Fig. 7).

In addition to the *ex*, the men sometimes wore a large square cotton cloth called the *pati*, knotted around the shoulders. This was more or less elaborately decorated according to the station of the wearer. It also served the poor as a covering for their beds at night.

Sandals made of untanned deer hide and tied with hemp cords completed the costume of the common people. On Classic-stage monuments, the sandals are shown as exceedingly elaborate (Fig. 8, *a-f*). One important difference may be noted between representations of ancient Maya sandals (Fig. 8, *g-j*) and those now in use. In ancient times the sandals were bound to the feet by two thongs, one passing between the first and second toes, the other between the third and fourth toes (Fig. 8, *k*). Today, from the highlands of Guatemala to northern Yucatan, only the first of these thongs is still used (Fig. 8*l*).

The men wore their hair long with a bare spot burned on the top of the head. The hair was braided and wound around the head like a coronet, except for a queue which fell behind. Warriors painted themselves black and red, prisoners were painted in black

Fig. 7.—Examples of Maya breechclouts, or *ex*, from the monuments of the Classic stage.

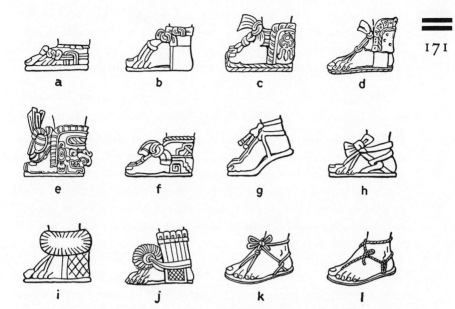

FIG. 8.—Maya sandals, or *xanab*: (*a*, *b*, *c*, *d*, *e*, *f*) examples of sandals from Classic monuments; (*g*, *h*, *i*, *j*) examples of sandals from the Postclassic monuments; (*k*) ancient method of fastening sandals with two cords, one passing between the first and second toes, the other between the third and fourth toes; (*l*) modern method of fastening sandals with a single cord passing between the first toe and the second toe.

and white stripes, and the priests were painted blue. In preparation for one of the most important ceremonies of the year, the celebrants painted with a blue pigment everything from the utensils of the priests down to the spindles with which the women wove. The priests and sacrificial victim depicted in a fresco from the Temple of the Warriors at Chichen Itza are painted blue from head to foot (Plate 28*f*). Many of the balls of *pom* incense found in the Well of Sacrifice at Chichen Itza were also painted a bright turquoise blue. Blue was the color associated with sacrifice among the late Postclassic Maya just as it was among the Mexicans, from whom they may have derived this association.

Paint was also used in tattooing:

Those who do the work, first painted the part which they wish with color, and afterwards they delicately cut in the paintings, and so with blood and coloring-matter the marks remained on the body. This work is done a little at a time on account of the extreme pain, and afterwards also they were quite sick with it, since the designs festered and matter formed. In spite of all this they made fun of those who were not tattooed.

Several accounts of the principal garment worn by Maya women have come down to us, but none is clear. Landa says:

The women of the coast and of the Provinces of Bacalar and of Campeche are more modest in their dress, for, besides the covering which they wore from the waist down [a kind of skirt], they covered their breasts, tying a folded *manta* [*pati*] underneath their armpits. All the others did not wear more than one garment like a long and wide sack, opened on both sides, and drawn in as far as the hips, where they fastened it together, with the same width as before.

Herrera writes: "They wore a dress like a sack, long and wide, open on both sides and sewn as far as the hips." A third early writer states: "The Maya women wore their kind of petticoats, which is like a sack open at both sides, and these, tied at the waist, covered their private parts." A cotton kerchief was worn over the head, "open like a short cowl, which also served to cover their breasts."

Although none of these descriptions is complete, together they give a fair idea of the costume of the Maya women of Yucatan at the present time (Plate 26). Today this garment is known as the *huipil*, an Aztec word. It is a white, loose-fitting cotton dress, of the same width from top to bottom. It is sewn at the sides, with holes for the arms and a square opening for the head. The armholes, neck opening, and bottom of the garment are beautifully embroidered in cross-stitch. This garment, with its unusual embroidery, is almost certainly a survival from ancient times (Plate 26, *c* and *d*).

Underneath is worn a very full, long petticoat (Maya *pic*), which hangs below the huipil. This is sometimes embroidered around the bottom, but always in white. A Maya woman never leaves her house without her *rebozo* (Maya *booch*), a scarf which she wears draped around her neck or thrown over her head; this may be a survival of the cotton kerchief mentioned above. Today

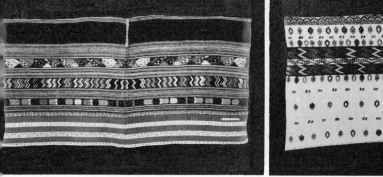

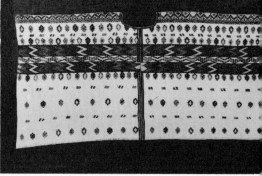

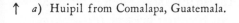
a) Huipil from Comalapa, Guatemala.

↑ b) Huipil from San Pedro Sacatepequez, Guatemala.

↑ c) Huipil from Tixcacal, Quintana Roo.

↑ d) Huipil from Mérida, Yucatan.

PLATE 26.—HUIPILES, OR DRESSES OF MAYA WOMEN FROM GUATEMALA (a AND b) AND FROM QUINTANA ROO AND YUCATAN (c AND d)

slippers of European style are worn by the women, but formerly they no doubt used sandals for festive occasions, going barefoot the rest of the time.

Women and girls wore their hair long and took great care of it. The hair was done in various ways, the style for married women differing from that of the young girls. The women, like their husbands, anointed themselves with a sweet-smelling red ointment, the odor of which lasted for many days. They tattooed themselves from the waists up, except for their breasts, the designs being more delicate than those tattooed on the men.

Much could be written about the dress of the rulers, nobility, and priesthood, based upon the material in the sculptures, frescoes, and vase paintings (Plates 25, 63–69, 71, 72, and 91–94). The robes of the halach uinic, the festive and war apparel of the nobility, and the insignia and vestments of the priesthood were of great splendor. Yet these articles of dress, though elaborately decorated, were basically the same as the garments of the common man—the breechclout, cape, and sandals, with the addition of a headdress.

The breechclouts of the upper classes portrayed in the sculptures are of great intricacy. The ends are richly worked with feathers, and the part around the waist is heavily incrusted with ornaments. The simple square cotton pati of the common man becomes a magnificent cape of embroidered cotton stuff, jaguar skin, or even brilliantly colored feathers. The beautiful iridescent tail feathers of the quetzal seem to have been reserved for the nobility. The sandals became increasingly elaborate as the wearer rose in the social scale, until those of the chief priest, as represented on Classic-stage monuments, are extremely ornate.

It was in the headdresses, however, that the greatest magnificence was displayed. The framework was probably of wicker or wood, carved to represent the head of a jaguar, serpent, or bird, or even one of the Maya gods. These frames were covered with jaguar skin, feather mosaic, and carved jades, and were surmounted by lofty panaches of plumes. Sometimes the panache took the form of a stiffly feathered crest. It was always the most striking part of the costume, and indicated the rank and social class of the wearer.

Costume accessories consisted of collars, necklaces, wristlets, anklets, and knee bands. They were made of feathers, jade beads, shells, jaguar teeth and claws, crocodile teeth, and, in later times, of gold and copper. Other kinds of jewelry were nose ornaments, earrings, and lip plugs of jade, stone, obsidian, and less valuable materials. Ornaments of the lower classes were confined largely to simple nose plugs, lip plugs, and earrings of bone, wood, shell, and stone.

THE ROUND OF DAILY LIFE

The daily preparation of corn for household use is a major activity of Maya women, and doubtless was so in the past. This household duty may be divided into five steps:

1. The dried, shelled corn is first put into an olla (Maya *cum*) or cooking pot, with sufficient water and lime to soften the kernels. The mixture is brought nearly to the boiling point and kept at this temperature until the hull is softened, being stirred occasionally. The olla is then set aside and allowed to stand until the following morning. This softened corn is called *kuum* in Maya.

2. Sometime after breakfast the next morning, the kuum is washed until it is perfectly clean and free of hulls.

3. The kuum is then ground. In ancient times this was done by hand with stone grinders, but today hand-operated metal mills have generally replaced them. The ground corn, which is called *zacan* in Maya, is covered with a cloth and allowed to stand until later in the morning.

4. About an hour before the main meal of the day, a small round table about fifteen inches high, called the *banqueta*, is washed. This table always stands near the *koben* or typical Maya three-stone hearth. Next a round griddle (*xamach*) is also wiped clean, placed on the hearth, and allowed to heat. A section of plantain leaf (*u lee haas*), roughly six inches square, is heated on the xamach until it becomes soft and pliant; this is then placed on the banqueta with a pinch of ashes underneath to make it turn easily on the low table. After these preliminary preparations the Maya woman is ready to make her tortillas (*uah*).

5. She pinches off a lump of zacan about the size of a hen's egg and places it on the piece of plantain leaf. The left hand forms the edge of the tortilla while the right flattens the lump of zacan and, at the same time, gives it a rotary motion on the banqueta. A round, thin, flat cake rapidly takes form under her fingers. The almost continuous pats produce a typical sound, heard throughout all Maya villages in Yucatan at midday. When shaped, the tortilla is laid on the heated xamach to bake. It is next placed on the hot fagots of wood below the xamach until it puffs out, when the woman picks it up and flattens it again with a blow on the table. Finally the tortilla is placed in a gourd (*lec*) to keep it hot; the average Maya man usually eats nearly twenty at one meal, and demands that they be piping hot.

A sixteenth-century account of the eating habits of the ancient Maya has the following to say:

As to the meals which they ate in the time of their antiquity, they eat the same today. This is corn boiled in water and crushed. When made into dough, they dissolve it in water for a drink [*pozole*], and this is what they ordinarily drink and eat. An hour before sunset it was their custom to make certain *tortillas* of the said dough. On these they supped, dipping them into certain dishes of crushed peppers, diluted with a little water and salt. Alternately with this they ate certain boiled beans of the land, which are black. They call them *buul*, and the Spanish, *frijoles*. This was the only time they ate during the day, for at other times they drank the dissolved dough mentioned above.

The principal difference between ancient and modern Maya eating habits would appear to be in the hour for the main meal of the day. Formerly, to judge from this account, it was in the late afternoon "an hour before sunset," while now the main meal is usually eaten at noon, or early afternoon. There is also evidence that tortillas were not eaten in Yucatan before the Conquest.

Maya men and women even today do not eat together. The men of the family eat first and afterward the women and girls have their meal. The tortillas eaten at breakfast are those left over from the day before, but toasted crisp for the morning's meal. The fresh tortillas are not ready until the main meal of the day.

The men leave for the cornfields between four and five o'clock
in the morning, after which the women turn to their principal
task of the forenoon—preparing the zacan and making tortillas.
Any spare time they may have after this is devoted to other household duties.

For refreshment before his return to the house, the man working in the cornfields takes with him a lump of *pozole* wrapped in
a piece of plantain leaf. Pozole is much like zacan, only it is allowed to boil until it hardens into a thick mass. About ten, the
man stops work for a few minutes to mix a lump of pozole in a
cup made from half a gourd filled with water; the resulting drink
looks like milk. If he works until two or three in the afternoon,
he may drink pozole two or three times.

The men return from the fields in the early afternoon, after
which they eat the main meal of the day—fresh tortillas, beans,
eggs, a little meat if it is available, and perhaps a few vegetables
and chocolate, if the family can afford it. After this meal the man
takes his daily bath. Bathed and dressed, the men sit around talk-
ing until the evening meal, which is light—tortillas, beans, and
chocolate or *atole*, a hot drink made by mixing zacan with water,
sometimes sweetened with honey.

The family retires by eight or nine o'clock unless some special
business is afoot. Everybody sleeps in one room, in modern times
in hammocks but formerly on low platforms of poles. Landa says
in this connection:

And then they build a wall in the middle dividing the house length-
wise, and in this wall they leave several doors into the half which they
call the back of the house, where they have their beds, and the other half
they whitened very nicely with lime [this outer room would seem to have
been a sort of porch open at the front and sides] . . . and they have beds
made of small rods [saplings] and on the top a mat on which they sleep,
covering themselves with their *mantas* [*patis*] of cotton. In summer they
usually sleep in the whitened part of the house [that is, the porch], on one
of those mats, especially the men.

A seventeenth-century writer speaks of a bed in a house in the
lowlands of the Usumacinta River, made of a crude wooden frame-

work sufficiently large to hold four persons, while an eighteenth-century writer reports of the Yucatan Maya, "His bed is the floor, or a framework of boards, supported by four sticks."

Today the Indians of Yucatan, and most of the *mestizos*, sleep in hammocks. The hammock was probably imported by the Spaniards from the Caribbean region. It seems almost certain that had they been in general use at the time of the Conquest, Landa would have mentioned them, but he states explicitly that they "had beds made of small rods."

The food needs of the average Maya family today can be supplied in less than two months of eight-hour workdays. In ancient times it likely took much longer to fell the bush, plant a first-year cornfield, and keep it free of weeds. On the other hand, a cornfield can now be planted for only two successive years, but there are grounds for believing that formerly it could be planted for seven or eight seasons. In any event it is evident that the ancient Maya had a great deal of spare time when he was not engaged in raising food for his family's needs.

That this leisure time of the common people was highly organized by the nobility and priesthood is abundantly proved by the programs of public works which were carried out. These vast constructions of stone and mortar depended upon a highly organized and ably directed society. Much labor was needed to quarry the stone for these projects and to transport it to the building sites, to fell wood for the thousands of limekilns, and to gather gravel for the endless quantities of mortar. Time and skill were required to carve the worked-stone elements, to sculpture the monuments, and to construct the pyramids, temples, and palaces. And all this was in addition to supporting the ruler, the nobility, and the priesthood in economic idleness. In view of all that they did, the common people could have had but little time which they could call their own.

SICKNESS, DEATH, BURIAL, AND THE LIFE HEREAFTER

When a man was ill he summoned a priest, a medicine man, or a sorcerer—Landa lumps all three together. This curer of ills, by a combination of prayers, ceremonies, and administration of herbs, either cured or killed his patients, his reputation as a healer depending upon which of the two predominated. Yucatan has many medicinal herbs and plants, and an extensive pharmacopoeia was at the disposal of these sorcerer-doctors. Several seventeenth-century Maya manuscripts, listing many ills and their corresponding cures, have come down to us, and some of their remedies have merit. Many of them, too, smack of medieval European superstition mixed with Maya magic, as in the following remedy for toothache:

You take the bill of a woodpecker and bleed the gums a little with it; if a man, thirteen times; if a woman, nine times. [The gum] shall be slightly pierced by the bill of the woodpecker. Thus also a piece of a tree struck by lightning is to be grated with a fish-skin and wrapped in cotton-wool. Then you apply it to the tooth. He will recover by this means.

This bleeding of the gums might alleviate some kinds of toothache, but the "thirteen times in the case of a man" and the "nine times in the case of a woman" are surely ritualistic survivals from the ancient Maya, the former corresponding to the number of Gods of the Upper World and the latter to the number of Gods of the Lower World.

On the other hand, some of the native plants undoubtedly possess medicinal properties, as for example the *kanlol* (*Tecoma stans*), which grows in northern Yucatan. Two to ten drops of an extract made from this, taken hourly, is a strong diuretic and probably a mild heart stimulant as well.

Landa says:

There were also surgeons, or better said, sorcerers, who cured with herbs and many superstitious rites . . . The sorcerers and physicians performed their cures by bleedings of the parts, which gave pain to the sick man; . . . [the Maya] believed that death, sickness and afflictions came to them for their wrong doing and their sin; they had a custom of confessing themselves, when they were already sick.

According to the same authority, the Maya had great fear of death, and when it intervened their grief was excessive:

This people had a great and excessive fear of death and they showed this in that all the services, which they made to their gods, were for no other end, nor for any other purpose than that they [the gods] should give them health, life and sustenance. But when, in time, they came to die, it was indeed a thing to see the sorrow and the cries which they made for their dead, and the great grief it caused them. During the day they wept for them in silence; and at night with loud and very sad cries, so that it was pitiful to hear them. And they passed many days in deep sorrow. They made abstinences and fasts for the dead, especially the husband or wife; and they said that the devil had taken him away since they thought that all evils came to them from him [the devil], and especially death.

The body was wrapped in a shroud and the mouth filled with ground maize and one or more jade beads "which they use for money, so that they should not be without something to eat in the other life." The common people were buried under the floors or behind their houses; the houses of the poor were usually abandoned after a death. Idols of clay, wood, or stone were thrown into the grave, as well as objects indicating the profession or trade of the deceased.

The burial customs of the ruling classes were more elaborate. Landa says that the bodies of the nobles and persons of high esteem were burned, their ashes being placed in great urns and temples built above them. Excavations in the pyramid supporting the High Priest's Tomb at Chichen Itza, the substructures of Temples A-I and A-XVIII at Uaxactun, and the pyramid of the Temple of the Inscriptions at Palenque, among others, have established the fact that burials were made under the floors of the buildings they supported. Plate 27 shows a cross section of the Palenque tomb, discovered by Alberto Ruz.

Graves of important persons have also been found in small, stone-lined burial vaults with corbel-arched roofs, built under plaza floor levels at Chichen Itza, Palenque, Uaxactun, and Copan. Most of these pyramid and plaza subfloor burials were accompanied by elaborate mortuary furniture, exquisitely painted pottery vessels, carved jade beads and pendants, and ornately chipped objects of flint and obsidian.

PLATE 27.—CROSS SECTION OF THE RUZ TOMB

Ruz' discovery of the tomb in the Temple of Inscriptions at Palenque is one of the most notable of recent archaeological achievements. Others had investigated the building without detecting the tomb, but Ruz discovered that the inner walls of the temple did not end at their junction with the floor but continued on below it. This fact, coupled with his deduction that the holes in one large floor slab were fingerholds, led him to believe that the pyramid on which the temple stands might have another structure concealed within it. The slab was lifted, revealing a stairway completely blocked with rubble. Clearing the stairway presented a monumental task and there was no assurance that what lay below would justify the effort, but Ruz elected to try it. The work of clearing lasted from 1949 to 1952, and the stairway was found to end in one of the most elaborate tombs ever discovered in Mesoamerica.

In northern Yucatan, another burial custom among the nobility, according to Landa, was to enclose the ashes of the dead in hollow statues of pottery or wood. If a wooden statue, it was made to look like the dead man. The back of the statue's head was left hollow and here the ashes from a part of the cremated body were placed; the rest of the ashes were buried. These statues and crematory urns were preserved with great veneration among the family idols.

Among the Cocom, the ruling house of Mayapan, a special burial custom obtained. The bodies of dead Cocom lords were boiled until the fleshy parts could be completely removed from the bones. The back half of the head was sawed off, leaving the front half intact. Then, where the fleshy parts of the face had been, a new face was built up with resin. These restored faces were kept, together with the wooden effigies, in the oratories of their houses with the family idols. They were held in great veneration and respect, and on feast days offerings of food were made to them so that the lords might lack for nothing in their afterlife.

Archaeology partially supports Landa's statement, since in dredging the Well of Sacrifice at Chichen Itza a skull was recovered which had the crown cut away. The eye sockets were filled with wooden plugs, and there were the remains of painted plaster on the front. There also has recently been found, in the Department of El Quiché, Guatemala, the front part of a human skull covered with a thick coat of lime plaster, which was modeled to represent a human face.

RELIGION AND DEITIES

RISE AND DEVELOPMENT

DURING THE several thousand years since the Maya exchanged their nomadic life for a sedentary one, their religion had undergone corresponding changes. At first the Maya religion was probably a simple nature worship, a personification of the natural forces which surrounded them and whose interplay formed the background against which the Maya lived their nomadic lives.

Such a religion required little formal organization—no priesthood, no elaborate ceremonials, not even specialized places of worship. Each family head was probably the family priest, and the family temple was little more than a temporary hut set close to the equally temporary dwellings of the family. Much the same condition, for example, still exists among the Lacandon Maya in the forests of the Usumacinta Valley in eastern Chiapas.

Later, agriculture was introduced, bringing fixed dwellings and more leisure time; religion became more organized and the gods more specialized. A priesthood grew up whose business it was to interpret the will of the gods to the people; the need for more formal temples arose; religion became a business of the few. Fixed homes made possible more permanent ceremonial centers and encouraged the erection of more ambitious sanctuaries and the development of an elaborate ritual.

During the centuries which elapsed between the introduction of agriculture and the invention of the Maya calendar, chronology, and hieroglyphic writing, probably in 7.0.0.0.0 or 7.6.0.0.0 of the Maya Era (353 or 235 B.C.), the Maya religion, doubtless, changed very slowly. These centuries saw the beginnings of individualized gods, a growing priesthood, a richer ritual, and more elaborate sanctuaries, though still not of masonry. This second period was probably contemporaneous with the Mamom ceramic phase at Uaxactun.

However, with the introduction of the calendar, chronology, and writing, all of priestly invention, Maya religion underwent important modifications, again in the direction of greater complexity and formalization. A religious philosophy gradually took shape, devised by a professional priesthood and built around the increasing importance of astronomical manifestations. This change, while it probably began as early as the third century before Christ, first becomes archaeologically apparent with the earliest appearance of sculptured stone monuments at Uaxactun about 8.14.0.0.0 (A.D. 317). These in turn probably coincided with the introduction of corbeled roof vaulting and the beginnings of Tzakol pottery, also found first at Uaxactun.

Something fundamentally important took place in northern central Peten sometime during the three or four centuries immediately preceding and following the beginning of the Christian Era. Was this cultural impetus due to some outside influence, or was it of autochthonous origin? Perhaps we shall never surely know.

As early as the fourth century after Christ, Maya culture was firmly established in northern central Peten. Maya religion had become a highly developed cult based upon a fusion of the primitive personification of nature with a more sophisticated philosophy, built around a deification of the heavenly bodies and a worship of time. This religion, while shared by the common people, was highly esoteric in nature. It was interpreted and served by a closely organized priesthood composed of astronomers, mathematicians, prophets, and ritualists, and, as it grew more complex, by skilled administrators and statesmen.

Judging from the generally peaceful tenor of Classic-stage sculptures, Maya religion throughout this period must have been a more lofty faith, not debased as it was in later times by wholesale human sacrifice. Only two representations of human sacrifice are known for this period, both from Piedras Negras. Just as the

Classic stage was the peak of Maya culture, so was it also the noblest period of Maya religion, before the beliefs and practices had degenerated into bloody orgies.

There are no archaeological reasons for believing that the Maya religion suffered any fundamental changes during the Classic stage, but in the Postclassic, during the Puuc and Mexican periods, sweeping changes were introduced.

A number of sixteenth-century Spanish writers affirm that the Mexicans introduced idolatry, which probably was meant to include human sacrifice as well:

> The old men of these provinces [Yucatan] say that anciently, near to eight hundred years ago, idolatry was not practiced, and afterwards when the Mexicans entered it and took possession of it, a captain, who was called Quetzalquat [Quetzalcoatl] in the Mexican language, which is to say in ours, plumage of the serpent . . . introduced idolatry into this land and the use of idols for gods, which he had made of wood, of clay and of stone. And he made them [the Maya] worship these idols and they offered many things of the hunt, of merchandise and above all the blood of their nostrils and ears, and the hearts of those whom they sacrificed in his services . . . They say that the first inhabitants of Chichenyza [Chichen Itza] were not idolators, until a Mexican captain Ku Kalcan [Kukulcan] entered into these parts, who taught idolatry, and the necessity, so they say, to teach and practice it.

Herrera, the official historian of the Indies for the Crown of Spain, leaves no doubt about this point, stating bluntly that "the number of people sacrificed was great. And this custom was introduced into Yucatan by the Mexicans."

The archaeological evidence also supports the interpretation that idolatry included the practice of human sacrifice. At Chichen Itza, the great Mexican-Maya metropolis of the Postclassic, probably the whole cult of the Well of Sacrifice, where so many human victims were offered, dates from the Mexican period. Of the eight representations of human sacrifice known in the Maya area, four occur at Chichen Itza: two in frescoes in the Temple of the Jaguars (Plate 28e), one in a fresco in the Temple of the Warriors (Plate

28*f*), and the fourth on a gold disk from the Well of Sacrifice. Two others are found in the hieroglyphic manuscripts: the Codex Dresdensis (Plate 28*c*) and the Codex Tro-Cortesianus (Plate 28*d*), both also dating from the Postclassic. The other two are those previously noted at Piedras Negras in the Classic stage. In view of such evidence, documentary as well as archaeological, there is little, doubt that the sanguinary character of Maya religion as found by the Spaniards in the early sixteenth century was due chiefly to Mexican influence and was introduced into Yucatan by the Mexican invaders in the tenth century.

The Maya religion suffered its final change when the Spaniards forcibly substituted Christianity for the old pagan beliefs and practices in the middle of the sixteenth century. The few survivals of the ancient faith that have remained are not from the esoteric cult and complex theology of the priestly class, but the belief in the simple gods of nature—the Chacs, or rain gods of fertility. The homely everyday beliefs of the common people have outlived the formalized gods of priestly invention.

This is not surprising. The more sophisticated gods, who were the creatures of the professional priesthood, were forgotten as soon as the priests who had created and served them had passed away. And it was precisely upon the priesthood that the full weight of the Spanish Conquest fell most crushingly. The Christian god was a jealous god, and his ministers quickly saw to it that the native priests either gave up their old beliefs or were exterminated. With them went the old esoteric religion, learning, and philosophy, while the simpler faith of the common people, which was more generally shared, has in part survived to the present day.

These survivals, as we now find them, are a motley mixture of Catholic saints and pagan deities. In Yucatan, the archangel Gabriel and other Christian saints become the Pauahtuns of ancient Maya mythology, the guardians of the four cardinal points; the archangel Michael leads the Chacs, the former rain gods. In British Honduras it is St. Vincent who is the patron of rain and St. Joseph the guiding spirit of the cornfields.

PLATE 28.—SCENES OF HUMAN SACRIFICE AS REPRESENTED ON THE
MONUMENTS, CODICES, AND WALL-PAINTINGS

(a) Stela 11, Piedras Negras, Peten, Guatemala; (b) Stela 14, Piedras Negras;
(c) Codex Dresdensis; (d) Codex Tro-Cortesianus; (e) Temple of the Jaguars,
Chichen Itza, Yucatan, Mexico; (f) Temple of the Warriors, Chichen Itza.

The creator of the world, according to ancient Maya belief, was a god named Hunab, or Hunab Ku, who was the father of Itzamna, the Maya Zeus: "They worshipped a single god who was named Hunab and Zamana, which [Hunab] is to say one only God." Hunab Ku means precisely that in Maya: *hun*, "one," *ab*, "the state of being" and *ku*, "god." This creator god was so remote from everyday affairs that he seems to have figured little in the life of the people. According to the Popol Vuh, the sacred book of the Quiche Maya of highland Guatemala, the creator fashioned mankind out of corn.

The Maya also believed that there had been several worlds before the present one, and that each had been destroyed by a deluge. Landa records this tradition but fails to state the number of worlds thus destroyed:

Among the multitude of gods which this people adored, they worshipped four, each of whom was called Bacab. They said they were four brothers whom God [Hunab Ku], when he created the world, placed at the four points of it, to hold up the sky, so that it should not fall. They also said of these Bacabs, that they escaped when the world was destroyed by the deluge. They gave to each one of them other names and [thus] designated by them the part of the world where God placed him [each one] to bear up the heavens.

In confirmation of this tradition, the end of the world by a deluge is graphically depicted on the last page of the Codex Dresdensis (Fig. 9). Across the sky stretches a serpent-like creature with symbols of constellations on its side and signs for solar and lunar eclipses hanging from its belly. From its open jaws, as well as from the two eclipse signs, a flood of water pours earthward. Below the heavenly serpent, the Old Woman Goddess with long talon-like fingernails and toenails, the patroness of death and destruction, holds an inverted bowl from which also gushes a destroying flood. At the bottom stands Ek Chuah, the black God of War, the Moan bird of evil omen on his head. In his right hand he holds two javelins and in his left a long staff, all pointing downward.

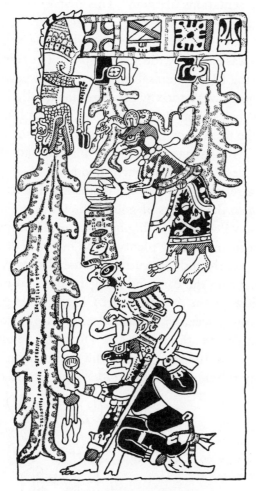

Fig. 9.—Destruction of the world by water.
Page 74, Codex Dresdensis.

The modern Maya of northern Yucatan believe there have
been three worlds previous to this one. The first world was inhabited by dwarfs—the *saiyam uinicob* or "adjuster men," who
are thought to have built the great ruined cities. This work was
done in darkness, for the sun had not yet been created. As soon
as the sun rose for the first time, the dwarfs were turned to stone,
and their images are still to be seen in the ruined cities today; per-

haps the so-called Atlantean figures found at Chichen Itza (Plate 73*d*) are representations of them. This first world was ended by a universal deluge, the *haiyococab*, or "water over the earth." The second world was inhabited by people called the *dzolob* or "offenders," and was ended by the second flood. The third world was populated by the Maya themselves, the common people or *mazehualob*; this world was ended by the third flood, called the *hunyecil* or *bulkabal*, which means "the immersing." This last deluge was followed by the present or fourth world, peopled by a mixture of all the previous inhabitants of the peninsula, and this too will eventually be destroyed by a fourth flood.

The Maya religion had a strong dualistic tendency, the eternal struggle between the powers of good and evil over the destiny of man. The benevolent gods, bringing thunder, lightning, and rain, fructify the corn and ensure plenty. The malevolent ones, whose attributes are death and destruction, cause drought, hurricanes, and war, which ruin the corn and bring famine and misery. This contest is depicted in the codices, where Chac, the rain god, is shown caring for a young tree, while behind him follows Ah Puch, the death god, who breaks the tree in two (Fig. 10). This balance of good against evil in the struggle for the soul of man is a contrast found in many religions, some far older than Christianity.

FIG. 10.—The rain god nourishes a tree; the death god uproots it. Page 60, Codex Tro-Cortesianus.

The Maya conceived the world as having thirteen heavens, arranged in layers, the lowest being the earth itself. Over each presided one of the Thirteen Gods of the Upper World or *Oxlahuntiku*—meaning in Maya, *oxlahun*, "thirteen," *ti*, "of," and *ku*, "god." There were nine underworlds, also arranged in layers, over each of which presided its own god, one of the *Bolontiku* or Nine Gods of the Lower World—meaning in Maya, *bolon*, "nine," *ti,* "of," and *ku,* "god." The ninth and lowest underworld was Mitnal, ruled by Ah Puch, the Lord of Death.

To the ancient Maya the principal object of religion was to procure life, health, and sustenance. A number of early authorities express this idea: "They worship idols ... in order to petition [the gods] for health and good seasons"; or again in the following prayer: "All powerful god, these sacrifices we make to thee and we offer thee these hearts so that thou mayest give us life and temporal goods." Sacrifices were made "in order to buy food from the gods so that they [the people] might have much to eat."

The gods were invoked and placated by a number of different offices. Almost all important ceremonies began with fasts and abstinences. They were scrupulously observed, and to break one's fast was considered a great sin. These preparatory purifications, which also included sexual continence, were mandatory upon the priests and those who assisted directly in the ceremonies, but were voluntary for others. In addition to fasting and continence, their abstinences included giving up flesh foods and the use of salt and chili pepper.

Sacrifices were an important part of Maya worship; they ranged from simple offerings of food to all kinds of ornaments and valuables, and, in Postclassic times, to the practice of human sacrifice. The offerings varied according to the urgency of the occasion. If the sacrifice was to cure a sickness or to avert some minor trouble, offerings of food or ornaments might be made. In times of great common need human victims were sacrificed, especially in order to bring rains.

Bloodletting and scarification played a leading part in religious observance. Although Landa says that only the men indulged in these practices, the Codex Tro-Cortesianus shows both a man and a woman in the act of drawing blood from their ears (Fig. 11). The blood thus obtained, as well as that of human and animal sacrificial victims, was liberally sprinkled over the idols.

They make sacrifices of their own blood, sometimes cutting the edges [of their ears] in pieces, and thus they left them as a sign [of their devotion]. Other times they pierced their cheeks, other times the lower lips;

again they scarify parts of the body; or again they perforate their tongues in a slanting direction from side to side, passing pieces of straw through the holes, with horrible suffering; and yet again they slit the superfluous part [the foreskin] of the virile member, leaving it like their ears, which deceived the general historian of the Indies [Oviedo] into saying that they practiced circumcision. . . . The women do not practice these blood-lettings although they were very devout; furthermore, of all things that they have, whether it be birds of the sky, animals of the earth, or fish of the sea, they always anointed the face of the demon [their idols] with the blood of these.

FIG. 11. — Bloodletting rite.
Page 95, Codex Tro-Cortesianus

The burning of incense formed an indispensable part of every religious ceremony. It was made principally of copal (*pom*), a resin extracted from the copal tree (*Protium copal*) and less frequently of rubber, chicle, and another resin called *puk ak* in Maya; such trees were grown on special plantations. The incense was highly prized and formed an important article of trade. It was made into small cakes, decorated with crosshatching and painted a bright turquoise blue. Scores of such cakes were recovered in the dredging of the Well of Sacrifice at Chichen Itza. The priest's assistants prepared balls of fresh incense, laying them out on small boards made for the purpose, as the Lacandon Maya of Chiapas still do today. The incense was then burned in specially shaped pottery vessels, which had the head or figure of some deity modeled on the outside.

Pom burns with a heavy, black smoke and a fragrant odor. If the hearts of large animals were not available for offerings, Landa says, imitation hearts were sometimes molded out of pom incense: "And if they were not able to have large animals like tigers [jaguars], lions [pumas], or crocodiles, they fashioned hearts out of their incense." Landa's statement has been corroborated by the discovery of a human-shaped heart, made of some vegetable substance, in the center of one of the incense cakes recovered from the Well of Sacrifice. Faint memories of the ancient faith and its holy places linger among modern Maya in remote regions. The Lacandon still burn pom incense in typical Maya incense burners in the principal temple at the ruins of Yaxchilan (Plate 30*b*). The Maya of eastern Yucatan still offer incense in the sanctuary of the principal temple at the ruins of Tulum on the east coast of the peninsula.

Another religious observance was dancing. There were many kinds, varying with the different ceremonies, but social dancing was entirely unknown. Each sex had its own dances, and only rarely did men and women dance together. In one of their war dances some eight hundred dancers took part:

There is another dance [*holcan okot*] in which eight hundred Indians, more or less, dance with small banners, taking long war-steps to the beat [of a drum], among them there is not one who is out of step.

In another dance, great skill was shown in catching reeds with a little stick:

One is a game of reeds, and thus they call it *colomche,* which means that. In order to play it, they form a large circle of dancers, whom the music accompanies, and two of them enter the circle in time to the music, one with a handful of reeds with which he dances holding himself upright; the other dancer crouches, both of them always inside the circle. And he with the reeds throws them with all his strength at the other, who with great skill, catches them, by means of a small stick. Having finished throwing, they return in time to their places in the circle, and others go out to do the same thing.

Dancing was very popular; another sixteenth-century writer says:

There were many other dances of which there would be more than one thousand kinds, and they considered this as an extremely important thing and so great a number of people assemble to see it that more than fifteen thousand Indians would gather, and they came from more than thirty leagues [75 miles] to see it, because, as I say, they considered it an extremely important affair.

The Maya believed in the immortality of the soul and an afterlife. According to Landa, the future was divided into a place of rest and a place of suffering, although there is some suspicion of Catholic influence in his statement.

Suicides by hanging, warriors killed in battle, people who were sacrificed, women who died in childbirth, and the priests when they died went directly to the Maya Paradise:

> They also said and held it as absolutely certain that those who hanged themselves went to this heaven of theirs; and thus there were many who on slight occasions of sorrows, troubles or sicknesses, hanged themselves in order to escape these things and to go and rest in their heaven, where they said that the Goddess of the Gallows, whom they call Ixtab, came to fetch them.

The Maya Paradise is described as a place of delights, where there was no pain or suffering, but an abundance of food and drink. There grew the *yaxche* or sacred tree of the Maya (the ceiba), in the shade of which they could rest forever from labor. Those whose lives had been evil descended into a lower region called Mitnal — the Maya Hell. There devils tormented them with hunger, cold, weariness, and grief. Hunhau, the Lord of Death, was regarded as the prince of the devils, and presided over this bottommost Hell. The Maya believed that neither Paradise nor Hell would ever end, since the soul itself could not die but must go on forever.

THE PANTHEON

ITZAMNA, LORD OF THE HEAVENS (GOD D[1])

Discounting Hunab Ku, the creator, who does not appear to have played an important part in the life of the common people,

---

[1] The German scholar, Paul Schellhas, has classified the deities represented in the three Maya codices, giving each a letter designation. In his classification, Itzamna is God D.

the great Itzamna, son of Hunab Ku, stood at the head of the Maya pantheon. In the codices, Itzamna is represented as an old man with toothless jaws and sunken cheeks (Plate 29*a*). He has two name glyphs—one which may be a conventionalized representation of his head, and another which contains as its main element the day sign Ahau. This day sign meant "king, emperor, monarch, prince, or great lord," so the second of Itzamna's name glyphs declares his position as head of the pantheon. He was patron of the day Ahau, the last and most important of the twenty Maya days.

Few recognizable Classic-stage representations of Maya deities have survived. Most of the figures presented in the sculptures, frescoes, and vase paintings of the period are probably those of rulers, priests, and warriors. The pictures of Maya gods shown here are taken from the three known Maya hieroglyphic manuscripts, which date from the Postclassic. However, it seems probable, in view of the cultural continuity of the Classic and Postclassic stages, that the Maya pantheon remained largely the same for both periods, except for two important exceptions: (1) the introduction of a new deity named Kukulcan from Mexico in the tenth century; and (2) the increasing importance of the rain god, Chac, in Yucatan as compared with Peten; this latter region has a much higher rainfall than Yucatan, and it was not necessary to call upon the rain god as frequently.

Itzamna was Lord of the Heavens, and also Lord of Day and of Night. In these latter capacities he is intimately associated with Kinich Ahau, the sun god or "Lord of the Eye of the Sun" (God G), who was especially worshiped at Izamal in northern Yucatan, and with Ixchel, the moon goddess (Goddess I). Kinich Ahau may be only a special manifestation of Itzamna in the latter's capacity as Lord of the Day. Itzamna, the inventor of writing and books, is said to have been the first priest to name the places in Yucatan and to divide the lands there. These activities by their very nature indicate that the cult of Itzamna did not originate in Yucatan but was brought from somewhere else. Since we know that both the priesthood and hieroglyphic writing first developed in the Classic stage, it is probable that he was transplanted from the Peten. As the first priest and inventor of writing, he is clearly a god who went back to the beginnings of Maya history and who probably always stood at the head of the pantheon.

During the important ceremonies in connection with the Maya New Year, Itzamna was especially invoked to avert calamities. In the month of Uo, at a ceremony in his honor in his manifestation as the sun god, the priests consulted the sacred books to learn the auguries for the coming year. In the month of Zip he was invoked as the god of medicine, together with his wife Ixchel. In the month of Mac he was worshiped by the old men in a ceremony with the Chacs. Itzamna was a benevolent deity and always the friend of man. He is never connected with destruction or disaster and never appears in the codices associated with the symbols of death.

CHAC, THE GOD OF RAIN (GOD B)

Chac, the God of Rain, is represented in the codices with a long nose and two curling fangs which project downward from his mouth. His headdress is usually a knotted band (Plate 29*b*), and his name glyph has an eye which, in the Codex Tro-Cortesianus, is T-shaped ⊥ . This element, it has been suggested, represents tears streaming from the eye, and may symbolize pouring rain and hence fertility. This sign is also the glyph for the day Ik, of which the rain god was probably the patron deity.

Chac was a universal deity of first importance. If we judged only by the number of his representations in the codices, he would have to be regarded as even more important than Itzamna. Pictures of Chac occur 218 times in the three codices; Itzamna occurs only 103 times and is not found at all in the Codex Peresianus.

Chac was regarded not only as a single god but also as the four gods of the cardinal points, each having its associated color: Chac Xib Chac, the Red Man—Chac of the East; Sac Xib Chac, the White Man—Chac of the North; Ek Xib Chac, the Black Man—Chac of the West; and Kan Xib Chac, the Yellow Man—Chac of the South. This concept is analogous to our belief concerning the Holy Trinity, or three Gods in one.

In the months of Chen or Yax a great festival was held in

honor of the Chacs, which was called the *ocna*, meaning "enter the house." The four gods known as the Bacabs, who were closely associated with the Chacs, were consulted to determine a propitious day for the ceremony, which was devoted to renovation of the Temple of the Chacs. During this ceremony, held once a year, the idols and incense burners were renewed, and, if necessary, the temple itself was rebuilt. A tablet commemorating the event was set into the temple wall.

Just as Itzamna was associated with the sun god, so Chac seems to have been associated with the wind god; this wind god may be only a special manifestation of the rain god, and may have had no separate existence.

The rain god was a benevolent deity like Itzamna, associated with creation and life. For the ordinary Maya farmer whose paramount interest was his cornfield, Chac was the all-important deity, and his friendly intervention was sought more frequently than that of all the other gods combined. The mask panels with long curling noses found throughout the Maya area, but especially in Puuc architecture, are probably representations of the head of this god (Plate 60, *a* and *b*).

THE GOD OF CORN (GOD E)

The third deity in frequency of representation in the codices is the corn god or the god of agriculture, who occurs 98 times in the three manuscripts. He is always represented as a youth (frontispiece), sometimes with an ear of corn as his headdress (Plate 29*c*). Occasionally this ear is shown sprouting from the glyph for the day Kan, which itself is the symbol for corn in the codices. Kan was also the day of which this god was the patron. Of all the gods represented in the codices this deity shows the greatest amount of head deformation. His name glyph is his own head, which merges at the top into a highly conventionalized ear of corn, surmounted by leaves.

This god was the patron of husbandry and is shown engaged in a variety of agricultural pursuits. He, or a priest impersonating him, is occasionally depicted in Classic-stage sculpture scattering grains of the cereal on the head of the Earth Mother. Like the corn he typified, he had many enemies and his destinies were controlled by the gods of rain, wind, drought, famine, and death. In one place he is shown under the protection of the rain god and in another in combat with a death god.

Although his specific name as the God of Corn is unknown, in later Postclassic times his identity seems to have merged with that of a more general agricultural deity known as Yum Kaax, Lord of the Forests, and at least some of his functions were probably taken over by the more powerful Chac. Like Itzamna and Chac he was a benevolent deity, a god of life, prosperity, and abundance.

AH PUCH, THE GOD OF DEATH (GOD A)

The fourth god in frequency of representation is the God of Death, who occurs 88 times in the three codices. He has a skull for a head, bare ribs, and spiny vertebral projections; if his body is clothed with flesh, it is bloated and marked with black circles, suggesting decomposition (Plate 29*d*). The principal accessories of the death god are his sleigh-bell ornaments. These sometimes appear fastened in his hair or to bands around his forearms and legs, but more often they are attached to a stiff rufflike collar (Plate 29*d*). These bells, of all sizes and made of copper and sometimes of gold, were found in quantity during the dredging of the Well of Sacrifice at Chichen Itza, where they had presumably been thrown with the sacrificial victims (Plate 101*b* and Fig. 55, *d*, *e*, and *f*).

Like Itzamna, whose antithesis he is, Ah Puch has two name glyphs and is the only other deity thus distinguished. The first glyph represents the head of a corpse with its eyes closed in death; the second is the head of the god himself, with truncated nose, fleshless jaws, and a flint sacrificial knife as a prefix. A frequent sign associated with the God of Death is not unlike our own percentage sign ℀ . The God of Death was patron deity of the day Cimi, which means "death" in Maya.

In the case of Ah Puch, we are also dealing with a deity of first importance, as attested by the frequency of his representations in

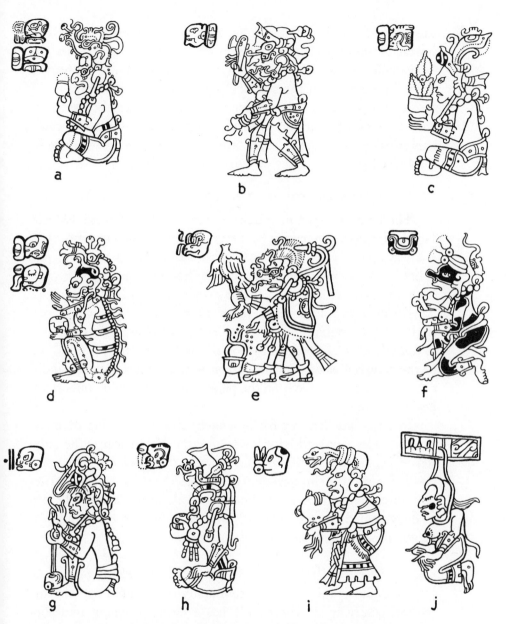

PLATE 29.—PRINCIPAL DEITIES OF THE MAYA PANTHEON AS
REPRESENTED IN THE CODICES

(*a*) Itzamna, head of the Maya Pantheon (God D); (*b*) Chac, the rain god
(God B); (*c*) Yum Kax, the corn god (God E); (*d*) Ah Puch, the death god
(God A); (*e*) the wind god, perhaps Kukulcan (God K); (*f*) the war god
(God M); (*g*) the god of sudden death and of human sacrifice (God F); (*h*)
Xaman Ek, the North Star god (God C); (*i*) Ixchel, wife of Itzamna and the
goddess of childbirth and weaving (Goddess I); (*j*) Ixtab, the goddess of suicide.

the codices. As the chief demon, Hunhau, he presided over the lowest of the nine Maya underworlds. Even today the modern Maya believe that, as Yum Cimil, the Lord of Death, he prowls around the houses of the sick, looking for prospective prey.

Ah Puch was a malevolent deity. He was frequently associated with the God of War and Human Sacrifice, and his constant companions were the dog, the Moan bird, and the owl, all of which were considered to be creatures of evil omen and death.

XAMAN EK, GOD OF THE NORTH STAR (GOD C)

The fifth most common deity in the codices is Xaman Ek, the North Star god, who occurs 61 times in the three manuscripts. He is always portrayed (Plate 29*h*) with a snub-nosed face and peculiar black markings on his head. He has only one name glyph, his own head, which has been likened to the head of a monkey. This head, with a different prefix than that of his own name glyph, is also the hieroglyph for the cardinal point North, thus tending to confirm his identification as God of the North Star. The nature of the occurrences of his name glyph in the manuscripts also indicates that he must have been the personification of some important heavenly body.

In one place Xaman Ek is spoken of as "the guide of merchants." He may well have been, since the North Star is the only star in the latitudes of Peten and Yucatan that does not change its position radically through the year. Merchants are also said to have offered pom incense to him at altars along roadsides. He was a benevolent deity and is found in association with the rain god; he was probably patron of the day Chuen.

EK CHUAH, THE BLACK WAR CAPTAIN (GOD M)

Ek Chuah is the sixth most commonly represented deity in the codices, occurring 40 times. He has a large, drooping underlip and is usually shown painted black, the color of war (Plate 29*f*). His name glyph is an eye rimmed with black. This god seems to have had a twofold and somewhat contradictory character; as God of War he was malevolent, but as God of Traveling Merchants he was friendly. In the former capacity he appears with a lance in hand, occasionally engaged in combat and even vanquished by another war god. We have also seen him with Ixchel, armed with javelins and lance, taking part in the destruction of the world by water (Fig. 9). As a friendly god, he appears with a bundle of merchandise on his back like an itinerant merchant, and in one place he is shown with the head of Xaman Ek, the North Star and "guide of merchants." Ek Chuah was also the patron of cacao, and those who owned cacao plantations held a ceremony in his honor in the month of Muan. In one aspect he seems to have been hostile to man, in another, friendly — a two-faced deity like the Roman Janus.

THE GOD OF WAR, OF HUMAN SACRIFICE, AND VIOLENT DEATH (GOD F)

This deity occurs 33 times in the codices, and always in connection with death. His constant characteristic is a black line partly encircling his eye and extending down his cheek (Plate 29g). His own head, with the number 11 in front of it, is his name glyph. He may be the patron of the Maya day Manik, the sign for which is the grasping hand. He is sometimes shown in company with Ah Puch, the God of Death, at scenes of human sacrifice. He was also a war god in his own right and is shown burning houses with a torch in one hand while he demolishes them with a spear in the other. The concept of a war god, a god of death by violence and by human sacrifice, all seem to be combined in this deity.

THE GOD OF THE WIND, POSSIBLY KUKULCAN (GOD K)

The suggested association of the famous Maya-Mexican culture hero Kukulcan with the Maya God of the Wind is not surely established. The wind god is rarely portrayed in the codices. There are less than a dozen representations of him altogether and not one in the Codex Tro-Cortesianus, a late Postclassic manuscript. In view of the predominant position held by Kukulcan in early Postclassic times, it seems strange that, if the wind god were Kukulcan, more representations of him should not have been found.

The association of the wind god with Chac, the rain god, is very close. We see Chac offering the head of the wind god, in connection with a katun-ending ceremony in the Codex Peresianus (Fig. 16). The identification of the wind god as Kukulcan rests largely upon an identical association in Aztec mythology of Quetzalcoatl with Ehecatl, the wind god, who sweeps the path of the rain god. Since the Maya wind and rain gods are also closely associated, and since both the Maya wind god and Quetzalcoatl-Ehecatl, the Aztec wind god, both have large, foliated noses, there may be some connection between the Maya wind god and Kukulcan. This connection is only suggested, and Chac himself, the principal Maya rain god, has also been identified as Kukulcan by several authorities. Some believe the connection between the wind god and the rain god is so close as to indicate that the former is only a special manifestation of the latter and should not be regarded as a separate god. His name glyph (Plate 29*e*) is frequently found in connection with that of Chac. He was patron of the day Muluc, and was a benevolent deity.

IXCHEL, GODDESS OF FLOODS, PREGNANCY, WEAVING, AND PERHAPS OF THE MOON (GODDESS I)

Ixchel was an important personage in the Maya pantheon, but apparently more often unfriendly than not. We have already seen her as an angry old woman destroying the world by flood (Fig. 9); again, in Plate 29*i*, she is a personification of water as a destroyer, and of floods and cloudbursts. She is usually portrayed surrounded by symbols of death and destruction, a writhing serpent on her head, and crossbones embroidered on her skirt.

But Ixchel seems to have had a friendlier side. She was the consort of Itzamna, Lord of the Heavens, and since her husband occasionally appears as the sun god, she would seem to have been the moon goddess. She was also the patroness of pregnancy and the inventor of weaving.

IXTAB, GODDESS OF SUICIDE

The ancient Maya believed that suicides went directly to Paradise. There was a special goddess who was the patroness of those

who had taken their lives by hanging—Ixtab, Goddess of Suicide.
She is shown in the Codex Dresdensis (Plate 29*j*) hanging from
the sky by a halter which is looped around her neck; her eyes are
closed in death, and a black circle, representing decomposition,
appears on her cheek.

PATRON GOD SERIES

THE THIRTEEN GODS OF THE UPPER WORLD AND THE
NINE GODS OF THE LOWER WORLD

The ancient Maya conceived of some of their deities not only
as single entities but as composite or multiple in character. Chac,
as we have seen, was considered as a single god and at the same time
as four gods. Similarly the Oxlahuntiku, or Thirteen Gods of
the Upper World, although regarded collectively as a single deity,
were considered to be thirteen separate gods; the Bolontiku, or
Nine Gods of the Lower World, were also regarded in this dual
capacity.

In certain myths preserved in the Book of Chilam Balam of
Chumayel, this unity and composite character of the Oxlahuntiku
and Bolontiku are clearly set forth, while in the inscriptions of the
Classic stage the dual conception of the Bolontiku is repeatedly
emphasized. Each of the nine Bolontiku was, in turn, the patron
of a day of the Maya calendar, and it was believed that these nine
gods followed each other in endless succession throughout time.
Thus, if God x were patron of the 1st day, he would again be patron
of the 10th day, the 19th day, etc.; and if God y were patron of
the 2d day, he would again be patron of the 11th, the 20th, etc.
We do not know what the nine Bolontiku looked like, since no
representations of them have yet been identified in the codices, but
their name glyphs have been identified (Fig. 12).

Against an inner wall of Temple 40 at Yaxchilan there seems
to have been a row of nine seated anthropomorphic figures, each
about two feet high, which may have represented these nine gods,
but unfortunately all of them have been destroyed except for
their ankles and feet. Along the eastern base of the tower of the
Palace at Palenque were found the badly destroyed remains of

First	Second	Third
Fourth	Fifth	Sixth
Seventh	Eighth	Ninth

FIG. 12.—Name glyphs of the Nine Gods of the Lower World.

nine similar figures, but all details by which either series might have been identified have disappeared.

We do not even know the name glyphs for the thirteen Oxlahuntiku, although together with the Bolontiku they must have constituted one of the most important groups of the Maya pantheon. It has been suggested that the thirteen head-variant numerals of the Maya arithmetical system are in reality the heads of these gods.

THE THIRTEEN GODS OF THE KATUNS

There were thirteen different katuns or 20-year periods, each having its special patron. Although the names and name glyphs of this group of gods are unknown, they seem to be shown in the fragmentary Codex Peresianus, one side of which presents a succession of katuns with their corresponding patron deities. Some of these may be recognized, such as the rain god and the wind god in the representation of Katun 7 Ahau (Fig. 16).

GODS OF THE NINETEEN DIVISIONS (MONTHS) OF THE YEAR

Another series of deities whose names we do not know are the patrons of the nineteen months of the Maya year. Here again, however, we do know most of their corresponding name glyphs (Fig. 13). Some of these are the signs of heavenly bodies, others the heads of animals or birds, and still others forms of unknown meaning.

GODS OF THE TWENTY DAYS

Another series of patron deities was that of the twenty gods who presided over the Maya days. Itzamna was the patron of the days called Ahau; Chac, of the Ik days; the corn god, of the Kan

FIG. 13.—Name glyphs of the patron gods of the nineteen Maya months.

days; Ah Puch, of the Cimi days; Xaman Ek, of the Chuen days; the God of War and Human Sacrifice, of the Manik days; the wind god, of the Muluc days. The remaining thirteen days doubtless had their own patron deities, which have not been identified as yet.

GODS OF THE FOURTEEN NUMERALS O AND 1–13

Another important series of gods were the patrons of the fourteen head-variant numerals. The numerals are the heads of these fourteen deities, each of whom was associated with one of the numbers. Ah Puch, the God of Death, was patron of the number 10, which is depicted as the fleshless skull of the god himself (Plate 30a). The sun god was the patron of the number 4, and Chac, the rain god, patron of the number 13. The heads of the numbers 1–13 inclusive, as already suggested, may be those of the thirteen Oxlahuntiku.[2]

RITES AND CEREMONIES

GENERAL NATURE

There were many ceremonies for individual and group needs, but a similarity of pattern runs through all of them: (1) preliminary fasting and abstinences, symbolic of spiritual purification; (2) selection by priestly divination of an auspicious day for the rite; and at the ceremony itself; (3) an expulsion of the evil spirit from the worshipers; (4) incensing of the idols; (5) prayers; (6) the sacrifice, if possible, of some living thing, animal or human. In all such sacrifices the victim's blood was smeared on the idol of the god in whose honor the ceremony was being held. The priests themselves were also smeared with blood, their hair being clotted, gory mops. Most of the ceremonies closed with feasting and gen-

[2] These number gods are also depicted as the numerical coefficients in the exceedingly rare full-figure glyphs, found only in seven inscriptions in the Maya hieroglyphic writing: (1) Lintel 48, Yaxchilan; (2) Stela D, Copan; (3) Temple 26, Copan; (4, 5) Stela D, east and west sides, Quirigua (Plate 72b); (6) Zoömorph B, Quirigua; and (7) Altar of Zoömorph O, Quirigua (Plate 27b).

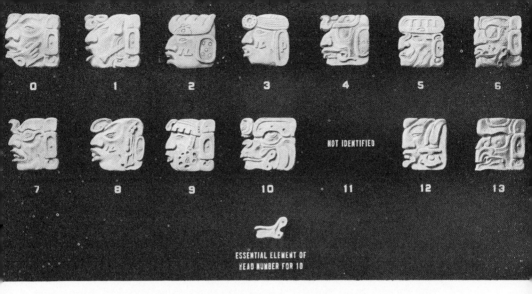

0   1   2   3   4   5   6

7   8   9   10   11 NOT IDENTIFIED   12   13

ESSENTIAL ELEMENT OF
HEAD NUMBER FOR 10

a) Head-variant numerals.

PLATE 30.—HEAD-VARIANT NUMERALS AND
LACANDON AT THE RUINS OF YAXCHILAN

b) The man holds a prayer board on which are small nodules of pom to be burned
as a religious offering.

eral drunkenness, the latter, according to the early Catholic fathers, being the inevitable conclusion of every Maya ceremony.

HUMAN SACRIFICE

Human sacrifice was performed in several ways; the most common and perhaps the most ancient was by removing the heart. The intended victim, after being stripped, painted blue (the sacrificial color), and having a special peaked headdress set on his head, was led to the place of sacrifice. This was usually either the temple courtyard or the summit of the pyramid supporting the temple. The evil spirits were first expelled and the altar, usually a convex stone that curved the victim's breast upward, was smeared with the sacred blue paint. The four *chacs*, also painted blue, next grasped the victim by his arms and legs and stretched him on his back over the altar. The *nacom* advanced with the sacrificial flint knife and plunged it into the victim's ribs just below the left breast. Thrusting his hand into the opening, he pulled out the still beating heart and handed it to the *chilan* or officiating priest, who smeared blood on the idol to whom the sacrifice was being made. If the victim had been sacrificed on the summit of a pyramid, the chacs threw the corpse to the court below, where priests of lower rank skinned the body, except for the hands and feet. The chilan, having removed his sacrificial vestments, arrayed himself in the skin of the victim and solemnly danced with the spectators. If the sacrificial victim had been a valiant and brave soldier, his body was sometimes divided and eaten by the nobles and other spectators. The hands and feet were reserved for the chilan, and, if the victim was a prisoner of war, his captor wore certain of his bones as a mark of prowess. Women and children were as frequently sacrificed as men.

Archaeological corroboration of this ceremony is found several times in the wall paintings at Chichen Itza (Plate 28, *e* and *f*). One such scene (Plate 28*f*) portrays a human sacrifice to Kukulcan, the Feathered Serpent, patron deity of this city. A lower coil of the serpent-god's body forms the sacrificial altar, while the upper coils and the head rise in front of the doorway of his temple. Only

two chacs are shown, perhaps because of difficulties in handling
the perspective involved in drawing one figure directly behind
another. The chilan stands between the altar and the god, his
upraised hand holding the sacrificial knife. Several of these knives
have been recovered from the Well of Sacrifice. One has a blade
of finely chipped flint and a handle of wood, carved in the likeness of two intertwined serpents, their bodies overlaid with gold
(Fig. 14).

FIG. 14.—Sacrificial knife from the Well of Sacrifice, Chichen Itza, Yucatan,
Mexico.

In other representations of human sacrifice (Plate 28, *a-d*)
the victim's breast is shown as already opened. Rising out of it
is a portrayal of the dead man's soul, conceived in one case as a
tree ascending toward the heavens, with a bird perched on its
branches (Plate 28*c*).

Another form of human sacrifice was by bow and arrow:

If he [the victim] was to be sacrificed by arrows they stripped him
naked and anointed his body with a blue color, and put a pointed cap on
his head. When they had reached the victim, all of them, armed with bows
and arrows, made a solemn dance with him around the stake, and while
dancing they put him up on it and bound him to it, all of them keeping
on dancing and looking at him. The foul priest in vestments went up and
wounded the victim with an arrow in the parts of shame, whether it were
a man or woman, and drew blood and came down and anointed the face
of the idol with it. And making a certain sign to the dancers, as they passed
rapidly before him [the prisoner] still dancing, they began one after another to shoot at his heart, which had been marked beforehand with a white
sign. And in this manner they made his whole chest one point like a hedge-
hog of arrows.

This type of sacrifice is depicted in an incised drawing from the
walls of Temple II at Tikal (Fig. 15), probably scratched there

long after the city had been abandoned. The same ceremony is also shown in the Mexican codices, and was probably an importation from central Mexico in late Postclassic times.

An unusual ceremony of human sacrifice was practiced in the Well of Sacrifice at Chichen Itza. In times of famine, epidemic, or prolonged drought, victims were hurled into this great pocket

FIG. 15.—Graffitti from Temple II at Tikal, Peten, Guatemala, showing arrow-shooting ceremony.

in the limestone. The Well of Sacrifice (Plate 42*b*) is roughly oval; it varies in width from 150 to 190 feet and is 65 feet deep from the ground level to the surface of the water. The depth of the water is another 65 or 70 feet, and the sides of the well are either vertical or undercut. Pilgrimages were made from great distances to attend these sacrifices and valuables were hurled into the well with the living victims in order to appease the angry rain gods. The cenote is connected with the Castillo, the principal temple dedicated to Kukulcan, by a stone causeway 1,000 feet long and 20 feet wide, varying in height from 3 to 15 feet above the ground level. Says Landa:

Into this well they have had, and then [middle-sixteenth century] had, the custom of throwing men alive, as a sacrifice to the gods in times of drought, and they believed they did not die though they never saw them again. They also threw into it many other things, like precious stones and things that they prized. And so if this country had had gold, it would be this well that would have the greater part of it, so great was the devotion which the Indians showed for it.

This prediction has been confirmed by modern archaeology. In 1905–8 the Peabody Museum of Archaeology and Ethnology of Harvard University carried on dredging operations in the Well of Sacrifice, bringing to the surface a treasure of sacrificial offerings. These articles include gold and copper repoussé plates, masks, cups, saucers, and gold jewelry. Many copper sacrificial bells of different sizes were found, and small ceremonial axes. There were numbers of polished jade beads as well as carved jade ornaments, sacrificial knives, and several throwing sticks. Fragments of cotton textiles were found, and ornaments of carved bone and shell. There were also about fifty human crania, and human long bones. Some of the latter were carved, perhaps for use as trophies of war. Most numerous of all were the cakes of pom incense, usually found in the bottoms of crude pottery vessels and painted a bright turquoise blue.

Study of the gold and copper objects found in the Well of Sacrifice indicates that they were brought to Chichen Itza from points as far distant as Colombia and Panama to the south and from as far north as the state of Oaxaca and the Valley of Mexico.

In addition to its use as a place where offerings and human sacrifice were made, there was also a prognosticative element in these ceremonies. The victims, especially children, their hands and feet unbound, were thrown into the well by their masters at daybreak. If any survived the plunge, a rope was lowered at midday to haul them out and they were asked by the lords what manner of year the gods had in store for them. If a child did not survive the ordeal, "all that lord's people [that is, the master of the child and his retainers] as well as the lord himself threw large stones into the water and with great hue and cry took flight from there."

THE THIRTEEN KATUN ENDINGS

An old and important ceremony, going back to the beginnings of the Classic stage, was the erection of the katun stone or monument at the end of each katun or 7,200-day period. Each of the thirteen differently named katuns had its own patron deity and its special rites. Although this ceremony started as a katun-ending rite at Uaxactun in 8.16.0.0.0 (357), as the Classic stage developed it soon came to be celebrated twice each katun, at the halfway point and at the end. The celebration at the intermediate lahuntun, or 3,600-day-period ending, was ceremonially of lesser significance, but the one at the katun ending was of great importance. In a few cities of the Classic stage, notably Quirigua and Piedras Negras, the quarter-katun endings as well, i.e., the hotun or 1,800-day-period endings, were also commemorated. In late Postclassic times, however, when we have a number of contemporary references to this ceremony, it was again celebrated only on the katun endings.

One of the most constant features of the ceremony, and one which persisted for nearly twelve centuries (357–1519), was the erection of a monument inscribed with hieroglyphics which gave the date in Maya chronology and additional astronomical, chronological, and ritualistic data. Usually there is also a figure panel showing a ruler or priest, often with accompanying assistants and prisoners.

In late Postclassic times the ceremony was celebrated, according to Bishop Landa, in this fashion: Take, for example, the Katun 7 Ahau, which ran from 1323 to 1342, and which is possibly represented on page 6 of the Codex Peresianus (Fig. 16). During the first half of this 20-year period (1323–32), the idol of Katun 7 Ahau ruled alone in the temple, although he had already been a guest there for the ten years previous to his actual rule. During the second half (1332–42) of Katun 7 Ahau, the idol of the following katun, 5 Ahau, who was to rule from 1342 to 1362, was placed in the same temple as a guest and was shown respect as the successor of the idol of Katun 7 Ahau. In 1342, when the rule of 7 Ahau was finished, his idol was removed and the idol of 5 Ahau was left to rule alone for ten years (from 1342 until 1352). Then the idol of Katun 3 Ahau, who was to succeed 5 Ahau in 1362, was placed in the temple as guest for ten years (1352–62), until 3 Ahau should rule alone, beginning in 1362. Thus the idol of each katun was worshiped for thirty years—the first decade as the guest of his predecessor, the second decade when he ruled

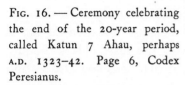

FIG. 16. — Ceremony celebrating the end of the 20-year period, called Katun 7 Ahau, perhaps A.D. 1323–42. Page 6, Codex Peresianus.

alone, and the third decade when he shared the rule with his successor.

NEW YEAR CEREMONIES

Another important group of ceremonies centered around the Maya New Year. At the time of the Spanish Conquest the Maya year-bearers, the days upon which a New Year could begin, were Kan, Muluc, Ix, and Cauac. Each was associated with one of the cardinal points: Kan years with the East, Muluc years with the North, Ix years with the West, and Cauac years with the South. The New Year ceremonies began in the closing five days of the preceding year—the Uayeb or unlucky days, when everyone stayed at home lest misfortune should befall him. The celebrations corresponding to the four kinds of Maya New Years, although differing in details, follow the same general pattern.

Kan years.—The New Year ceremonies for Kan years began during the five closing days of the preceding or Cauac year. A pottery idol of a god called Kan U Uayeb was set up temporarily on a pile of stones at the south entrance to the town, because south was the cardinal point of the dying Cauac year. A lord was chosen at whose house all the feasts connected with the ceremony were to be held, and here an idol, Bolon Dzacab ("Nine Generations"), who was to be patron of the new Kan year, was erected. Bolon Dzacab was an agricultural god who has been identified with the God of the Winds (God K). Next the whole community went to the south entrance where the idol of Kan U Uayeb had been set up, and there the priest incensed it with a mixture of ground corn and pom; cutting off the head of a turkey, he offered the fowl to the idol. The idol, amidst rejoicing and dancing, was then carried to the house of the lord who was donor of the feast. Here the idol of Kan U Uayeb was placed in front of that of Bolon Dzacab and many gifts of food and drink were offered to them. Afterward these offerings were distributed among those present, the officiating priest being given a haunch of venison. The devout drew blood from their ears and smeared the idols with it, offering heart-shaped loaves of corn meal and squash seeds to the idol of Kan U Uayeb.

The two idols were kept at the lord's house for the five days of Uayeb. It was believed that failure to incense them regularly during this period would be followed by special sicknesses which afflicted mankind during Kan years. As soon as the five Uayeb days had passed, the idol of Bolon Dzacab, patron of the Kan year, was taken to the temple; that of Kan U Uayeb was set up at the east gate, East being the cardinal point associated with Kan years. Here the idol of Kan U Uayeb stood until the end of the Kan year over which it presided. Kan years were considered good ones "because the Bacab Hobnil who ruled with the sign Kan, they said, had never sinned as had his brothers [especially the two who presided over the Ix and Cauac years], and it was on this account that no calamity came to them in it [a Kan year]."

Later in the year, if misfortunes began to happen, the priests ordered another idol to be made and erected to the god Itzamna Kauil. This was placed in the temple; three balls of rubber were burned before it, and a dog or, if possible, a man was sacrificed to it. This sacrifice was effected by hurling the victim from the summit of the pyramid onto a pile of stones in the court below. The heart was removed and offered to the new idol, together with

gifts of food. This second ceremony closed with a dance given by
the old women of the community, dressed in special garments.
Landa says that this ceremony was the only one celebrated in a
temple at which women could be present.

Muluc years.—In Muluc years, which followed Kan years, an
idol called Chac U Uayeb was taken to the east entrance where the
idol of Kan U Uayeb had been left the year before. The same
ceremonies were repeated, but in Muluc years the idol set up in
the house of the lord chosen to give the feast was called Kinich
Ahau, the sun god. The same dances were performed, offerings
of food and incense were made and, when the five unlucky days
were over, the idol of Chac U Uayeb was carried to the north entrance and set up on one of the two piles of stone. Muluc years
were thought to be good years because the Bacab who presided
over them was believed to be "the best and greatest of the Bacab
gods." If the Muluc years turned out badly, however, the priests
turned to a god called Yax Cocay Mut, "the green firefly pheasant,"

Fig. 17.—Woman on stilts.
Page 36, Codex Tro-Cortesianus.

of whom an image was made and worshiped. The special evils that
were prone to happen in Muluc years were a scarcity of water and
an abundance of sprouts in the corn. The old women had to per-
form a special dance on high stilts (Fig. 17) and to offer dogs made
of pottery with food placed on their backs.

Ix years.—In Ix years the idol Sac U Uayeb was erected at the north entrance of the town and a statue of Itzamna, the patron of the Ix year, was set up in the house of the lord selected to give the feast. The same series of rites was performed and at the end of the year the idol of Itzamna was carried to the temple and that of Sac U Uayeb to one of the piles of stone at the west gate. Ix years were considered unfavorable; people were especially prone to fainting fits and troubles of the eyes. There were supposed to be hot suns, drought, famine, thefts, discords, changes of rulers, wars, and plagues of locusts. If any of these calamities occurred, the priests ordered an idol made to Kinich Ahau Itzamna and again the old women executed a special dance.

Cauac years.—In Cauac years an idol called Ek U Uayeb was made and carried to the west entrance of the town, and another of Uac Mitun Ahau was placed in the house of the lord who was giving the New Year's feast that year; the same ceremonies followed in other years were repeated. Uac Mitun Ahau may be translated "Lord of the Sixth Hell" or Lower World. When the ceremonies had been performed the idol of Uac Mitun Ahau was carried from the house of the lord to the temple, and the idol of Ek U Uayeb was carried to the south entrance of the town, where it was installed for the coming year.

Cauac years were considered to be the most dangerous of all; they were years when heavy mortality was to be expected, as well as hot suns, flocks of birds, and swarms of ants to devour the young seeds. But again the priests came forward with their remedy. This time the people had to make idols of four gods—Chic Chac Chob, Ek Balam Chac, Ah Canuol Cab, and Ah Buluc Balam—which were installed in the temple with ceremonies such as burning a huge fire of fagots and dancing on the embers in bare feet.

Throughout the year other ceremonies were celebrated to propitiate various gods to obtain rain or good harvests, to ensure success in hunting, trading, war, and other activities. Most of these have long since been forgotten, and only a few of the most important are discussed here.

The month of Pop.—On the Maya New Year's Day, the first day of the month of Pop, which fell on July 16 of the Julian calendar in the year 1556 (July 26 of the Gregorian calendar), a solemn renovation ceremony was held in which all the articles in daily use were renewed. Houses were swept clean and old utensils were thrown out upon the town refuse pile. The four chacs who were to serve the priest for the ensuing year were chosen and the priest himself prepared the balls of incense for the New Year ceremony.

The month of Uo.—During this second month, the priests, physicians, sorcerers, hunters, and fishermen celebrated festivals to their respective patron gods. A priest consulted the sacred books to learn the auguries for the coming year and, after feasting and drinking, the festivities closed with a dance in honor of the month. The special ceremonies of these five vocations were continued into the following month of Zip.

The months of Zotz and Tzec.—During the fourth month, Zotz, the owners of beehives began to prepare for their feast, which was held in the following month, Tzec. Their divine intercessors were the four Bacabs, and Hobnil, the Bacab who was patron of the Kan years, was their special friend. Incense was burned and pictures of honey were painted on the incense boards. The object of the feast was to increase the yield of honey, and the owners of hives contributed an abundance of it, from which a wine was brewed with the bark of the *balche* tree; heavy drinking of this beverage concluded the ceremony.

The month of Xul.—On the sixteenth day of the sixth month, Xul, which began on November 17 (Gregorian), one of the most important festivals of the Maya year was celebrated, in honor of Kukulcan. This ceremony was formerly observed all over Yucatan, but after the fall of Mayapan in 1441 it was held only at the Xiu capital of Mani. Other provinces sent gifts, among them the magnificent banners of featherwork used in the rite.

People from surrounding towns and villages assembled at

Mani on the day of the feast, having prepared for it by preliminary fastings and abstinences. At evening a great procession of lords, priests, common people, and clowns, the latter a special feature of the celebration, set out from the house of the lord who was giving the feast and proceeded to the Temple of Kukulcan. The exorcisms and prayers were made, the feather banners were broken out from the summit of the temple-pyramid, and the participants spread out their personal idols of wood and clay in the court in front of the temple. A new fire was kindled, incense was burned, and offerings were made of food, cooked without salt or chili pepper, and of a beverage composed of ground beans and squash seeds.

The lords and all those who had fasted stayed at the temple for the remaining five days and nights of the month, making offerings to their idols, praying, and performing sacred dances. During these five days the clowns passed among the houses of the well-to-do, playing their comedies and collecting gifts, which were divided among the lords, priests, and dancers. The banners and idols were then gathered up and taken to the house of the donor lord, from whence each participant departed for his own home. It was believed that Kukulcan himself descended from heaven on the last day of the feast to receive the offerings of the worshipers. This feast was called *chic kaban*, which may mean "clown-named."

The months of Yaxkin and Mol.—During the seventh month, Yaxkin, preparations were made for another general ceremony in honor of all the gods, which was celebrated in the eighth month, Mol, on a day fixed by the priests. It was called, according to Landa, *olob zab kamyax*, which is probably a corruption of the Maya phrase *yolob u dzab kamyax*, meaning "they wish to administer the receiving of the blue color." After the people had assembled in the temple and the exorcism and incensing had been carried out, the principal object of the ceremony, which was to anoint everything with the sacred blue ointment, was begun. All sorts of utensils and even the doorposts of the houses were smeared with blue ointment. The boys and girls of the town were assembled, and the backs of their hands were struck nine times to make them skillful in the pursuits of their fathers and mothers. An old woman called the *ixmol* or "conductress" did this for the girls and a priest did it for the boys. The beekeepers also celebrated a second festival in the month of Mol in order that the gods should provide flowers for the bees.

Another important ceremony was held in Mol, or in some other month if the priests found the omens of Mol were not propitious. It was called "making gods," and was for the purpose of making the wooden idols. The sculptors who carved these idols were fearful of their own art, since it was thought very dangerous to make representations of the gods. They consented to do it with great reluctance, fearing that some member of their families would fall ill or die. As soon as the sculptor who was to make the idols had been selected, the priest, the four chacs, and the sculptor began to fast. The man for whom the idols were to be made built a thatched hut in the forest, cut the wood from which the idols were to be carved, and installed a covered pottery urn so that the idols could be decently kept under cover.

The wood used was always the same—cedar, the most easily carved of all native woods. The Maya word for cedar is *kuche*, which means "god tree," perhaps because such idols were made from it. Incense was taken to the hut to offer to four gods, called *Acantuns*, each of whom presided over one of the cardinal points. Instruments for scarification were provided, and tools for carving.

The priest, the chacs, and the sculptor were shut up in the hut and went to work, first cutting their ears and smearing the images of the Acantuns with blood, incensing, and praying. This was kept up until the idols were finished, while the man for whom they were being made carried food to the hut. Absolute continence was required of all, and no outsider was allowed to approach the place.

The month of Chen.—By the next month, Chen, the idols were finished. The man for whom they had been made paid the priest, chacs, and sculptor with gifts of food and beads, and removed the idols to an arbor in his own yard. Here the priest and sculptor cleaned themselves and the priest blessed the idols with prayers. The evil spirits having been exorcised and incense burned, the idols were wrapped in cloth, placed in a basket, and turned over to the owner, who received them with great devotion and reverence. The ceremony, as usual, closed with feasting and drinking.

The month of Yax.—A renovation ceremony, already described in connection with the rain god, Chac, was celebrated in the month of Yax. Clay idols and incense burners were renewed, probably with ceremonies similar to those described in connection with the making of wooden idols.

The month of Zac.—During this eleventh month, the hunters again celebrated a festival like the one in the month of Zip, to make amends to the gods for any blood they might have shed in the chase. Any bloodshed, except in sacrifice, was believed to be an abomination for which atonement had to be made.

The months of Ceh and Mac.—There is no special ceremony described for the twelfth month, Ceh, but in the next month, Mac, the old men celebrated a feast in honor of the four Chacs and Itzamna. This was called the Tupp Kak, or "the killing of the fire." A great hunt was organized, in which many animals and birds were caught. On the day of the ceremony these were brought to the courtyard of the temple, where a great pile of fagots was set up. After the usual exorcisms and incensing, the animals and birds were sacrificed and their hearts thrown into the fire. When the hearts were consumed the chacs extinguished the fire and the ceremony proper began. For this feast only the lord who gave it was obliged to fast. All assembled in the court of the temple, where a stone altar had been built with a stairway on one side. When the altar had been ceremonially purified, mud was smeared on the bottom step and the sacred blue ointment on the other steps. Incense was burned and the Chacs and Itzamna were invoked with prayers and offerings; eating and drinking closed this ceremony as all others. The Tupp Kak was celebrated in order to obtain a year of good rains; the month Mac fell in the latter part of March and early April, not long before the beginning of the rainy season, and it was thought that the ceremony would assure plenteous rains for the corn.

The months of Kankin and Muan.—No special ceremony is reported for the fourteenth month, Kankin, but in the following month, Muan, a festival in honor of Chac Ek Chuah (God of Cacao) and Hobnil (Bacab of the Kan years), was celebrated by owners of cacao plantations. A dog with cacao-colored spots was sacrificed on one of the plantations, incense was burned, blue iguanas, blue feathers, and game were offered to the idols of these gods, and the long pods of the cacao beans were given to each official who participated in the rite. When the offerings and prayers were over, the ceremony closed with the usual feasting and drinking, but this time with no drunkenness. Bishop Landa says, "there were three drinks of wine for each one and no more."

The month of Pax.—In the month of Pax there was a ceremony called Pacum Chac, "the recompensing of Chac," in honor of a god called Cit Chac Coh, "Father Red Puma." Judging from the nature of the ceremony, this god was a patron of warriors. This was a general ceremony; the lords and priests of the smaller towns and villages went to the larger centers, where the celebration was held in the Temple of Cit Chac Coh. For five days preceding the festival, prayers, gifts, and incense were offered at the temple. Sometime before the fifth day, everyone went to the house of the war captain, the elected nacom, and with great pomp bore him in a palanquin to the temple, where he was seated and incensed. The remainder of the five days were spent in feasting, drinking, and dancing the *holcan okot* or dance of the warriors. After the first five days, the ceremony proper began, and since it was a rite to secure victory in war it was celebrated with great solemnity.

The ceremony opened with the same ordeal by fire as practiced in the month of Mac, which was followed by prayers, offerings, and incensing. The lords carried the nacom on their shoulders in his palanquin around the temple, incensing him as they went. A dog was sacrificed and its heart offered to the idol of Cit Chac Coh. The chacs opened a large jar of wine, which ended the festival. The other celebrants escorted the nacom back to his home, where everybody but the nacom himself got ceremoniously drunk. The next day the nacom distributed quantities of incense among the

TABLE VI

List of Ceremonies, Their Objectives, and Corresponding Patron Gods and Sacred Dances Celebrated During the Year, According to Bishop Landa

Month	Patron of Month	Name of Ceremony	Patron God or Gods	Object of Ceremony	Group or Groups Participating in Ceremony	Name of Dance
Pop	Jaguar	....	All gods	New Years rites and renewal of all utensils	General	....
Uo	God of Number 7	Pocam	Kinich Ahau Itzamna	Ascertain prognostications for the year	Priests, physicians, sorcerers, hunters, fishermen	Okot uil
			Ixchel, Itzamna, Cit Bolon Tun, Ahau Chamahez	To these gods of medicine for their help	Physicians, sorcerers	Chan tuniah
Zip	A serpent-god	....	Acanum, Suhui Dzipitabai	To these gods of the hunt for successful hunting	Hunters	....
			Ah Kak Nexoy, Ah Pua, Ah Cit Dzamal Cun	To these gods of fishing for successful fishing	Fishermen	Chohom
Zotz	Bat	....	No special ceremonies reported; devoted to preparation for those of the following month			
Tzec	God of the Day Caban (?)	....	Four Bacabs, but especially Hobnil, Bacab of Kan years	To the god of bees for an abundance of honey	Owners of bee hives	....
Xul	Unknown ;	Chic Kaban	Kukulcan	Blessing of the idols	General	Sacred dances
Yaxkin	Sun	....	No special ceremonies reported; devoted to preparation for those of the following month			

Month / God	Ceremony	God(s)	Purpose	Participants	
Mol ... An old god (?)	Olob zab kamyax	All gods	Anointing all utensils with sacred blue ointment	General	....
			For flowers for the bees	Owners of bee hives	....
		Four Acantuns	Making new idols of the gods	Individual having new idols made for him	....
Chen ... Moon	Idol-making ceremonies continued				
Yax ... Venus	Ocna	Chac	Renovation of Temple of Chac	General	....
Zac ... God of the Uinal, or 20-day time period		Acanum, Suhui Dzipitabai	To appease gods of hunt for having shed blood in the chase	Hunters	....
Ceh ... New Fire	No special ceremony reported				
Mac ... A young god (?)	Tupp Kak	Chac, Itzamna	To secure rains for the corn and a good year	Old men	....
Kankin .. Unknown	No special ceremony reported				
Muan ... A young god (?)		Chac Ek Chuah Hobnil	Successful year for the cacao plants	Owners of cacao plantations	....
Pax ... A god with a Roman nose	Pacum Chac	Cit Chac Coh	To obtain victory in war	Warriors	Holcan okot
Kayab					
Cumhu . A young god (?) unknown	Sabacil Than		For pleasure and diversion	General	Dances
Uayeb ... Unknown		Kan (yellow) U Uayeb, Chac (red) U Uayeb, Sac (white) U Uayeb, Ek (black) U Uayeb	Preparation for the New Years ceremonies, one each for the four kinds of years: Kan, Muluc, Ix, and Cauac	General	....

participants in the feast, and urged them to observe all the festivals of the coming year with diligence and fidelity in order that the year should be prosperous.

The closing months of Kayab, Cumhu, and Uayeb.—A fairly strenuous program of religious ceremonies had been going on for the first sixteen Maya months and a need was felt for some relaxation before the exacting rites of the New Year began. The lighter festivities, held during the last three months—Kayab, Cumhu, and Uayeb—were called the *sabacil than* and were celebrated in this manner:

> They sought in the town among those who were the richest for someone who would be willing to give this festival, and advised him of the day, in order that these three months that remained before the New Year should have more diversion. And what they did was to assemble in the house of him who gave the festival, and there they performed the ceremonies of driving out the evil spirit, and burned copal [pom] and made offerings with rejoicings and dances, and they made wine-skins of themselves, and this was the inevitable conclusion. And so great was the excess which there was in the festivals during these three months that it was a great pity to see them, for some went about covered with scratches, others, bruised, others with their eyes enflamed from much drunkenness, and all the while with such a passion for wine that they were lost because of it.

In judging Landa's constant complaints about the drunkenness of Maya ceremonies, it must be remembered that every observance of the ancient religion was anathema to him. The bishop was as bigoted as the Maya priests he condemns, and his observations about the drunken orgies with which he says these ceremonies always concluded should probably be taken with a grain of salt. (For a résumé of the ceremonies and dances of the Maya year see Table VI.)

GROWTH OF THE PANTHEON

The Maya had a number of gods, though the most powerful and the most frequently invoked were those already described. Not more than a dozen deities enjoyed most of the worship, the aid of the others being sought only if specific need for their help arose.

Originally the Maya religion was a relatively simple personification of the forces of nature which immediately influenced the
lives of the common people. With the introduction of corn culture, the pantheon was enlarged to admit agricultural and fertility deities whose continued good will now became necessary for
the first time. Later, when the Maya civilization began to take
shape with the invention of the calendar, chronology, and hieroglyphic writing, a further expansion of the pantheon became necessary to make room for the new crop of astronomic and calendric
deities, whose functions were more specialized than those of the
nature gods. The newer gods also required the services of a professional priesthood to worship them and to interpret their wishes.
And so matters continued for more than six centuries. The Maya
religion grew more esoteric, the gods more specialized, the priesthood more highly organized, and ritual more complex, but still
without excessive human sacrifice or the general use of idols.

Authorities are agreed that both mass human sacrifice and
idolatry were introduced into Yucatan by the Maya-Mexican invaders under Kukulcan during the tenth century of the Christian
Era. Some human sacrifice was practiced during the Classic stage,
but it was rare. It was not until the Puuc and Mexican periods of
the Postclassic that hecatombs of human victims were offered to
the gods after the fashion then prevailing in central Mexico.

The Classic-stage Maya were not, generally speaking, worshipers of images in a literal sense. Authorities again agree that
idolatry as such was also a Maya-Mexican importation into Yucatan, and the number of idols is said to have been enormous. Landa
states: "They had a very great number of idols and of temples
which were magnificent in their own fashion, and besides the community temples, the lords, priests and leading men also had oratories and idols in their houses, where they made their prayers
and offerings in private." And again, "They had such a great
quantity of idols, that those of their gods were not enough, for
there was not an animal or insect of which they did not make a
statue." Another seventeenth-century Spanish priest, in writing
of Tayasal on Lake Peten Itza, the last independent Maya strong-

hold, says: "They have many other public idols, as there are nearly as many as there are priests' houses and the streets of the district." Another writer in 1562 mentions that "there must have been more than 100,000"; the royal *alcalde mayor* of Mérida, writing three years later, raises this number to "almost a million of them." Even discounting such obvious exaggeration, the early writers agree that there were great numbers of idols, almost everyone having his own private collection.

Among this multitude of gods, many were the creation of the professional priesthood. The common man, whose toil made possible the whole complicated governmental, social, and religious structure, turned most frequently to Chac, the rain god, since by Chac's good will he lived, and by Chac's wrath he was undone.

HIEROGLYPHIC WRITING, ARITHMETIC, AND ASTRONOMY

H. G. WELLS in his *Outline of History* says that the invention of a graphic system is the true measure of civilization, and Edward Gibbon, in his *Decline and Fall of the Roman Empire*, claims that the use of letters is the principal characteristic which distinguishes civilized people from savages. By such standards, the Maya were the most civilized people of the New World in pre-Columbian times, since they alone originated a system of writing.

THE DEVELOPMENT OF WRITING

Writing seems to have passed everywhere through three stages of development:

1.—*Pictorial or representative writing*, wherein a picture of the idea is portrayed. Thus a deer hunt is represented by the picture of a deer and a man throwing a spear at it. This is called pictographic writing.

2.—*Ideographic writing*, wherein characters stand for ideas rather than representing pictures of them. In ideographic writing the characters employed are usually little more than conventionalized symbols. In Chinese writing, the ideograph for "trouble" is the conventionalized symbol for a woman, repeated twice, standing under a gate.

3.—*Phonetic writing*, wherein the characters have lost all resemblance to the objects they originally portrayed, and denote only sounds. Phonetic writing may be further divided into (*a*) syllabic writing, in which each character stands for a syllable, and (*b*) alphabetic writing, in which each of the characters stands for a single sound. Egyptian hieroglyphic writing is an example of the former; modern alphabets are examples of the latter.

Maya hieroglyphic writing is ideographic, since its characters represent ideas rather than pictures or sounds. It has been thought by some that there are phonetic elements included in Maya writing.

MAYA WRITING ONE OF THE EARLIEST EXAMPLES
OF A GRAPHIC SYSTEM

One of the important facts about the Maya hieroglyphic writing is that, barring such purely pictorial efforts as the paleolithic cave paintings or the American Indian pictographs, it may represent the earliest stage of a formal graphic system that has come down to us. This does not mean that the Maya hieroglyphic writing is the oldest graphic system known. Although the earliest Egyptian and Sumerian inscriptions go back to the fourth millennium before Christ, the earliest known Maya writing was done after the beginning of the Christian Era. However, early Egyptian hieroglyphics had already advanced to a semiphonetic stage. In addition to the many ideographs present, perhaps half the characters are phonetic, mostly syllabic. A similar condition obtains in the earliest cuneiform writing.

The Maya "Rosetta Stone" is the *Relación de las cosas de Yucatán*, written about 1566 by Bishop Diego de Landa.

At the time of the Spanish Conquest of Yucatan, Maya hieroglyphic writing was still in use. Maya civilization toward the end of the Postclassic had passed into a decline, but knowledge and use of hieroglyphic writing among the priesthood and ruling class continued to the time of the Conquest and later.

Landa, in his *Relación*, gave a brief description of the Maya calendar, drawings of the signs for the different days and months, and some general information about it. His chief source of calendric information was Nachi Cocom, who had been a native prince before the Conquest and who was well versed in hieroglyphic writing.

The bishop, though he regards the whole matter as "the work of the devil," nevertheless attempted a phonetic transliteration of Maya glyphs into the Latin alphabet, and an explanation of Maya calendrics. With Landa's information as a basis, about one-

third of the hieroglyphs, largely the chronological sections, can ⠒⠁
now be read.

STORY TOLD BY THE MAYA INSCRIPTIONS

The Maya inscriptions treat primarily of chronology, astronomy, and religious matters. They are not records of personal glorification, like the inscriptions of Egypt, Assyria, and Babylonia. They are so completely impersonal that it is unlikely that the name glyphs of specific men were ever recorded upon the monuments.

The first and most important part of the Classic Maya inscriptions was the dedicatory date of each monument, the so-called Initial Series, usually recorded at the beginning of each inscription. This date was inscribed to the day.

Each of the nineteen divisions of the 365-day calendar year had its own deity. The name glyph of the patron god in whose month the Initial Series date fell is recorded in the first hieroglyph of each text in the majority of inscriptions (Fig. 13). The name glyphs of the Nine Gods of the Lower World are also recorded on most monuments immediately following the record of the days over which they presided (Fig. 12).

Very early in the use of the Maya calendar the priests undoubtedly saw that a calendar year with a fixed length and no provision for the extra quarter-day each year would start to gain upon the true year. This increase would amount to fifteen days in sixty years. If this discrepancy had continued uncorrected for any length of time, the significant dates of the farmers' year would quickly have become displaced. The time for burning the bush for their cornfields, instead of falling toward the end of the dry season, would have crept backward through the months until presently their calendar would have been telling them to burn at the height of the rainy season. The priests doubtless foresaw this difficulty and solved it.

They must have reasoned like this: "Let us permit our calendar year to gain on the true year as fast as it will. We will allow our calendar to function without change, but when we erect a monument, we will engrave upon it, in addition to the official calendar date of its dedication, a calendar correction for that particular date. In this way, no matter what month our calendar may register, we shall always know, whenever we erect a monument, the position of its corresponding date in the true year."

The Maya priests followed this procedure throughout the Classic stage by means of a corrective count which has been called the "Secondary Series." As monuments were erected on the hotun, lahuntun, or katun endings, the correction necessary to bring the recorded Maya year into harmony with the solar year was clearly set forth. This correction increased as time went on, the error accumulating at the rate of one day every four years.

The priests' awesome knowledge of the movements of the heavenly bodies must have been a source of tremendous power to them. It proved to the ignorant masses that the priesthood held close and intimate communion with their greatest deities and so must be obeyed.

Beyond the calendrics, what do the Maya inscriptions tell? We cannot answer this question yet, but judging from the glyphs which have been deciphered we may be justified in guessing that the remainder probably refer to ceremonial matters, offerings, and deities. We may eventually find hieroglyphs for a group of special moon gods and for Venus in her different phases. Some of the unknown signs no doubt represent deities; others, the offerings with which they were to be propitiated or the rites with which they were to be worshiped.

MAYA CALENDAR

TZOLKIN OR SACRED YEAR OF 260 DAYS

The people must all have been familiar with the sacred year of 260 days, the *tzolkin* or "count of days." This time period determined for everyone the pattern of ceremonial life. The ancient Maya regarded his birthday as the day of the tzolkin upon which he was born, and the god of that particular day was his patron saint. Among the Cakchiquels of the highlands of Guatemala a man also took his given name from his tzolkin birth date.

The sacred year was not marked off into months, but was a succession of 260 days, each designated by prefixing a number from 1 to 13 to one of twenty Maya day names. These are given below, and their corresponding hieroglyphs are shown in Figure 18.

Ik	Manik	Eb	Caban
Akbal	Lamat	Ben	Eznab
Kan	Muluc	Ix	Cauac
Chicchan	Oc	Men	Ahau
Cimi	Chuen	Cib	Imix

The tzolkin had no day name without an accompanying number. Since each of the day names had a number prefixed to it, the calendar ran: 1 Ik, 2 Akbal, 3 Kan, 4 Chicchan, 5 Cimi, and so on. The fourteenth name, Men, had the number 1 again; next came 2 Cib; and so on. The first name, Ik, on the second time around, had the number 8. Not until every one of the thirteen numbers had been attached in turn to every one of the twenty day names was a tzolkin complete. Since 13 and 20 have no common factor, 260 days had to elapse before 1 Ik recurred and a new tzolkin began.

In order to give any day in the Maya Calendar Round its complete description it was also necessary to add to the tzolkin designations the corresponding position in the *haab* or 365-day calendar year which it occupied.

CALENDAR YEAR OF 365 DAYS

The Maya civil year or haab was composed of 19 months—18 months of 20 days each, and a closing month of 5 days, making a total of 365 positions in the calendar year. These 19 monthly divisions are given below and their corresponding hieroglyphs are shown in Figure 19.

Pop	Tzec	Chen	Mac	Kayab
Uo	Xul	Yax	Kankin	Cumhu
Zip	Yaxkin	Zac	Muan	Uayeb
Zotz	Mol	Ceh	Pax	

In order to show how the 260 days of the tzolkin were combined with the 365 positions of the haab let us represent them graphically

232

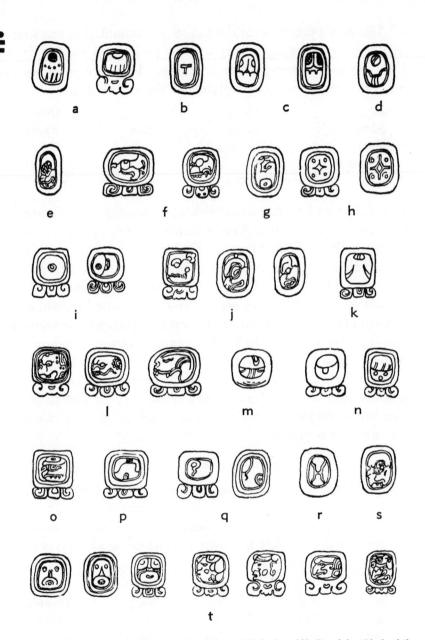

Fig. 18.—Glyphs for the twenty Maya days: (*a*) Imix; (*b*) Ik; (*c*) Akbal; (*d*) Kan; (*e*) Chicchan; (*f*) Cimi; (*g*) Manik; (*h*) Lamat; (*i*) Muluc; (*j*) Oc; (*k*) Chuen; (*l*) Eb; (*m*) Ben; (*n*) Ix; (*o*) Men; (*p*) Cib; (*q*) Caban; (*r*) Eznab; (*s*) Cauac; (*t*) Ahau.

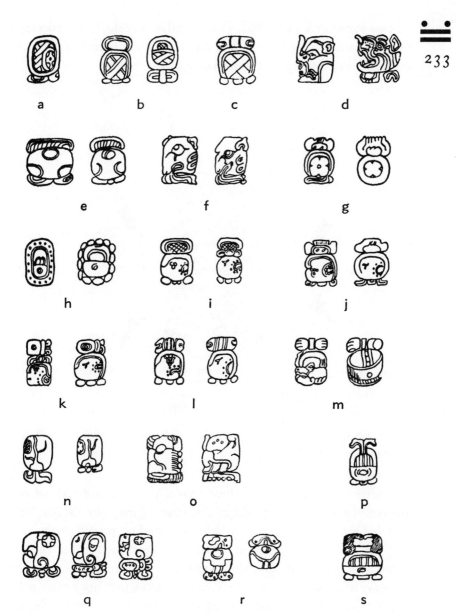

Fig. 19.—Glyphs for the nineteen Maya months: (*a*) Pop; (*b*) Uo; (*c*) Zip; (*d*) Zotz; (*e*) Tzec; (*f*) Xul; (*g*) Yaxkin; (*h*) Mol; (*i*) Chen; (*j*) Yax; (*k*) Zac; (*l*) Ceh; (*m*) Mac; (*n*) Kankin; (*o*) Muan; (*p*) Pax; (*q*) Kayab; (*r*) Cumhu; (*s*) Uayeb.

on two cogwheels (Fig. 20). The smaller wheel, *A*, has 260 cogs, one for each day of the tzolkin, and the larger wheel, *B*, has 365 cogs, one intercog space for each day of the haab.

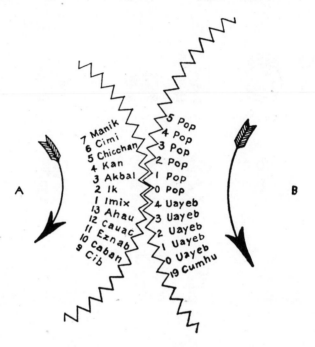

FIG. 20.—Diagram showing the enmeshing of the 365-day civil year (*B*) with the 260-day sacred year (*A*).

Before we can enmesh these two wheels we must know two further facts about the Maya calendar. First, the Maya New Year's Day was written 0 Pop. Pop was the first month of the year and the first position in that month was written 0 rather than 1, as we would write it. But this is the way we number the hours of the day: when we say one o'clock, in reality the first hour after noon is gone and we are about to start the second hour. Similarly, although the Maya haab months were 20 days in length, the days were numbered from 0 to 19.

The second fact is that only 52 of the 260 differently named days of the tzolkin could ever occupy the first position of the haab,

or of any of its months. These are days in which the names Ik, ■ ■
Manik, Eb, and Caban appear. Since each of these four names had
numbers 1 to 13 prefixed to it in turn, only 52 (4 × 13) days of
the tzolkin could begin the Maya civil year or any one of its months.
These 52 possible New Year's Days, or year-bearers, fell, during
the Classic stage, upon the following days:

1 Ik	1 Manik	1 Eb	1 Caban	1 Ik
2 Manik	2 Eb	2 Caban	2 Ik	2 Manik
3 Eb	3 Caban	3 Ik	3 Manik	etc, etc.
4 Caban	4 Ik	4 Manik	4 Eb	
5 Ik	5 Manik	5 Eb	5 Caban	
6 Manik	6 Eb	6 Caban	6 Ik	
7 Eb	7 Caban	7 Ik	7 Manik	
8 Caban	8 Ik	8 Manik	8 Eb	
9 Ik	9 Manik	9 Eb	9 Caban	
10 Manik	10 Eb	10 Caban	10 Ik	
11 Eb	11 Caban	11 Ik	11 Manik	
12 Caban	12 Ik	12 Manik	12 Eb	
13 Ik	13 Manik	13 Eb	13 Caban	

At the time of the Spanish Conquest, however, the days with
which the Maya New Year began had shifted forward two positions, presumably because of faulty counting in Postclassic times.
Instead of beginning with days named Ik, Manik, Eb, or Caban,
they began with days named Kan, Muluc, Ix, or Cauac.

CALENDAR ROUND

We are now in a position to mesh the two wheels in Figure 20.
Let us do this so that the cog of Wheel *A*, named "2 Ik," will
fit into the space on Wheel *B* corresponding to "0 Pop," giving the
complete designation of this particular day as "2 Ik 0 Pop." Now
our problem is to find out how many complete revolutions each
wheel will have to make before "2 Ik" will again enmesh with
"0 Pop."

We must first ascertain the least common denominator of 260
and 365. Both numbers are divisible by 5; 260 gives a quotient of

52, and 365 gives a quotient of 73, so the least common multiple of 260 and 365 is 5 × 52 × 73, or 18,980. Therefore, Wheel *A* will make 73 revolutions and Wheel *B* will make 52 revolutions before the two wheels have returned to their original positions, a total of 18,980 elapsed days, or about 52 years.

Once every 52 civil years, then, any given year-bearer coincided with the first day of the year. Thus any Maya who lived more than 52 years began to see New Year's Days of the same name repeat themselves. We do not know the ancient Maya name or hieroglyph for this 52-year period, but modern students of the Maya calendar have called it the Calendar Round.

None of the peoples of Mesoamerica who borrowed their calendars from the Maya made use of time periods longer than this 18,980-day period. The Aztecs, for example, conceived time as an endless succession of these 52-year periods and gave to them the name *xiuhmolpilli*, meaning "year bundle" or complete round of the years.

The Aztecs had two special glyphs for this period, arising from their beliefs concerning it. The first was a knot (Fig. 21*a*) indicating that the bundle of 52 years had been tied up, and the second was the fire drill and stick for kindling the Sacred Fire (Fig. 21*b*).

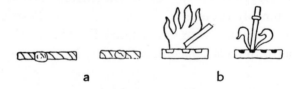

a   b

Fɪɢ. 21.—Aztec glyphs for the *xiuhmol pilli* or 52-year period: (*a*) two examples of the knot; (*b*) two examples of the stick and drill for kindling the sacred fire.

The Aztecs believed that the world would come to an end at the close of one of these 52-year periods, and on the last night of the xiuhmolpilli, the population of Tenochtitlan (Mexico City) withdrew to the hills surrounding the city to await the dawn. When the sun rose on that morning, there was general rejoicing, the Sacred Fire was rekindled, the houses were cleaned and set in order, and the business of life was resumed. The gods had given mankind another 52-year lease on life.

In order to escape rapidly mounting calendric chaos, the Maya priests devised a simple numerical system which even today stands as one of the brilliant achievements of the human mind.

Some time during the fourth or third centuries before Christ, the priests devised a system of numeration by position, involving the conception and use of the mathematical quantity of zero, a notable intellectual accomplishment.

The unit of the Maya calendar was the day or *kin*. The second order of units, consisting of 20 kins, was called the *uinal*. In a perfect vigesimal system of numeration, the third term should be 400 (20 × 20 × 1) but at this point the Maya introduced a variation for calendric reckoning. The third order of the Maya system, the *tun*, was composed of 18 (instead of 20) uinals, or 360 (instead of 400) kins. This was a closer approximation to the length of the solar calendar.

Above the third order the unit of progression is uniformly 20, as will be seen from the numerical values of the nine known orders of time periods:

20 *kins*	= 1 *uinal* or	20 days
18 *uinals*	= 1 *tun* or	360 days
20 *tuns*	= 1 *katun* or	7,200 days
20 *katuns*	= 1 *baktun** or	144,000 days
20 *baktuns*	= 1 *pictun* or	2,880,000 days
20 *pictuns*	= 1 *calabtun* or	57,600,000 days
20 *calabtuns*	= 1 *kinchiltun* or	1,152,000,000 days
20 *kinchiltuns*	= 1 *alautun* or	23,040,000,000 days

* The period of the fifth order, the *baktun*, was originally called the "cycle" by modern investigators. The ancient name for this period, however, was probably *baktun* as given above.

MAYA GLYPH FORMS

Every Maya hieroglyph occurs in two forms in the inscriptions: (1) the normal form and (2) a head variant, this being the head of a deity, man, animal, bird, serpent, or some mythological creature. Very rarely there is a third form where the glyph is a full figure.

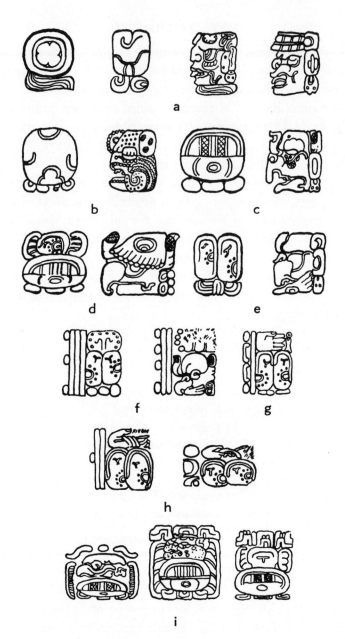

Fig. 22.—Glyphs for the nine known Maya time periods: (*a*) *kin*; (*b*) *uinal*; (*c*) *tun*; (*d*) *katun*; (*e*) *baktun*; (*f*) *pictun*; (*g*) *calabtun*; (*h*) *kinchiltun*; (*i*) *alautun* or Initial Series introducing glyph.

The glyphs for the nine time periods are given in Figure 22, with normal forms at the left and head variants at the right. Head variants have not yet been identified for the last three periods.

MAYA NUMERICAL NOTATIONS

The ancient Maya used two types of notation in writing their numbers: (1) bar-and-dot numerals, and (2) head-variant numerals. In the first notation, the dot ● has a numerical value of 1 and the bar ——— a numerical value of 5, and by varying combinations of these two symbols, the numbers from 1 to 19 were written (Fig. 23). The numbers above 19 were indicated by their positions and will be described later.

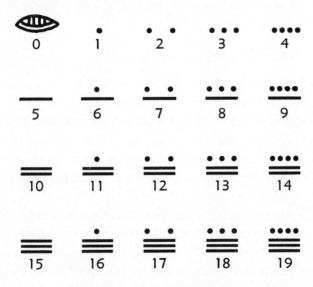

FIG. 23.—Glyphs for 0 and the numbers 1 to 19 inclusive.

Maya bar-and-dot notation was simpler than Roman notation and superior in two respects. To write the numbers from 1 to 19 in Roman notation, it is necessary to employ the symbols I, V, and X, and the processes of addition and subtraction: VI is V plus I, but IV is V minus I. In order to write the same numbers in Maya bar-and-dot, it is necessary to employ only the dot and the bar, and one arithmetical process, that of addition.

240

The second notation employed in writing Maya numbers used different types of human heads to represent the numbers from 1 to 13, and zero. The Maya head notation is comparable to our Arabic notation, where ten symbols represent zero and the nine digits. These Maya head-variant numerals are heads of the patron deities of the first fourteen numbers (Plate 30*a*).[1] The head variant for 10 is the death's head, and in forming the head variants for the numbers from 14 to 19 the fleshless lower jaw (Plate 30*a*) is used to represent the value of 10. For example, if the jaw is applied to the lower part of the head for 6, which is characterized by a pair of crossed sticks in the large eye socket, the resulting head will be that for 16. It is probable that the heads representing numbers 1 to 13 are those of the *Oxlahuntiku* or Thirteen Gods of the Upper World.

MAYA VIGESIMAL SYSTEM OF MATHEMATICS

In writing bar-and-dot numbers above 19, the ancient Maya used a positional system of numeration. In our decimal system, the positions to the left of the decimal point increase by tens. In the Maya vigesimal system the values of the positions increase by twenties from bottom to top. An exception is made in counting time, when, as already noted, the third position is 18 instead of 20 times the second.

To illustrate this, let us see how the Maya would have written the number 20, which is 1 complete unit of the second order and no units of the first order. This necessitates a symbol for zero in the lowest position to show that no units of the first order are involved; for this we shall use the conventionalized shell, one of the commonest symbols for zero. Thus, by placing a shell ◍ in the lowest position to denote 0 units of the first order and a dot • in the second position to denote 1 unit of the second order, the number 20 can be written (Fig. 24). The manner of writing other numbers is also shown in Figure 24, including two numbers written in the chronological count. The simplicity of Maya addition is also obvious in Figure 24: 10,951, the sum of the numbers in the two

---

[1] The head variant for the number 11 has not yet been surely identified.

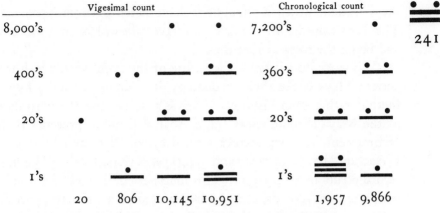

FIG. 24.—Examples of Maya positional mathematics.

preceding columns, is obtained simply by combining the dots and bars of 806 and 10,145 into a new figure.

MAYA CHRONOLOGY

STARTING POINT OF THE SYSTEM

Most peoples have eventually realized the necessity of having a fixed point from which their chronological records could be counted, but the ancient Maya may have been the first to reach this basic concept. The events selected by different peoples as starting points for their chronologies may be classified into two general groups: (1) those starting from specific historical events, and (2) those starting from hypothetical events.

The most familiar chronology of the first group is our own Christian Era, with its starting point at the birth of Christ. The Greeks reckoned time by four-year periods called Olympiads from the earliest Olympic Festival of which the winner's name was known, that of 776 B.C.

There are other chronologies which begin with an event whose nature makes the starting point hypothetical. Here may be included the chronologies which reckon time from a supposititious date of the creation of the world. The "Era of Constantinople," the chronological system used in the Greek Church, begins with the Creation, which is thought to have taken place in 5509 B.C. The Jews consider the Creation to have taken place in 3761 B.C. and begin their era at that time.

While we do not know the nature of the event with which the ancient Maya began their chronology, it is almost certainly hypothetical rather than historical. This is true because the zero date of the Maya chronological era, 4 Ahau 8 Cumhu, precedes their earliest contemporary records—the Leyden Plate and Stela 9 at Uaxactun—by 3,433 years and 3,440 years respectively. The first record occurs in 8.14.3.1.12. This long period, devoid of any contemporaneous records, may be interpreted as a priestly approximation rather than as a chronological era which had endured for three thousand years before its first records appear.

It has been suggested that the observations on which the Maya calendar was based began in 7.0.0.0.0, or 7.6.0.0.0 of the Maya Era—either 2,760 or 2,878 years after its zero date. From the absence of all early records we may conclude that the astronomer-priests who devised Maya chronology selected an arbitrary starting point 7 *baktuns* earlier than the date of actual inauguration. It may have commenced with a suppositious event like the creation of the world, or it may have been counted from the supposed date of the birth of the gods; the question is still undetermined.

THE INITIAL SERIES, OR LONG COUNT

The Initial Series method of dating was so named by the English archaeologist and explorer, A. P. Maudslay. The name of this time count derives from its position at the beginning of the inscription.

Ernst Förstemann, the German archaeologist, in 1887 first worked out the details of the Initial Series count as they are presented in the codices. J. T. Goodman, the American archaeologist, first deciphered this time count in 1890 from the inscriptions on the monuments, basing his work on Maudslay's reproductions of Maya sculptures. Goodman's discoveries are in perfect agreement with Förstemann's findings. The Maya Initial Series time count can now be read as clearly as our own calendar.

At the beginning of the Initial Series stands a large glyph, usually four times as large as the other glyphs in the inscription, which has been called the introducing glyph (Fig. 25). The only part of this large initial glyph which varies is the central element, of which there are nineteen different forms, one for each of the months of the civil year. This variable central element is probably the name glyph of the deity who presided over the month in which each date fell.

Maya inscriptions are read from left to right and top to bottom. Following this order, the first five glyphs are the number of *baktuns, katuns, tuns, uinals,* and *kins* which have elapsed from the starting point of Maya chronology.

The unit of the Maya Initial Series is the day and that of our chronology is the year, but the two systems are not unlike in their methods of recording. When we write the date Monday, December 31, A.D. 1956, we mean that 1 period of one thousand years, 9 periods of one hundred years, 5 periods of ten years, and 6 periods of one year have elapsed since the birth of Christ. When the ancient Maya wrote the Initial Series 9.17.0.0.0 13 Ahau 18 Cumhu (Fig. 25) they meant that 9 periods of 144,000 days (9 baktuns), 17 periods of 7,200 days (17 katuns), 0 periods of 360 days (0 tuns), 0 periods of 20 days (0 uinals), and 0 periods of 1 day (0 kins) had elapsed since the starting point of their chronology. The tzolkin designation of the terminal date, in this case 13 Ahau, is usually found in the sixth position after the introducing glyph, immediately following the last time period (the kins) of the Initial Series number (Fig. 25).

The glyph following the Initial Series terminal date, the one in the seventh position after the introducing glyph, is usually called Glyph G. It has nine forms, one corresponding to each of the *Bolontiku* or Nine Gods of the Lower World, and refers to the particular god who was patron of the day reached by the accompanying Initial Series number. In the Initial Series here described, this was the sun god, patron of the Ninth Day (Fig. 25). Following this glyph is another of unknown meaning, Glyph F. It is the last sign of the Initial Series, except for the month part of the terminal date, which follows the last glyph of the Supplementary Series.

THE SUPPLEMENTARY SERIES, OR MOON COUNT

Between Glyph F and the month glyph (the position of the day in the calendar year) of the Initial Series, there is usually a group of six glyphs which have been called the Supplementary Series. They give information (1) about the age of the moon on the date recorded; (2) the length of the lunar month in which the Initial Series date fell, here 29 days; (3) the number of the particular lunation in the lunar half-year period, here 2; and some other undetermined points.

By means of their simple but efficient numerical system, expressed in the Initial Series or Long Count, the ancient Maya were able to fix any date in their chronology so exactly that it could not recur before a cycle of 374,440 years had passed—a major achievement for any chronological system.

THE SECONDARY SERIES, OR CALENDAR-CORRECTION FORMULA

A third count in the Maya inscriptions is the Secondary Series, which seems to have been a calendar-correction formula, somewhat like our leap-year correction. From the outset the Maya civil year began to gain upon the true year, and since the Maya had no elastic month like our February, some other method had to be devised for keeping the calendar year of 365 days from running ahead of the true year of 365¼ days.

In addition to the dedicatory date of the monument, other dates are often included in the inscription. To express a single day by means of the Initial Series, ten different glyphs were necessary. This method of dating was accurate but cumbersome, and its repetition for every additional date in an inscription was superfluous. If one date in an inscription was fixed by means of its Initial Series, other dates could be calculated from it. Such derived dates have been called Secondary Series.

Grotesque head in center is the only variable element of this sign. This is the name glyph of the deity who is patron of the month (here Cumhu) in which the Initial Series terminal date falls

Initial Series

9 *baktuns* (9 × 144,000 days = 1,296,000 days)	17 *katuns* (17 × 7,200 days = 122,400 days)
0 *tuns* (0 × 360 days = 0 days)	0 *uinals* (0 × 20 days = 0 days)
0 *kins* (0 × 1 day = 0 days)	13 Ahau (day reached by counting forward above total of days from starting point of Maya Era)

Supplementary Series

Glyph G9 Name glyph of the deity who is patron of the Ninth Day in the nine-day series (The Nine Gods of the Lower World)	Glyph F Meaning unknown
Glyphs E and D Glyphs denoting the moon age of the Initial Series terminal date, here "new moon"	Glyph C Glyph denoting position of current lunar month in lunar half-year period, here the 2d position
Glyph X3 Meaning unknown	Glyph B Meaning unknown
Glyph A9 Current lunar month, here 29 days in length. Last glyph of the Supplementary Series	18 Cumhu (month reached by counting forward above total of days from starting point of Maya Era). Last glyph of the Initial Series

Fig. 25.—Examples of an Initial and a Supplementary Series: east side of Stela E, Quirigua.

The Secondary Series seem to have worked like this. Let us take the date 9.16.0.0.0 2 Ahau 13 Tzec of the Maya Era (A.D. 751, May 9). Counting from July 26 (Gregorian)—the Maya New Year's Day, o Pop—the month position 13 Tzec actually fell on October 27 in 751, 171 days later than the Maya calendar indicated. In order to correct this error, the following calendar-correction formula was applied—8 uinals and 11 kins, which was the Maya way of expressing 171 days. This period was then counted forward from 9.16.0.0.0 2 Ahau 13 Tzec to reach a new date 9.16.0.8.11 4 Chuen 4 Kankin (751, October 27). This was the position which 13 Tzec had originally occupied but which by 9.16.0.0.0 occurred 171 days earlier. By this date the position in the year originally represented by 13 Tzec (October 27) now fell on May 9. Without correction to the solar year, the Maya calendar would have been useless for agricultural purposes.

THE U KAHLAY KATUNOB, OR SHORT COUNT

By the middle of the Late Period of the Classic stage (731), Initial Series dating began to pass out of current use, and was replaced by an abbreviated system which modern students call "period-ending dating." In this method only a specific time period and the date upon which it ended are stated. In it the ten glyphs needed to express the Initial Series 9.16.0.0.0 2 Ahau 13 Tzec are reduced to three (Fig. 26). While not computed over such a long period as an Initial Series, a period-ending date was exact to a day within a cyclic period of nearly 19,000 years.

a   b   c

FIG. 26.—Period-ending date: Katun 16 ending on 2 Ahau 13 Tzec, corresponding to the Initial Series 9.16.0.0.0 2 Ahau 13 Tzec. (*a*) End of Katun 16; (*b*) 2 Ahau; (*c*) 13 Tzec.

By late Postclassic times the Maya chronological system suffered further abbreviation, and this time so sharply that accuracy
within a period of only 256 years could be achieved. This new
system was called the *u kahlay katunob* or "Count of the Katuns."
Maya students call it the "Short Count."

In our previous example, the Initial Series date 9.16.0.0.0
2 Ahau 13 Tzec, a katun ending of the Long Count, the day
upon which this katun ended was 2 Ahau. In the *u kahlay katunob*
everything was eliminated except this ending day; all other time
periods were suppressed. This particular katun was known simply
as Katun 2 Ahau.

This method of dating had the merit of requiring only one
glyph to express it—any given day Ahau—plus the understanding that this day ended some katun of the Long Count. Such abbreviated katun-ending dates were accurate only to within 256¼
years, which meant that any given katun ending recurred at such
an interval. If a Katun 2 Ahau ended in 751, another Katun 2 Ahau
would end in 1007, and another in 1263. There were only thirteen
differently designated katuns in this method of dating (1 Ahau,
2 Ahau, 3 Ahau, etc.), and since each katun was 19.71 years long,
a katun of any given designation would return after a lapse of
13 katuns, 13 × 19.71 years, or 256¼ years.

Each katun of the *u kahlay katunob* was named after its last
day, but the numbers did not follow each other in ascending numerical sequence. They assumed an order in which the number
of the day Ahau with which each successive katun ended was
two less than that of the last day of the preceding katun:
Katun 13 Ahau, Katun 11 Ahau, etc. This round of the katuns
was represented graphically by the ancient Maya as a wheel, the
periphery of which was divided into sections, one for each of the
13 differently numbered katuns.

Bishop Landa describes and illustrates one of these katun
wheels (Fig. 27):

Not only did the Indians have a count for the year and months, as has
been said and previously set out, but they also had a certain method of
counting time and their affairs by their ages, which they counted by twenty-

year periods, counting thirteen twenties, with one of the twenty signs of their months, which they call Ahau, not in order, but going backward as appears in the following circular design. In their language they call these [periods] katuns, with these they make a calculation of their ages that is marvelous; thus it was easy for the old man of whom I spoke in the first chapter [of Landa's original manuscript] to recall events that had taken place three hundred years before. Had I not known of these calculations, I should not have believed it possible to recall thus after such a period.

Fig. 27.—Katun wheel. After Bishop Landa.

The direction of movement is counterclockwise, in order that the katuns shall pass the cross at the top in the proper sequence—the days Ahau decreasing by two each. The words in the center of Landa's wheel read:

They call this count in their language *uazlazon katam* [more properly *uazaklom katun*] which means the round [or return] of the epochs [katuns].

The katun from which this round was counted seems to have been a Katun 8 Ahau. The repetition of the sequence began after each Katun 8 Ahau was completed, and these katuns were called the *uudz katunob*, or the katuns which are doubled back.

Each of the thirteen katuns had its patron deity, its prophecies, and its special ceremonies. A series of eleven katuns, part of a *u kahlay katunob*, are presented in the Codex Peresianus, beginning with a Katun 4 Ahau (perhaps A.D. 1224–44) and closing with a Katun 10 Ahau (perhaps 1421–41). One of the intermediate katuns, a Katun 7 Ahau (perhaps 1323–42) has been reproduced in part in Figure 16, page 213.

The *u kahlay katunob* or Short Count was a kind of historical synopsis presented in a succession of twenty-year periods, and so long as the sequences remained unbroken it was accurate enough for ordinary purposes. At the time of the Spanish Conquest, this record, if we can trust its ordering, stretched back through sixty-two katuns, to the beginning of Baktun 9 (A.D. 435), a period of eleven centuries.

THE THREE KNOWN MAYA HIEROGLYPHIC MANUSCRIPTS

Only three original pre-Columbian Maya codices or hiero-glyphic manuscripts have survived the fanaticism of the Spanish priesthood and the vicissitudes of time and weather. In central Mexico, more than four hundred native manuscripts have come down to us, about fifty being of pre-Columbian origin. But of the Maya native books only three have survived: the Codex Dres-densis, the Codex Tro-Cortesianus, and the Codex Peresianus.

Landa in speaking of the Maya codices says:

These people also made use of certain characters or letters, with which they wrote in their books their ancient affairs and their sciences, and with these and drawings and with certain signs in these drawings, they under-stood their affairs and made others understand them and taught them. We found a great number of books in these characters, and, as they contained nothing in which there was not to be seen superstition and lies of the devil, we burned them all, which they regretted to an amazing degree and caused them affliction.

The Maya codices were made of the bark of a tree called in Maya *copo* (*Ficus cotonifolia*), pounded into a pulp and held together with a natural gum as a bonding substance. Each was made in a long strip and folded like a screen. The Codices Tro-Cortesianus and Peresianus are the same size, the individual leaves being about 9¼ inches high and 5 inches wide. The Codex Dresdensis is a little smaller, its leaves being about 8 inches high by 3½ inches wide. A coating of fine white lime was applied to both sides of this bark paper strip, and on the smooth finish thus obtained columns of glyphs and pictures of gods and ceremonies were painted in several colors. The pages were divided into horizontal sections by red lines, and the order of reading was from left to right, always in the same horizontal section until the matter being treated was finished. These so-called "chapters" sometimes extended across eight consecutive folds. The codices were bound between decorated boards, and when completely opened they were quite long. The Codex Tro-Cortesianus is 23½ feet long and has 56 leaves, or 112 pages. The Codex Dresdensis is 11¾ feet long and has 39 leaves, or 78 pages, 4 of them blank. The Codex Peresianus, which is only a fragment, is 4¾ feet long and has 11 leaves or 22 pages.

Some of the Aztec, Mixtec, and Zapotec codices from central Mexico were made of deerskin, and others of cotton stuffs, but if these materials were ever used in Maya hieroglyphic manuscripts no examples of them have survived, nor does Landa mention them.

Unfortunately, none of the known Maya codices treats of history as such. The Codex Dresdensis is essentially a treatise on astronomy. The Codex Tro-Cortesianus is primarily a textbook of horoscopes to assist the priests in making their divinations. The fragmentary Codex Peresianus is basically ritualistic, one side being completely given over to a katun sequence and its patron deities and ceremonies. The Spanish and native writers of the sixteenth century agree that the Maya recorded their history in hieroglyphic manuscripts, but unfortunately none of the three known codices is of a historical nature.

None of the codices was found under archaeological conditions in the Maya area. The climate of the Yucatan Peninsula is so moist, and the mildew so destructive, that it is doubtful whether a codex could have survived had it been buried.

The Codex Dresdensis was found in Vienna in 1739, and was given to the Royal Library at Dresden; its earlier history is unknown. Since this manuscript was obtained in Vienna, and since Austria and Spain had a common sovereign at the time of the Conquest, it is possible that some Spanish priest or soldier sent this codex back to Spain. From Spain it possibly followed the emperor to Austria, where much of the Moctezuma treasure and the letter from Cortez to Charles V have been discovered. The Codex Dresdensis is now in the State Library at Dresden, Germany. A sample page has been shown in Figure 9, page 189.

The Codex Tro-Cortesianus, divided into two unequal sections, was discovered in Spain during the 'sixties of the last century. Although the sections were found in different places, students have proved that they are parts of the same manuscript. The larger section was owned by Señor Juan de Tro y Ortolano, of Madrid; the smaller section belonged to Señor José Ignacio Miró, who acquired it in Extremadura and called it the Codex Cortesianus, believing that it had been brought there by Cortez. Since Francisco de Montejo and many of his men came from Extremadura, Montejo himself or one of his soldiers may have brought the whole codex from Yucatan. Both sections, rejoined and called the Codex Tro-Cortesianus, are now in the Museum of Archaeology and History at Madrid; page 45 from this manuscript is shown in Figure 28.

The Codex Peresianus was found in the Bibliothèque Nationale at Paris in 1860, in a basket of old papers in a chimney corner, its existence apparently forgotten. It was wrapped in a piece of torn paper with the word "Perez" written on it, and because of this was named the Codex Peresianus. This manuscript is only a small part of the original codex, and is in much worse condition than the other two. The plaster coating around the margins of the pages has fallen off, taking with it all the pictures and glyphs except those

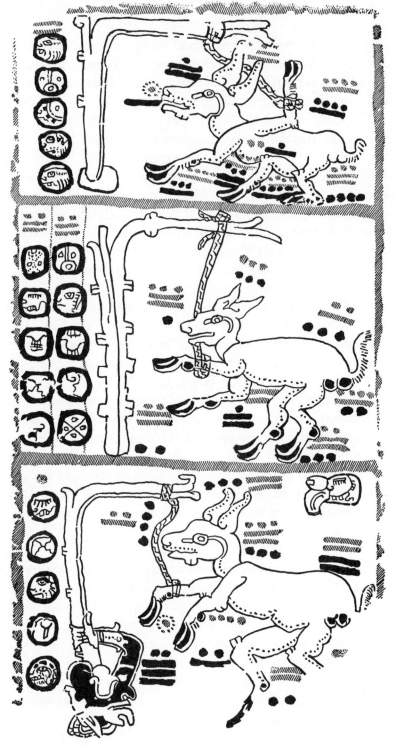

Fig. 28.—Design showing the snaring of a deer. Page 45, Codex Tro-Cortesianus.

in the middle of the pages (Fig. 29). The Codex Peresianus is still in the Bibliothèque Nationale.

It has been pointed out that the Maya year-bearers—the days on which the Maya New Years could begin—were, during the

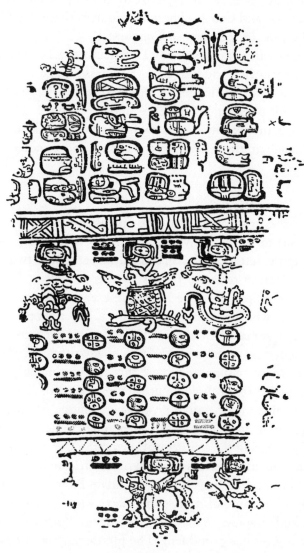

FIG. 29.—Three signs of the Maya zodiac (middle section): the scorpion, the turtle, and the rattlesnake. Page 24, Codex Peresianus.

Classic stage, days in which the names Ik, Manik, Eb, and Caban appeared. By the time of the Spanish Conquest more than twelve centuries later, two shifts forward had taken place in the year-bearers: first, a shift of one day to the set named Akbal, Lamat, Ben, and Eznab; later, a second shift of one day to the set named Kan, Muluc, Ix, and Cauac. These last four were the year-bearers in use at the time of the Spanish Conquest.

The year-bearers in the Codex Dresdensis are Ik, Manik, Eb, and Caban, following the usage of the Classic-stage monuments. There are no sure day names in the Codex Tro-Cortesianus, so this manuscript presents no evidence upon the point. The Codex Peresianus has the intermediate set of year-bearers Akbal, Lamat, Ben, and Eznab, midway between the Classic and Conquest-period series.

THE BOOKS OF CHILAM BALAM

One of the first concerns of the Spanish priesthood after the Conquest was to teach the Maya Indians to write their own language, using the letters of the Spanish alphabet. Only two symbols had to be added in order to render sounds present in Maya that were wanting in Spanish. The Portuguese *x* was used to represent the *sh* sound, which is common in Maya, for example, Uxmal, pronounced Ushmal. An inverted *c* (ɔ), now written *dz*, rendered the sound *dz* or *tz* as in Ah Ɔun, now written Ah Dzun.

The natives were supposed to use this new writing only for purposes of the Christian religion, but they managed to record in it a considerable amount of native prophecies, myths, rituals, current events, and, most important of all, chronological synopses of their own history. During the century following the Conquest a number of these native manuscripts were written in northern Yucatan. They have been called the "Books of Chilam Balam." *Chilam* (or *Chilan*) was the name of a class of priests who were soothsayers, prophets, and oracles. *Balam*, which means "jaguar," signifies something mysterious or hidden. The phrase may be freely translated "The book of the soothsayer of hidden things."

Originally there must have been many of these native manuscripts, but only a few have survived. They were distinguished one from another by the addition of the name of the town where each was written. Fragments of ten or twelve are known, of which the most important are the Books of Chilam Balam of Mani, Tizimin, Chumayel, Kaua, Ixil, Tusik, and the Codex Perez, which is a nineteenth-century compilation containing rescripts from others which are now lost.

Historically, the most significant sections of the Books of Chilam Balam are the *u kahlay katunob* or native chronicles, which set forth briefly the leading events of Maya history. There are five of these chronicles preserved in the Books of Chilam Balam—one in the Mani manuscript, one in the Tizimin manuscript, and three in the Chumayel manuscript. Of these, the Mani, the Tizimin, and the first Chumayel *u kahlay katunob* give the most accurate summaries of Postclassic history. There is in fact little doubt that the *u kahlay katunob* of the Books of Chilam Balam are literal translations of Maya historical codices, the originals of which are now lost.

THE POPOL VUH AND THE ANNALS OF THE CAKCHIQUELS

In the highlands of Guatemala, among the Quiche and Cakchiquel Maya, a similar body of native literature developed, written in the Quiche and Cakchiquel languages, using the letters of the Spanish script.

The Popol Vuh or "Book of the Quiche" is the most outstanding work of this nature among the southern Maya. It preserves fragments of the cosmogony, religion, mythology, migration traditions, and history of the Quiche, who were the most powerful Maya people of the southern highlands. The elegance of the language and the literary style of the Popol Vuh emphasize the loss we have suffered in the annihilation of Quiche learning by the Spanish Conquest.

The Annals of the Cakchiquels treats more of the history of that people and less of their cosmogony, mythology, and religion. It covers a longer time than the Popol Vuh of the Quiche, and describes events of the Conquest and the post-Conquest periods.

The Maya had a fixed calendar year of only 365 days with which to measure an astronomical phenomenon which, according to modern measurements, requires 365.2422 days to complete. The Maya priests realized the discrepancy between their calendar year and the true solar year and by means of the Secondary Series took care of the accumulated error. The calendar-correction formula worked out by the astronomer-priests at Copan in the sixth or seventh century was slightly more accurate than our Gregorian leap-year correction, which was not introduced until 1582, as the following tabulation will show:

Length of the year according to modern astronomy......365.2422 days
Length of our old, uncorrected Julian year...........365.2500 days
Length of our present, corrected Gregorian year........365.2425 days
Length of the year according to ancient Maya astronomy.365.2420 days

THE MOON

The Maya had also made advances in measuring the exact length of a lunation. According to the perfected observation of modern astronomers, this period is 29.53059+ days. Since Maya arithmetic had no fractions, how did the priests measure such a complex fraction as $\frac{53,059}{100,000}+$ of a day? The result was accomplished much as we keep our own calendar year in harmony with the true year by the leap-year correction. We have three years of 365 days each, followed by a fourth which is 366 days long. Centuries which are divisible by 400 are leap years; the others are not. Our process gives a slight overcorrection every four years, compensated for by a slight undercorrection once every century. This system of checks and balances keeps the calendar closely in harmony with the natural year.

At first, the Maya may have tried out a revolution of the moon composed of 30 days, but they soon saw that the actual new moons were falling short of this. Next, they allowed 29 days for a lunation, only to discover that the moons were exceeding 29 days in length. When this happened, they may next have tried alternating lunations of 29 and 30 days.

But even this correction failed them, although more slowly. Every two lunations of this kind gave an average lunation of 29.5 days, but the exact figure is 29.53059+ days. This kind of lunar calendar gained on the actual phenomenon at the rate of $\frac{3,059}{100,000}+$ of a day every lunation, an error which reached one entire day in every 2⅔ years. Finally, an accurate lunar calendar was developed by the age-old process of trial and error.

On pages 51 to 58 of the Codex Dresdensis, 405 consecutive lunations (about 32¾ years) are presented, arranged in 69 groups. These groups are usually composed of six lunations each, but occasionally have only five. In the 60 six-lunation groups, each totals either 178 days or 177 days, depending upon whether three or four 30-day months have been used, giving $30 + 29 + 30 + 29 + 30 + 30 = 178$ days, or $30 + 29 + 30 + 29 + 30 + 29 = 177$ days. Each of the 9 five-lunation groups totals 148 days, or $30 + 29 + 30 + 29 + 30 = 148$. These pages of the Codex Dresdensis are a solar eclipse table, since the closing days of each of these groups are days upon which, under certain conditions, a solar eclipse would be visible somewhere on the earth. The extra 30-day lunar months are so skillfully interpolated that nowhere throughout these 405 successive lunations does the discrepancy between the calendar placement and the actual appearance of new moons amount to one day.

ASTRONOMICAL OBSERVATORIES

It may be asked how the ancient Maya achieved such a high degree of astronomical accuracy without the instruments upon which modern astronomers depend. However, if the lines of sight are sufficiently long, accuracy to within less than a day's error may be achieved in fixing the synodical or apparent revolution, as opposed to sidereal or true revolution, of many of the heavenly bodies. Maya temples are sufficiently high to obtain clear lines of sight from their summits to distant points on the horizon. A pair of crossed sticks was set up inside the temple on top of a pyramid. From this as a fixed observation point, the place where the sun, moon, or planets rose or set was noted with reference to some natural feature on the horizon. When the heavenly body under observation rose or set behind this same point a second time, it had made one complete synodical revolution.

Although the three known Maya codices have no representations of observatories, pictures of them are found in the Mexican codices. Figure 30*a* shows an observatory from the Codex Bodley. In the doorway of a temple is a pair of crossed sticks, and looking out through them is the head of a man. In Figure 30*b*, also from the Codex Bodley, an eye appears in the notch made by a pair of crossed sticks in the temple doorway. Another picture in the Codex Bodley shows an eye between two crossed sticks, a star descending into a notch, and two observers (Fig. 30*c*); the projection at the left of the platform represents a pair of crossed human legs and a celestial eye. With such simple instruments as crossed sticks, the ancient Maya probably also predicted eclipses and the heliacal risings and settings of the Morning and Evening Stars.

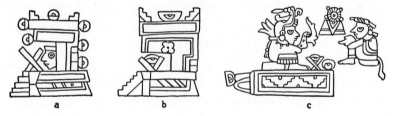

Fig. 30.—Representations of astronomical observatories in the Codex Bodley.

VENUS

Venus was one of the most important stars observed by the ancient Maya astronomers. There seem to have been at least two names for it: *Noh ek,* "the great star"; and *xux ek,* "the wasp star." Landa mentions Venus as the Morning Star but gives no specific name for it: "They used the Pleiades and Gemini as guides by night, so as to know the hour of the Morning Star."

The planet Venus makes one synodical revolution in almost exactly 583.920 days. The individual revolutions run in series of five—approximately 580, 587, 583, 583, and 587 days each, but any five consecutive revolutions average close to 583.920 days each. The Maya called this period 584 days, but they knew that this value was a little too high.

Venus in its synodical revolution divides into four periods: (1) after inferior conjunction it is Morning Star for roughly 240 days; (2) it then disappears for about 90 days during superior conjunction; (3) it reappears as Evening Star for another 240 days; (4) it disappears again for 14 days during inferior conjunction. The Maya astronomer-priests arbitrarily assigned slightly different values to these four phases of Venus, although the total number of days in one synodical revolution always remained 584 days. According to Maya astronomy, Venus was Morning Star for 236 days; invisible during superior conjunction for 90 days; Evening Star for 250 days; and invisible during inferior conjunction for 8 days—making a total of 584 days. It has been suggested that the lengths of these four Venus phases were arbitrarily fixed to agree with lunations.

Ascribing 584 days to one synodical revolution of Venus made it a little too long. The Maya priests were aware of this error of 8/100 of a day every 584 days and knew how to correct it. One of their important ceremonial periods was a time unit composed of 5 synodical revolutions of Venus ($5 \times 584 = 2,920$ days). They also had discovered that this period was equal to 8 of their calendar years ($8 \times 365 = 2,920$ days), a coincidence which was useful to them. It combined 8 solar years with 5 Venus years and supplied a convenient period for correcting the Venus calendar, which was falling behind the apparent Venus year at the rate of 2/5 of a day every 8 calendar years.

As presented in the Codex Dresdensis, the Venus calendar is really three distinct calendars, each composed of 65 synodical revolutions of the planet. Each Venus calendar is equal to 104 calendar years, but there is an overlap between the first and second, and another overlap between the second and third. The corrections were inserted at these points, at which the calendar Venus-year of 584 days overran the synodical Venus-year. By the end of the 57th Venus-solar period of this first calendar, the accumulated error had reached 8 days. By dropping back 8 days from this date, the zero date of the second calendar is reached. At the end of the 61st Venus-solar period of the second calendar, an error of 4 days had accumulated, and by dropping back 4 days from this point in the second calendar, the zero date of the third calendar is reached. By the use of this table the Venus-solar period was kept in harmony with the movements of the planet for 384 years before the accumulated error began to render the table useless.

OTHER STARS AND CONSTELLATIONS

The Pleiades were called *tzab*, the Maya word for the rattles of a rattlesnake, perhaps because of their fancied resemblance. Gemini was called *ac*, "the tortoise."

It has been suggested that the ancient Maya may have had their own zodiac, composed of thirteen houses, and that this Maya zodiac may be represented on pages 23 and 24 of the Codex Peresianus. If so, the first three signs, or houses, seem to have been Scorpion, Tortoise, and Rattlesnake. These are the first three figures shown hanging from a constellation band in the middle section of page 24 (Fig. 29).

The North Star was also of great importance. Its apparent immobility and the orderly procession of the other constellations around it made it a dependable beacon.

ARCHITECTURE

NATURE OF THE MAYA CITIES AND POPULATION

THERE IS NO evidence thus far that the archaeological sites of the Classic stage are the ruins of cities and towns; there is on the other hand much evidence that they were religious centers to which the Maya resorted only for ceremonies. The Maya seem to have lived in small groups probably only of family size, in thatched huts scattered over the countryside.

By the time the first Spaniards visited the Yucatecan Maya this situation had changed. Landa, in describing a sixteenth-century Maya town, says:

Before the Spaniards had conquered that country [Yucatan] the natives lived together in towns in a very civilized fashion. They kept the land well cleared and free from weeds, and planted very good trees. Their dwelling-place was as follows—in the middle of the town were their temples with beautiful plazas, and all around the temples stood the houses of the lords and priests and then [those of] the most important people. Thus came the houses of the richest, and of those who were held in the highest estimation nearest to these, and at the outskirts of the town were the houses of the lowest class.

The striking change from a dispersed living pattern to one of concentrated town settlement took place, with little question, after the Toltecs came into Yucatan, and is described in chapter v.

Our best information on the living patterns of the Classic-stage Maya comes from the study of the domestic settlements near Uaxactun, which was carried out as follows: A large cross was laid out on the ground with its center at the main group of ruins, each arm being 400 yards wide and 1 mile long from the central point to its end. Each arm was divided into 68 squares, 100 yards to a side;

261

each square contained 10,000 square yards, making a total of 272 squares for the four arms of the cross, or 2,720,000 square yards. It was thought that these squares would give a fair sample of the land in the immediate vicinity of the ceremonial and governmental center. Each square was examined carefully for traces of artificial construction, especially for vestiges of house sites, which would appear only as low mounds a foot or two above the ground level. The houses themselves, built of thatch and sapling, would have disappeared within a decade after the city was abandoned.

The survey showed that 43 per cent of the area examined was composed of logwood swamps or other uninhabitable terrain, leaving 57 per cent available for human occupation. Of this area, 400,000 square yards (14.7 per cent) were occupied by Groups A and E, the largest of the eight plaza-complexes at Uaxactun. This left a remainder of 1,140,000 square yards (114 squares) or about 42.3 per cent of the total area examined for domestic housing. These 114 squares contained 52 house mounds and 50 water reservoirs (*chultuns*), though no specific relationship between their locations could be ascertained.

Since the known occupation of Uaxactun lasted over a thousand years it seems likely that only a fraction of the house locations were occupied at one time. Although the normal Maya thatch house does not last more than about thirty years it is also probable that house mounds are often the result of several rebuildings of a house. Assuming occupancy of one out of eight houses, with five persons per house, gives a density of 136 persons per square mile. This density should be further lowered if it is taken into account that the normal Maya homestead consists of two or more houses and that about one-third of the house mounds near Uaxactun were in groups.

It is impossible to say how large an area was served by the religious and governmental center at Uaxactun, but it must be remembered that Tikal, the largest known Classic Maya center, is only ten miles away. This argues for a restricted drawing area for Uaxactun as well as an unusual density of population in the Uaxactun-Tikal region.

The problem of the population of the Maya lowland area may be attacked from an entirely different approach, that of the carrying capacity of the land. The modern state of Yucatan has an average population density of about 30 persons per square mile. Statistics over a recent ten-year period show that although a considerable percentage of the land is now planted to henequen, an export crop, the imports of corn amount to only about 2 per cent of the total required to sustain the native population, for whom this is still the chief staple.

If we accept a figure of 30 persons per square mile as the average carrying capacity over the whole lowland area—even with a possible error to half or double that density—we are faced with an amazing disparity between this area and a highland area such as the Valley of Mexico, where population density at the time of the Spanish Conquest is with some reliability estimated at about 500 per square mile. Theories that cultural advancement is proportional to population density are popular among present-day archaeologists, but do not easily explain the pre-eminence of the Classic Maya among New World cultures.

A comparison of the amount and quality of human labor required to build religious centers is useful as a check against the archaeological and agricultural approaches given above.

The Pyramid of the Sun, which is the largest structure in the Valley of Mexico and the second largest in Mesoamerica, contains about a million cubic meters of earth. It is estimated that the spare-time labor available from a population of 10,000 working over a twenty-year period would allow the amassing of this huge temple substructure. Such manpower could probably have been recruited within easy walking distance of Teotihuacan because of the dense population possible in the valley.

The largest of the Maya pyramids ranges little over 50,000 cubic meters in volume. This is a twentieth of the Pyramid of the Sun, a proportion surprisingly (perhaps even coincidentally) close to our population density estimates for the two areas (500 compared to 30). It thus seems clear that at our density estimates there were enough Maya to build the religious centers even taking into account the extra labor necessary to gather wood for limekilns and to carve the great amount of carefully cut masonry and elaborate sculpture characteristic of Maya buildings.

The kind of labor required to raise the Maya temples suggests an insight into the characteristics rather than the density of the Maya population. Without question the Maya labor force included a large percentage of skilled artisans, woodsmen, lime burners, masons, architects, and sculptors, in comparison with the relatively small proportion of skilled labor required to raise such a huge but simply formed mass as the Pyramid of the Sun.

The Puuc area in the state of Yucatan is a particularly rewarding area for population study because of the limited water supply. Pottery samples from the four largest sites of the area—Uxmal, Kabah, Labna, and Sayil—show that these ceremonial centers, in marked contrast to some 15 other sites sampled in Yucatan, had an occupational span limited to only about 250 years at the end of the Classic stage. A sudden influx of population into the Puuc area seems to have depended upon the development of a technique to store drinking water.

Although in the northern Yucatan plain the water table is high enough so that water can be easily obtained throughout the year from natural cenotes or from shallow wells which the Maya dug, the Puuc area contains almost no water sources during the six-month dry season. Water is hauled at times to this area to supply even the sparse modern population of about 5 persons per square mile. Yearly rainfall is, however, well above that of the northern plain and the area has a reputation for agricultural fertility.

The Puuc area is notable for the occurrence of *chultunes,* Maya cisterns carved into the limestone bedrock or built into the stone fill of the plazas of the ceremonial centers. Chultunes are usually hemispheroid, with a flat bottom and a hole about 40 centimeters in diameter at the top. They show signs of an interior coat of plaster, and invariably underlie the remains of a plastered floor, so sloped as to drain into the cistern. The chultun mouth often is covered by a carefully beveled stone lid set flush with the floor surface, presumably to eliminate the danger of falling in. The chultunes are found in major numbers under the plazas of ceremonial centers, and are also characteristic of the small domestic sites which dot the area, but are not found on the Yucatan plain to the north. The size of chultunes is quite constant, with an average capacity of about 7,500 gallons. According to computations based on monthly rainfall figures for the Puuc, and upon the water consumption of individuals in this area, a chultun could have comfortably supplied about 25 people with drinking and cooking water the year around, and the chultunes in one of the larger centers could have supplied between 2,000 and 6,000 people permanently. A single chultun would thus have furnished sufficient water for an extended family if settled in a residential site—and the sites observed are of a size which makes occupation by such a group likely.

The four major Puuc ceremonial centers — Uxmal, Kabah, Sayil, and Labna—form a chain about 20 miles long. If it be assumed that they were used for periodic worship by the population within a 10-mile radius, they must have served an area of about 750 square miles, or 22,500 people, if population be computed at 30 per square mile. This figure corresponds neatly to the water utilization figures given above. The samples of pottery from these ceremonial centers came from the ground along the bases of plazas, where it had accumulated when discarded from above. It included cooking pots, but little evidence of any but domestic pottery. Without doubt it came from Maya families picnicking on the ceremonial plazas, gathered for religious and perhaps other community functions.

The various lines of evidence seem to check each other, and to form a picture of a relatively light and surprisingly dispersed population. This sort of a population patterning is extremely unusual if not unique among known high cultures. The economic inducements and compulsion which could readily be applied by the rulers of concentrated urban settlements to obtain the co-operation of the people for community work are not readily applicable in this situation; in fact the Maya show a long history of non-cooperation in governmental projects since the Spanish Conquest.

During the nineteenth-century War of the Castes, the Maya farmers simply moved into the southern jungle areas when military control was attempted. The strong priestly control of Classic times which resulted in the magnificent Puuc centers must have been of a noneconomic nature. The remarkably rich and closely integrated Maya religion must have provided the impetus for the great amount of voluntary labor required.

The Classic-stage Maya settlement pattern differs markedly from the modern Yucatecan living patterns described by Redfield and his associates. It is hard to reconstruct a folk-urban continuum among a people who lived in the country, but spent many days per year worshiping in the "city." The great strength of Classic-stage Maya society is well documented in the surprisingly uniform and elaborate religious architecture, iconography, calendrics, and art, over an area which dwarfs other New World archaeological regions in size. However, the weakness which permitted Maya Classic culture to disintegrate in the central area, and to fall ready prey to what must have been a relatively small number of Toltec invaders in the north, must still be sought in the system itself rather than in outside influences.

The effects of Mexican mainland influence on the way of life of the Postclassic Yucatecans were obviously great. The Puuc area was abandoned, seemingly at the height of its cultural development. The cataclysmic nature of this event is obvious if it be remembered that this area shows the largest, most concentrated, and most elaborate mass of architecture of pre-Columbian America. A tremendous burst of religious construction at Chichen Itza followed the Puuc abandonment. It is likely that the Puuc was vacated under some compulsion such as the destruction of the chultunes, which, as we know archaeologically, ceased to be built at this time.

There are no known Postclassic sites south of the Yucatan plain. The two major sites, Chichen Itza and Mayapan, are in areas notable for concentration of cenotes of such size as to guarantee water for a large and concentrated population. At Chichen Itza there is no evidence that the settlement pattern is different from that of the

Puuc sites; the people seem to have remained scattered in residence, coming to the religious center at intervals for ceremonies.

At Mayapan, however, a striking and very significant change can be seen. The recent Carnegie Institution program has shown that the site was a genuine city rather than a religious center. A stone wall designed for defense encloses an area of 1.4 square miles. Within this area are a major religious precinct and some 2,100 definitely identified house ruins, a concentration of many times the density of that around Uaxactun. Mayapan unquestionably consisted of people who were near neighbors, as the classic Maya never had been. Religious ceremonies had ceased to be their only occasion for gathering in groups.

The change from Maya living patterns to Mexican was not, however, complete. The Toltec towns were built of contiguous walled houses, separated only by courts and irregular passages, while at Mayapan the country homestead seems to have survived, adapted to the narrowing confines of city life much like the houses of retired farmers in a small American town. Each Mayapan house, or group of two or three houses, stands in a yard surrounded by a low dry-stone wall. Landa seems to describe such homesteads in sixteenth-century Yucatan:

. . . and they had their improved lands planted with wine trees and they sowed cotton, pepper and maize, and they lived thus close together for fear of their enemies, who took them captive, and it was owing to the wars of the Spaniards that they scattered to the woods.

The walled yard is still a regular feature of Maya town life, a source of vegetables, fruit, and honey, and a further evidence of the strength of tradition among the Maya.

CLASSIFICATION OF THE CENTERS OF POPULATION

The basic criteria in classifying the Maya religious centers according to their relative importance would seem to be: (1) their respective areas; (2) the number and extent of the architectural remains; and (3) the number and excellence of their sculptured monuments. Even such obvious standards of comparison, however, are open to serious objections and lead to conflicting results. Some sites are outstanding because of the size, number, and decoration of their buildings, but they have few sculptured monuments. Others have relatively insignificant architectural remains, but numerous and notable sculptured monuments. Moreover, we do not know what sites were distinguished by the excellence of their ceramic wares, jade carving, featherwork, and weaving, though these crafts were highly esteemed by the ancient Maya. For the purposes of a rough classification, however, we will use the three criteria given here.

A classification into four groups has been made in Table VII, and is shown in Plate 19, where the first-, second-, third-, and fourth-class centers are represented by different symbols.

Before describing some of the important centers, a further word of explanation about Table VII is necessary. All except eleven of the sites listed in this table have this point in common: regardless of their sizes, they all have one or more hieroglyphic inscriptions. The exceptions are Holmul, in the central region, and Mani, T'ho, Izamal, Sotuta, El Tabasqueño, Chunchintok, Hochob, Ppustunich, Civiltuk, and Acanceh in the northern region.

Although there are only four Class 1 sites listed in Table VII (Tikal, Copan, Chichen Itza, and Uxmal), there are two others—Calakmul in the central Peten region and Coba in northeastern Yucatan—which perhaps should also be included in Class 1. Calakmul has more monuments (103) than any other city of the Maya civilization, and Coba has extensive architectural remains, as well as numerous sculptured stelae (24). Both sites, however, have been assigned to Class 2. In spite of the mass production of monuments at Calakmul, the individual sculptured stelae are for the most part of little esthetic merit; although there are many buildings at Coba, its twenty-four sculptured stelae are mediocre in character, and not to be compared with, for example, the monuments at Copan.

Of the nineteen centers listed in Class 2, twelve are in the heart of the Peten; one (Tonina) is in the southwestern highlands; one

TABLE VII

269

Classification of the Centers of the Maya Civilization According to Their Supposed Degrees of Relative Importance in Ancient Times

Class 1	Class 2	Class 3	Class 4	
Tikal	Calakmul	Balakbal	Uolantun	Bonampak
Copan	Coba	Xmakabatun	Kaxuinic	El Amparo
Chichen	Uaxactun	Chochkitam	El Encanto	Quexil
Itza	Xultun	Ucanal	Ixkun	Jonuta
Uxmal	La Honradez	Tzimin Kax	Yaltitud	Tila
	Nakum	Seibal	Benque Viejo	Comitan
	Naranjo	Altar de	Chunhuitz	Tenam
	Yaxchilan	Sacrificios	Cancuen	Quen Santo
	Piedras	Itsimte	Aguas Calientes	Ichpaatun
	Negras	Polol	El Caribe	Santa Rita
	Naachtun	Tayasal	La Amelia	Corosal
	Quirigua	Yaxha	Laguna Perdida	Dzilam
	El Palmar	Lubaantun	Motul de San	Jaina
	Rio Bec	Pusilha	José	Ichmul
	Palenque	Tzibanche	Ixlu	Tabi I
	Tonina	Uxul	San Clemente	Dzibilnocac
	Kabah	Becan	La Florida	Cave of Loltun
	Sayil	Oxpemul	Rio Amarillo	Ikil
	Etzna	Xamantun	Los Higos	Pechal
	Santa Rosa	Alta Mira	Oxlahuntun	Pasión del
	Xtampak	Comalcalco	Tzendales	Cristo
		Chuctiepa	Lacanha	El Tabasqueño
		Chinkultic	El Cayo	Chunchintok
		Tulum	La Mar	Hochob
		Labna	Chinikiha	Ppustunich
		Mayapan	El Tortuguero	Civiltuk
		Oxkintok	Santo Ton	Acanceh
		Keuic	Santa Elena	Dzibilchaltun
		Holactun	Poco Uinic	Chama
		Xculoc		
		Huntichmul I		
		Nohpat		
		Tzocchen		
		La Milpa		
		Holmul		
		Yaxuna		
		Mani		
		T'ho		
		Izamal		
		Sotuta		
4 sites	19 sites	39 sites	54 sites	

(Rio Bec) is in the Chenes area of central Campeche; and five are in northern Yucatan.

The chief difficulty in making the classification shown in Table VII was to distinguish between small Class 2 and large Class 3 sites. The question may well be raised whether it would not be better to group all Class 2 and Class 3 sites together, and have only three classes. The principal objection to such a procedure is that it involves grouping together sites of such widely differing importance as Yaxchilan, Piedras Negras, and Palenque on the one hand, and Chochkitam, Becan, and Tzocchen on the other. Rather than include such important cities as the first three in the same group with such relatively unimportant ones as the last three, it seems much better to hold to the original fourfold classification.

One point should be borne in mind concerning the Class 4 sites: in assigning sites to this class, neither their areas nor the size and number of their architectural remains have been taken into consideration. Assignments to this class have been made solely upon the basis of their having hieroglyphic inscriptions, though not more than four or five each.

DESCRIPTIONS OF THE MORE IMPORTANT MAYA SITES

Unfortunately the ancient names of the majority of the cities of the central area have been lost, with the possible exception of Copan. This site was called Copan as early as the sixteenth century, when the Spaniards first reached the region, but it had long since been abandoned and there are grave doubts as to whether this was its original name. As to the names of the other Classic-stage centers, probably not one antedates the close of the eighteenth century. Many of them have been named by modern archaeologists during the last fifty years.

The situation is only slightly better for the northern area. We know the original names of about half a dozen sites from the Books of Chilam Balam—Chichen Itza, Chakanputun, Uxmal, Mayapan, Izamal, Coba, and T'ho (the modern Mérida)—but the ancient names of many others have long since been forgotten.

The largest and probably the oldest center of the Maya civilization was Tikal in northern central Peten (Plate 31a). The temple and governmental precincts cover almost a square mile, but beyond this there are smaller plazas, surrounded by ruined buildings, which extend outward with decreasing frequency for two or three miles. Tikal may be divided into nine groups, A–I, of which the most important is Group A (Plate 32). This group is built on an artificially leveled tongue of land between two ravines. It is connected by a graded stone causeway with Group G to the southeast, and by a longer causeway crossing the north ravine with Groups E and H to the north; Groups D and H are connected directly by a third causeway. Group I, not included on the map, lies southeast of Group G, to which it is connected by a causeway.

The outstanding architectural characteristic of Tikal is its six great pyramid-temples, the highest constructions in the Maya area (Plate 31a). From the ground level to the tops of their roof combs, the temples measure as follows: Temple I, 155 feet; Temple II, 143 feet; Temple III, 178 feet; Temple IV, 229 feet (see Plates 52b and 70b); and Temple V, 188 feet.

These enormous constructions are also noteworthy for their fine wood carvings. The twelve doorways in these temples were originally spanned by lintels of sapodilla wood, eight of them carved with magnificent representations of religious ceremonies. Most of these have either been destroyed or removed to foreign museums; the finest is now in the Museum of Archaeology at Basle, Switzerland (Plate 33a). Figure 31 shows part of another lintel; the figure of a halach uinic is seated on his throne, while rising behind him is the figure of a jaguar.

While the architecture of Tikal is imposing, stone sculpture is undistinguished except for that of the Early Period (317–593). Of the eighty-six stelae known at Tikal, only twenty-one are sculptured. It has been suggested that the unsculptured stelae were originally covered with plaster and painted with figures and hieroglyphs, but proof is lacking. Of the twenty-one sculptured stelae at Tikal, all but five date from the Early Period.

↑ *a*) Tikal, Guatemala.

↑ *b*) Copan, Honduras.

↑ *c*) Quirigua, Guatemala.

PLATE 31.—PAINTINGS OF CITIES OF THE CLASSIC STAGE BY CARLOS VIERRA

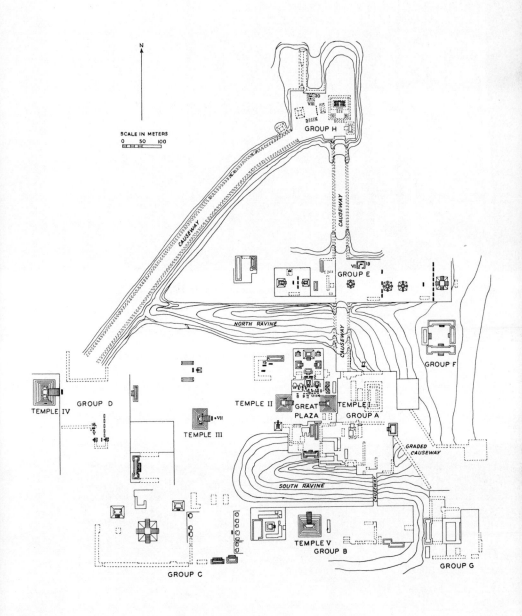

PLATE 32.—Map of the Central Section of Tikal

↑ *a*) Wooden lintel, Temple IV, Tikal.

PLATE 33.—SCULPTURES OF THE CLASSIC STAGE

↓ *b*) Sanctuary tablet, Temple of the Cross, Palenque.

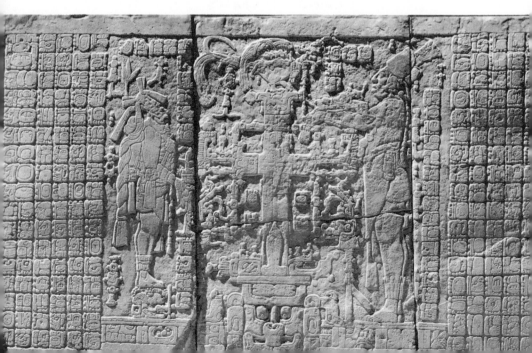

Fig. 31.—Part of a wooden door lintel from Temple IV, Tikal, Peten, Guatemala. Now in the British Museum, London.

The second largest center in the southern half of the peninsula was Copan, the scientific center of the Classic stage. This city consists of a main group and sixteen dependent subgroups, one seven miles distant from the ceremonial center. The Main Structure (Plates 31*b*, 34, and 37*a*) covers about seventy-five acres and is composed of the Acropolis and five adjoining plazas. The Acropolis is an architectural complex of pyramids, terraces, and temples, which by reason of constant additions has grown into one great masonry mass. It covers twelve acres of ground and rises 125 feet at its highest point. It supports the three finest temples in the city: Temple 26, dedicated in 756 on completion of the Hieroglyphic Stairway; Temple 11, also erected in 756 in memory of an important astronomical discovery made at Copan (the determination of the exact length of the intervals between eclipses); and Temple 22, dedicated in 771 to the planet Venus.

There are five courts or plazas at the Main Structure: (1) the Main Plaza, (2) the Middle Court, (3) the Court of the Hieroglyphic Stairway, and, on the Acropolis, (4) the Eastern Court, and (5) the Western Court. The Main Plaza, 250 feet square and surrounded on three sides by tiers of stone seats, has a pyramid at the center of the fourth side. There are nine sculptured monuments in this court alone, and a number of elaborately carved altars.

The Court of the Hieroglyphic Stairway is 310 feet long by 125 feet wide; at one end, just behind Stela M and its altar, rises the Hieroglyphic Stairway, 33 feet wide and composed of 62 steps. The faces of these steps are sculptured with 1,500 to 2,000 individual glyphs, the longest inscription in Maya hieroglyphic writing (Plate 35*c*). At the middle point of every twelfth step there is a large seated anthropomorphic statue. This monumental sculptured stairway leads to Temple 26.

Both the East and West Courts on the Acropolis proper have floor levels considerably above the general ground level. The East Court has the beautiful Jaguar Stairway (Plate 35*a*) on its western side, flanked by figures of rampant jaguars; their bodies were originally incrusted with disks of polished black obsidian to simulate the

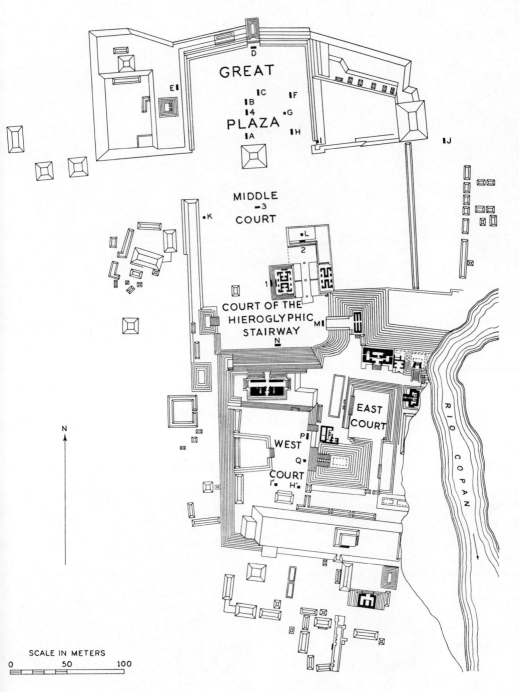

GREAT

PLAZA

MIDDLE
COURT

COURT OF THE
HIEROGLYPHIC
STAIRWAY

EAST
COURT

WEST
COURT

RIO COPAN

N

SCALE IN METERS

0   50   100

PLATE 34.—MAP OF THE CENTRAL SECTION OF COPAN

↑ *a*) Jaguar Stairway, East Court, the Acropolis.

PLATE 35.—VIEWS OF COPAN

↓ *b*) Figure from the Jaguar Stairway.   ↓ *c*) Hieroglyphic Stairway, Temple 26.

spots of a jaguar (Plate 35*b*). The West Court has a fine Reviewing Stand, Stela P—the latest monument of the Early Period
(Plate 67*d*)—and several handsome altars.

One of the most interesting archaeological features at Copan
is the cross-section of the Acropolis exposed by the Copan River
(Plate 36). Since the city was abandoned in the early ninth century, the Copan River has changed its course and has cut away a
great portion of the eastern base of the Acropolis, exposing a vertical face 118 feet high at the highest point and nearly 1,000 feet
long at the base. This is the largest archaeological cross-section in
the world, and a number of earlier plaza floor-levels can be clearly
distinguished in it.

The Carnegie Institution of Washington has been working at
Copan in co-operation with the government of Honduras since
1935. The course of the Copan River has been changed to its
original channel so that the Acropolis is no longer threatened with
destruction (Plate 37*a*). More than a dozen fallen and broken
monuments have been repaired and re-erected (Plate 68), much
enhancing the appearance of this group of ruins. Temples 11, 21*a*,
22, 26, and the Ball Court (Structures 9 and 10) have been excavated and repaired, and several tunnels have been driven through
the Acropolis in order to find whether it contained earlier constructions.

One of the most significant discoveries at Copan was the finding
of two small fragments of gold, the feet of a hollow figurine, in
the foundation of Stela H dedicated in 782. These are the only
pieces of metal ever recovered from a Classic-stage site (Fig. 55*c*).

There is evidence that Copan was a great center of learning in
the Classic stage, especially in the field of astronomy; the formulas
of the astronomer-priests for determination of the true length of
the solar year and of the eclipse periods were more accurate than
those of any other center.

CHICHEN ITZA

The greatest Postclassic metropolis and sacred city was Chichen
Itza in northeastern Yucatan. The city reached its zenith in the

PLATE 36.—SECTION OF THE ACROPOLIS AT COPAN, EXPOSED
BY THE COPAN RIVER

↑ *a*) Copan.

PLATE 37.—AIR VIEWS OF CLASSIC-STAGE SITES

↓ *b*) Coba, Quintana Roo.

↑ *a*) Chichen Itza.

PLATE 38.—AIR VIEWS OF YUCATECAN SITES

↓ *b*) Uxmal.

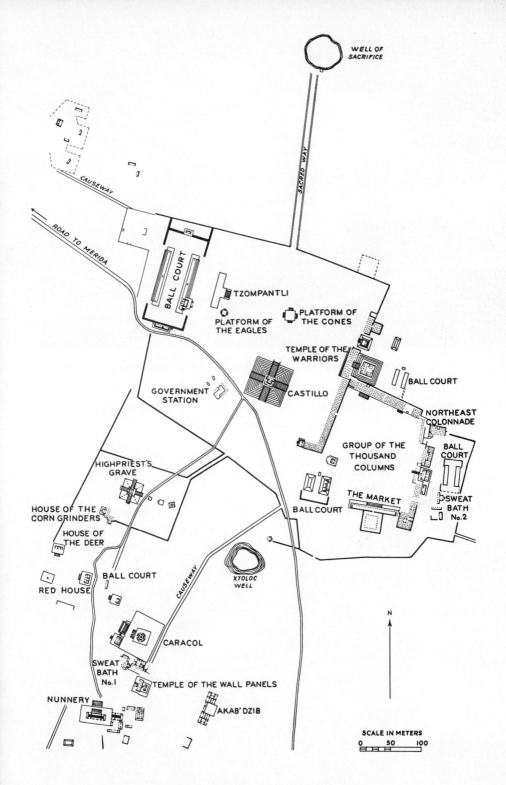

WELL OF
SACRIFICE

SACRED WAY

CAUSEWAY

ROAD TO MERIDA

BALL COURT

TZOMPANTLI

PLATFORM OF
THE EAGLES

PLATFORM OF
THE CONES

TEMPLE OF THE
WARRIORS

GOVERNMENT
STATION

CASTILLO

BALL COURT

NORTHEAST
COLONNADE

HIGHPRIEST'S
GRAVE

GROUP OF THE
THOUSAND
COLUMNS

BALL
COURT

HOUSE OF THE
CORN GRINDERS

THE MARKET

SWEAT
BATH
No.2

HOUSE OF
THE DEER

BALL COURT

BALL COURT

RED HOUSE

XTOLOC
WELL

CAUSEWAY

N

CARACOL

SWEAT
BATH
No.1

TEMPLE OF THE WALL PANELS

NUNNERY

AKAB'DZIB

SCALE IN METERS
0   50   100

PLATE 39.—MAP OF THE CENTRAL SECTION OF CHICHEN ITZA

↑ *a*) Temple of the Warriors, showing Northwest Colonnade in foreground.

PLATE 40.—VIEWS OF CHICHEN ITZA

↓ *b*) Temple of the Warriors, showing feathered-serpent columns.

eleventh and twelfth centuries under Mexican rulers who had established themselves there in the tenth century (Plate 45*b*). The civic and religious precincts cover an area nearly two miles long by a mile wide. While extending over a greater area than Tikal, the groups at Chichen Itza are less numerous, smaller, and more scattered (Plates 38*a*, 39, and 45*b*).

The architecture shows two distinct styles: (1) a Maya period, the buildings of which date from the eighth to tenth centuries, and (2) a Toltec period, the buildings of which date from the eleventh and twelfth centuries and show many architectural features imported from central Mexico.

One of the striking architectural features at Chichen Itza are the pyramid-temples with feathered-serpent columns. Seven of these pyramids are known, of which the Castillo, or principal Temple of Kukulcan, is the largest and possibly the oldest (Plate 44*a*). One, the Temple of the Chac Mool, is buried in the pyramid supporting the later Temple of the Warriors. These serpent-column temples were dedicated to Kukulcan, the Feathered Serpent, who was the patron deity of Chichen Itza. The style seems to have been an importation from central Mexico during the tenth century (Plates 40*b* and 41*b*).

There are seven ball courts known at Chichen Itza: six that were still in use when the city was last occupied, and an earlier one buried under a later terrace behind the Monjas. The ball courts vary in size; the largest, which is in the northern part of the city, is 545 feet long by 225 feet wide on the outside, while the actual field of play is 480 feet long by 120 feet wide (Plate 41*a*); the smallest court behind the Red House is only 65 feet long and 20 feet wide. A stone ring was usually set into the middle of each long facing wall, and the object of the game was to drive the ball through one of the rings, the openings of which were perpendicular to the ground. The balls were solid rubber, and the description of them given by the early Spanish historians marks the first European notice of rubber. The ball could not be thrown by the hand but had to be struck by the elbow, wrist, or hip, and leather pads were fastened to these parts of the body. The winning stroke was made so rarely that, by an ancient rule of the game, the player making it had forfeited to him all the clothing and jewelry of the spectators. When the ball was thus driven through the ring, all the spectators took to their heels to avoid paying the forfeit, and the friends of the lucky player ran after them to exact it.

Another distinctive feature at Chichen Itza is the use of great colonnades, some of them 400 feet long (Plates 40a and 61b). Thrones have been found in them, and it has been suggested that they were used as council halls. Colonnades completely surround the Court of the Thousand Columns, a great open plaza of four and a half acres, which may have been the market place of the ancient city. There are so many colonnades in this part of Chichen Itza that it has been called the Group of the Thousand Columns.

One of the most important structures is an astronomical observatory (Plate 42a). This round tower, called the Caracol, is 41 feet high and surmounts a rectangular terrace 31 feet high. The tower has a central core of masonry in which a spiral staircase winds up to a small observation chamber near the top of the building. The Spanish name for such a stairway is *caracol*, because of its fancied resemblance to the convolutions of a snail shell. The square openings through the thick walls of the chamber (Fig. 32) fix certain astronomically important lines of sight. For example, one line of sight through the west wall bisects the setting sun on March 21, the vernal equinox; other lines coincide with the moonset on this same date. The observation room near the top is still partially preserved.

Chichen Itza is probably better known than any other city of the Maya civilization because of the extensive excavations and restorations carried on there by the Ministry of Public Education of the Mexican government and by the Carnegie Institution of Washington since 1924. Quite a large number of buildings have been excavated and repaired, wall paintings and sculptures have been uncovered, and many archaeological specimens brought to light. Among the more spectacular discoveries were a handsome turquoise mosaic plaque (Plate 43a) and the Red Jaguar throne, a life-sized statue of a jaguar, painted a brilliant red and studded with seventy-three disks of jade in imitation of the markings of the jaguar (Plate 73c). The mosaic plaque, found in a covered stone urn, was excavated from beneath the floor of the Temple of the Chac Mool and the Red Jaguar throne was discovered in the temple buried beneath the Castillo (Plate 44a).

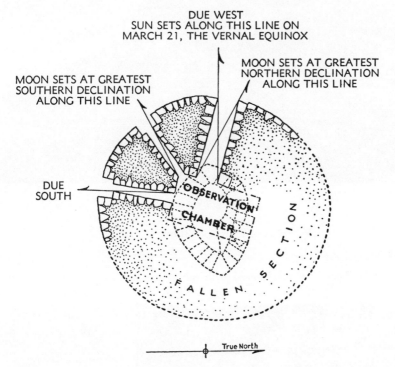

DUE WEST
SUN SETS ALONG THIS LINE ON
MARCH 21, THE VERNAL EQUINOX

MOON SETS AT GREATEST
NORTHERN DECLINATION
ALONG THIS LINE

MOON SETS AT GREATEST
SOUTHERN DECLINATION
ALONG THIS LINE

DUE
SOUTH

OBSERVATION
CHAMBER

SECTION

FALLEN

True North

Fig. 32.—Plan of the Caracol, Chichen Itza, Yucatan, Mexico, showing its use as an astronomical observatory.

In the northern part of the city there are two large natural wells or cenotes, which no doubt contributed greatly to the importance of this site in ancient times—the Xtoloc Cenote, which was formerly the water supply of Chichen Itza, and the Well of Sacrifice (Plate 42b). During the Mexican Period of the Postclassic, Chichen Itza was the most sacred city in Yucatan. Pilgrims came there from all parts of Mesoamerica, and sacrifices of every sort were hurled into the depths of this well.

↑ *a)* Ball court.

PLATE 41.—VIEWS OF CHICHEN ITZA

↓ *b)* Temple of the Jaguars, south end of east wall of ball court.

↑ *a*) *Caracol* or astronomical observatory.

PLATE 42.—VIEWS OF CHICHEN ITZA

↓ *b*) The Sacred *Cenote* or Well of Sacrifice.

a) Turquoise mosaic disk found in the Temple of the Chac Mool, inside the pyramid of the Temple of the Warriors. →

PLATE 43.—TURQUOISE MOSAIC DISK

b) Limestone box in which the disk was found. →

↑ *a*) The Castillo or principal temple.

PLATE 44.—VIEWS OF CHICHEN ITZA

↓ *b*) Dance platform in front of the Castillo.

↑ *a*) Palenque (Classic Stage).

↑ *b*) Chichen Itza (Postclassic Stage).

↑ *c*) Uxmal (Late Classic Stage).

PLATE 45.—PAINTINGS OF CLASSIC- AND POSTCLASSIC-STAGE CITIES,
BY CARLOS VIERRA

Uxmal (Plates 38*b* and 45*c*) is located in a cuplike valley just behind the Puuc hills that sweep up from the southwest and southeast, coming to a point just south of the modern town of Maxcanu.

The most beautiful Puuc-style buildings in Yucatan are to be found at Uxmal (Plates 24*a*, 46–48, and 51, *a*, *c*, and *d*). In this region the Mexican influence, so strongly noticed at Chichen Itza, is almost nonexistent; there are no serpent-column temples and no colonnades, nor does any building at Uxmal have the sloping base so common at Chichen Itza.

The cutting and fitting of the individual elements of the stone mosaic façades at Uxmal reached a perfection not equaled elsewhere. The edges are sharply cut, the surfaces smoothly dressed, and the elements are fitted exactly in the intricate patterns of the mosaics. Although to our thinking the term mosaic refers to something small, the elements of these mosaic façades are sometimes a yard in length and may weigh several hundred pounds. The Governor's Palace surmounts a triple terrace 50 feet high and covering five acres of ground; the palace itself is 320 feet long, 40 feet wide, 26 feet high, and contains twenty-four chambers. The elaborate mosaics decorating its four façades are composed of twenty thousand elements (Plate 24*a*).

Equally imposing are the Nunnery Quadrangle and adjacent House of the Magician (Plates 46–48). The Quadrangle is composed of four buildings with sculptured façades, arranged around the sides of a court 250 feet long by 200 feet wide. This court is entered through a central arcade in the building on its south side (Plate 46*b*). The structure on the north side surmounts a terrace 18 feet high and is reached by a stairway 90½ feet wide; architecturally it is the most important unit of the quadrangle, though the two flanking units, the so-called East and West Ranges (Plate 47, *a* and *b*) are scarcely less impressive. The quadrangle probably served as a residence for the priests, who officiated in the unfortunately misnamed "House of the Magician" (Plate 48), which was the highest construction and principal temple at Uxmal.

Although Puuc architecture predominates at Uxmal, a Chenes

strain is also noticeable. This is especially apparent in the west façade of the House of the Magician, which is Chenes in general character (Plate 48).

Although Chichen Itza covers more ground than Uxmal, the architectural effect of the latter city is more imposing because its six largest groups are concentrated in a relatively small area and their effect is more immediate. The largest groups at Uxmal (Plate 49) are: (1) the Governor's Palace (Plate 24a); House of the Turtles; Ball Court and Great Pyramid (Plate 51a); (2) the Nunnery Quadrangle (Plates 46 and 47) and House of the Magician (Plate 48); (3) the South Group; (4) the Cemetery Group; (5) the Northwest Group; and (6) the House of the Old Woman and associated structures.

The region south of the two ranges of hills that converge just northwest of Uxmal (Plate 1) is called the Puuc. During the ninth and tenth centuries, this section of Yucatan supported the densest population in the northern half of the peninsula, a population which was gathered around many ceremonial centers. The second largest of these centers, Kabah, was located nine miles southeast of Uxmal and connected to it by a stone causeway. The most interesting structure at Kabah is the so-called Palace of the Masks (Plate 56a), which is 151 feet long and contains ten chambers arranged in two rows of five each. The chambers of each pair are built directly behind each other, with a single outside doorway.

The exteriors of most Puuc-style buildings are devoid of sculptural decoration below the medial molding, the intricate mosaics being concentrated in the upper half of the facades. The Palace of the Masks, however, is different in this respect. It stands on a low platform, the face of which is decorated with a single row of mask panels; above this is a carved molding, surmounted by the lower half of the façade, which is composed of three rows of mask panels running across the front of the building. Above an elaborate medial molding there are again three rows of mask panels, the topmost row being surmounted by a terminal molding.

Another unique feature at Kabah is the stone arch (Plate 56b). It stands apart from any other building, at the beginning of the

↑ *a*) The Nunnery Quadrangle, looking north.

PLATE 46.—VIEWS OF UXMAL

b) South wing of the Nunnery Quadrangle; Palace of the
↓   Governor in the background.

↑ *a*) East wing of the Nunnery Quadrangle.

PLATE 47.—VIEWS OF UXMAL

↓ *b*) West wing of the Nunnery Quadrangle.

PLATE 48.— HOUSE OF THE MAGICIAN, UXMAL

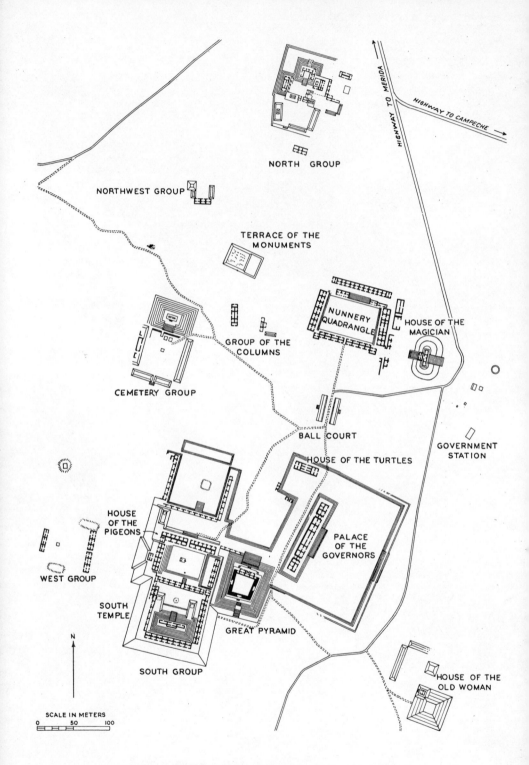

HIGHWAY TO MERIDA

HIGHWAY TO CAMPECHE

NORTH GROUP

NORTHWEST GROUP

TERRACE OF THE
MONUMENTS

NUNNERY
QUADRANGLE

HOUSE OF THE
MAGICIAN

GROUP OF THE
COLUMNS

CEMETERY GROUP

BALL COURT

GOVERNMENT
STATION

HOUSE OF THE TURTLES

HOUSE
OF THE
PIGEONS

PALACE
OF THE
GOVERNORS

WEST GROUP

SOUTH
TEMPLE

GREAT PYRAMID

N

SOUTH GROUP

HOUSE OF THE
OLD WOMAN

SCALE IN METERS

0   50   100

PLATE 49.—MAP OF THE CENTRAL SECTION OF UXMAL

causeway leading to Uxmal, and has a span of fifteen feet. Its
use is unknown; it may have been erected as a triumphal arch, or
it may have been dedicated to one of the gods.

UAXACTUN

While lack of space prevents an extensive description of all
the Class 2 cities, a few words may be said about the more important ones.

Uaxactun is noteworthy to the archaeologist for five reasons:

1. It has the oldest monument yet discovered in the Maya
area (Plate 16)—Stela 9, dating from 8.14.10.13.15 (A.D. 328).
In addition, it has ten of the thirteen known stelae dating from
Baktun 8, toward the end of which the Maya began to erect stone
monuments.

2. The Carnegie Institution of Washington carried on intensive archaeological studies at this site for twelve years (1926–37),
and invaluable scientific data were gathered. Archaeological material of all kinds was collected, including some of the finest polychrome pottery ever found in the Maya area. Due to these excavations, more is known about Uaxactun than about any other city of
the Classic stage.

3. Owing to such extensive work, direct associations between
architectural types and ceramic phases, together with their corresponding dates in Maya chronology, have been so carefully worked
out for Uaxactun that they may serve as standards of comparison
throughout the Maya area.

4. The first astronomical observatory for the Classic stage was
found and identified at Uaxactun, and this led to the later discovery of between twelve and eighteen similar observatories at
other Classic-stage sites. These observatories seem to have been
used primarily for determining the positions of the equinoxes and
solstices. A pyramid was built on the west side of a court, facing
due east (Fig. 33). On the opposite side, three temples were
erected on a terrace, their façades running north and south and
arranged so as to establish the following lines of sight when observed from the stairway of the pyramid on the west side. From

this observation point the sun, on its way north, rose directly behind the middle temple (E-II in Fig. 33) on March 21, the vernal
equinox; it rose behind the north front corner of the north temple
(E-I in Fig. 33) on June 21, the summer solstice; behind the middle temple again on its way back south on September 23, the au-
tumnal equinox; and behind the south front corner of the south
temple (E-III in Fig. 33) on December 21, the winter solstice.
This assemblage of buildings was a practical instrument for determining the longest and shortest days of the year, and the two intermediate positions when day and night are of equal length.

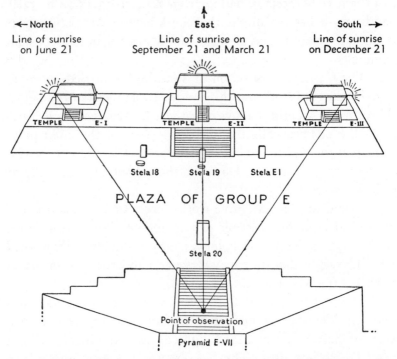

Fig. 33.—Diagram of the astronomical observatory at Group E, Uaxactun, Peten,
Guatemala, for determining the dates of the solstices and equinoxes.

5. A fine Classic-stage wall painting was found in Structure
B-XIII at Uaxactun, and probably represents a religious ceremonial (Plate 50). The figure of a woman is seated on a dais in
a flat-roofed building, while outside stand twenty-five other people.
Below this scene is a horizontal band of 72 day signs (not shown

Left half ↑

PLATE 50.—DRAWING OF A WALL PAINTING IN STRUCTURE B-XIII, UAXACTUN

↓ Right half

PLATE 51.—VIEWS OF UXMAL, AND ALTAR FROM TIKAL

(a) North face of temple near summit of the Great Pyramid, Uxmal; (b) Altar VIII, Tikal; (c) stone mask step in front of building near summit of the Great Pyramid, Uxmal; (d) detail of masks on corner of the same building.

↑　*a*) General view of Piedras Negras.

PLATE 52.—RESTORATIONS OF CLASSIC-STAGE CITIES

↓　*b*) Model of Temples II, III, and IV, at Tikal.

PLATE 53.—STELA 10 (FRONT), SEIBAL, PETEN

← *a*) Stela 12 (T-26), Tonina, Chiapas.

← *b*) Stela E, Quirigua, Guatemala.

c) Stela 40, Piedras Negras, Guatemala, showing the corn god. →

PLATE 54
SCULPTURES OF THE
CLASSIC STAGE

in Plate 50), which begins with the day 12 Imix, and ends with the day 5 Eb; this is evidently part of a tzolkin or sacred year of 260 days. The fresco is painted in red, orange, yellow, gray, and black on a white background, and was in an excellent state of preservation. It probably dates from the Early Period of the Classic stage and is the oldest known wall painting in the Maya area.

PALENQUE, YAXCHILAN, AND PIEDRAS NEGRAS

Palenque (Plate 45a), Yaxchilan, and Piedras Negras were the three largest cities of the Usumacinta Valley and were also those where sculpture reached its esthetic peak. This development in sculpture started at Palenque as early as 9.10.10.0.0 (642), and probably depended in part on the fact that the Palenque sculptors had available a superior grade of fine-grained limestone. Also, the stuccowork at Palenque is equaled nowhere else in the Maya area (Plate 77). The low-relief tablets of limestone are characterized by a delicacy of line, beauty of composition, and brilliance of technique that compare favorably with the best low-relief sculptures of ancient Egypt. Although excellent low reliefs were produced at Palenque from 9.10.10.0.0 to 9.17.13.0.0 (643–783), the peak of artistic achievement was reached in 9.13.0.0.0 (692), when wall tablets were dedicated in three temples.

With the exception of Copan, which was first described in 1576 by Diego García de Palacio, *Oidor* of the *Audiencia Real* of Guatemala, Palenque has been known longer than any other city of the Classic stage.

The Palace Group is one of the outstanding constructions in the Maya area. Its individual ranges of rooms, its high, square tower, and its many subterranean chambers and passages make it unique. The graceful proportions of the city's several pyramid-temples—the Temples of the Cross, Foliated Cross, Sun, Inscriptions, Count, and Beau-Relief—give Palenque a high degree of architectural elegance. The crypt recently discovered beneath the Temple of the Inscriptions (Plates 27, 98–100) is unique in its magnificence, and also demonstrates that Classic Maya pyramids were at least occasionally constructed as tombs.

Yaxchilan, the second of these three cities, also reached its peak of artistic production about 9.13.0.0.0 (692), and maintained this level of achievement until 9.14.15.0.0 (726). During this time four outstanding temples were erected—Structures 21, 23, 42, and 44. These buildings were richly embellished with twelve sculptured·stone lintels, three in each building (Plate 71).

Piedras Negras (Plate 52a) reached a similar level of sculptural brilliance at about the time Yaxchilan was at its peak. The period culminated in 9.16.10.0.0 (761), in Wall Panel No. 3, from Temple O-13 (Plate 69a). This fine panel, made of warm ivory-colored limestone, combines balance and harmony of design with pre-eminent technical perfection.

The practice of erecting period markers at the ends of the successive hotuns, or 1,800-day periods, was more consistently followed at Piedras Negras than at any other Maya center. From 9.8.15.0.0 to 9.19.0.0.0 (608 to 810), each of the twenty-two consecutive hotun endings was celebrated by the erection of a sculptured monument, and not one of these monuments is now missing.

CALAKMUL, NARANJO, AND NAKUM

These three central Peten cities are interesting more for their size than for the distinction of their buildings and monuments. Calakmul has more stelae than any other site in the Maya area, and occasionally several monuments were set up at one time. In 9.15.0.0.0 (731) seven stelae were erected to commemorate the katun ending. But even at the height of the Late Period, the Calakmul monuments were of no particular artistic merit. The emphasis both in sculpture and in the extensive architecture seems to have been on quantity rather than on quality. An interesting feature at Calakmul is a sculptured limestone outcropping 21 feet long by 17 feet wide. Seven captive figures with their hands bound behind their backs are carved on the top of this ledge, the largest figure measuring 9 feet high.

Naranjo, which is considerably smaller than Calakmul, has numerous architectural remains and forty-seven stelae (thirty-six sculptured), but again neither buildings nor monuments are especially noteworthy.

Nakum was a large and important center. Its architectural remains are more extensive than those of Naranjo, but fewer than those of Calakmul. It has fewer monuments, however—only fifteen stelae (three sculptured)—than either Calakmul or Naranjo. There is some basis for believing that Nakum was founded only shortly before the end of the Classic stage, which may account for the scarcity of monuments; the three dated stelae at Nakum are all late, and date from 771, 810, and 849.

PERIPHERAL CITIES OF QUIRIGUA, TONINA, AND COBA

Quirigua (Plate 31c), though one of the smallest second-class cities, has a splendid series of monuments. There are twelve sculptured stelae, four sculptured zoömorphs or great boulder-like mythological animals, and one temple. This series of seventeen hotun markers covers a period of about sixty-five years from 9.15.15.0.0 to 9.19.0.0.0 (A.D. 746–810), and one hotun ending, 9.17.5.0.0 (775), was marked by the erection of two stelae. At other sites a certain flamboyancy of design and execution crept in toward the close of the Late Period, but at Quirigua the hardness of the local stone held the sculptors to simpler designs. This gives the Quirigua monuments a greater dignity and nobility, and renders them more attractive to the modern eye.

The largest block of stone ever quarried by the ancient Maya was found at Quirigua—that from which Stela E, dedicated in 9.17.0.0.0 (771), was fashioned. This giant shaft of sandstone measures 35 feet long, 5 feet wide, 4 feet 2 inches thick, and weighs 65 tons (Plate 54b).

The largest center in the southwest highlands was Tonina, which, so far as its monuments are concerned, was the least typical of all Maya Classic-stage centers. The sixteen Tonina stelae (fifteen sculptured) are all short compared with those of other Maya cities. The average Maya stela was between 8 and 10 feet high, while none of the Tonina stelae is more than 7 feet. They also differ from other Maya stelae in another important respect: they are carved in the complete round, like statuary (Plate 54a). Except for their relatively small size, the Tonina stelae resemble the figures on the Quirigua and Copan stelae (Plates 54b and 68).

Coba was the earliest important Classic-stage city in northeastern Yucatan, and dates to 9.9.10.0.0 (623). Coba is the next to largest Class 2 center known. It is located amidst five small lakes, a rare physiographic feature in the almost waterless plain of northern Yucatan. The largest, Lake Coba, is about a mile long and half a mile wide (Plate 37*b*).

The city is notable for the following characteristics:

1. Its location around the shores of the five lakes.

2. Its long period of occupation. It was founded in 9.9.10.0.0 (623) and was occupied, at least intermittently, until late Postclassic times, around the fourteenth or fifteenth centuries.

3. The presence of more Classic-stage stelae—thirty-two (twenty-three sculptured)—than at any other two cities in northern Yucatan combined.

4. The *sacbeob* or raised artificial roads, of which sixteen are known. This network of stone causeways connected the central section with its outlying groups.

The word *sacbe* (*sacbeob*, plural) means in Maya "artificial road"—*sac*, "something artificial, made by hand"; and *be*, "road." These limestone roads vary in height from 2 to 8 feet above the ground level (Plate 55*a*), and run in straight lines between the groups. The sides are built of roughly dressed stone and the tops covered with a natural lime cement called *sahcab*, which hardens under wetting and pressure. The roads are about 15 feet wide and vary in length from less than a mile to 62.3 miles. The longest causeway (Plate 19) runs generally westward from Coba to Yaxuna and is straight except for a few slight deviations. Two causeways which intersect each other just south of the isthmus between the two largest lakes at Coba appear as two straight lines across the forest in the air photo in Plate 37*b*.

An interesting discovery in connection with the Coba-Yaxuna highway was the finding of an ancient Maya road roller. This cylinder of limestone, now broken in two pieces (Plate 55*b*), measures 13 feet long, 2 feet 4 inches in diameter, and weighs 5 tons. It is large enough for fifteen men to have pushed it at one time, and when rolled along the highway it must have packed the surface into a hard layer.

An important deduction may be made from this causeway. It was built from east to west, from Coba to Yaxuna, which may indicate that when it was constructed—probably in the early part of the Late Period of the Classic stage—Coba was the largest city in northeastern Yucatan. This is apparent from the fact that of the seven changes in direction of the highway the first six are made within twenty miles of Coba in order to pass through smaller settlements dependent on it.

ARCHITECTURE

ORIGIN

Maya architecture is as distinctive as Greek, Roman, or Gothic. It has local variations, but fundamentally it is of a single type.

It has been suggested that the Maya thatched hut, with its sharply pitched roof of two slopes, was the prototype of the corbel-arched stone buildings. This theory is not improbable. The thatched hut of the common people, which has remained the same for two thousand years, is rectangular with rounded ends and is about 22 feet long by 12 feet wide. The walls are made of saplings daubed with mud, or of undressed stone, and are not more than 7 feet in height. Resting on them, a framework of poles rises another 12 or 15 feet to support the sharply pitched two-slope roof of thatch (Plate 57a).

Representations of such houses occur in wall paintings and façade decorations of the Postclassic (Plates 57b and 94, and Fig. 54). The actual foundations of one have been discovered in one of the early levels of the palace (Structure A-V) at Uaxactun. The resemblance between the thatched huts and the stone buildings, when viewed from the inside, is so close as to suggest that the interior slopes of the thatched roofs may have given rise to the idea of the stone corbeled roof vaults.

Materials for stone masonry were abundant. There was an easily worked building material, the local limestone, which was also burned to yield lime, and there were many deposits of gravel,

↑ *a*) Side of causeway at highest point.

PLATE 55.—STONE CAUSEWAY CONNECTING COBA, QUINTANA ROO,
AND YAXUNA, YUCATAN

↓ *b*) Stone roller, found on top of the causeway.

↑ *a*) Palace of the Masks, the principal building.

PLATE 56.—VIEWS OF KABAH, YUCATAN

↓ *b*) The arch.

↑ *a*) Maya house, Hacienda Tanlum, Yucatan.

PLATE 57.—MAYA THATCH AND SAPLING HOUSE

b) Reproduction of Maya house in stone as façade decoration.
↓ South wing of the Nunnery Quadrangle, Uxmal.

↑ *a*) Human type.

PLATE 58.—STUCCO MASKS, PYRAMID E-VII-SUB, UAXACTUN

↓ *b*) Serpentine type.

which was used in mortar. Given the high intelligence and strong religious fervor of the ancient Maya, it was almost inevitable that they should develop a great religious architecture. Beyond the immediate needs of their domestic economy, no other activity consumed so much of their time and energy.

THE OLDEST EXAMPLE OF MAYA ARCHITECTURE

There were presumably no stone buildings in the early Formative stage at Uaxactun, but late in the period low stone walls begin to appear. It is doubtful that stone buildings proper were erected at the beginning of this period; the walls found in association with early Chicanel pottery were probably retaining walls for low platforms, which supported superstructures of perishable materials. Toward the close of the period, however, we find the first large stone construction, a pyramid for supporting a temple of saplings and thatch.

The earliest known example of Maya stone architecture is the stucco-covered pyramid, E-VII-sub, at Uaxactun (Plate 17*b*), which is remarkable for its state of preservation. Shortly after it was finished, it was covered by a rough-rubble, masonry pyramid, E-VII (Plate 17*a*), which protected and preserved it. The sides of this later construction were also decorated with great stucco masks (Plate 58). The top of the later pyramid was so small that it obviously could not have supported a stone building, nor did E-VII-sub support one. Four postholes were found in the lime-plaster flooring of E-VII-sub and these had no doubt held the corner posts of a thatch and sapling structure.

This stucco-covered pyramid, ascended by a stairway on each side and decorated with sixteen large stucco masks (Plate 58), is a marvel of early Maya architecture. Although built of masonry, it is only a substructure, and may antedate the first stone buildings.

CORBELED STONE ROOF VAULTING

With the introduction of the stela complex and Tzakol pottery at Uaxactun about 8.14.0.0.0 (317), we find the earliest corbeled stone roof vaulting in the Maya area. Perhaps as early as 8.12.0.0.0 (278) the first corbeled vaults were constructed. The earliest examples of roof vaults are crude. They are formed of rough, unshaped, flat stones, laid in a thick bed of mortar and pebbles; the under slopes or soffits of the arches are covered with a thick coat of rough plaster (Fig. 34, *d* and *g*).

After its introduction at Uaxactun, the use of corbeled roof vaults seems to have spread. It had reached the extreme southeast at Copan by 9.0.0.0.0 (435); northwestern Yucatan at Oxkintok by 9.2.0.0.0 (475); northeastern Yucatan at Tulum by 9.6.10.0.0 (564); and the Usumacinta Valley by 9.10.0.0.0 (633) or perhaps earlier.

Before the end of the Classic stage in 10.3.0.0.0 (889), the corbeled roof vault had penetrated to every part of the lowland Maya area. Its use seems to have been restricted to this area, and it is not found in any of the adjacent regions. Its westernmost occurrence is at Comalcalco in the state of Tabasco, and its southeasternmost occurrences at Papalguapa and Asunción Mita in southeastern Guatemala. The corbeled vault does not occur in the highlands of Guatemala except in the roofing of a few scattered tombs, and its more extensive use may have been prohibited by the intense earthquake activity there.

LIME-CONCRETE AND BEAM ROOFS

In addition to corbeled roof vaults, flat lime-concrete and beam roofs are also found in Maya architecture. They have been discovered for the Classic stage at Piedras Negras, Uaxactun, and Tzimin Kax; for the Postclassic, at Chichen Itza and at such relatively late sites along the east coast of Yucatan as Tulum and Chac Mool. The lime-concrete roofs were constructed on top of crossbeams, the interbeam spaces being filled with a temporary wattlework of saplings. On this framework, a lime-concrete roofing was built up to the thickness of a foot or more, and when it had set firmly the wattlework was removed. This method of roofing is common in Yucatan today. The residue of such a roof is hard to identify in excavation since it disintegrates into small stones and a

Fig. 34.—Cross-sections of Maya corbeled vaults; (*a*) Monjas Annex, Chichen Itza; (*b*) section of ordinary arch with flat capstones and undressed sides, characteristic of the Classic; (*c*) viaduct, Palenque; (*d*) Temple E-X, Uaxactun; (*e*) section of ordinary arch with flat capstones and dressed sides, characteristic of the Postclassic; (*f*) section of ordinary arch with flat capstones, dressed sides, and curved soffit slopes; (*g*) Palace (Structure A-V), Uaxactun; (*h*) arcade through Governor's Palace, Uxmal; (*i*) trifoil arch, Palace, Palenque; (*j*) second story, Monjas, Chichen Itza.

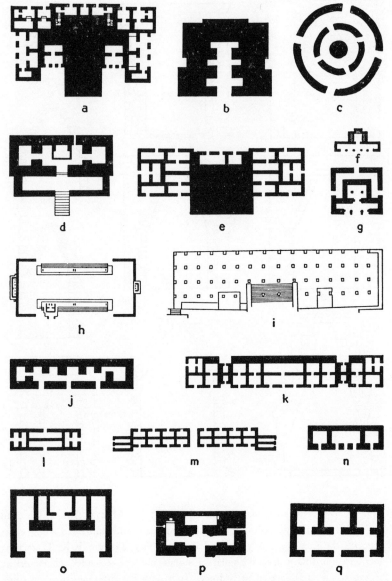

Fig. 35.—Maya ground plans: (*a*) Palace, Santa Rosa Xtampak; (*b*) Temple IV, Tikal; (*c*) Caracol or astronomical observatory, Chichen Itza; (*d*) Temple E-II, Uaxactun; (*e*) Akabtzib, Chichen Itza; (*f*) vapor bath No. 2, Chichen Itza; (*g*) Castillo or principal Temple of Kukulcan, Chichen Itza; (*h*) ball court, Chichen Itza; (*i*) Northwest Colonnade, Chichen Itza; (*j*) Structure 33, Yaxchilan; (*k*) Governor's Palace, Uxmal; (*l*) House of the Turtles, Uxmal; (*m*) House of the Pigeons, Uxmal; (*n*) Structure 21, Yaxchilan; (*o*) Temple of the Sun, Palenque; (*p*) Temple 22, Copan; (*q*) Red House, Chichen Itza.

powdery lime. However, in most cases where vault stones are
not found in excavating masonry buildings, it is safe to assume that
the structures had been roofed with concrete and beams.

DESCRIPTION OF BUILDINGS

Practically all Maya buildings were placed on substructures,
which varied in height depending upon the use of the buildings
they supported. They ranged from low terraces 2 to 6 feet high
for palaces and domiciliary buildings, to pyramids as much as 150
feet high for the temples (Temple IV at Tikal). The substructures
were ascended by broad, steep stairways on one or more sides. The
buildings were usually set back on the summits, leaving a wide
space between their façades and the stairways giving access to them.
At the back and sides, however, they were built close to the edges
of the substructures.

Maya facades are usually divided into two main horizontal
zones by a medial molding which runs entirely around the building about halfway up the wall; a similar molding runs around the
top of the building (Plates 46*b* and 47). The flat roofs are made
of hard lime concrete and are usually a little higher in the center
to facilitate drainage. At Copan, Chichen Itza, and Uxmal there
are sometimes projecting drains to carry off the water.

On top of the roof, parallel with the front of the building and
over the central axis, there is sometimes a high reticulated wall
which runs the entire length of the building. These roof combs are
sometimes as high again as the building itself, and are purely for
decorative purposes.

Ground plans vary according to the purpose of the building
(Fig. 35). Temples (Fig. 35*b*) usually have only two chambers,
one behind the other, and are entered by a doorway in the front
wall. The inner chamber was the sanctuary, while the outer chamber was used for less sacred ceremonies (Fig. 35*q*). In the palace
type of building, there are generally two long ranges of chambers,
one behind the other. If there are exterior doorways only in the
front wall, the inner chambers are reached through doorways in
the back walls of the outer chambers. Sometimes the back range

of chambers may be entered directly through doorways in the back wall of the building (Fig. 35, *e* and *m*). In this case, doorways are rarely found in the long central wall separating the two ranges, or in the transverse partition walls. This applies especially to the "palaces" of the northern area, but at Piedras Negras (central area) doorways in both the medial and transverse walls are not infrequent.

There are no windows, though occasionally the upper half of the façade may be pierced by small rectangular openings. A number of ground plans are shown in Figure 35; they exhibit considerable variety, but most of them classify into a few basic forms, of which the two most common are the temple and the palace types.

No matter how skillfully the Maya cut and dressed their individual building blocks, both exterior and interior walls were covered with lime plaster, which hid all joints. Especially in the Yucatan buildings, no attempt was made to offset joints.

In the smaller towns and villages of northern Yucatan limekilns are made as they were in ancient times, and the local limestone is still burned to make lime. A place in the forest is selected and cleared. Fagots of wood are cut and laid in a circle varying from 10 to 20 feet in diameter, with their lengths parallel to the radii of the circle. A hole about a foot in diameter is left in the center, and the pile of wood is built to a height of about 4 feet (Plate 62*a*). On top of it, beginning about a foot back from its outer edge, broken pieces of limestone are heaped to a height of another 2 feet.

When this is finished, the kiln is fired by dropping leaves and rotten wood into the bottom of the center hole and igniting them. The fire works from the bottom up and from the inside of the kiln outward. The Maya believe that two precautions are vital to a successful burn: first, there must be no wind, so the kiln will burn evenly; and second, no women must be allowed to approach the spot; should one touch the kiln the burn will be a failure. It takes thirty-six hours for a kiln to burn completely, and when a good burn has been achieved the limestone fragments are reduced to a pile of powdered lime (Plate 62*b*).

Not only temporal differences but marked regional variations developed in the twelve hundred years during which the Maya erected stone buildings. These variations are reflected in different types of assemblages and in details of construction, as well as in styles of decoration. However, Maya architecture is singularly homogeneous, considering the long span of time which it covered and the large area where it flourished.

CLASSIFICATION OF BUILDINGS

An attempt has been made in Table VIII to classify Maya buildings and other constructions according to their probable uses. Such a classification cannot be rigid, since many cases might fall equally well into some other group. In general, however, the characteristics of the buildings are so obvious that the classification is fairly exhaustive.

DECORATION OF BUILDINGS

In the early part of the Classic stage, the buildings do not seem to have been heavily decorated. Façades were usually vertical, with medial and top moldings made of projecting courses of rough stone, finished with coats of plaster (Plate 59, *a* and *b*). Some Classic-stage buildings of the central area, especially at Copan, Palenque, and Tikal, have sloping façades above the level of the medial molding. Later, the area between the medial and top moldings began to be sparingly decorated with stucco. This type of façade decoration reached its highest development in the Classic stage at Palenque, where both the upper and lower zones of the façade were ornamented with elaborate designs. These designs were modeled in hard lime stucco, applied to rough stones projecting from the façade.

In the central area there seems to have been very little carved-stone decoration in the upper half of the façade, except at Copan and Quirigua. Sculpture was occasionally employed in exterior decoration—in wall panels (Piedras Negras), on ramps flanking stairways (Palenque, Copan, Quirigua), and on the risers of steps. These steps are sometimes carved with hieroglyphic inscriptions (Copan, Quirigua, Palenque, Yaxchilan, Naranjo, Seibal, Etzna,

TABLE VIII

CLASSIFICATION OF MAYA BUILDINGS AND OTHER CONSTRUCTIONS ACCORDING TO THEIR PROBABLE USES

Kind of Building, or Construction	Examples		Corresponding Plates in This Book	
	Central Area	Northern Area	Central Area	Northern Area
Pyramid-temples	Temples I, II, III, IV, V, Tikal; Temple 26, Copan; Temple of the Inscriptions, Palenque	Castillo, Chichen Itza; House of the Magician, Uxmal	II, III, and IV, Plate 52a; IV, only, Plates 70b, 33a; Palenque, Plate 27	Plates 44a, 48
Small temples	Structures 20, 21, 33, 42, 44, Yaxchilan	Red House, Chichen Itza; House of the Old Woman, Uxmal		
Palaces	Palace, Palenque; Palace (Structure A-V), Uaxactun	Monjas, Chichen Itza; Governor's Palace, Uxmal		Plate 24a
Astronomical observatories	Structures E-I, E-II, E-III, E-VII, Uaxactun; Structures II, III, IV, VIII, Naachtun	Caracol, Chichen Itza; Round Tower, Mayapan	E-VII, only, Plate 17, a and b	Plate 42a
Ball courts	Structures 9 and 10, Copan; Structure 14, Yaxchilan	Ball court, Chichen Itza; Ball court, Uxmal		Plate 41, a and b
Colonnades	Structure J-2, Piedras Negras; Structure 74, Yaxchilan	Northwest Colonnade, Chichen Itza; Colonnade, Ake		Plate 40a
Dance platforms	Structures 66, 78, 79, 80, 82, Tikal	Dance platform in front of Castillo, Chichen Itza; Structure 8, Tulum		Plate 44b
Peristyle courts	Not yet found	Market place and Structure 2-D-6, Chichen Itza		

Vapor baths	Structure P-7, Piedras Negras	Structures 3-E-3 and 3-C-17, Chichen Itza	Plate 56b
Arches or gateways....	Not yet found	Arch, Kabah; Portal, Labna	
Shrines	Not yet found	Small structure at edge of Well of Sacrifice (Structure 1-D-1), Chichen Itza; Structure 7, Tulum	
Skull platforms	Not yet found	Place of the Skulls, Chichen Itza; Platforms in Cemetery, Uxmal	Plate 61a Plate 73f
Monumental stairways..	Jaguar Stairway, Copan; Hieroglyphic Stairway (Structure 5), Yaxchilan	Not yet found	Plate 35, a and b
Reviewing stands	North side, West Court, Copan	Not yet found	
Square stadiums for public spectacles	Great Plaza, Copan; Ceremonial Plaza, Quirigua	Not yet found	
City walls	Becan*	Mayapan; Tulum	
Causeways	Coba-Yaxuna; Coba-Kukicaan	Uxmal-Kabah; Izamal-Kantunil	Plate 55a
Foundation platforms..	Terrace of Group A, Tikal; Terrace of Group A, Uaxactun	North terrace, Chichen Itza; Terrace of the Governor's Palace, Uxmal	Plate 38b
Bridges and aqueducts..	Pusilha; Becan; Palenque	Not yet found	

* A moat also has been found around this site.

La Amelia). The use of interior sculptural decoration in Classic buildings is relatively uncommon. Its most notable occurrences are on the sanctuary tablets at Palenque (Plate 33*b*), on doorjambs and flanking interior doorways at Copan, and on the risers of interior steps and as wall decorations at Quirigua.

In the northern area, however, sculptural decoration is more commonly used. In the Chenes region in central Campeche and western Quintana Roo, façades are elaborately decorated both above and below the medial molding, and are the most ornate in the Maya area. The Puuc area, north and northwest of the Chenes, was the most fertile and densely populated section of northern Yucatan during late Classic times. In this area, sculpture is largely confined to the upper zones of façades (Plates 24*a*, 46*b*, and 47), though a sculptured lower zone is occasionally found (Plate 56*a*). The designs are largely geometric (Plate 60), though occasional human, animal, bird, and serpent figures are tenoned into the upper halves of the facades.

In the Puuc region the individual elements of the mosaics are the most skillfully carved and fitted. Here architecture reached heights never attained before nor equaled again. Sculpture, so highly developed in the central area, was little cultivated as an independent art in the northern area. It became subordinate to architecture and was restricted almost exclusively to façade embellishment. Sculpture suffered because of this limitation. While Puuc architecture reached new levels of beauty and dignity, the few sculptures are for the most part heavy and awkward.

A later architectural phase is the mixed Maya-Toltec architecture, which reached its highest expression at Chichen Itza. The feathered serpent, Kukulcan (the Mexican Quetzalcoatl) dominates the scene. The chief temples were erected in his honor, and his likeness sprawls over columns and balustrades. The buildings are characterized by battered (sloping) bases, and their roofs are ornamented with stone frets. Some types of structures are definitely of Mexican origin, such as the Tzompantli, or Place of the Skulls, where the skulls of sacrificial victims were impaled on wooden stakes. The Tzompantli at Chichen Itza is an open plat-

↑ *a*) The Labyrinth (Structure 19), Yaxchilan, Chiapas.

PLATE 59.—CLASSIC-STAGE FAÇADES

↓ *b*) Temple of the Five Stories (Structure 10), Tikal.

↑ *a*) Corner mask panel from the House of the Magician, Uxmal.

↑ *b*) Mask panel at top of west stairway, House of the Magician, Uxmal.

PLATE 60.—LATE CLASSIC-STAGE FAÇADES, PUUC PERIOD

↓ *c*) The Church, Nunnery group, Chichen Itza.

↑ *a*) Tzompantli, or Place of the Skulls, Chichen Itza.

PLATE 61.—POSTCLASSIC-STAGE FAÇADES, MEXICAN PERIOD

↓ *b*) Colonnade, interior of the Market, Chichen Itza.

↑ *a*) Before burning.

PLATE 62.—MAKING A LIMEKILN AT CHICHEN ITZA

↓ *b*) After burning.

form about 185 feet long, 40 feet wide, and 6 feet high; its sides
are decorated with sculptured representations of skulls fixed upon
stakes (Plate 61a). Toltec-period buildings and substructures at
Chichen Itza are decorated with human and animal motifs, but
little use is made of the geometric elements common in Puuc architecture. Large reclining human statues, the so-called Chac Mool
figures, stand at the portals of the temples (Plate 73a). Maya-
Toltec architecture is also characterized by the frequent use of
great colonnades. These may be 200 or 300 feet long, with four
or five ranges of corbeled vaults. Against their back walls are
sculptured thrones, flanked by benches (Plates 40a and 61b).
Architecture has become less massive, but more open and graceful.

SCULPTURE AND MODELING

MATERIALS AND TOOLS

LIMESTONE, being the most plentiful, was the principal stone used in ancient Maya sculptures. A few sites like Quirigua, Pusilha, and Tonina employed sandstone, the native rock in their localities, and Copan used andesite, a volcanic tuff. However, these are exceptions.

Wood, stucco, and clay were also employed in Maya sculpture and modeling, although less commonly than stone. Wood was used for carved door lintels (Plate 33a) and chamber beams (Plate 53e), and some idols were carved from Spanish cedar in the Postclassic stage, but none of them has survived. Idols were also modeled from clay, particularly in the form of incense burners, and stucco found extensive use in architectural decoration.

We get our first glimpse of Maya chronology on the stone stelae of the early fourth century, when the hieroglyphs are already a perfected device for recording time. No preliminary steps in writing have yet been found, which may indicate that the earlier stages were recorded on wood or some other perishable medium.

The tools of the Maya sculptors were principally of stone, although wooden mallets may also have been used. The principal tools were chisels and hammerstones. The chisels (Fig. 36) are from two to six inches in length and have one cutting edge, the opposite end being rounded. It is likely that the flaked flint chisels, found so plentifully in some Maya sites, were used for stone cuttings. The hammerstones are roughly spherical in shape and vary from two to three inches in diameter.

The native limestone is relatively soft as it occurs in the ground, but hardens after exposure. It was quarried with comparative facility, and was easily carved while still fresh from the quarries. The sandstone of Quirigua, Tonina, and Pusilha was also soft in its

FIG. 36.—Maya stone chisels.

native state, but the andesite used in Copan is of about the same hardness before being quarried as afterward. Andesite is so fine-grained and even-textured that it is admirably adapted to carving; however, it has one serious drawback—it contains nodules of flint which are so hard that stone chisels could not have worked them. When such nodules were encountered they were either removed, leaving a depression in the face of the monument, or they were left protruding. Examples of both practices may occur on the same monument. Sometimes, when the inclusion was too difficult to remove entirely, the projecting part was battered off. In the case of the human head in the Initial Series introducing glyph on Stela 2 (Fig. 37), clever manipulations incorporated a stubborn nodule into the design itself. The heads represented in Maya inscriptions almost always face the observer's left, but this profile faces to the right. By thus reversing the direction, this flinty inclusion fell in the right position to serve as an earplug.

FIG. 37.—Initial Series introducing glyph on Stela 2, Copan, Honduras.

Maya sculpture was doubtless finished by abrasion and then painted, usually a dark red. This red pigment was probably made from an oxide of iron obtained from anthills, which abound in the forest. Blue was the next most common color. The pigments were ground and probably mixed with copal, for the paint still adheres to the stone in many places with the tenacity of a good varnish. Although the colors have for the most part worn off, traces of the original paint can still be found where the relief is high and under-cut.

In quarrying the shafts of stone from which the stelae were made, advantage was taken of natural cleavage planes in the rock. This is best seen in the case of some of the Quirigua stelae, the cross-sections of which are trapezoidal in shape, with no single corner a true right angle. The method of quarrying at Calakmul (Plate 76) was to free the blocks from the surrounding limestone by digging down along their sides and ends, preparatory to prying them loose from the bedrock. Several of the Quirigua stelae still show "quarry stumps" on their plain undressed butts (Plate 76a).

William Henry Holmes sketched a quarry site near the ruins of Mitla (Fig. 38), which shows blocks of stone in various stages of being freed from the native rock.

Fig. 38.—Quarry at Mitla, Oaxaca, Mexico. After Holmes.

The French artist, Jean Charlot, has made four original draw-ings illustrating the principal steps in making a Maya stela: (1) quarrying the shaft, (2) transporting it, (3) erecting it, and (4) sculpturing it. The first step has been described above (Plate 64*a*), and the second is shown in Plate 64*b*. The forests of Peten abound in hardwood trees, sections of which would have served admirably for rollers, and fiber-yielding plants for making ropes and cables are equally common. The erection of the shaft is shown in Plate 65*a*. A masonry socket to fit the butt of the shaft was made. Then, probably by means of a ramp and an A-frame of beams, the shaft was pulled upright and the fourth side of the socket filled in. It is important to note that the shafts were brought from the quarries in an unfinished state. They were carved after being set up (Plate 65*b*).

STONE SCULPTURE

The earliest stone sculptures in the Maya area are the group of monuments at Uaxactun in northern central Peten, which date from the fourth century A.D. The human figures on these monuments are always shown in the same position—head, legs, and feet in profile; torso and arms in full front; and feet in tandem. This is the earliest position of the human figure in Maya art. It is found exclusively at Uaxactun and seems to have passed out of use even there before the close of Baktun 8 (435).

The next position is a little more natural. The toes of the back foot are advanced slightly, overlapping the heel of the front foot, but the rest of the body remains unchanged. This position also appears first at Uaxactun before the close of Baktun 8 (435). The profile presentation of the human figure persisted throughout Maya history with little change and is the most common position in Maya art.

To Uaxactun or possibly to Tikal belongs credit for having first sculptured the human figure in full front view. The earliest certain example of this is on Stela 26 at Uaxactun, dedicated in 9.0.10.0.0 (445). This monument was discovered beneath the floor of Shrine II in one of the earliest levels of Structure A-V. The figure on its front would almost appear to have been intentionally rubbed off (Plate 63*b*), but it is still possible to distinguish the lower half of the face, the arms, and the feet. A possibly earlier example of a figure in front view is found on Stela 4 at Tikal (Plate 63*a*), which may have been dedicated as early as the close of Baktun 8.

The full front view of the human figure is restricted to Tonina (Plate 54*a*), Copan, Quirigua (Plates 54*b* and 68*b*), Piedras Negras, Palenque, Yaxchilan, Naachtun, and Seibal. It reached its greatest perfection at Copan and Quirigua, while the front view of the human figure seated cross-legged is best expressed at Piedras Negras.

The four Piedras Negras monuments, shown in Plate 66, constitute a fine series for the study of the human figure seated cross-legged in a niche. The earliest of these four monuments, Stela 25, was dedicated in 9.8.15.0.0 (608). The figure sculptured on this monument is wooden and lifeless (Plate 66*a*) and the niche is too shallow to permit treatment of the figure in high relief. On Stela 6, dedicated in 9.12.15.0.0 (687), this same composition was attempted again (Plate 66*b*). Considerable advance in sculpture had been made, and the niche is deeper, permitting the figure to be treated more successfully. The face is well done but out of proportion to the rest of the body. By the time this composition was attempted on Stela 11, dedicated in 9.15.0.0.0 (731), notable improvement had been made (Plate 66*c*). The niche has become so deep that the proportions of the seated figure are more lifelike, and the details are beautifully executed. The design was again sculptured on Stela 14, dedicated in 9.16.10.0.0 (761), which is perhaps the finest stela at this site (Plate 66*d*). The niche is sufficiently deep to present the figure in the half round; its anatomical proportions are correct, and details are exquisitely carved. This monument also presents a masterly combination of high- and low-relief carving.

The front presentation of the standing human figure was brilliantly achieved at Copan and Quirigua. The figures at the latter site are probably more to modern taste because they are more restrained, although this restraint in design may have been accidental, owing to the greater intractability of the Quirigua sandstone.

Returning to Preclassic sculptures, the human figures portrayed

← *a*) Stela 4, Tikal.

b) Stela 26, Uaxactun. →

← *c*) Stela 5, Uaxactun.

d) Stela 2, Tikal. →

PLATE 63
MONUMENTS OF THE EARLY
PERIOD OF THE CLASSIC
STAGE

↑   *a*) First step. Quarrying the shaft.

PLATE 64

FOUR STEPS IN THE MAKING OF A MAYA MONUMENT, AFTER TH

↓   *b*) Second step. Transporting the shaft.

↑ *a*) Third step. Erecting the shaft.

ɪɢɪɴᴀʟ Dʀᴀᴡɪɴɢꜱ ʙʏ Jᴇᴀɴ Cʜᴀʀʟᴏᴛ

PLATE 65

b) Fourth step. Sculpturing the shaft.
→

← *a*) Stela 25, erected A.D. 608.

b) Stela 6, erected A.D. 687. →

← *c*) Stela 11, erected A.D. 731.

d) Stela 14, erected A.D. 761. →

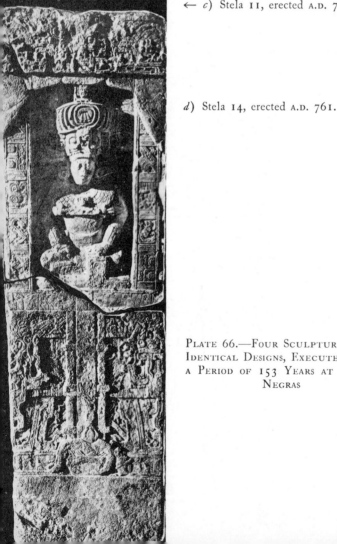

PLATE 66.—FOUR SCULPTURES WITH
IDENTICAL DESIGNS, EXECUTED OVER
A PERIOD OF 153 YEARS AT PIEDRAS
NEGRAS

are stilted and out of proportion, but by the end of the period
advances had been made toward a more naturalistic presentation. The proportions of the body became more lifelike and its positions easier.

The last vestiges of archaism disappeared early in the Late Period, from about 630 to 730, though in provincial centers some sculptors did not follow the prevailing naturalistic trends of this period. The figures on Stela 21 at Naachtun (Plate 67*c*), dedicated in 687, are dumpy and misshapen for such a late date. The contrast between this monument and Stela A at Copan (Plate 68*b*), dedicated in 9.15.0.0.0 (731), is arresting. Such stylistic differences between monuments erected so close together in time may be explained by the backwardness of smaller centers as compared to the creative brilliance of the larger centers. The farther away from centers of esthetic inspiration peripheral settlements are located, the longer it takes them to catch up with the "big cities" in clothes and customs and in architecture and art.

The century and a half from 731 to 889 of the Late Period of the Classic stage witnessed the most brilliant development of New World sculpture in pre-Columbian times. This period was in many ways the golden age of the Maya civilization, and its cultural flowering is perhaps best exemplified in sculpture. By this time four centuries of sculptural achievement lay behind, and technical difficulties had long since been mastered; creativity was free to express itself within the framework of its traditions and experience.

Among the wealth of sculptures from the Late Period, it is difficult to select those which are most typical. One of the most beautiful monuments at Piedras Negras, Stela 14, has already been illustrated (Plate 66*d*). Another almost equally striking monument, Stela 12 (Plate 18*c*), dedicated in 9.18.5.0.0 (795), shows profile presentation of the human figure exclusively.

At Palenque, in the crypt below the Temple of the Inscriptions, the carving of the slab covering the sarcophagus is exceptional for its delicacy and sureness of line (Plate 100, *b* and *d*).

One of the most beautiful sculptures produced is Wall Panel

No. 3 from Structure O-13 at Piedras Negras (Plate 69*a*). This masterpiece was executed in 9.16.10.0.0 (761) and is a perfect combination of high and low relief. In a number of places on the panel, arms and legs are sculptured in the full round. The composition represents a priest seated on a throne, the back of which is a mask panel; he is flanked on each side by three standing figures. On the ground before the throne seven figures are seated cross-legged, facing an altar. The figure on the extreme right is the only one in the composition that has its face still preserved. Miss M. L. Baker has made a restoration of this wall panel (Plate 69*b*), although her drawing uses the three-quarter view of figures, a stylistic device which never occurs in Maya art. The original is in the National Museum of Archaeology and History at Guatemala City.

A University of Pennsylvania expedition discovered a throne in Palace J-6 at Piedras Negras (Fig. 39) which was almost identical with that represented in the wall panel, although the two front supports of the throne on the wall panel are undecorated (Plate 69*a*), while those of the actual throne are covered on three sides with hieroglyphic inscriptions (Plate 70*a*). It was dedicated in 9.17.15.0.0 (785), twenty-five years later than the wall panel, and was so located in the principal hall of the palace that it could be seen from any point in the court below.

At Yaxchilan sculpture reached its highest point in the lintels of Structure 23—Lintels 24, 25, and 26, the first two of which are now in the British Museum. Lintel 24 (Plate 71*b*) is the most outstanding example of sculptural art at Yaxchilan in harmony of composition, balance of design, and brilliance of execution. Structure 23 was dedicated in 9.14.15.0.0 (726). The finest monuments at Yaxchilan—Stelae 1, 3, 4, 7—fall little short of the lintels, though most of them date about thirty-five years later, when Yaxchilan was already past the peak of its artistic achievements.

There is more Late Period sculpture at Copan than at any other city of the Classic stage. Many fine monuments were sculptured there: Stelae A (Plate 68*b*), B, C, D, F, H (Plate 68*a*), M, N, and 4, and Altars Q, R, S, and T. There were also some other spectacular constructions: Temples 11, 22, and 26, the Jaguar

← *a*) Stela 27 ,Yaxchilan, erected A.D. 514.

b) Stela 25, Naranjo, Guatemala, erected A.D. 615. →

c) Stela 21, Naachtun, Guatemala, erected A.D. 687. ←

d) Stela P, Copan, erected A.D. 623. →

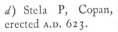

PLATE 67
SCULPTURES OF THE
EARLY AND LATE PE-
RIODS OF THE CLASSIC
STAGE

a) Stela H, Copan, erected A.D. 782.

b) Stela A, Copan, erected A.D. 731.

PLATE 68.—SCULPTURES OF THE CLASSIC STAGE

↑　*a*) Wall Panel, as found.

PLATE 69.—WALL PANEL NO. 3, TEMPLE O-13, PIEDRAS NEGRAS

↓　*b*) Pen-and-ink restoration by M. Louise Baker.

↑ *a*) Throne in Palace J-6,
Piedras Negras.

b) Model of Temple IV,
Tikal.   →

PLATE 70
THRONE AND MODEL OF A
TEMPLE

Stairway (Plate 35*a*), and the Reviewing Stand. All were erected and carved between 731 and 782. The longest hieroglyphic inscription in the Maya area—the Hieroglyphic Stairway of Structure 26 (Plate 35*c*)—was dedicated in 9.16.5.0.0 (756). The exquisite head and torso of the corn god illustrated in the frontispiece was also carved during this half-century.

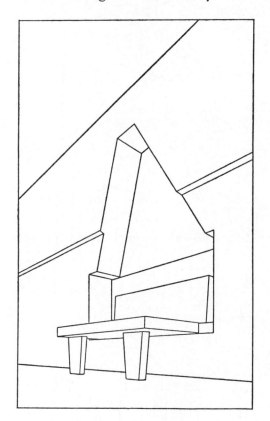

Fig. 39.—Location of throne in Palace J-6, Piedras Negras.

Quirigua, although a medium-sized site, has twenty-two sculptured monuments. Two have already been described—Stela E (Plate 54*b*), A.D. 771, and the altar of Zoömorph O. A third monument which deserves particular mention is Zoömorph P (Plate 72*c*). This massive boulder-shaped piece of sandstone measures 9 feet 8 inches long, by 11 feet 6 inches wide, by 7 feet 3 inches

Fig. 40.—Front view
of Stela 10, Xultun.

high, and is completely covered with an intricate sculptured design; it was dedicated in 9.18.5.0.0 (795). Perhaps the finest glyphs ever carved on stone are to be found at Quirigua, especially those on Stela F (Plate 72a), dedicated in 9.16.10.0.0 (761), and the rare full-figure glyphs on Stela D (Plate 72b), dedicated in 9.16.15.0.0 (766).

By the end of Baktun 9 (830), however, the crest had been passed and there followed an artistic recession from which the ancient Maya never recovered.

Examples of late Classic-stage sculpture reflect this decline. Stela 10 at Xultun (Fig. 40), dedicated in 10.3.0.0.0 (889), is one of three monuments erected on this katun ending. The loss in inspiration and technical skill is evident, and the composition is cluttered and flamboyant. The figures are poorly proportioned and a mass of detail obscures the design.

In Yucatan during late Classic times, distinctive local sculptural styles developed. There are sixteen sculptured stelae at Uxmal, but even the best of them, Stela 7 (Fig. 41), is overly ornate as compared with the sculptures of the Classic stage. Here also was found a well-executed human head emerging from the jaws of a conventionalized serpent (Plate 74, c and d), with tattooing on its right cheek. The head can hardly be called independent sculpture, however. It is attached to the façade of a range of chambers at the western base of the pyramid supporting the House of the Magician and formed an element of the architectural decoration. This head is now in the National Museum of Anthropology and History at Mexico City.

During the Postclassic stage, sculpture was confined almost exclusively to the embellishment of architecture. At Chichen Itza no Postclassic stelae have been found, but there are the following categories: (1) the so-called Chac Mool figures, (2) jaguar thrones, (3) standard bearers, and (4) Atlantean figures. The first are reclining human figures (Plate 73a) with heads turned to the right or left. At least a dozen have been discovered at this site, and two of them still retain inset pieces of polished bone to represent the whites of the eyes, the fingernails, and toenails. Each holds a stone

Fig. 41.—Front view
of Stela 7, Uxmal.

plate clasped by the two hands and resting on the abdomen, and this
position suggests that their function might have been to receive
offerings.

The jaguar thrones are life-sized figures of jaguars with flat
backs to serve as seats. Sculptured representations of them are
found at Tikal, Piedras Negras, Palenque, and Xultun, but the
actual thrones have been found only at Uxmal and Chichen Itza
(Plate 73c). They also occur in the frescoes in the Temple of the
Warriors at Chichen Itza.

The standard bearer constitutes the third type of statue; its
purpose was to support a staff from the top of which hung a feather
banner. These standard bearers are in the form of small human
figures about three feet high (Plate 73b), with the forearms extended horizontally in front, the hands forming a hole through
which the staff passed. Another standard bearer found at Chichen
Itza shows a figure kneeling on its left knee and grasping the staff
in its right hand (Plate 73e).

The fourth group, the Atlantean figures, are anthropomorphic
statues with arms raised above their heads. They were used to
support daises or door lintels in the temples (Plate 73d).

Wood carving seems to have reached its most perfect expression
at Tikal in the door lintels of the five pyramid-temples at that site.
Such a perishable material as wood could hardly have survived the
damp climate of the Maya area except in very sheltered positions,
and the only wooden objects recovered are from places which are
protected from the weather.

A photograph of the most complete lintel has been illustrated
in Plate 33a and a drawing of part of another is shown in Figure 31.
The lintels are each composed of from four to ten beams of sapodilla with an over-all length of from 7 to 17½ feet. The design
on the lintel in Plate 33a shows an elaborately decorated serpent,
its body arching in the middle to form a central niche. The head is
to the left, and issuing from its open mouth is the upper body of
a god; the serpent's tail is at the right, terminating in two scrolls.
A hieroglyphic inscription fills the upper left and right corners of
the composition, and across the top between the glyph panels

Fig. 42.—Design on carved wooden lintel, Temple of the Jaguars, Chichen Itza.

stretches a great bird with spreading wings, the *kukul* (quetzal) or Sacred Bird of the Maya. In the niche formed by the upward curl of the serpent's body is the figure of a priest seated on a throne. This lintel originally spanned one of the doorways of Temple IV, which was dedicated in 9.16.0.0.0 (751). Another Classic-stage lintel was found in Temple VII at Tzibanche, west of the southern end of Lake Bacalar (Plate 19). This has an inscription of eight hieroglyphs but no figures, and probably dates from the early Late Period, perhaps about 9.9.5.0.0 (618).

Occasionally the wooden poles spanning the vaults have also been carved. One of these was found at Tikal in a fourth-story rear chamber of the Palace of the Five Stories (Plate 53*e*).

Carved wooden lintels have been found at Chichen Itza and Uxmal. The best-preserved lintel at Chichen Itza spans the inner doorway of the Temple of the Jaguars on top of the west wall of the ball court (Fig. 42). Each of the two beams forming this lintel has the same design carved upon it: the sun disk, with a human figure inside it, and outside it another human figure enveloped in the coils of a feathered rattlesnake. Both figures face a centrally placed altar. The lintels in the Castillo at Chichen Itza were carved originally, but most of the low relief has been hacked off with machetes.

An account of travel in the Maya area has been left by John Lloyd Stephens, the American diplomat and amateur archaeologist who visited Uxmal in 1840 and 1841. He found a sapodilla beam in the Governor's Palace which he took to the United States when he left Yucatan. It was subsequently destroyed by a fire in New York—an irreparable loss. Stephens says it was the only beam at Uxmal which was carved, and the inscription might have dated this structure, one of the most beautiful in pre-Columbian America.

Other small objects of carved wood were taken from the Well of Sacrifice at Chichen Itza, among them the handle of a wooden sacrificial knife, carved in the likeness of two intertwined rattlesnakes (Fig. 14). A chipped-flint blade was hafted to this and its handle is covered with a thin sheet of gold.

Stucco seems to have been widely used in the exterior decoration of Classic-stage buildings and also to a lesser extent in Postclassic façades. Stuccowork reached its highest development at Palenque and the tablets and panels there are the finest examples of this plastic art in the Maya area. Two panels from the west façade of House D of the Palace are illustrated in Plate 77, *a* and *b*.

In the sealed crypt which Alberto Ruz discovered in the Temple of the Inscriptions, the walls are decorated with handsomely modeled reliefs of nine figures, which possibly represent the *Bolontiku*, the Nine Gods of the Lower World. Under the sarcophagus itself were two excellently modeled stucco heads, which illustrate the Classic Maya ideal of beauty (Plate 98, *b* and *c*).

Even provincial centers within the Palenque sphere of influence showed this mastery of the stucco technique. Some years ago a tomb was found at Comalcalco, about one hundred miles northwest of Palenque. On three walls were representations of standing human figures in stucco, three to a side; two, as restored, are shown in Plate 78, *a* and *b*; the same two, as found, in Plate 78*c*. Although less finely executed than the stucco figures at Palenque, these Comalcalco figures are not without considerable merit. The best example of stuccowork in northern Yucatan is at Acanceh. Here in the upper half of a façade are the remains of a handsome stucco panel, composed of animals, birds, and serpents (Plate 79). When this was uncovered forty years ago, the frieze still retained many traces of its original coloring, with a bright turquoise blue predominating. This frieze dates from early Classic times. In Postclassic times Tulum furnishes the only examples of stucco decoration, in the form of recessed panels above the doors of buildings.

CLAY MODELING

The practice of making modeled clay heads goes back to a very early period in Mesoamerican art. Such heads have been found in quantity in the prehistoric cemetery beneath the lava flow at San Angel and Tlalpan outside Mexico City, probably dating from the

a) Lintel 25, from Structure 23. →

↓ *b*) Lintel 24, from Structure 23.

PLATE 71.—SCULPTURED LINTELS,
YAXCHILAN

← *a*) Stela F, Quirigua.

b) Stela D, Quirigua. →

PLATE 72.—SCULPTURES OF
THE CLASSIC STAGE

↓ *c*) Zoömorph P, Quirigua.

PLATE 73.—SCULPTURES OF THE POSTCLASSIC STAGE (*a–e*)
AT CHICHEN ITZA, AND (*f*) AT UXMAL

(*a*) Chac Mool; (*b*) anthropomorphic support for a banner; (*c*) Red Jaguar Throne; (*d*) Atlantean figure altar support; (*e*) support for a banner; (*f*) altar in the so-called cemetery.

PLATE 74.—SCULPTURES OF THE POSTCLASSIC STAGE AT
CHICHEN ITZA AND UXMAL

(a) Seated figure, Northwest Colonnade, Chichen Itza; (b) same figure, profile; (c) head
emerging from the mouth of a serpent, House of the Magician, Uxmal; (d) same head, profile.

← *a*) Door jamb, Structure 2C6, Kabah, Yucatan.

b) Door jamb, Structure 2C6, Kabah. →

PLATE 75
SCULPTURES
OF THE
POSTCLASSIC
STAGE

←*c*) Lintel, Structure 2, Xculoc, Campeche.

d) Lintel, Structure 2, Xculoc. →

↑　*a*) Quarry stumps on base of Stela J, Quirigua.

PLATE 76.—QUARRYING OPERATIONS (CLASSIC STAGE)

↓　*b*) Two partially quarried shafts, Calakmul, Campeche.

↑

House D of the Palace Group,
west façade.

←

PLATE 77.—STUCCOWORK FROM PALENQUE

a) Figures
on wall of
tomb as re-
stored.
←   →

PLATE 78
STUCCO-
WORK FROM
COMALCALCO,
TABASCO

b) Figures
on wall of
same tomb as
found. ↓

↑ *a*) Figure of squirrel.

PLATE 79.—STUCCOWORK FROM ACANCEH, YUCATAN

↓ *b*) Figures of bat, eagle (?), jaguar (?), and serpent.

↑ *a*) Archaic clay head, "black dirt" stratum.

↑ *b*) Another example of the same type.

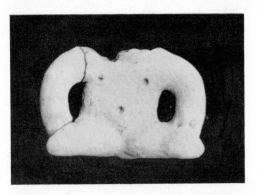

↑ *c*) Archaic female torso, "black dirt" stratum.

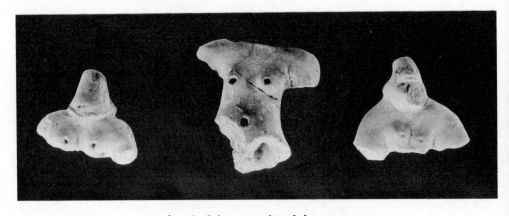

↑ *d*) Other examples of the same type.

PLATE 80.—UAXACTUN CERAMICS, MAMOM PHASE

PLATE 81.—CLAY MODELING FROM THE CLASSIC AND POSTCLASSIC
STAGES AMONG THE LACANDON

(a) Effigy pipe, Temple of the Warriors, Chichen Itza; (b) head from incense burner, Mayapan; (c) figurine made from an ancient mold, found near the Rio Chixoy, Chiapas; (d) modern Lacandon incense burner, Chiapas.

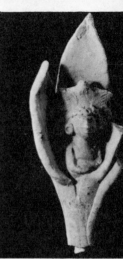

PLATE 82.—CLAY FIGURINES FROM
THE ISLAND OF JAINA, CAMPECHE

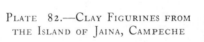

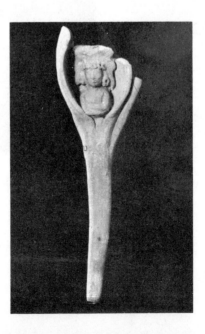

first millennium before Christ. Similar heads have been found in the earliest layer showing human occupation at Uaxactun (Plate 80, *a* and *b*). The Uaxactun heads are quite crude: the eyes are round holes punched in almond-shaped depressions; the eyebrows appear as shallow lines; the face is modeled without skill. Found with these early heads, which probably date to the first millennium before Christ, are crudely shaped torsos (Plate 80, *c* and *d*).

A few examples of heads and torsos have been found which may be ascribed to the early part of the Late Period, but a number of fine clay figurines have been recovered that date from late in the period. Some of these were modeled by hand and then baked, but others were made in molds of baked clay. A few of these ancient molds have been found. The finest is a one-piece mold of the front of a seated female figure about 8 inches high; a modern cast of it is shown in Plate 81*c*. This mold was found near the west bank of the Chixoy or Salinas River in the eastern part of the state of Chiapas, Mexico, and the statuette made from it recalls the best stuccowork at Palenque. The cast is now in the Peabody Museum, Harvard University.

Another Classic-stage center where figurines and heads of baked clay reached a high degree of perfection was Jonuta on the lower Usumacinta River. Excellent figurines were also made at the Island of Jaina (Plate 82), off the west coast of the northern peninsula. While modeled clay heads and figurines are found everywhere in the region covered by the Maya civilization and occur throughout Maya history, they seem to have reached their highest perfection during the eighth and ninth centuries A.D., in Campeche and Tabasco.

Figurines of early Postclassic times are unknown. A finely modeled pipe of this period, imported from west Mexico and found in the North Colonnade at Chichen Itza, is illustrated in Plate 81*a*. The length of this pipe is 20½ inches; the bowl is 2¼ inches high, flaring to a diameter of 3 inches at the top. In front of the bowl there is a modeled bird's head; this head is hollow and contains a pellet of clay which makes the pipe rattle when moved.

Just behind the bowl there is another appliquéd decoration in strips of clay. The color is a warm terra-cotta red and the pipe has a polished finish.

Incense burners were common in late Postclassic times; these have modeled clay heads and figurines appliquéd to their exterior walls. One from an incense burner found at Mayapan is shown in Plate 81*b*; this dates from the fifteenth century. The features show considerable skill in modeling, but the clay is poorly baked and the painted decorations are crudely applied.

The technique of appliquéing modeled heads to incense burners still persists among the remnants of the Lacandon Maya in eastern Chiapas (Plate 81*d*).

Between the "black dirt" heads from the lowest occupational level at Uaxactun down to the Lacandon incense burner of today (Plate 81*d*), there is a lapse of at least two thousand years. Plastic art has evidently flourished for a very long time.

≡

CERAMICS

POTTERY, THE BEST GUIDE TO CULTURAL DEVELOPMENT

OF ALL the imperishable remains of former cultures which man has left behind him, his pottery best reflects his cultural progress and presents a guide to its sequence. A welter of pottery fragments litters the sites where man formerly lived, and they may be analyzed by the same technique as that worked out by geologists for studying the geological periods through which the earth has passed. This technique, called stratigraphic sequence, works on the general principle that what happened or was made first was deposited first; therefore, the oldest pottery will be found at the bottom of the refuse heaps.

Around the settlements of pottery-making peoples there gradually accumulated refuse heaps of broken pottery, mingled with other debris. These heaps are usually found in exposed places, and the perishable materials in them have largely disappeared. Except in sheltered refuse heaps in unusually dry climates, only such indestructible objects may be found as stone, shell, bone, and—most important for the chronologic records—potsherds.

These refuse heaps were always located near the settlements that made them, and may sometimes measure many feet in depth; a cross-section of such a deposit gives a reliable ceramic history of the settlement near which it accumulated. Such stratified deposits of pottery fragments give dependable relative ceramic sequences, but do not, however, furnish an absolute chronology.

This technique for the relative dating of ceramic types has been most highly perfected for the Pueblo Indian cultures of the southwestern United States. There is another factor present in this region which makes even more accurate dating possible, and this is supplied by the roof beams of the houses. The exact ages of these

367

beams may be determined by a study of their growth rings according to a method developed by Dr. A. S. Douglass of the University of Arizona. Once the time span of the settlement has been determined in this way, it is possible to determine more accurately the relative ages of the ceramic wares found there.

In the Maya area, stratified deposits showing ceramic sequence are even more varied than those in the Pueblo region of the United States. In addition to refuse heaps, stratification of ceramic fragments has been found under plaza floors and in superimposed architectural units and tombs. All these sources have been found at Uaxactun, and have provided a relative chronology for central Maya ceramic types. This chronology gives us a framework for the Peten region, a sequence for Copan has recently been published, and additional materials from Piedras Negras and Palenque have been excavated. A volume based on excavations at fifteen sites in Yucatan is now in press. In the Guatemala highlands, Formative and early Classic pottery from Kaminaljuyu have been described, as well as good ceramic sequences from Zacualpa and Zaculeu. The variation in the pottery from these regions is striking enough to indicate that a large number of additional excavations are necessary to learn the whole Maya ceramic development. There are, however, enough interregional similarities throughout to allow the presentation of an over-all picture of development, fixed in time at various points by associated Maya calendric dates.

In the dated Maya monuments we may someday have an absolute chronological yardstick. The dates of many of these monuments have been exactly determined in terms of Maya chronology, and it remains only to align Maya with Christian chronology to have as accurate dating as that afforded by tree rings.

Such are the variety, complexity, number, and specialization of Maya ceramic wares, however, and so close their association with exactly dated monuments that, when the whole story has been pieced together and all the existing evidence gathered in, we shall probably know more about the ceramics of the Maya area, of the cities or localities where the different wares originated, of their distribution and disappearance from the Maya picture, than we shall ever know about the ceramics of any other people of ancient America.

With little question, the art of pottery making was not invented in the Maya lowlands. Guatemala highland Formative pottery shows elaboration which suggests that this area, a likely point of origin of maize agriculture, was also a focal point in early ceramic development. Here in earliest Formative times (Las Charcas phase) is found pottery with simple, one-color painted designs, shoe-shaped cooking pots, *comales*, bowls with grater bottoms, and a peculiar cup-shaped vessel with long, tripod legs, which lasted in use through all periods in some areas of Mesoamerica. Both cylindrical and flat clay stamps, effigy whistles in animal form, and hand-modeled figurines are found. In the next phase in order (Sacatepequez) new colors and forms are added, and in the long final Formative phase in highland Guatemala (Miraflores) there is a continuing history of ceramic development which includes the growth in popularity of tripod legs on bowls, resist-painted designs, and great enrichment and variation in ceramic forms and decoration. Hand-modeled figurines appear in some quantity. Whistling vessels and stirrup-spouted vessels, both forms chiefly known from Peru, appear in this phase.

The three Formative-stage phases in the Guatemala highlands show a continuous development with no evidence of change due to foreign influence. In general, the closest counterparts to this development lie in the Mexican highlands. Large temple substructures and magnificently furnished tombs characterize the Miraflores phase, indicating that by then the priestly hierarchy was well organized. Other arts and crafts during Formative times are as highly developed as are the ceramics.

In the Maya lowland area, Formative ceramics are not so fully known, and those found are not so elaborate. However, this may be due to the fact that no early, rich tombs come from this area. The ceramics are almost exclusively monochrome, although finely burnished and meticulously shaped, but the form and decorative repertories are limited.

Formative pottery is quite similar throughout the Maya lowland area, even in the distant Maya-speaking Huastec region. The striated, unslipped cooking pot is a ubiquitous form, arguing for common cooking practices which lasted through the whole time span of the Maya pre-Hispanic culture. The distribution of the *comale*, a flat platter used for roasting tortillas, suggests that this food was largely restricted to the highland area until the Conquest.

CLASSIC STAGE

The hallmark of the Classic stage in the central Maya area is the evolution of polychrome pottery. Over much of Mesoamerica in late Formative times, orange slipped pottery was decorated by painting in red, outlined by an incised line. In the first polychromes, black or white painted outlining was substituted for the incising. Earlier designs were simple and largely geometric. In the mainland Mexican area, Classic pottery was chiefly monochrome, but in the central Maya area were developed the most elaborate and exquisitely designed painted pottery of the New World. The earliest polychromes (early Tzakol phase) were decorated in geometric style. Later (Tepeu phase) naturalistic designs, some of them narrative in character, were painted. The pottery designs doubtlessly copied the Maya manuscripts, the production of which must have been a major activity of the priests of this period. The ceramics show finer draftsmanship than the three Maya codices which are extant, but the glyphic inscriptions on the pottery were for the most part painted by illiterate although proficient craftsmen. This suggests that hieroglyphic writing was, during Classic times as at the Conquest, a priestly monopoly, a specialty requiring long training. The finest naturalistic polychrome was made in the southern valleys of the central area in late Classic times. In the western end of the central area, incised and plano-relief decoration was highly developed. Classic-stage Maya pottery does not in general show the extreme conservatism of Maya sculpture and calendrics during this period. Changes in secular culture seem to have been uninhibited by the conservatism characteristic of highly formalized religion.

TABLE IX

SELECTED CERAMIC SEQUENCES FROM THE MAYA AREA

Stage	Dates According to 11.16.0.0.0 Correlation		Central Area			Highlands	Yucatan
	Christian	Maya	Uaxactun	San José	Copan		
Preclassic (Formative)			Mamom			Las Charcas	Early
						Sacatepequez	Formative Middle
				I			
			Chicanel			Miraflores	Late
			disjunction				
			Incised Dichrome Horizon				
Classic (Initial Series)	A.D. 300	8.14.0.0.0	I	Beginnings of Polychrome Pottery			Early
		9.0.0.0.0	2 Tzakol	II	Early Classic	Esperanza	Middle
	A.D. 500		3				Regional
		9.10.0.0.0	I	III	Full Classic		Late
			2 Tepeu	IV			Early
			Mold-Made Figurines				
		10.0.0.0.0	3	V	disjunction	Amatle-Pamplona	Florescent Full
	A.D. 1000	10.10.0.0.0	Plumbate and X Fine Orange Traded				
				Postclassic		Qankyak	Early
Postclassic (Mexican)		11.0.0.0.0	Little evidence of Postclassic occupation			Xinabahul	Mexican Middle Late
		11.10.0.0.0	Figurine Incensarios				
	A.D. 1500	12.0.0.0.0	Conquest of the Itza (1697)			Spanish Colonial	

During the second half of the Classic stage, figurines appear in the central Maya area; their center of development seems to be along the Gulf of Campeche in the states of Tabasco and Campeche. The finest lots of figurines come from the Island of Jaina, although good examples also come from the region of Palenque and Jonuta. The figurines range in height from 4 to 10 inches. They are made of a fine-textured orange clay, and often bear a white wash, with traces of paint in blue and other colors. They are usually found in graves. There are two types: one solid and hand-modeled, the other with mold-pressed front and plain clay back; the latter often contains pellets to make a rattle, or a whistle and stops to form an ocarina. Detailing on these figurines is amazingly fine; tattooed designs are shown clearly on faces no larger than a thumbnail. Without question these are the most intricate and detailed work in clay in pre-Columbian America. Figurines, flageolets, and other small pottery objects, generally similar in style to the Jaina mold-made figurines, are found over a larger area, including the Peten, Puuc, and La Venta regions.

In the northern Yucatan plain the ceramics contemporaneous to the central Classic stage show a sharply marked division into two traditions: the earlier (Regional stage) pottery is closely similar to the pottery of the central area; the later (Florescent stage) stems from developments in the Puuc–Chenes–Rio Bec area, where a separate tradition developed in early or mid-Classic times. Regional-stage pottery consisted of monochromes which are strikingly similar to those of the Peten, but polychrome was little used; along the western border a thus far unique but highly developed ceramic assemblage is found. The presence of central-Maya-style ceramics in the north suggests that this area was culturally peripheral to the Peten, where the earliest Classic Maya stelae and architecture have been found. Yucatan has, however, produced the best documented ceramic sequences leading from Maya Formative into Regional, and sizable middle and late Formative temple substructures. These are the work of well-organized communities of considerable size. It is also notable that every archaeological site sampled on the northern plain has produced late Formative ceramics. The religious centers of northern Yucatan were thus established well before the "Maya civilization" developed, and continued to be occupied until after the collapse of the Peten centers.

The Florescent-stage ceramics follow those of the Regional stage in Yucatan, but they had a specific point of origin, and they spread during a considerable time period before they replaced the Regional ceramics over the whole northern end of the peninsula. The distinguishing and diagnostic Florescent potteries are the slate-wares, characterized by a waxy gray to brownish slip, occasionally ornamented with a pale, crudely applied grayish paint. Despite their drab coloring, they are characterized by a fine smooth finish, careful forming, and technical excellence. They seem to be the product of a carefully organized, competent group of craftsmen, whereas the Peten polychromes are creations of talented individuals. A further evidence of the "industrialization" of Maya pottery is found in the use of the *k'abal* among modern Yucatecans. The k'abal is a wooden cylinder which rests on a smooth board and is spun between the soles of the potter's feet. With the k'abal the operator can vary the process of forming a pot from the simple scraping and spreading technique used by Indians over large areas of the Americas, to a procedure very close to the wheel throwing used by Old World potters as early as 3000 B.C. Although the potter's wheel was never used in pre-Columbian America, vessels made on a k'abal have the even, elaborate contours characteristic of wheel-made pottery, and such characteristics are found on much pre-Conquest Maya ceramics.

The exact region of origin of the Yucatecan slatewares is unknown, but may likely have been the Chenes area. To the south in the Rio Bec area the few available data indicate that the archaeological sites are sharply differentiated both architecturally and ceramically from the Peten-style ruins to the south of them. A sort of cultural frontier seems to have existed here along a well-defined line, formed perhaps by expansion of two political groups— Peten to the south, Chenes–Rio Bec to the north. The Puuc-region ceramics are a variation of Chenes style, showing indications, as does the architecture, of a later dating. It would seem that the Puuc area was colonized relatively late by people from neighboring areas, perhaps only after cistern storage of water was evolved (see chapter V). Puuc-style buildings and ceramics are found on Chenes sites, and vice versa; there was certainly no frontier here, and it is likely that all three areas—Puuc, Chenes, Rio Bec—had common cultural origins, constant interconnections, and that the Puuc was the last of these regions to be settled.

It was probably after 9.18.0.0.0 (A.D. 790) that Florescent ceramics and Puuc-Chenes-style architecture came to dominate all of northern Yucatan to the extinction of earlier ceramics and architecture. The spread of slatewares was gradual; there is evidence that for a period of at least a hundred years and perhaps longer, slatewares of Chenes type were used with Regional monochromes. The correlation of vessel shapes and wares in these deposits is revealing, certain vessel forms occurring only in slateware, others only in monochrome. It seems likely that trade took place among various communities during this period, each with its specialty in pottery wares and forms, much as native goods are traded now in the area. There is evidence for the same sort of community specialization and trade among the Puuc sites.

The vessel types in the Maya area during the Initial Series period are quite similar throughout. In slipped ware there were two size ranges of jars, one large enough to carry a full backload of water, the other of two- to three-quart capacity. Hemispheroid basins are common, and low platters are found in some areas; both have thickened rims. Bowls are of two types, both smaller than the preceding shapes. Basal break bowls hold one to three quarts; their bottoms are nearly flat, their sides are flaring, and they have specialized supports, either a ring or three legs. Hemispheroid bowls hold a pint to a quart and have either a flattened bottom or a ring base. The unslipped, externally striated cooking pots have been described above. *Incensarios* for religious ceremonies were also unslipped, but they were decorated with appliqué and painted with white clay or plaster. Among the thin, finely made, and elaborately decorated vessels which were so widely traded, the common-

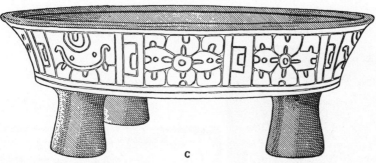

Fig. 43.—Examples of Fine Orange ware from the Postclassic; (*a*) from Uxmal; (*b* and *c*) from Chichen Itza.

↑ *b*) Bowl from Dzan.

↑ *a*) Excavated fragment, Uxmal.

PLATE 83.—SLATEWARE, PUUC PERIOD,
FROM NORTHERN YUCATAN

↓ *c*) Jar, provenance unknown.

d) Engraved vase found near Ticul. ↓

Plate 84.—Plumbate Ware, Mexican Period, from
Northern Yucatan

↑ *a*) Coarse red ware tripod bowls, northern Yucatan.

↓ *b*) Incense burner found near Chichen Itza.

PLATE 85
LATE
DECADENT
WARES,
PERIOD OF
DISINTEGRATION

est shape is cylindrical; some flare slightly, some are barrel-shaped.
Thin, decorated hemispheroid bowls with flaring ring bases also
belong in this group.

This is a simple repertory of pottery forms, perhaps mirroring
a simple way of life. The Maya seem to have channeled their love
of the rich and ornate exclusively into their religion.

POSTCLASSIC STAGE

The Postclassic ceramics of Chichen Itza aid our understanding
of the Toltec conquest. In their materials and craftsmanship they
are direct descendants of the Florescent ceramics which preceded
them, but in form and decoration they are slavish and rather poor
copies of the Fine Orange pottery imported by the Toltecs from
Veracruz. Following the Toltec period there were changes in the
preparation of pottery clay and later a change to the red slip color
which is still used in Yucatan. Later still, the introduction of a new
form of cooking pot suggests the bringing in of foreign women in
numbers, and the introduction of figurine incensarios indicates a
striking change in religious custom.

The Spaniards made fewer changes in the ceramics of Yucatan
than did the Toltecs. Glaze was never introduced, nor has the
potter's wheel displaced the k'abal. The vessel forms also have
remained amazingly constant, perhaps a reflection of the surprisingly slight changes in Maya folk life in general. The period from
A.D. 1350 to 1950 has been probably the most conservative in the
ceramic history of Yucatan. Since Toltec conquest this area changed
from the most progressive in the New World to a cultural backwater.

MISCELLANEOUS ARTS AND CRAFTS

TEXTILES

NO CLASSIC-STAGE textiles have survived and only a few from the Postclassic. Fragments of white cotton cloth, thought to date from before the Conquest, are reported from Tenam in eastern Chiapas; the supposed late Postclassic dating of this cloth is based upon the associated pottery. Numerous small pieces of carbonized cloth were recovered from the Well of Sacrifice at Chichen Itza. They show many complicated weaves, and date from late Postclassic times.

These are the only specimens of ancient Maya textiles that have yet been discovered, but the Classic and Postclassic sculptures bear witness to their former abundance and variety. The modern Maya of the highlands of Guatemala have a rich textile art which no doubt derives from their pre-Conquest ancestors. The Lacandon Maya of eastern Chiapas still practice spinning and handloom weaving, crafts that have disappeared in northern Yucatan only during the past generation or two.

Classic-stage sculptures indicate that the cotton fabrics of that period were of rich and complicated weave, and elaborate embroidery seems to have been employed. A few representations of these textiles, taken from the monuments, are shown in Figure 44, *a*, *b*, *c*, and *d*. Textiles from the Postclassic stage are illustrated in Figure 44, *e*, *f*, *g*, and *h*.

Hand-woven cotton materials (*patis*) of fixed length and width were used as articles of trade in ancient times and after the Conquest became the principal form of tribute (*mantas*) exacted from the Indians.

The Lacandon, whose living conditions closely resemble those of the ancient Maya, still spin cotton thread and weave a coarse cloth, using the same techniques as did their ancestors.

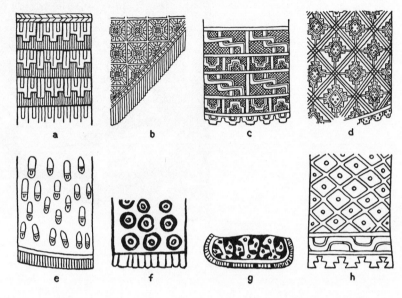

a   b   c   d

e   f   g   h

FIG. 44.—Classic textiles (*a, b, c, d*) taken from the monuments; and Postclassic textiles (*e, f, g, h*) from wall paintings and pottery.

Spinning and weaving is done by the women. They gather the cotton and spin it into thread, using as a spindle a slender pointed stick about 10 inches long, weighted near the lower end with a disk of pottery. These disks, or spindle whorls, are all that has survived of ancient Maya spinning and weaving implements. They gave balance and weight to the spindle as it was twirled in the right hand, while the lower end of the spindle rested in a gourd on the ground; the unspun cotton was held in the left hand or thrown over the left shoulder (Plate 86*a*).

The Maya loom was of the same general type as those of other American Indian groups. One wooden rod is fastened to each end of the warp to keep the cloth stretched to the desired width. A thick hemp cord (*yamal*), attached to each end of the lower rod,

a) Spinning. →

← *b*) Weaving.

PLATE 86.—SPINNING AND WEAVING
AMONG THE LACANDON MAYA, CHIAPAS

passes behind the weaver, permitting her to tighten the warp by leaning backward. The upper rod is attached to a tree or post. The strip of cloth may be made as long as eight feet, and as it lengthens it is wound around the upper rod. The weaver sits as far back from the post as possible in order to hold the loom horizontally at the required tension (Plate 86*b*). The looms are 2½ to 3 feet wide, and when wider cloth is desired two strips are sewed together. An ancient representation of this technique appears in the Codex Tro-Cortesianus (Fig. 45), where Ixchel, patroness of the art, is shown weaving.

Fig. 45.—The goddess Ixchel weaving. Page 79, Codex Tro-Cortesianus.

The towns and villages of Guatemala are still characterized by the different kinds of cloth they weave and by their traditional designs. Although wool has been introduced since the Conquest, most native clothing is still made of hand-loomed cotton cloth. Today silk is generally used for embroidery, but colored cotton threads and feathers were used in earlier times. There are no identical designs, but in each village there is general conformity to the traditional pattern (Plate 26, *a* and *b*).

The color symbolism used by the Guatemala Indians in their designs still bears some relation to that used by the ancient Maya. Black represents weapons because it is the color of obsidian; yellow symbolizes food because it is the color of corn; red represents blood; and blue means sacrifice. The royal color is green because that is the color of the quetzal bird, whose plumage was reserved for the rulers.

In coloring textiles the thread is dyed rather than the finished fabric. Although aniline dyes are now replacing organic and mineral colors, a few are still in use. Perhaps the most highly prized native dye was a deep purple obtained from a mollusk found along the Pacific coast (*Purpura patula*, Linnaeus and Lamarck), a relative of the Mediterranean mollusk which gave the famous "royal purple of Tyre."

In Yucatan the type of embroidery used by the modern Maya is cross-stitch (*xoc bil chui* or "threads that are counted"). The earlier designs may have been geometric like those still used in central Quintana Roo (Plate 26*c*), but geometric designs are now largely replaced by floral motifs (Plate 26*d*).

But native weaves and colors are everywhere giving way to machine-made fabrics and aniline dyes. Except in the highlands of Guatemala, the native textile art has almost disappeared.

BASKETRY AND MATTING

No early Maya baskets have been discovered, but they are depicted in Classic-stage graphic art. An elaborate basket appears in Lintel 24 at Yaxchilan (Fig. 46*a*). The upper half is in a twilled

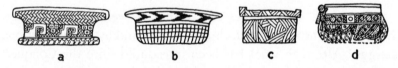

a   b   c   d

FIG. 46.—Classic and Postclassic baskets from the monuments, wall paintings, and pottery: (*a*) on Lintel 24, Yaxchilan; (*b* and *c*) on the Nebaj Vase; (*d*) fresco in the Temple of the Jaguars, Chichen Itza.

technique, the middle section shows a design of stepped frets and small squares, and the bottom seems to be ornamented with featherwork. Representations of two late Classic-stage baskets are shown in Figure 46, *b* and *c*, from the Nebaj Vase. A Postclassic basket from a wall painting in the Temple of the Jaguars at Chichen Itza (Fig. 46*d*) is more elaborate but less effective.

Modern Maya baskets are relatively crude. Some are woven from thin, tough vines; these are large and coarse and are used for carrying corn. Split-cane baskets, smaller and more neatly woven, are used in the home.

No pieces of matting have survived, but imprints have been found on pottery and plaster. A small heap of disintegrated material, apparently the remains of a palm-fiber mat, was found below the plaza floor at Uaxactun. The imprint of another piece was found in the temple beneath the Castillo at Chichen Itza; the Red Jaguar throne had rested upon this matting. The weave of this Postclassic piece was identical with that of mats which are still made in Mérida.

Mats seem to have played an important role in ancient Maya life. A piece of matting with the sun symbol beside it (Fig. 19*a*) is the hieroglyph for the first month of the ancient Maya year, *Pop*, which means "matting." Sitting on a mat was a mark of authority, and throughout the Book of Chilam Balam of Chumayel the words "mat" and "throne" are used interchangeably. The sequence of the hieroglyphic inscriptions on the backs of Stela J at Copan (Fig. 47*b*) and Stela H at Quirigua (Fig. 47*a*) follow the weave of a mat pattern in the order of their reading.

Baskets and matting must have been common among the ancient Maya, and the materials from which they were made occur in abundance throughout the area.

PAINTING

Painting was a fine art among the ancient Maya, and reached a high degree of excellence. Frescoes were used in wall decoration, and painting was also used in the decoration of ceramics and in illustrating the codices.

The Maya palette was extensive. There were several reds, ranging from an opaque purplish red to a brilliant orange. A coppery tan color was used extensively for outlining, while varying mixtures of red with opaque white gave a number of pinks. The yellows ranged from a pale greenish yellow to a dark yellow. A dark brown resulted from mixing yellow and black. There seems to have been but a single blue; this was painted over an opaque ground to obtain a Prussian blue or laid directly on white plaster

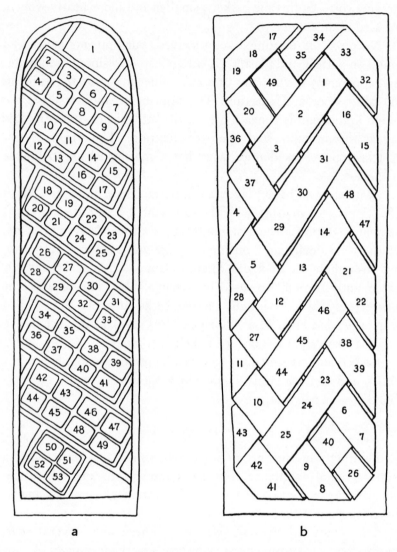

Fig. 47.—Mat patterns shown on the backs of Postclassic monuments; the glyph sequence in these inscriptions follows the pattern of a mat. (*a*) Stela H at Quirigua; (*b*) Stela J at Copan.

for a bright cerulean blue. There are many greens, from olive to almost black. No basic green has been found and the different shades probably result from varying mixtures of blue and yellow.

A brilliant, lustrous black was used for outlining, and an opaque white for mixing.

The substance with which the colors were mixed in many examples seems to have been viscous. Chemical analyses of the pigments in the Chichen Itza frescoes show no trace of this carrying substance. It was probably organic and has disappeared with time. It may have been the resin of the *pom* tree from which copal varnish now is made.

The colors were of both vegetable and mineral origin. There are a number of trees in the Yucatan Peninsula which yield excellent dyes. Analysis of Chichen Itza pigments shows that they are largely of mineral origin, but this may be due to the fact that vegetable colors are more perishable. The reds are made from hematite and the yellows from ocherous earths and clays. Charcoal and other carbonized organic matter was the essential ingredient of the black pigment. The strong blue, although its exact nature has not been identified, was inorganic—probably some mineral clay.

The brushes with which these pigments were applied have not been found, but the quality of the painting indicates their excellence. Some brushes were so delicately made that fine tapering lines could be drawn with them, while coarser brushes were used for filling in backgrounds and broader spaces. The brushes were probably made of fine feathers or of hair.

The oldest painting in the Maya area is the fresco in Structure B-XIII at Uaxactun, excavated by the Carnegie Institution in 1937 (Plate 50). This building dates from the Early Period (prior to A.D. 593) and had undergone several changes in ancient times; some of its chambers show beam-and-mortar roof construction. The fresco is in black, red, orange, yellow, and gray, and measures 9 feet 10 inches wide by 4 feet 1 inch high. Twenty-six human figures are shown, arranged in two horizontal panels and interspersed with several panels of hieroglyphs. Beneath the lower figure panel is a horizontal line of seventy-two day signs (not shown in Plate 50) beginning with the day 12 Imix and ending with 5 Eb. The composition doubtless portrays some important ceremony.

Hieroglyphic inscriptions are painted on interior walls of the palace at Palenque, and the walls of the shrine in Structure 33 at Yaxchilan show traces of scrolls and figures in red and blue.

By far the most spectacular, as well as the most informative, Maya murals yet discovered are those of Bonampak, Chiapas. These paintings, discovered in 1946 by Giles Healey, cover the three vaulted chambers of a building. They are in excellent condition, preserved by the formation of a heavy coat of stalactitic limestone which has resulted from constant seepage of water during more than 1,000 years—they are dated as of Classic stage, at about A.D. 790.

The scenes, room by room, show the holding of a religious ceremony. Room 1 shows the robing of the priests, the gathering of an orchestra, and a series of conferences. Room 2 continues with a raid to obtain human victims and their ceremonial sacrifice on the stairs of a temple substructure. Room 3 shows the culmination of the rites by a dance in magnificent costumes on the steps of a pyramid, and a bloodletting ceremony by the high priest and his family. The murals contain a number of hieroglyphic texts which date and perhaps explain the pictures and give the names or titles of the participants.

The murals stand in sharp contrast to the sculpture of the stelae, where the principal figure remained stylized in attitude and accouterments for over 500 years. The scenes are narrative in a forthright yet sensitive style. Naturalism was held so important to the artist that the faces of certain of the participants in the murals can be recognized from room to room as they recur in parts of the story. The moods of the scenes vary: postures and facial expressions are relaxed during the preparation for the ceremony, ferocious in the raid, cold and forbidding during the sacrifice. Foreshortening and superposition give an effect of depth. The naturalism is stronger and the drafting more skillful than in any Old World art of the same period.

The first overpowering effect of the Bonampak murals is the magnificence of costuming. Headdresses of delicate featherwork nearly double the height of each principal performer, and the variety of materials used is dazzling—featherwork, cut stone, furs,

↑ *a*) Doorways (left to right) of Rooms 1, 2, and 3. The façade of the building still shows stuccowork and niches above the entrances, the central one containing fragments of a statue.

PLATE 87.—THE TEMPLE OF THE MURALS AT BONAMPAK

b) Floor plan, showing thickness of walls and comparative size of dais and ↓ floor space.

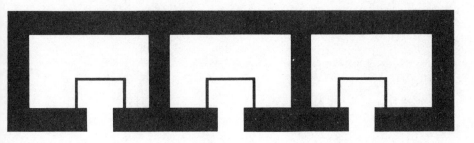

↑ *a)* A view from the back, toward the entrance.

PLATE 88.—INTERIOR OF ROOM 2, TEMPLE OF THE MURALS, BONAMPAK

↓ *b)* Upper mural of the front wall.

Plate 89.—Sacrificial Figures from the Mural of Room 2

PLATE 90.—ATTENDANTS IN THE SACRIFICIAL CEREMONY

intricate woven fabrics. The next impression is that of complete lack of self-consciousness in the performers. There is much gossiping, and a relaxed and individual posture in each figure. It is hard to believe that these people were repressed by a strictly ordered series of ranks, even though the splendor of their costuming varies through a considerable range.

The detailed information given by these murals on the life of the Maya priestly class is tremendous, and will increase as our knowledge for their interpretation increases. One point of interest is the participation of the wife and children of the chief priest in the ceremonies—it had previously been supposed that only men were participants. The practice of human sacrifice was also thought to be entirely or nearly restricted to Postclassic times, but it obviously took place on a considerable scale at Bonampak.

Some of the best paintings of the Classic stage are on the polychrome vases and bowls of the Late Period found at Uaxactun, Holmul, and in the Chama region along the Chixoy River. The finest were found in a stone-lined tomb in Structure A-I at Uaxactun. This must have been the burial of a person of high rank, judging from the magnificence of his burial offerings. The skeleton lay at full length, with the head pointing to the north and both hands clasped against the right shoulder (Fig. 48). At the head stood a painted vase, the extended design of which is shown in Plate 91. The background is a brilliant orange-red; the figures are outlined in black and painted with black and several shades of yellow. Around the top is a line of glyphs, and glyph panels are interspersed between the figures. The principal panel of sixteen glyphs is the center of the design, with all the figures facing it. These glyphs denote a mathematically incorrect Maya date, 7.5.0.0.0 8 Ahau 13 Kankin. It is possible that the date intended was 8.5.0.0.0 12 Ahau 13 Kankin, which would involve two relatively simple changes in the original inscription, but even these corrections give an unlikely date (A.D. 254). Stylistically the vase dates about five hundred years later.

The design shows a priest seated on a throne, facing the central glyph panel. Behind him stands an attendant, painted black and

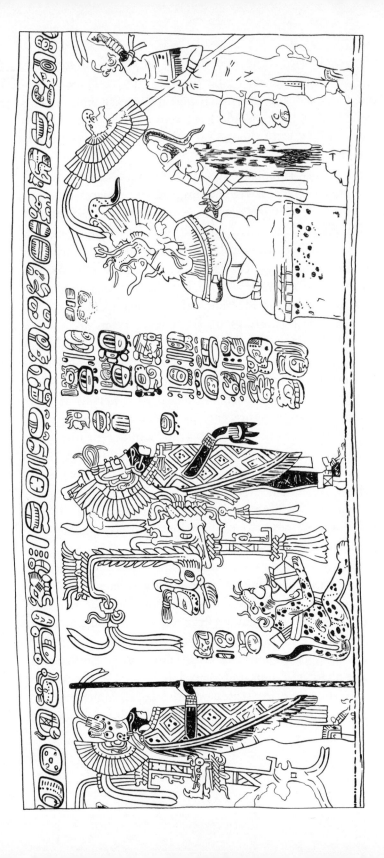

PLATE 91.—CLASSIC-STAGE POLYCHROME VASE PRESENTING
AN INITIAL SERIES DATE, UAXACTUN

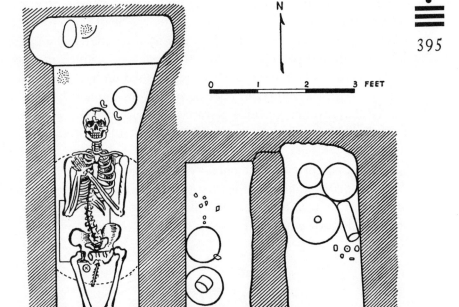

Fig. 48.—Sketch of the burial place of a high priest or principal lord in Structure A-I, Uaxactun, Peten, Guatemala; for a description of the mortuary furniture, see text.

holding an eccentric-shaped flint (see Plate 107a); another figure holds a feather canopy over the priest's head. To the left of the glyph panel are three figures. The two standing figures are also painted black; one carries an eccentric-shaped flint and the other holds a spear; both wear elaborate cloaks. Between them is a seated jaguar offering two bowls, one inverted over the other.

This tomb also contained other polychrome vessels of equal beauty. There were eleven pieces of pottery, nine of them painted. The flat plate with three legs (Fig. 49) is an especially fine piece. The background is terra cotta and the design is outlined in black and painted in black and red. A dancer, poised on his toes, is executing a step; his right arm rests lightly on his hip and his left is turned outward in a graceful gesture. The sure sweep of line and the admirable fitting of the design to the circular space indicate mastery of the art. This plate has a small hole broken in the bottom, apparently a ceremonial "releasing of the spirit" of the vessel so that it might accompany the owner on his journey to the other world. Two other painted plates from this same tomb are shown in Figures 50 and 51.

Fig. 49.—Polychrome plate from tomb in Structure A-I, Uaxactun, Peten.

Fig. 50.—Polychrome plate from tomb in
Structure A-I, Uaxactun, Peten.

Fig. 51.—Polychrome plate from tomb in
Structure A-I, Uaxactun, Peten.

a) The Chama vase.

PLATE 92
CLASSIC-STAGE POLYCHROME VASES FROM THE
CHIXOY VALLEY, GUATEMALA

b) The Ratinlinxul vase.

A famous painted vase from the upper Chixoy Valley in Guatemala is shown with its design extended in Plate 92*a*. The colors are black, red, and brown on a background of pink. Seven figures, interspersed with as many glyph-panels, are portrayed. The two principals face each other and are painted black; the one on the right wears a jaguar-skin cloak. Three of the remaining figures carry fans. Personal characteristics are faithfully rendered, which makes it likely that the figures are portraits.

A similar vase from Nebaj is almost as well done (Plate 93*a*). This has five human figures, five glyph panels, and four larger glyphs at the back of the design. Two figures sit on a dais, with the priest occupying the central position.

A third vase from Ratinlinxul in the same region shows a priest borne in what appears to be a basketry palanquin suspended from carrying poles on the shoulders of retainers (Plate 92*b*). A dog stretches himself realistically below the palanquin. Five retainers follow: the first carries a jaguar-cushioned throne; the next three carry supports for the palanquin when at rest; and the last grasps a fold of cloth in his left hand.

Among the codices, the brushwork of the Codex Dresdensis (Fig. 9) is of the highest quality; the lines are bold and fluid. The Codex Peresianus (Figs. 16 and 29) is not quite so well done but the difference is not great. The Codex Tro-Cortesianus (Fig. 28), however, is much inferior to the others; both figures and glyphs are poorly drawn. All these codices are suspected to be Postclassic copies of Classic-stage originals.

The central capstones in corbel-vaulted chambers were sometimes painted with designs of human figures with single rows of glyphs above and below them. These painted capstones are not common and are confined exclusively to northern sites; all probably date late Classic (Figs. 52 and 53). Wall paintings are also more common at northern centers than in the central area and have been found at Chichen Itza, Tulum, Santa Rita Corozal, Chacmultun, and Santa Rosa Xtampak (Plate 19).

The frescoes from the Temple of the Warriors, the Temple of the Jaguars, and the Monjas at Chichen Itza all date from

a) The Nebaj vase, Chixoy Valley, Guatemala.

PLATE 93.—POLYCHROME VASES (a) FROM THE CLASSIC STAGE
AND (b) FROM THE POSTCLASSIC STAGE

b) Vase from northern Yucatan.

Fig. 52.—Painted capstone from Temple of the Owl, Chichen Itza, Yucatan.

Plate 94.—Wall Painting of a Fishing Village from the Temple of the Warriors, Chichen Itza

the Toltec period, and show obvious Mexican influence. Two scenes
of human sacrifice have been illustrated (Plate 28, *e* and *f*) and a
wall painting of a coastal village from the Temple of Warriors is **403**
shown in Plate 94. The sea occupies the lower third of this pic-

Fig. 53.—Painted capstone from tomb, Chichen Itza, Yucatan.

ture, and there are three canoes, each with an oarsman in the prow
and two men fishing. A variety of marine life swarms in the water.

404 On shore at the right there is a flat-roofed temple, a feathered
serpent rising from the inner chamber and two worshipers kneeling in the outer chamber. There are several thatched houses of
typical Maya design interspersed with trees. A number of people
go about their daily tasks and the whole picture is peaceful and
domestic.

Another mural from the Temple of the Jaguars portrays a
vigorous assault on a Maya village (Fig. 54). Only two of the
attackers show in the lower left corner; a serpent curls behind one
of them, apparently his patron deity. The defending warriors
swarm out of their village and behind them, among the thatched
houses, are the women. The composition is full of action and there
are no superfluous lines.

A mural from the Temple of the Warriors shows another
battle. A temple stands in a lake in the upper left corner and several fish, a snail, a crab, and a jaguar appear in the water. Half a
dozen nude captives, painted with stripes and their arms tied behind their backs, are being led off by warriors or priests. Other
warriors seem to be defending a temple in the lower right corner
(Plate 25).

The wall paintings at Tulum and Santa Rita Corozal are religious in character. They date from late Postclassic times, and show
such striking resemblances to Mixtec art as to assure a common
religion in the two areas.

A few painted vases have been found in Yucatan, although
they may not have been made there; one of the best is shown in
Plate 93*b*. At the right is a tree whose trunk shows the outline of a
human face; a figure is seated on each of the two branches while
a serpent coils around the trunk. At the right is a standing figure
who is blowing on a conch shell. Beneath the branches two deer
are seated, the one at the right completely swathed in bandages.
The left half of the composition shows two figures facing a deer,
which seems to be shedding its horns. The figure in front of the
deer grasps an antler, and the deer has a blanket on its back deco-

FIG. 54.—Detail from wall
painting of a battle, Temple
of the Jaguars, Chichen Itza,
Yucatan.

rated with crossbones. The three figures at the left all wear short jaguar-skin skirts or kilts. Above the deer hovers a white bird of prey with hawklike beak. The scene may represent a ceremony held at the time the deer shed their horns, which in Yucatan takes place in March.

LAPIDARY ART

The finest examples of Maya lapidary art are carved jades, the earliest of which were made during Preclassic times. The earliest dated piece is the Leyden Plate, engraved in 320 (Plate 15), on which the carving is little more than incised. The figure and the glyphs are well done for the early period at which they were executed, but the quality of line appears slightly blurred.

Another early piece from Copan, carved perhaps two hundred years later, shows improvement in technique. This piece (Plate 95*a*), a three-inch pendant, shows a seated human figure in left profile. The hole for the suspension cord enters at the mouth of the figure and emerges at the back of the neck; the drilling was done from both sides. The carving is rounded and the style is pleasing.

A fine piece of early Classic carved jade was excavated at Kaminaljuyu, the archaeological site on the outskirts of Guatemala City. Although this site lies outside the Classic Maya area, the Maya origin of this piece (Plate 95*b*) is unmistakable. It presents a standing human figure instead of a seated one, and the design is more elaborate. This piece is 6 inches high; the body appears in front view and the head and headdress in left profile. The head has a typical Maya profile and the headdress is formed by the head and foreleg of a crocodile.

A finer piece is a jade head (Plate 95, *c* and *d*), which dates from A.D. 674. Although found at Chichen Itza, it was probably carved at Piedras Negras, where the unusual non-period-ending date which it presents, 9.12.2.0.16 (674), is recorded three times; this date appears nowhere else in the Maya area. It is 3¾ inches high, and is hollowed out behind. The headdress is formed of a

a) Early Period pendant, Copan.
←

PLATE 95
CARVED JADES
(CLASSIC STAGE)

↑ c) Pendant of Piedras Negras style.

↑ d) Profile view.

←

b) Pendant, Kaminaljuyu.

e) Pendant, Piedras Negras.

↑ f) Profile view.

PLATE 96.—CARVED JADES
(CLASSIC STAGE)

a) Plaque showing Maya ruler. →

b) Statuette from Temple A-XVIII, Uaxactun. ↓

↓ *c*) Profile.

PLATE 97.—CARVED JADES
(POSTCLASSIC STAGE)

a) Carved head and necklace from cache lying on the Red Jaguar Throne, Chichen Itza.   →

b) Head from cache under Castillo Stairway, Chichen Itza.   ↓

↓ *c*) Figure from same cache.

jaguar head, and the inscription is incised on a flat edge surrounding the hollow at the back.

    A jade head of unknown provenance is shown in Plate 95, *e* and *f*. This belongs to the latest part of the Classic stage, when jade carving was at its best. The features are classic Maya and the technique is excellent.

The plaque shown in Plate 96*a* also dates from very late in the Classic stage. It is wedge-shaped, perforated longitudinally near the top, and is about 4 inches high. A handsomely dressed priest is seated on a throne, body in front view and head in left profile. The headdress consists of a serpent with opened jaws from which emerges a small figure with a grotesque face. Another figure kneels before the throne, and an elaborate "speech scroll" issues from the priest's mouth. The color of this piece is a lovely blue-green. It is almost certainly of Maya origin, although it was found near San Juan Teotihuacan, twenty-five miles northeast of Mexico City.

The jade statuette of a human figure carved in the full round is shown in Plate 96, *b* and *c*. It was found under the stairway leading to Temple A-XVIII at Uaxactun. The eyes are rectangular and painted a brilliant red. There are a number of small holes drilled in the figure, possibly for attaching ornaments. This statuette, which weighs 11½ pounds, is the largest piece of carved jade found in the Maya area. A large boulder of unworked solid jade weighing slightly over 200 pounds was discovered under the stairway of a pyramid at Kaminaljuyu. It is water-worn and apparently has had many small pieces sawed from it, perhaps for making into ornaments.

Three pieces of engraved jade from Chichen Itza are shown in Plate 93; although somewhat inferior to the jades previously illustrated, they are excellently carved. The two largest were found in a stone box at the base of the stairway which leads to the early temple buried inside the Castillo pyramid at Chichen Itza.

The Ruz tomb at Palenque yielded a carved jade of excellent workmanship (Plate 98*a*). The figurine, which was found in the sarcophagus itself, represents Kinich Ahau, the sun god.

↑ *a*) Jade figurine.

PLATE 98.—OBJECTS FROM THE RUZ TOMB, PALENQUE

↓ *b*) Stucco mask.   ↓ *c*) Stucco mask of Classic-type profile.

↑ *a*) The interior.

PLATE 99.—SARCOPHAGUS FOUND IN THE RUZ TOMB, PALENQUE

↓ *b*) Detail of relief on the outer surface.

↑ *a*) Entry.   ↑ *b*) Stucco figures on wall.

PLATE 100.—INTERIOR OF THE CRYPT, TEMPLE OF THE
INSCRIPTIONS, PALENQUE

↓ *c*) View toward entry steps.   ↓ *d*) View from steps.

Natural deposits of jade have never been found in Meso-america, though geologists believe that there were two principal sources of supply: (1) the mountains of southern Mexico in the states of Guerrero and Oaxaca and (2) the highlands of western Guatemala. Pieces of jade were probably found as water-worn pebbles or boulders in streams, varying in weight from a few ounces to several hundred pounds. The shape and size of the original piece often influenced the design into which it was carved. A study of Middle American jades by mineralogists of the Carnegie Institution of Washington has shown that American jades are true jade-ites, though their chemical composition differs from that of Chinese jadeite. This variation is not sufficient to place them outside the true jadeite group, but it makes them differ somewhat in appearance from Chinese jades. American jade is not so translucent as Chinese jade; it varies from dark green to light blue-green, through all shades of gray and into white; it is also more mottled than Chinese jade.

American jade is extremely hard—6.5 to 6.8 in the mineralogical scale, the diamond being graded 10—and when we consider that the ancient Maya had no metal tools, their mastery of jade carving is a technical achievement. Pieces of jade were sawed by drawing cords back and forth through grooves and by using stone particles and water as a cutting agent. Holes were bored from both ends with drills of bone or hardwood, again using finely crushed stone and water as the cutting agent, with the perforations meeting in the middle. Hollow bird bones were used for drilling circles and segments of circles. In the finer pieces a modeled effect was probably achieved by careful incising, followed by deepening and smoothing the grooves.

MOSAICS

Few mosaics from either the Classic or Postclassic have survived. Mirrors made of fitted pieces of iron pyrites attached to backs of wood or stone have been found at Piedras Negras and Kaminaljuyu. There are suggestions of jade mosaics in Classic-stage reliefs, and a fine mask has been reconstructed from the jade pieces found in the Ruz tomb at Palenque.

Examples of turquoise mosaic from the Postclassic are four disks found buried in ceremonial caches at Chichen Itza. These were not made in Yucatan, which lacks deposits of turquoise, but were brought from central Mexico, where the technique was common during the fourteenth to sixteenth centuries.

The first was found by the Carnegie Institution of Washington in a covered limestone jar (Plate 43*b*) beneath the floor of the Temple of the Chac Mool, which was later incorporated into the pyramid of the Temple of the Warriors. The backing of this disk had been made of wood which was almost rotted away. The restored disk is in the National Museum of Anthropology and History, Mexico City (Plate 43*a*). Three similar disks were found by the Mexican government in the buried temple under the Castillo at Chichen Itza—two in the same box with the carved jades illustrated in Plate 97, *b* and *c*, and the third on the seat of the Red Jaguar Throne. One of the first two disks is in the Museum of Archaeology and History at Merida; the last still rests on the seat of the Red Jaguar Throne (Plate 73*c*).

METALWORK

The only metal objects recovered from a Classic-stage center under archaeological conditions are a pair of legs belonging to a small, hollow figurine made of a gold-copper alloy (Fig. 55*c*), which were found at Copan. Analysis of this alloy, as well as the casting technique employed, suggests that it was made in Costa Rica or Panama. The legs were recovered from the dirt fill of the foundation vault under Stela H, dedicated in 782 (Plate 68*a*). The other parts of the figurine were not located, and the pieces recovered may have found their way into the vault some time later than the dedicatory date.

Metal objects from the Postclassic are also infrequent. The greatest number recovered have been dredged from the Well of Sacrifice at Chichen Itza, though copper bells have been found elsewhere.

Gold and copper objects from the Well of Sacrifice include disks decorated in repoussé technique (Fig. 56, *a*, *d*, and *e*), cup and saucer (Fig. 56*c*), necklaces, bracelets (Fig. 56*b*), masks, pendants (Plate 101, *a* and *c*), rings (Fig. 55, *a* and *b*), earplugs, bells (Fig. 55, *d*, *e*, and *f*, and Plate 101*b*), and beads. The style and workmanship of many of the smaller objects indicate that they were also made in Costa Rica and Panama.

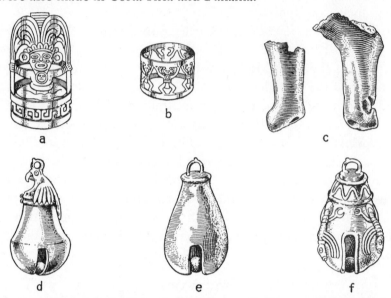

a
b
c
d
e
f

F IG. 55.—Examples of metalwork from Copan, Honduras, and from Chichen Itza, Yucatan: (*a*, *b*) gold finger rings and (*d*, *e*, *f*) copper bells, all dredged from the Well of Sacrifice; (*c*) pair of legs of gold found in the cruciform vault below Stela H.

Most of these metal objects probably reached Chichen Itza as articles of trade. Chemical analyses have established that they came from as far south as Colombia, Panama, Honduras, and Guatemala, and from as far west and north as Chiapas, Oaxaca, and the Valley of Mexico. The copper pieces which contain tin and arsenic came from Oaxaca and the Valley of Mexico; those containing only tin are from Honduras. The purest copper came from Guatemala and Chiapas.

All objects which show casting are of foreign origin. The only technique with which Maya goldsmiths were familiar was hammering and repoussé work. It is probable that the gold used in the few objects actually made at Chichen Itza was obtained by

← *a*) Pendant.

b) Bell. →

PLATE 101.—POSTCLASSIC-STAGE GOLDWORK. WELL OF SACRIFICE, CHICHEN ITZA

↓ *c*) Three portions of mask.

Fig. 56.—Gold and copper objects from the Well of Sacrifice, Chichen Itza, Yucatan: (*a*, *d*, and *e*) disks decorated in repoussé technique; (*b*) gold bracelet; (*c*) gold cup and saucer.

reworking cast-gold objects of foreign origin. These local pieces are usually thin disks decorated with scenes of battle. The scenes represent conflicts between the Maya of Chichen Itza and the Mexican conquerors. The central designs from three such disks are reproduced in Figure 57. The figures are similar to those in the reliefs and frescoes of the Toltec Period at Chichen Itza, and the disks probably date from that period.

a

b

FIG. 57. — Central designs of three gold disks in repoussé technique from the Well of Sacrifice, Chichen Itza, Yucatan: (*a, b*) two Mexican warriors, right, armed with spears and spear throwers, and two Maya warriors with feather capes at the left; (*c*) the two Maya warriors retreating at the right, before the two pursuing Mexicans.

c

The most common metal objects recovered from the Well of Sacrifice are small copper bells of the sleigh-bell type. These bells were a common ornament of the death god (Fig. 55, *d*, *e*, and *f*) and are usually associated with him.

FLINT CHIPPING

Flint chipping was a fine art among the ancient Maya. Substela caches of eccentric-shaped flints (Plate 102, *a* and *b*) and blades (Plate 102*c*) are often found buried under Maya monuments. Perhaps the finest examples of this craft are the elaborate but delicately chipped staff heads excavated at El Palmar in Quintana Roo (Plate 102*d*) and at Quirigua (Plate 102*e*). A small piece broken from the bottom of the El Palmar flint was not found, but in its original condition it was a completely closed design. Three human heads in profile are shown on the Quirigua piece.

FEATHERWORK

A few examples of Aztec featherwork have been found, but none of the ancient Maya work has survived. The graphic art of the Classic and Postclassic periods shows how rich and highly developed it must have been, and early Spanish writers frequently allude to it.

The forests of the Yucatan Peninsula teem with birds of gorgeous plumage, and the highlands of Guatemala are the habitat of the beautiful quetzal. Feathers were utilized in making panaches, crests, capes, and shields. They were also used for pendant decorations to spears and scepters, and in canopies, fans, and personal ornaments. Featherwork was also used in embroideries and fringes for cotton fabrics.

One of the loveliest examples is the panache of the headdress worn by the priest on Wall Panel 3 at Piedras Negras (Plate 69). Such long plumes must have been the tail feathers of the quetzal. A similar headdress is worn by the priest on Stela 12 at Piedras Negras (Plate 18*c*), who also wears a short feather cape. The graceful and slightly stylized treatment of the featherwork lends distinction to these fine reliefs.

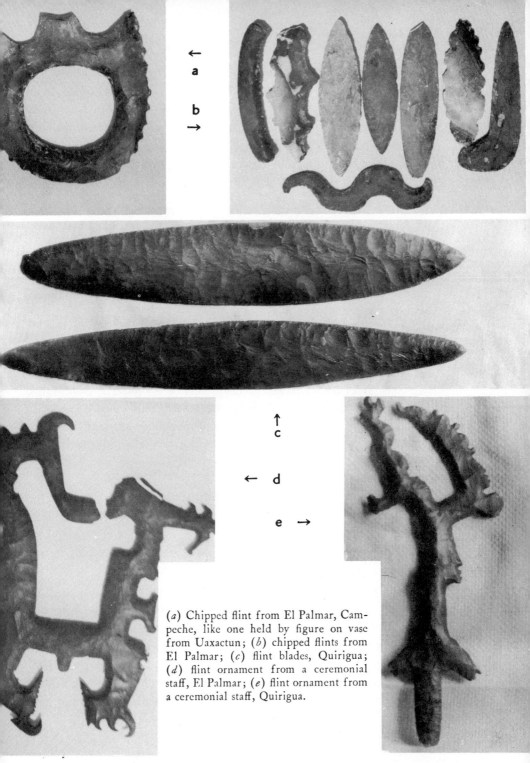

(a) Chipped flint from El Palmar, Campeche, like one held by figure on vase from Uaxactun; (b) chipped flints from El Palmar; (c) flint blades, Quirigua; (d) flint ornament from a ceremonial staff, El Palmar; (e) flint ornament from a ceremonial staff, Quirigua.

PLATE 102.—ECCENTRIC CHIPPED FLINTS (CLASSIC STAGE)

Northern area representations of featherwork show an inferior technique, and it is probable that this art was also declining. Some featherwork is shown on the wooden lintels from the Temple of the Jaguars at Chichen Itza (Fig. 42), and another example from Xculoc, Campeche, is illustrated in Plate 75, *c* and *d*.

Father Sahagun, our greatest authority on the Aztec, tells us that they had two kinds of featherwork:

> They [the Aztec] make the devices which they wear on their backs in dancing, all the costumes of the dance, and the trappings with which they dance [of feathers] and they executed the craft and profession of feather-workers in two different ways: the first kind of work consists of fastening the feathers to the background with paste in order thus to finish the work; the second way consists in doing the work and finishing it with the help of thread and cord.

In describing this latter technique Father Sahagun writes further:

> There is another kind of work, the handicraft of thread and cord. In this way they make their fans out of the plumes of the quetzal, their feather bracelets, the devices they wear on their backs and other things, their tunics blazoned with their arms etc.; and in addition pendants, panaches, balls, tassels of feathers, with all of which they adorn themselves and decorate their fans.

He also says that this art was relatively recent among the Aztec, especially the use of the brightly colored feathers of tropical birds. These came from the southern provinces, which were not subjugated until the reigns of the last two Aztec emperors before the Spanish Conquest.

Early Spanish writers indicate the importance of this craft among the Quiche Maya of the Guatemala highlands, who had aviaries where birds were bred for their plumage. Fuentes y Guzman, the seventeenth-century historian of Guatemala, says that the Quiche rulers at Utatlan had "places set apart for the breeding of ducks, for the sake of their plumage which they employed in weaving." Another early authority, describing the same place, states:

The throne of the king was notable because it had a canopy of very rich plumes and above this protection or covering, other coverings of different colors, in such a way as to give an effect of great majesty. The prince, or he who was to succeed, had three canopies and the other brothers or sons, two.

In addition to weaving feathers into their cotton fabrics, the Maya attached them to wood and wicker frames for headdresses. Father Moran in his manuscript dictionary of Pokomam defines the word *mayut* as a "framework of wood adorned with plumage, which they wear on their backs in their dances." In the Museum of the Cinquantennaire in Brussels there is an ankle-length cape of macaw feathers built on a framework of wickerwork; this cape supposedly belonged to Moctezuma II. A quetzal-plume headdress, certainly belonging to the same ruler, is in the former Imperial Museum in Vienna.

Feathers, cotton fabrics, sea shells, and semiprecious stones were used not only personally but as articles of trade and to pay legal penalties; in Postclassic times turquoise, copper, and gold were similarly used:

they exchanged *mantas* [*patis*] of cotton for gold and for certain axes of copper, and gold for emeralds, turquoises and plumes. [And again] At the end [the man who had committed the injury] was sentenced to pay a certain quantity of rich plumes, or *mantas*, or cacao, which went to the treasury.

The most highly prized feathers were the tail plumes of the quetzal, which were reserved for royal use. According to Bartolomé de Las Casas, either to capture or kill one was a capital offense:

in the province of Vera Paz [Guatemala], they punish with death him who killed the bird with the rich plumes [the quetzal] because it is not found in other places, and these feathers were things of great value because they used them as money.

AN APPRAISAL OF THE MAYA CIVILIZATION

By Betty Bell

PROFESSOR BRAINERD, whose task in preparing this concluding chapter has fallen upon me, spoke often of the enigma of the Maya civilization. In this summary and appraisal, I will try to present the unresolved riddles as he saw them.

In recent years, archaeologists and social anthropologists have shown increasing interest in the causes for the development of civilization, and in formulating theories of social and cultural change. A number of analyses have been aimed at determining whether there are any characteristics common to all civilizations, and any series of developmental stages through which they have all passed. The material culture, subsistence basis, technology, religion, social and political structure, and intellectual achievements of the ancient civilizations have been studied, and the causes for their decline have also been ascertained.

Many anthropologists now believe that there are certain criteria by which civilizations can be judged—certain traits common to all of them and certain stages through which they all seem to have passed. In general, progress toward civilization is thought to have been marked by increasing complexity in all aspects of culture and this developmental process is thought to have resulted everywhere in certain distinguishing features by which civilization can be defined. The causes for the decline of civilization, of course, have not been everywhere the same. The decline may have been due to external factors such as military conquest, or to internal weaknesses—or to a combination of both—but intensive study will often give at least some indication of the causes.

The Maya, however, cannot easily be made to fit into the pattern which has been developed. As Dr. Brainerd saw it, they present three problems:

1. While their developments in some fields have seldom been surpassed, the Maya lacked a number of traits which have come to be accepted as prerequisites to civilization, and they seem not to have passed through a number of the supposedly necessary developmental stages. Their status as a high civilization cannot be denied, but they lack many of the criteria by which such civilizations are usually defined. If theories of social evolution postulate that certain characteristics are everywhere necessary for the development of a complex society, how are we to account for the Maya?

2. Once the Maya civilization was developed, what kind of authority ruled it? Almost nothing is so far known of Classic-stage political structure. There is no evidence for the ramified political organization and centralized authority which elsewhere marked complex societies. Some method of control must be assumed to be necessary—but what method operated to keep the Maya civilization functioning smoothly through so long a time?

3. The Classic stage was notable for a high degree of homogeneity and stability. In the absence of any strong political authority, this argues for a peaceful and well-adjusted populace, unanimous in its agreement on the cultural values and goals and on the means for attaining them. But despite this presumed placidity, the causes for the decline of Classic-stage civilization must be sought within the society itself; there is no evidence that external pressures hastened its fall. What, then, caused this discontent, this sudden change? Or was it rather the result of some hidden but long-enduring weakness in the society, the culmination of several centuries of small dissatisfactions and the gradual erosion of the sense of cultural community?

In the light of present knowledge, no final answers can be given to any of these questions. We can here summarize the features of Maya civilization, appraise its achievements, and suggest tentative answers—but the enigma remains. Definitive answers must wait upon future studies and investigations, although the answers may never be forthcoming.

CHARACTERISTICS OF MAYA CIVILIZATION

Let us first recapitulate the features of Maya civilization—its remarkably advanced characteristics and its undeniably primitive ones, as well as its still unknown features.

In comparison with the subsistence bases of other comparably high civilizations, Maya subsistence techniques were almost primitive, and were comparable to the agricultural practices of the Neolithic period in the Old World. The Maya occupied an environment unlike that of most other early high civilizations, and this environment precluded development of the more advanced agricultural techniques upon which most early civilizations have been based. The type of agriculture made necessary by this environmental limitation required the Maya to live scattered throughout the areas surrounding the ceremonial centers. There is as yet no evidence for the concentration of the population into large, permanent settlements of closely packed dwellings. However great their size or elaboration, the sites seem to have been principally the foci of religious ceremonies which drew the populace in from the surrounding countryside, rather than true urban centers.

The character of the Maya area also enforced a degree of isolation unusual among high civilizations. While the dense jungle of the central Maya area may not have been as impassable to the foot-traveling Maya as it is to machine-bound moderns, it must still have cut them off to a large extent from the outside contacts through which new ideas and inventions are diffused, and hindered the development of a large-scale trade which could have supplied resources lacking in the area.

Maya technology was also of a sort which can only be considered rather primitive. Metal was apparently unknown until the Postclassic and then it appears only as jewelry and ornaments, largely imported from other areas. Metal tools were completely unknown; stone tools were used for everything from the cutting of slabs for stelae and building blocks to the execution of the most delicate carving. The wheel was also unknown; there were no wheeled vehicles, nor even the potter's wheel. It might appear that the rollers which were used on the causeways should have suggested the principle of the wheel, but the invention of wheeled vehicles seems to be closely related to the availability of animals for motive power, and the Maya lacked all domestic animals except the dog. This lack of the wheel, however, is general throughout the aboriginal New World, for nowhere except in Peru was there a native domestic animal large enough to serve as a beast of burden or a potential puller of vehicles.

Despite the marked primitiveness of some aspects of their civilization—its isolation, scattered population, simple agriculture, and meager technology—the Maya developed other cultural features to a point of complexity and elaboration unequaled among other early civilizations of the New World. Although the true arch was never developed, the invention of the corbeled arch permitted the construction of large temples and palaces, occasionally multistoried. The outstanding characteristic of Maya architecture, however, is its emphasis upon skillful and elaborate decoration rather than upon size. The reticulated roof-combs of Tikal and the beautifully carved mosaic façades of Uxmal alike show a preoccupation with the esthetic refinements of architecture rather than with sheer imposing mass. Maya graphic art was also well developed. While the stone sculptures tend to be formal and stylized, and the designs too intricate for modern taste, the skill of their execution is undeniable. The figures on the ceramics are more freely and informally rendered, and many designs, such as that on the famous polychrome plate from Uaxactun (Fig. 49), show a degree of sophistication which compares favorably with the most modern ceramic design. Some of the figures in the Bonampak murals, moreover, exhibit a degree of naturalism which Western European art did not achieve until several centuries later.

The Maya religion, which was a focal point for so much of the culture, was complex and formalized. It had a well-developed cosmogony, a large pantheon of gods, and an elaborate cycle of rituals. The Maya had the concept of a creator-god, although he does not seem to have played an important role in the lives of the common people, and of several worlds prior to this one, all of which had been destroyed by floods. In addition to major deities such as the Lord of the Heavens, the gods of rain and corn, and numerous others, each of the thirteen levels of the upper world and the nine levels of the lower world had its patron god. There were also patron deities for each of the katuns, the nineteen divisions of the haab, the twenty day-names of the tzolkin, and the numerals 0 to 13.

The katun endings, the New Year, and each of the months were marked by appropriate ceremonies, which included fasting and abstinence, exorcism, prayers, and sacrifice. Although human sacrifice existed during the Classic stage, the sacrifices were principally of animals and birds; the extensive human sacrifice which characterized Postclassic-stage religion was a Toltec innovation.

This religious complexity is a far remove from the simple pantheon of nature gods which probably existed in the Preclassic. It reflects the increasing complexity of the culture itself, and the growth of a professional priesthood which formalized the religion, elaborated the rituals, and maintained its dominant position in the society by its claim to interpret the wishes of an ever-increasing number of gods.

The most notable characteristic of Maya civilization, however, was its achievements in the abstract intellectual fields of writing, astronomy, mathematics, and calendrics. Alone of New World civilizations, the Maya developed what can truly be considered a system of writing, in which the characters were not merely pictographs or mnemonic devices. Maya hieroglyphic writing was long thought to be entirely ideographic, but recent studies have indicated that many of the elements of the glyphs may be syllabic. It was thus at least in the process of becoming a phonetic system, its characters coming to represent sounds rather than objects or ideas.

Unfortunately, a great deal of Maya writing remains undeciphered, and those portions which have been deciphered have yielded largely calendric or astronomical information. The stelae record the endings of time periods, and the three existing fragmentary codices deal with astronomy, ritual, and divination. Some of the countless codices which Landa prided himself on having destroyed may well have contained the history of the Maya.

Using the simplest of equipment, the Maya calculated the length of the solar year with an accuracy equal to that of modern astronomy, and devised correction formulae to adjust the discrepancy between the true year and the calendar year which is handled by our leap-year correction. They worked out an accurate lunar calendar and calculated the synodical revolutions of Venus, in each case devising means for correcting the accumulated error.

The Maya vigesimal system of mathematics was a positional system and embodied the concept of zero, a notable abstract intellectual achievement. Elsewhere, this mathematical concept is known to have been developed only in the early Hindu civilization. The ancient civilizations of Mesopotamia employed a positional system of arithmetic, but it seems to have been in existence for centuries before the concept of zero diffused to them from the Hindu world. The ancient civilizations of the Mediterranean area derived many of their cultural features from the civilizations of the Middle East, but they did not take over the well-developed system of computation. This sort of mathematical complex did not penetrate Western Europe until the time of the Arab invasions in the early Middle Ages, several centuries after the Maya had developed their own accurate and flexible system.

The basis of the Maya calendric system was the 260-day tzolkin, with its named and numbered days, and the 365-day haab, with its named months and numbered positions within each month. These two meshed calendars repeated cyclically, and could return to a given starting point only after a lapse of 52 years. The stelae inscriptions, however, involved longer time periods, which, with one exception, were based on the vigesimal system of multiples of twenty. Using these longer periods, the Maya counted the elapsed time since the hypothetical starting date of their chronology. They also recorded in the inscription the fact that the stela was erected on a certain numbered and named day of the tzolkin which occupied a certain position in a particular month of the haab; the accompanying supplementary series recorded lunar information for that date. The information given by these Initial Series or Long Count inscriptions is thus so specific that a day fulfilling all of the prescribed requirements could not recur for 374,440 years.

One of the unknown factors in Maya civilization is the type of authority which governed it during its almost 600 years of existence. Religion was of central importance to the Maya; there is little doubt that it was uniform throughout the area, and that the priests of the various centers must have co-operated closely on religious matters. It is impossible to say how far this control penetrated into political matters. The remarkable homogeneity of Classic-stage civilization would seem to indicate some kind of hegemony over the area, either civil or religious. Priestly control may have sufficed to maintain order, or there may have been some centralized political authority which has so far not been detected.

The other unknown factor, of course, is the reason for the decline of Maya civilization. It was quite clearly not due to outside pressures. There is still no evidence of internal weakness, although it must have existed. It is difficult to believe that so solidly established a civilization could be overturned abruptly, but if dissatisfactions had been accumulating slowly through the centuries, they left no mark by which they can be identified.

TWO THEORIES OF SOCIAL EVOLUTION

There are certain variations in current definitions of civilization, but all definitions include most of the following requirements: a surplus of food produced by farmers to support nonfarmers; concentrated human settlements (cities); an improved technology; a formal political organization; a society organized into classes, some of which have the leisure for nonutilitarian pursuits; a formal religion and moral order; public works; writing.

From his research on the ancient civilizations of the Old World, archaeologist V. Gordon Childe has concluded that there is a developmental ranking, a causal relationship, among these factors which everywhere makes them prerequisites to the growth of civilization. Childe's most intensive studies have been of the civilizations of the Middle East, and there the evidence does seem to support his theory. In Mesopotamia, for example, large-scale irrigation agriculture was developed on the flood plains of the Tigris and Euphrates Rivers, and large permanent settlements grew up. The availability of surplus food permitted the support of full-time craft and religious specialists, and the existence of craft specialists in turn hastened technological progress. Outside contacts and the development of trade are also cited as necessary to an improved technology, for in this way the society might learn of new technical processes and could also supply resources which might be lacking in its environment.

Religion grew more complex and formalized. The priests were at first the rulers of the cities, later being supplanted in part by the growth of a monarchy and a hierarchy of civil officials. Each city-state was originally an autonomous unit, but as control passed more into civil hands, military conquest and political organization welded a number of city-states into empires.

Within the city-state, order was maintained largely by the ruler's control over the irrigation system which was so vital to the group's existence. The concentration of population facilitated control by a central authority; the populace could more easily be taxed for the support of the priests, nobles, and king, and conscripted for labor on the palaces and temples.

As social organization became more complex, some classes of society were freed from subsistence activities and had leisure to devote to nonutilitarian pursuits. The priests, supported by the populace, developed mathematics and writing, although it might be argued that these were not entirely devoid of utility since they were developed in connection with keeping accounts of the offerings made to the temples.

In Childe's opinion, then, culture develops with an increased technological efficiency and integrative ability, and an increased control of knowledge. But he believes that the great variety of cultures revealed by ethnographic and archaeological research is a handicap if the objective is to establish general stages in the evolution of cultures. In order to discover general laws descriptive of the evolution of all societies, he feels, we must omit or discount the features peculiar to particular habitats or environments.

432   Anthropologist Julian Steward believes that this view fails to account for the development of particular patterns among different societies, and he proposes instead a theory of multilinear evolution. This theory admits the existence of distinctive cultural traditions, but does not assume that such traditions are necessarily unique; there is reason to believe that knowledge gained from the analysis of one culture may provide insights useful to the analysis of another. Its emphasis lies not in the uniqueness of cultures but in the similarities that may be found among them. It recognizes that cultural traditions in different regions may be wholly or in part distinctive, and merely asks: "Are there any meaningful similarities between two or more cultures that can be formulated?"

Where such similarities are found, it may be possible to determine the causal factors, identical in each case, which led to their development. Such causal relationships need not be universally applicable, for multilinear evolution presents no pattern into which the cultures of all times and all places must be fitted. Rather, it compares cultural traditions in various parts of the world, attempts to develop a taxonomy of culture types, and to produce significant general statements about the developmental process of each type so discovered.

While Childe's theory ignores environmental variations and posits advanced agricultural techniques as being everywhere a prerequisite to the development of civilization, Steward takes account of such variations and suggests that the manner of a society's adaptation to a particular environment may be the significant factor in cultural development. Rather than establish an a priori pattern for the development of all cultures, he suggests a possible grouping on an ecological basis. In these terms, he would distinguish as a category or culture type the complex civilizations of Egypt, Mesopotamia, China, Northern Peru, and Highland Mexico, whose subsistence basis was a system of irrigation agriculture on arid lands. These civilizations, scattered as they are in space and time, show quite similar social, political, and technological developments, although the Inca and Aztec civilizations at the time of European contact had not reached the intellectual heights achieved by the Old World civilizations.

To this extent, Childe and Steward are in agreement. There does seem to have been a parallel development in these arid-land irrigation civilizations which suggests a causal relationship among their culture traits. They exhibit urbanization, similar degrees of technological advancement and social organization, a formalized religion, progress from a theocracy to political organization and a nation-state, and finally, programs of military conquest and empire building. But Steward does not agree that these traits can be considered universal criteria for civilization. He points out that this is but one type of environment, and one type of adaptation. If the manner of a society's adaptation to a particular environment is indeed the significant factor in cultural progress, there can perhaps be many different bases for complex civilizations, and many different paths leading to their development.

CHILDE'S AND STEWARD'S THEORIES APPLIED TO THE MAYA

Can the Maya be made to fit into Childe's scheme, which seeks to establish universal criteria and developmental stages for high civilizations? A glance at the characteristics of Maya civilization will show that it would be most difficult. They remain, as Dr. Brainerd remarked, an intractable exception.

Maya agriculture was of a rather primitive kind, and it would not have lent itself readily to the centralized control which could be exerted over irrigation systems. There is little doubt, however, that it was capable of producing surpluses, for it obviously supported such nonproducing groups as the priests and nobles. The quality of Maya art and architecture suggests the existence also of craft specialists, who could only be supported if surpluses were available. The free time which the Maya farmer presumably had after filling his family's subsistence needs may have been devoted not only to personal labor on the public works, but also to the production of food for trained artisans who did the highly skilled stone carving for which the Maya are famous.

Although urbanization seems in most areas to have been a significant factor in the development of a complex civilization, true urbanism, in the sense of densely populated settlements, was lacking in the Maya area during the Classic stage. The nature of their agricultural system obliged the Maya to live quite widely dispersed, gathering at the religious centers chiefly for ceremonies. The isolation of the area may have been an important factor in the maintenance of this kind of living pattern through a number of centuries, for such a scattered population, lacking fortified and defensible settlements, might otherwise have been extremely vulnerable to attack and invasion.

Increased technological efficiency is usually a concomitant of civilization, but Maya technology remained unchanged throughout its history. For lack of raw materials, metallurgy never developed; imported gold jewelry and ornaments appeared in the Postclassic stage, but metal tools never replaced stone tools. In the absence of domestic animals, the wheel was not invented, and the nature of the subsistence system offered no opportunity for the invention of improved agricultural equipment.

While Maya society was quite clearly organized into classes, no political organization has so far been detected. The remarkable homogeneity of Classic-stage civilization might indicate some overall political authority, but since religion was so pervasive and important, control might equally well have been theocratic during the entire period. Most high civilizations have evolved into political states, and many have eventually embarked upon programs of military conquest and empire building, but these developments did not appear among the Maya. There is evidence for a certain amount of internecine strife, but no evidence for organized warfare on a nationalistic basis.

The formalized religion which is characteristic of complex civilizations was highly developed among the Maya, and quite obviously the focal point of the culture. Since most Maya public works were religious edifices, the control which urbanization is said to facilitate in conscripting labor may not have been necessary. It is possible that the religion-conscious Maya worked willingly at such tasks.

The most notable Maya achievements, of course, were in abstract intellectual fields, and here they surpassed all other New World civilizations and equaled or surpassed many in the Old World. These achievements, inventions and possessions of the priesthood, seem to have been truly nonutilitarian, not connected with economic activities nor pursued in the hope of economic rewards. Writing, calendrics, astronomy, and mathematics were all parts of the Maya preoccupation with marking the passage of time, a preoccupation which is difficult to explain. The yearly calendar of necessary rituals presumably repeated itself endlessly, but it is not clear what significance the longer time periods had for the Maya, nor why it was so important for them to mark periodically the exact number of years, months, and days which had elapsed since the starting point of their chronology. It must, however, have had a great and central importance to have resulted in an intellectual system of such complexity.

Although the Maya civilization cannot be fitted into any universal criteria or series of developmental stages such as Childe postulates, it can perhaps be approached in Steward's terms, as an example of a highly successful adaptation to a particular environment. The Peten jungle seems an unfavorable setting for the development of a civilization, but the Maya transcended its limitations. The simple agricultural system which it enforced was made not only to fill subsistence needs but also to produce food surpluses. The relative poverty of natural resources prevented a great deal of technological advancement, but the existing technology was employed skillfully enough to fill the needs of a people whose emphasis was largely upon the esthetic refinements of their products rather than upon quantity or mass. The environment and subsistence system precluded any concentration of the population, but the Maya developed a social organization and mechanisms of social control which in other areas have been a consequence of urbanization. With this ecological adaptation successfully accomplished, with satisfactory agricultural, technological, and sociopolitical bases established, the Maya were able to turn their attention to the religious and intellectual developments which characterize most complex civilizations, and which became the hallmark of the Maya civilization in particular.

In a classification of this sort, which attempts to group cultures in terms of their environments and then to find even limited parallels in their development, the Maya must remain, at least for now, the only major culture within their particular ecological category. This may be due in part to the circumstances and difficulties of archaeological investigation. Most of the ancient high civilizations which are well known archaeologically have been located in the drier regions of the world, where climatic conditions have preserved sufficient material to permit quite substantial reconstruction of culture history. Such a degree of preservation is unlikely in humid regions, but more intensive archaeological work in these areas might yield enough information to allow at least limited comparisons of the Maya with other cultures in similar environments. Further archaeological investigation in the jungle regions of southeast Asia might provide material for such a comparison. The remains of at least one apparently high civilization have already been found there, at Angkor Vat in Cambodia. However, the ancient Cambodian civilization has not been studied as intensively as the Maya, and there is at present too little material available for a detailed comparison.

CLASSIC-STAGE GOVERNMENT

Much of Maya culture history has now been reconstructed, but the form of Classic-stage government is still problematical. The Classic stage was marked by a high degree of homogeneity and stability throughout the nearly six centuries of its existence. There were regional and temporal variations in such things as architecture and ceramics, to be sure, but the distinctive patterning of Maya culture remained unchanged. The extent of man's obedience to the unenforceable may indeed be one of the marks of civilization, but it is questionable if this alone could maintain order within so com-

plex a society. Some more formal method of control must be assumed to account for the stable and orderly character of Maya
civilization over so wide an area and through so long a time.

This widespread homogeneity suggests the presence of one supreme ruler over the area, but there is as yet no evidence for such
a centralized political authority. The absence of warfare has been
cited in the text as one of the characteristics of the Classic stage,
and this might indicate either the importance of religion in government or the presence of a strong civil authority. However, although
organized warfare was lacking, there undeniably was sporadic raiding between centers to obtain captives for slaves and for sacrifice.
This seems to suggest a certain autonomy for the various centers,
and to weaken the case for a central government, which presumably
could have prevented such occurrences.

The territorial rulers discussed in the text existed at the time
of the Spanish Conquest, but there is no evidence that they were
vestiges of some Classic-stage political authority. In all probability,
they were part of the political structure introduced by the Toltecs.
While much of the social organization and domestic life of the
people may have remained relatively unchanged since the Classic
stage, the Toltec invasion was in essence a military conquest and so
would undoubtedly have destroyed any political institutions which
it encountered.

Control may well have been theocratic. Religion was of central
importance in Maya life, and authority may have been exercised
by a closely co-operating group of priests, each of whom dominated
a particular religious center. If the society was thus controlled by
means of its adherence to a common religion, the religious bonds
were not strong enough to eliminate latent hostility—but at least
they were strong enough to ensure that such hostility did not become a disruptive force in the society.

If control was theocratic, it must simply have rested upon the
dominant role of religion and ritual in the lives of the common
people. The priests held no economically valuable knowledge such
as that held by the Egyptian priests, who were able to predict the
life-giving floods of the Nile. Nor did the Maya priests control

any important economic activity as did the Mesopotamian priests, who held a monopoly on the vital irrigation system. Perhaps possession of such specific information or power is not entirely necessary. Some anthropologists have suggested that man turns to religion for aid in matters where his limited empirical techniques are of no avail. The Maya subsistence economy depended upon a favorable combination of natural conditions which was quite outside the farmer's control. The people may well have been convinced that only propitiation of the gods by means of the proper ceremonies, under priestly direction, would ensure their continued well-being and perhaps their very existence. Whatever the means by which control was enforced, it does not seem to have been by the promise of rich economic rewards. The Maya economy was simple and self-sufficient, and apparently it was only necessary for the priests to guarantee its continued existence, although the ceremonial requirements for this guarantee became steadily more elaborate and perhaps even burdensome.

CAUSES FOR THE DECLINE OF MAYA CIVILIZATION

Despite this picture of stability and relative placidity, the causes for the inexplicable decline of Maya civilization must be sought within the society itself rather than in outside forces, either natural or human. Earthquake activity, disease, and climatic and vegetation changes have been disposed of as possible causes, and there is no evidence for warfare in the central Maya area. Yet after nearly six hundred years of activity, the great ceremonial centers of the Peten were abandoned. The people may have lived on in the areas around the centers, worshiping fewer gods with simpler ceremonies, but the great religious panoply, the complex cosmogony, the priestly hierarchy, were gone.

Why did this happen? The iconography indicates no change in the all-important religion, no discontentment with the old religion or substitution of a new one. Nor is there any suggestion of the social unrest which has precipitated so many changes in other civilizations. If the causes for the decline were cumulative, they cannot yet be identified in the archaeological record. It must be assumed

at present that the change was rather sudden, however strange that
seems in the light of religion's central role in Maya life.

It has been suggested by some authorities that perhaps the out-
wardly placid and well-adjusted populace had merely tired at last
of the burdens which its pervasive religion placed upon it. The
ceremonies may have become too expensive and the support of the
priestly hierarchy too burdensome in proportion to the rewards
which religion offered. A new philosophy of life may have arisen
which provided new values and goals, or the people may simply
have decided that life would go on regardless of priestly intervention with the gods—that their own prayers and offerings, made
directly, would ensure the coming of rain and the growing of
crops.

This social malaise, whatever its nature, must also have been
present in the centers of the northern area, at least to the extent
that it weakened the society sufficiently for it to be conquered a
short time later by a relatively small number of Toltec invaders.
The fact that the Toltec conquest was accompanied by a religious
evangelization also suggests some disabling weakness in the Maya
religion, or in the people's attitude toward it. Such a ready acceptance of many elements of Toltec religion hardly seems likely had
the people still been convinced of the importance of their existing
religion.

Thus, five centuries before the Spanish Conquest, this complex
civilization which had arisen in an environment unique among the
high cultures of the world, and which had flourished for centuries
despite its lack of some of the so-called prerequisites of civilization,
had fallen into decay.

APPRAISAL OF MAYA CIVILIZATION

Cultures must be judged not against some absolute scale of
achievement, but in relative terms—on the basis of their achievements within the framework of their limitations. In this sort of a
classification, the Maya must rank high. Their environment prevented the development of advanced agricultural and technological
processes, and inhibited the establishment of concentrated settle-

ments; and this lack of urbanization, in turn, may have prevented the development of complex political institutions and the formation of a political state. But set against this background of limitations and relatively primitive features, Maya esthetic and intellectual achievements have few equals.

The orientation of Maya civilization, its cultural patterning, gives it a unique position among early high civilizations. Others have excelled it in material culture, or have emphasized such traits as political organization or military conquest and empire building, but the remarkable traits of Maya culture are of an intellectual and esthetic order. It is impossible to ascertain the impetus behind this distinctive type of cultural development. So far as is known, it did not depend upon a strong governmental control which could channel cultural developments as it desired. It does not seem to have rested upon stern economic control, nor was it accomplished nor immediately preceded by the invention of new techniques for economic betterment, although this sort of developmental sequence is sometimes assumed to be necessary. The causes behind Maya intellectual progress do not fit easily into the sequences of advancement worked out for other early civilizations, which suggests that we do not yet fully understand the factors that lead a people in the direction of such progress.

While there is some particular emphasis in all cultures, some focal point around which much of the society is organized, this emphasis need not, perhaps, have been deliberately selected; it might equally well be influenced by the limitation of the number of choices available to the society. Thus it might be argued that the Maya cultural emphasis rested upon intellectual florescence at least in part because physical and developmental circumstances denied them the technological and political advancements which other societies emphasized. But this still does not explain Maya intellectual progress. Few if any other cultures with comparably primitive features, however satisfactory their adjustment to their environment, have focused to such a degree upon intellectual attainment. Perhaps the goad, if one be assumed necessary, was the overwhelming importance of Maya religion and the fact that intellectual developments

were the inventions of the religious specialists and were closely
connected with religious observances.

Whatever the causes of these developments, they are of a sufficiently high order to give the Maya an unchallenged position among complex civilizations. The esthetic refinements of Maya art and architecture, the accuracy of their astronomical system, the intricacy of their calendrics, and the skill and elaboration of their mathematics and writing, are unsurpassed by any other New World civilization and equaled by few in the Old World. The Maya must surely emerge for dispassionate comparison among the great world cultures.

APPENDIX

THE CORRELATION OF MAYA AND CHRISTIAN
CHRONOLOGIES

THE PROBLEM of correlation of Maya and Christian chronologies has long been intensively studied but still remains unsolved. The Goodman–Martínez Hernández–Thompson correlation has been the most generally accepted, but the Spinden correlation has recently received attention as a result of a series of radiocarbon tests of sapote wood from three Tikal lintels (one of which is illustrated in Plate 42). Radiocarbon dating cannot claim to establish its dates precisely, of course, and its margin of error becomes more critical with such relatively recent materials as these. However, since acceptance of the Spinden correlation would make the Classic-stage dates used in this book approximately 260 years earlier, the results of these tests are at least worth noting.

Each of the lintels bore the Maya date 9.15.10.0.0. In the GMT correlation this date is June 30, A.D. 741; in the Spinden correlation it is October 30, A.D. 481. One test was run by the Lamont Laboratories of Columbia University and two by the laboratories of the University of Chicago; the results are as follows:

> Lamont sample 113   A.D. 481 ± 120 years
> Chicago sample C-948   A.D. 469 ± 120 years
> Chicago sample C-949   A.D. 433 ± 170 years

While these dates indicate the ages of the samples, it is impossible to determine the age of the wood at the time the date was carved on it. The sapote is apparently a long-lived tree, and the trees which provided the wood for these lintels may have been of considerable age when they were cut. Moreover, most of the lintels are wider than the greatest diameter of the largest sapote, and are therefore composed of several beams. This makes it possible that a sample taken from one side of a lintel might yield a very different date than a sample taken from the opposite side.

Acceptance of the radiocarbon dates, and hence of the Spinden correlation, would necessitate a rather thorough revision of existing ideas, not only about the chronology of the Maya area but also about the relative chronologies of other New World areas. Crossties, based on archaeological evidence, have been established between the Maya area and central Mexico and between Mexico and the southwestern United States, and acceptance of the Spinden correlation would mean a corresponding readjustment of the dates now assigned to the cultures of these areas. However, the Spinden dates are more acceptable to many archaeologists of the southwestern United States than are those of the GMT correlation, for they give a longer time span for cultural developments which must now be compressed into a rather improbably short period.

The date now assigned to the end of the Classic stage in the Maya area is approximately A.D. 900; Spinden's correlation would make it A.D. 650. To fill the gap thus created, one of the following assumptions would no doubt be necessary: that the Classic stage endured for over two centuries after the cessation of dated stelae; that the Toltec horizon persisted for twice as long as is now believed; or that the period of disintegration between the Toltec era and the Spanish Conquest was more than two hundred years longer than it is now thought to have been. Such adjustments are far from satisfactory to most experts on the Maya area, and a great deal more study is unquestionably needed to resolve this incompatibility of opinion between the archaeologists and the physicists.

TABLE X

THE CORRELATION OF MAYA AND CHRISTIAN CHRONOLOGIES ACCORDING TO THE
GOODMAN-MARTINEZ HERNANDEZ-THOMPSON CORRELATION FORMULA

Katun and Half-Katun Endings in the Maya Long Count (the Initial Series)	Katun Endings in the Maya Short Count (the *u kahlay katunob*)	Gregorian Equivalents
8.14.0.0.0　7 Ahau 3 Xul	Katun 7 Ahau	A.D. 317, September 1
8.14.10.0.0　6 Ahau 13 Zip		A.D. 327, July 11
8.15.0.0.0　5 Ahau 3 Pop	Katun 5 Ahau	A.D. 337, May 19
8.15.10.0.0　4 Ahau 18 Pax		A.D. 347, March 28
8.16.0.0.0　3 Ahau 8 Kankin	Katun 3 Ahau	A.D. 357, February 3
8.16.10.0.0　2 Ahau 18 Zac		A.D. 366, December 13
8.17.0.0.0　1 Ahau 8 Chen	Katun 1 Ahau	A.D. 376, October 21
8.17.10.0.0　13 Ahau 18 Xul		A.D. 386, August 30
8.18.0.0.0　12 Ahau 8 Zotz	Katun 12 Ahau	A.D. 396, July 8
8.18.10.0.0　11 Ahau 18 Pop		A.D. 406, May 17
8.19.0.0.0　10 Ahau 13 Kayab	Katun 10 Ahau	A.D. 416, March 25
8.19.10.0.0　9 Ahau 3 Muan		A.D. 426, February 1
9.0.0.0.0　8 Ahau 13 Ceh	Katun 8 Ahau	A.D. 435, December 11
9.0.10.0.0　7 Ahau 3 Yax		A.D. 445, October 19
9.1.0.0.0　6 Ahau 13 Yaxkin	Katun 6 Ahau	A.D. 455, August 28
9.1.10.0.0　5 Ahau 3 Tzec		A.D. 465, July 6
9.2.0.0.0　4 Ahau 13 Uo	Katun 4 Ahau	A.D. 475, May 15
9.2.10.0.0　3 Ahau 8 Cumhu		A.D. 485, March 23
9.3.0.0.0　2 Ahau 18 Muan	Katun 2 Ahau	A.D. 495, January 30
9.3.10.0.0　1 Ahau 8 Mac		A.D. 504, December 9
9.4.0.0.0　13 Ahau 18 Yax	Katun 13 Ahau	A.D. 514, October 18
9.4.10.0.0　12 Ahau 8 Mol		A.D. 524, August 26
9.5.0.0.0　11 Ahau 18 Tzec	Katun 11 Ahau	A.D. 534, July 5
9.5.10.0.0　10 Ahau 8 Zip		A.D. 544, May 13
9.6.0.0.0　9 Ahau 3 Uayeb	Katun 9 Ahau	A.D. 554, March 22
9.6.10.0.0　8 Ahau 13 Pax		A.D. 564, January 29
9.7.0.0.0　7 Ahau 3 Kankin	Katun 7 Ahau	A.D. 573, December 7
9.7.10.0.0　6 Ahau 13 Zac		A.D. 583, October 16
9.8.0.0.0　5 Ahau 3 Chen	Katun 5 Ahau	A.D. 593, August 24
9.8.10.0.0　4 Ahau 13 Xul		A.D. 603, July 4
9.9.0.0.0　3 Ahau 3 Zotz	Katun 3 Ahau	A.D. 613, May 12
9.9.10.0.0　2 Ahau 13 Pop		A.D. 623, March 21
9.10.0.0.0　1 Ahau 8 Kayab	Katun 1 Ahau	A.D. 633, January 27
9.10.10.0.0　13 Ahau 18 Kankin		A.D. 642, December 6
9.11.0.0.0　12 Ahau 8 Ceh	Katun 12 Ahau	A.D. 652, October 14
9.11.10.0.0　11 Ahau 18 Chen		A.D. 662, August 23
9.12.0.0.0　10 Ahau 8 Yaxkin	Katun 10 Ahau	A.D. 672, July 1
9.12.10.0.0　9 Ahau 13 Zip		A.D. 682, May 10
9.13.0.0.0　8 Ahau 8 Uo	Katun 8 Ahau	A.D. 692, March 18
9.13.10.0.0　7 Ahau 3 Cumhu		A.D. 702, January 26

TABLE X (*Continued*)

Katun and Half-Katun Endings in the Maya Long Count (the Initial Series)	Katun Endings in the Maya Short Count (the *u kah-lay katunob*)	Gregorian Equivalents
9.14.0.0.0 6 Ahau 13 Muan	Katun 6 Ahau	A.D. 711, December 5
9.14.10.0.0 5 Ahau 3 Mac		A.D. 721, October 13
9.15.0.0.0 4 Ahau 13 Yax	Katun 4 Ahau	A.D. 731, August 22
9.15.10.0.0 3 Ahau 3 Mol		A.D. 741, June 30
9.16.0.0.0 2 Ahau 13 Tzec	Katun 2 Ahau	A.D. 751, May 9
9.16.10.0.0 1 Ahau 3 Zip		A.D. 761, March 17
9.17.0.0.0 13 Ahau 18 Cumhu	Katun 13 Ahau	A.D. 771, January 24
9.17.10.0.0 12 Ahau 8 Pax		A.D. 780, December 2
9.18.0.0.0 11 Ahau 18 Mac	Katun 11 Ahau	A.D. 790, October 11
9.18.10.0.0 10 Ahau 8 Zac		A.D. 800, August 19
9.19.0.0.0 9 Ahau 18 Mol	Katun 9 Ahau	A.D. 810, June 28
9.19.10.0.0 8 Ahau 8 Xul		A.D. 820, May 6
10.0.0.0.0 7 Ahau 18 Zip	Katun 7 Ahau	A.D. 830, March 15
10.0.10.0.0 6 Ahau 8 Pop		A.D. 840, January 22
10.1.0.0.0 5 Ahau 3 Kayab	Katun 5 Ahau	A.D. 849, November 30
10.1.10.0.0 4 Ahau 13 Kankin		A.D. 859, October 9
10.2.0.0.0 3 Ahau 3 Ceh	Katun 3 Ahau	A.D. 869, August 17
10.2.10.0.0 2 Ahau 13 Chen		A.D. 879, June 26
10.3.0.0.0 1 Ahau 3 Yaxkin	Katun 1 Ahau	A.D. 889, May 4
10.3.10.0.0 13 Ahau 13 Zotz		A.D. 899, March 13
10.4.0.0.0 12 Ahau 3 Uo	Katun 12 Ahau	A.D. 909, January 20
10.4.10.0.0 11 Ahau 18 Kayab		A.D. 918, November 29
10.5.0.0.0 10 Ahau 8 Muan	Katun 10 Ahau	A.D. 928, October 7
10.5.10.0.0 9 Ahau 18 Ceh		A.D. 938, August 16
10.6.0.0.0 8 Ahau 8 Yax	Katun 8 Ahau	A.D. 948, June 24
10.6.10.0.0 7 Ahau 18 Yaxkin		A.D. 958, May 3
10.7.0.0.0 6 Ahau 8 Tzec	Katun 6 Ahau	A.D. 968, March 11
10.7.10.0.0 5 Ahau 18 Uo		A.D. 978, January 18
10.8.0.0.0 4 Ahau 13 Cumhu	Katun 4 Ahau	A.D. 987, November 27
10.8.10.0.0 3 Ahau 3 Pax		A.D. 997, October 5
10.9.0.0.0 2 Ahau 13 Mac	Katun 2 Ahau	A.D. 1007, August 15
10.9.10.0.0 1 Ahau 3 Zac		A.D. 1017, June 23
10.10.0.0.0 13 Ahau 13 Mol	Katun 13 Ahau	A.D. 1027, May 2
10.10.10.0.0 12 Ahau 3 Xul		A.D. 1037, March 10
10.11.0.0.0 11 Ahau 13 Zip	Katun 11 Ahau	A.D. 1047, January 17
10.11.10.0.0 10 Ahau 3 Pop		A.D. 1056, November 25
10.12.0.0.0 9 Ahau 18 Pax	Katun 9 Ahau	A.D. 1066, October 4
10.12.10.0.0 8 Ahau 8 Kankin		A.D. 1076, August 12
10.13.0.0.0 7 Ahau 18 Zac	Katun 7 Ahau	A.D. 1086, June 21
10.13.10.0.0 6 Ahau 8 Chen		A.D. 1096, April 29
10.14.0.0.0 5 Ahau 18 Xul	Katun 5 Ahau	A.D. 1106, March 9
10.14.10.0.0 4 Ahau 8 Zotz		A.D. 1116, January 16

TABLE X (*Continued*)

Katun and Half-Katun Endings in the Maya Long Count (the Initial Series)	Katun Endings in the Maya Short Count (the *u kahlay katunob*)	Gregorian Equivalents
10.15.0.0.0 3 Ahau 18 Pop	Katun 3 Ahau	A.D. 1125, November 24
10.15.10.0.0 2 Ahau 13 Kayab		A.D. 1135, October 3
10.16.0.0.0 1 Ahau 3 Muan	Katun 1 Ahau	A.D. 1145, August 11
10.16.10.0.0 13 Ahau 13 Ceh		A.D. 1155, June 20
10.17.0.0.0 12 Ahau 3 Yax	Katun 12 Ahau	A.D. 1165, April 28
10.17.10.0.0 11 Ahau 13 Yaxkin		A.D. 1175, March 7
10.18.0.0.0 10 Ahau 3 Tzec	Katun 10 Ahau	A.D. 1185, January 13
10.18.10.0.0 9 Ahau 13 Uo		A.D. 1194, November 22
10.19.0.0.0 8 Ahau 8 Cumhu	Katun 8 Ahau	A.D. 1204, September 30
10.19.10.0.0 7 Ahau 18 Muan		A.D. 1214, August 9
11.0.0.0.0 6 Ahau 8 Mac	Katun 6 Ahau	A.D. 1224, June 17
11.0.10.0.0 5 Ahau 18 Yax		A.D. 1234, April 26
11.1.0.0.0 4 Ahau 8 Mol	Katun 4 Ahau	A.D. 1244, March 4
11.1.10.0.0 3 Ahau 18 Tzec		A.D. 1254, January 11
11.2.0.0.0 2 Ahau 8 Zip	Katun 2 Ahau	A.D. 1263, November 20
11.2.10.0.0 1 Ahau 3 Uayeb		A.D. 1273, September 28
11.3.0.0.0 13 Ahau 13 Pax	Katun 13 Ahau	A.D. 1283, August 7
11.3.10.0.0 12 Ahau 3 Kankin		A.D. 1293, June 15
11.4.0.0.0 11 Ahau 13 Zac	Katun 11 Ahau	A.D. 1303, April 25
11.4.10.0.0 10 Ahau 3 Chen		A.D. 1313, March 3
11.5.0.0.0 9 Ahau 13 Xul	Katun 9 Ahau	A.D. 1323, January 10
11.5.10.0.0 8 Ahau 3 Zotz		A.D. 1332, November 18
11.6.0.0.0 7 Ahau 13 Pop	Katun 7 Ahau	A.D. 1342, September 27
11.6.10.0.0 6 Ahau 8 Kayab		A.D. 1352, August 5
11.7.0.0.0 5 Ahau 18 Kankin	Katun 5 Ahau	A.D. 1362, June 14
11.7.10.0.0 4 Ahau 8 Ceh		A.D. 1372, April 22
11.8.0.0.0 3 Ahau 18 Chen	Katun 3 Ahau	A.D. 1382, March 1
11.8.10.0.0 2 Ahau 8 Yaxkin		A.D. 1392, January 8
11.9.0.0.0 1 Ahau 18 Zotz	Katun 1 Ahau	A.D. 1401, November 17
11.9.10.0.0 13 Ahau 8 Uo		A.D. 1411, September 26
11.10.0.0.0 12 Ahau 3 Cumhu	Katun 12 Ahau	A.D. 1421, August 4
11.10.10.0.0 11 Ahau 13 Muan		A.D. 1431, June 13
11.11.0.0.0 10 Ahau 3 Mac	Katun 10 Ahau	A.D. 1441, April 21
11.11.10.0.0 9 Ahau 13 Yax		A.D. 1451, February 28
11.12.0.0.0 8 Ahau 3 Mol	Katun 8 Ahau	A.D. 1461, January 6
11.12.10.0.0 7 Ahau 13 Tzec		A.D. 1470, November 15
11.13.0.0.0 6 Ahau 3 Zip	Katun 6 Ahau	A.D. 1480, September 23
11.13.10.0.0 5 Ahau 18 Cumhu		A.D. 1490, August 2
11.14.0.0.0 4 Ahau 8 Pax	Katun 4 Ahau	A.D. 1500, June 11
11.14.10.0.0 3 Ahau 18 Mac		A.D. 1510, April 20
11.15.0.0.0 2 Ahau 8 Zac	Katun 2 Ahau	A.D. 1520, February 27
11.15.10.0.0 1 Ahau 18 Mol		A.D. 1530, January 5

TABLE X (*Concluded*)

Katun and Half-Katun Endings in the Maya Long Count (the Initial Series)	Katun Endings in the Maya Short Count (the *u kah-lay katunob*)	Gregorian Equivalents
11.16.0.0.0 13 Ahau 8 Xul	Katun 13 Ahau	A.D. 1539, November 14
11.16.10.0.0 12 Ahau 18 Zip		A.D. 1549, September 22
11.17.0.0.0 11 Ahau 8 Pop	Katun 11 Ahau	A.D. 1559, August 1
11.17.10.0.0 10 Ahau 3 Kayab		A.D. 1569, June 9
11.18.0.0.0 9 Ahau 13 Kankin	Katun 9 Ahau	A.D. 1579, April 18
11.18.10.0.0 8 Ahau 3 Ceh		A.D. 1589, February 24
11.19.0.0.0 7 Ahau 13 Chen	Katun 7 Ahau	A.D. 1599, January 3
11.19.10.0.0 6 Ahau 3 Yaxkin		A.D. 1608, November 11
12.0.0.0.0 5 Ahau 13 Zotz	Katun 5 Ahau	A.D. 1618, September 20
12.0.10.0.0 4 Ahau 3 Uo		A.D. 1628, July 29
12.1.0.0.0 3 Ahau 18 Kayab	Katun 3 Ahau	A.D. 1638, June 7
12.1.10.0.0 2 Ahau 8 Muan		A.D. 1648, April 15
12.2.0.0.0 1 Ahau 18 Ceh	Katun 1 Ahau	A.D. 1658, February 22
12.2.10.0.0 13 Ahau 8 Yax		A.D. 1668, January 1
12.3.0.0.0 12 Ahau 18 Yaxkin	Katun 12 Ahau	A.D. 1677, November 9
12.3.10.0.0 11 Ahau 8 Tzec		A.D. 1687, September 18
12.4.0.0.0 10 Ahau 18 Uo	Katun 10 Ahau	A.D. 1697, July 27
12.4.10.0.0 9 Ahau 13 Cumhu		A.D. 1707, June 6
12.5.0.0.0 8 Ahau 3 Pax	Katun 8 Ahau	A.D. 1717, April 14

NOTES

CHAPTER I

IT HAS BEEN pointed out that the Maya civilization is unique in that it developed in a physical environment unlike that of any other high civilization, an environment seemingly unsuited to the advanced agriculture and population concentration which are often assumed to be prerequisites to the rise of such civilizations. Information on the geographical environments of Egypt, the Middle East, and the East, and their apparent effects upon the rise of high civilizations there, may be obtained from V. Gordon Childe's *New Light on the Most Ancient East* and *Man Makes Himself*; for the Indus Valley of India, from Stuart Piggot's *Prehistoric India*. The following suggested readings, taken from the Bibliography, will give additional information on the geography, climate, and plant and animal life of the Maya area.

Geography: Huntington (41), Sapper (129), Wadell (187); animal life: Griscom (33), Murie (88), Schmidt and Andrews (134), *Biologia Centrali-Americana* (6); plant life: *Botany of the Maya Area* (7); *Biologia Centrali-Americana* (6), Lundell (61), Standley (148); climate: Page (90, 91). Mangelsdorf and Reeves (68) discuss the problem of the origin of maize, and Pearse, Creaser, and Hall (94) present a zoological and hydrographic survey of the cenotes which were so important in northern Yucatan.

CHAPTER II

Dr. Norman McQuown, while generously giving help with the linguistics map and chart, does not see sufficient evidence for the threefold division which Dr. Morley presents. For other theories on Maya linguistics, including Dr. McQuown's, see his "The Classification of the Maya Languages" (62).

Gates (31) and Tozzer (177) provide grammars of Maya, while the *Diccionario de Motul* (24), attributed to an early Spanish priest, is a Maya-Spanish dictionary. Thompson (166) dis-

449

cusses the question of how much can be inferred about culture history and the probable contacts between two cultures from the presence of foreign loan words in a vocabulary.

Steggerda (149, 150) describes the physical characteristics of the modern Indians of Yucatan, while some descriptions of Maya physical types of the Conquest period appear in Landa's *Relación de las cosas de Yucatán* (53).

The life of a modern Maya village is discussed by Redfield and Villa R. (106), and Redfield (105) also describes village life in its relationship to tribal Indian communities and to larger urban centers in Yucatan.

Landa's *Relación* gives an excellent account of Maya life at the time of the Spanish Conquest, although it is colored throughout by his pious horror at the religion which formed a large part of that life, and which he was instrumental in destroying. The *Relación*, together with other documents, is available in an English translation by Gates (30) and in a comprehensively annotated translation by Tozzer (178).

General discussions of the background and culture of some of the early Mesoamerican peoples may be found in Radin (101) and La Farge and Byers (52). Material for a comparison of the Chorti Indians of Guatemala and the Lacandon Maya of Chiapas with the modern Maya of Yucatan is presented in the studies by Wisdom (195) and Tozzer (174), and for a comparison of a modern Mexican village with the Maya in La Farge (51).

CHAPTER III

There is no unanimity of opinion on the starting date of the Classic stage, and the date used here was selected from several possibilities. Some archaeologists feel that further investigation in southern Veracruz, the place of origin of the much debated Stela C (Tres Zapotes) and the Tuxtla statuette, might yield evidence for assigning a much earlier date to the beginning of the Classic stage.

The surprisingly elaborate Preclassic-stage remains in Guatemala are described by Brainerd (8) and Kidder, Jennings, and

Shook (48); the Formative Period of the Valley of Mexico, which equates roughly with the Maya Preclassic, is described by Vaillant (181).

Two early archaeological studies of Tikal are those of Maler (67) and Tozzer (175); findings at Uaxactun are discussed by Kidder (47), Ricketson (107), Ricketson and Ricketson (108), and Smith (139). The University Museum of the University of Pennsylvania has recently started a project of exploration and restoration at Tikal. The first season's work began in January 1956, under the general direction of John Dimick; field director is E. M. Shook of the Carnegie Institution of Washington and chief archaeologist is Linton Satterthwaite.

Additional information on early Maya dates in the Peten is found in Morley (82), and Morley and Morley (85) analyze the problem of the age and provenance of the Leyden Plate.

CHAPTER IV

Brainerd (8), Spinden (143), Thompson (169), and Gann and Thompson (29) give excellent accounts of the development, florescence, and decline of Maya civilization. One section of Thompson's book offers an interesting reconstruction of the life of the average Maya, while Brainerd discusses in some detail the possible causes for the inexplicable decline of the great Classic-stage centers. *The Maya and Their Neighbors* (74) and *The Civilization of Ancient America* (18) are collections of papers dealing in a more specialized fashion with various aspects of the early cultures of Mesoamerica.

The Chilam Balam of Chumayel is available in a translation by Roys (112), and the Chilam Balam of Tizimin by Makemson (64). The possible historical value of such documents is discussed by Morley (77).

More detailed studies of individual sites are those of Morley (79) and Gordon (32) for Copan; Morley (81) and Hewett (38) for Quirigua; Thompson, Pollock, and Charlot (171) for Coba; Satterthwaite (130, 131) and Mason (71) for Piedras Negras; and Ruppert, Thompson, and Proskouriakoff (120) for Bonampak.

Proskouriakoff's study of Maya sculpture (98) analyzes a large number of stelae, and shows the persistence through time of their subject matter, despite changes in the style of representation.

Stephens (151) and Maudslay and Maudslay (73) describe Maya sites in parts of Guatemala, Chiapas, and Honduras as they appeared to the early traveler, and also give an excellent picture of the Indian and village life of those regions in the middle and late nineteenth century.

CHAPTER V

Landa's *Relación* describes Chichen Itza and Mayapan as they appeared in the 16th century. Morris (86) offers a popular account of the problems of modern archaeological work at Chichen Itza, and more detailed studies of individual buildings there are given by Morris, Charlot, and Morris (87) for the Temple of the Warriors, Pollock (95) for the Casa Redonda, Ruppert for the Temple of the Wall Panels (115), the Caracol (116), and the Mercado (117). The east coast site of Tulum, which is relatively less well known, is described by Lothrop (58).

Covarrubias (22), Joyce (44), Keleman (45), and Toscano (172) provide material which will permit comparisons between Toltec and Maya art and architecture.

The most recent information on Mayapan is that given by Bullard (12, 13), Pollock (96), Proskouriakoff (99, 100), and Smith (140). Descriptions of particular types of buildings there are given by Shook (137), Shook and Irving (138), Smith (140), and Thompson (170); Jones (43) has mapped the structures at the site. The problem of the exact number of houses at Mayapan is still unsettled, but the latest excavations there (96) report a total of 4,140 buildings; platforms which show no traces of superstructures may have supported dwellings made of some perishable material. These excavations have also yielded evidence which suggests that the city was sacked and destroyed by hostile forces, as the old records imply.

CHAPTERS VI AND VII

These two chapters have been grouped together because the additional readings suggested cover the periods dealt with in both of them.

A number of the sources relating to these periods are in Spanish—Carillo y Ancona (15), Lizana (56), and Scholes *et al.* (135)—but an account in English of the Spanish conquest of Yucatan is available in Means (75).

The conquest of Yucatan unfortunately had no such participant-chronicler as did the conquest of Aztec Mexico, but the impact on the two native populations involved must have been much the same. Díaz del Castillo (23), who was a soldier in Cortez's army, tells of the actual conquest of the Aztecs, and much of his account of the destruction of native culture might equally well be applied to Yucatan. Sahagún (128), a sixteenth-century Spanish priest, interested himself sufficiently in the native culture of the Valley of Mexico to study and record much of it, and to add a few sharp words for the Spanish treatment of the Indians. Although not included in the Bibliography, Prescott's *History of Mexico*, which draws on a number of early Spanish documentary sources, also gives a good account of the Conquest-period Aztecs.

The pre-Conquest cultures of central Mexico are described by Thompson (159) and Vaillant (181).

CHAPTER VIII

A qualification of the description of Maya agriculture given in the text is presented here by Dr. Joseph Hester, who has made an intensive study (36) of the natural and cultural bases of ancient Maya subsistence economy.

"The 'simplicity' of Maya maize agriculture is more apparent than real. Actually, there are critical factors in many of the steps in making a milpa which could spell the difference between success, partial success, or complete failure. For example, potassium seems to be the most critical soil element in Yucatan maize agriculture, and is made most available from the soil by the burning of brush cut in clearing the milpa. The temperature of the fire must be within relatively narrow limits for optimum results. Too slow a fire is ineffective, and too hot a fire consumes the limited fuel inefficiently. Best results seem to be obtained when the cut brush is carefully distributed over the soil, and the field is fired when the proper conditions of both wind and atmospheric moisture prevail. This must also be done at a time which is carefully chosen with respect to planting time and the beginning of the rainy season. Burning too soon means that weeds may take over the milpa before planting can be done effectively; waiting too long may permit the irregular showers which precede the full rainy season to soak the cut brush to the point that it cannot be burned effectively when the time comes. The proper timing with respect to the approach of the rainy season and the moment for planting varies from north to south and from east to west; it may also not be possible without certain wind conditions. And there are years when a favorable set of conditions just does not occur. The farmer may be obliged to spend weeks waiting at his field for proper conditions, during which time he cannot be productively employed at any other important task.

"While it seems to be generally true of northern Yucatan that cornfield fires do not start forest fires, this may not apply equally well to the Peten and the east coast of the peninsula. Paradoxically enough, forest fires are a real concern in the Peten, even during the rainy season. Because of the excessive moisture the vegetation there often contains a much higher proportion of highly combustible volatile oils. Accidentally started fires have been reported in the Peten which raged out of control through miles of rain forest. The only comparable occurrences in northern Yucatan are henequen plantation fires, surely not an aboriginal problem.

"Over most of the Yucatan Peninsula the first native plants to infiltrate a cornfield are not grass, but leguminous shrubs. When unmolested, these tend to shade out all grasses within one to four years, depending upon the amount and annual distribution of rainfall at a given place. After this period the legumes in turn are shaded out by trees, many of which, like the acacia, also are

454

leguminous and calciphilic. Some of the taller grasses found in milpas are considered premium roof-thatching material, and sometimes these are actually sown from seed by the Maya farmer, along with maize and other cultigens, and often occupy the richest soil. Soils which naturally support grasses are generally too acid for maize, and in Yucatan are very limited in their distribution. There is no demonstrable evidence that grass is or ever has been a threat to maize agriculture on the Yucatan Peninsula.

"As there are variations in precipitation on the peninsula (increasing from north to south), there also are corresponding differences in native vegetation; both are reflected in limitations upon native agriculture. In northern Yucatan, where rain is less abundant, the maize growing season coincides closely with the rainy season and is limited to about seven months. Most frequently here a single crop of maize is planted, rarely two. To the south an increase in both precipitation and length of the rainy season permits from two to four crops per year. On the southern perimeter of the peninsula there may in some years be no distinct dry season and hence no clear interruption of the growing season. This is not to say that rainfall cannot become a critical factor in maize agriculture even in the wettest portions of the peninsula. There is, however, a noticeable increase in agricultural potential from north to south. Thus the chapter in this book on agriculture should be understood to apply most closely to northern Yucatan, where the only intensive studies of Maya maize agriculture have been made. Only with certain qualifications does it provide a picture of the agricultural economy in the southern lowland regions, where Maya civilization achieved its greatest elaboration.

"In the Peten a fallowing period of three to four years provides a growth of woody vegetation sufficient to furnish fuel for a good 'burn.' In northern Yucatan eight years is about the minimum, and frequently twelve or more years are necessary. Fields can thus be returned to agriculture more rapidly in the south.

"The Maya farmer now raises a surplus of maize which he sells or trades for cotton and other goods. Cotton now is grown only occasionally, and only as an ornamental, but in pre-Spanish times the acreage devoted to cotton was second only to maize. Thus the amount of corn required to feed a Maya family and their animals is not a simple index of the time actually spent aboriginally in agricultural pursuits. Furthermore, a long-term average of as much as 50 per cent of all the farmer's agricultural effort may not be productive, due to drought, infestation and deterioration or loss of stored grain, or to other factors. And in northern Yucatan the agricultural cycle is approximately fifteen months from the time of selection of a plot until final harvest of the first crop. Obviously the farmer will be working upon two or more milpas, in different stages of preparation or production, during the same season. An additional consideration is that even during the dry season the farmer seldom has as much as two weeks at one time completely free from milpa preparation, harvest, or care. In view of this, the '293 to 317 days' out of each year which the Maya farmer supposedly has, or had, for non-food-producing activities could more realistically be reduced to one-half or one-fourth or less of this time."

Discussions of the origin of maize may be found in Mangelsdorf and Reeves (68); of the origin of agriculture in America, in Spinden (144); and of the Maya utilization of wild plants, in Roys (111).

CHAPTER IX

There are few additional readings which might usefully be suggested here to augment the discussion of government and social organization among the ancient Maya, since, as the text points out, no direct evidence on these points has survived. Some inferences may be drawn from the pictorial art, but Classic-stage pictorial art is rare. A few of the more elaborately decorated ceramics show what seem to be ceremonial processions; the most extensive murals which exist for the period are those at Bonampak, and drawings of these in color appear in Villagra (185) and Ruppert, Thompson, and Proskouriakoff (120).

Landa gives a detailed account of Maya political and social

organization at the time of the Conquest, but by this time at least the political organization had no doubt been extensively altered by Mexican influences. Brainerd (8) and Thompson (169), in their general descriptions of Maya civilization, offer conjectural reconstructions of the social and governmental organization of the Classic stage. Tozzer's comparative study of the Maya and the Lacandons (174) gives more information on traces of a possible former clan system.

CHAPTER X

Virtually everything that is known about the everyday life of the ancient Maya has been derived from Landa's accounts in his *Relación* (178). The Maya whom Landa describes were those of the early Conquest period, but while political organization had no doubt changed greatly since the Classic stage, the daily life of the common people may well have been much the same. Landa was a careful observer and deserves due credit for having recorded so much valuable information about Maya life, but his *Relación* was written in large part as a justification for his treatment of the Indians when he was called before an ecclesiastical court in Spain, and he therefore exaggerates those aspects of native life which seemed abhorrent to the Spaniards. Thompson gives some hypothetical reconstructions of Classic-stage daily life in his *The Rise and Fall of Maya Civilization* (169).

For those interested in comparing the Aztec and Maya civilizations at the time of the Spanish Conquest, Díaz del Castillo (23) and Vaillant (181) give detailed descriptions of life in the Aztec capital, Tenochtitlan (the modern Mexico City). Little is known of the dress of the Maya common people beyond the descriptions given in Landa. The murals, such as those at Bonampak (120, 185) and in the Temple of the Warriors (87), and the figures on the stelae (98) show largely rulers, nobles, and priests.

The Annals of the Cakchiquels are available in a recent translation by Recinos and Goetz (103).

An alternative opinion on Maya subsistence practices, by Joseph Hester, is offered in the Note to chapter viii.

CHAPTER XI

Landa, of course, is the best source of material on the Maya religion of the Postclassic stage. The Codices Dresdensis (19), Peresianus (20), and Tro-Cortesianus (21) have been reproduced with texts in German, French, and Spanish, respectively, but these publications are now quite old and may be difficult to find. A more recent study on the Codices is that of Villacorta (184). Schellhas (133) discusses the representation of deities in Maya manuscripts; Thompson analyzes the symbolism of the Maya and Mexican religions (160) and the occurrence of the moon goddess and related deities in Mesoamerica (163).

For purposes of a comparison of Aztec and Maya beliefs and practices, Caso (16), Vaillant (181), and Díaz del Castillo (23) all describe the Aztec religion at the time of the Conquest.

Religious practices of the modern Lacandon Maya of Chiapas, who seem to retain many elements of the old religion, are discussed by Tozzer (174). Redfield (104) and Redfield and Villa R. (106) present material on the religion of the modern Maya of Yucatan, which is now a fusion of Catholic and native belief and practice.

CHAPTER XII

The statement that Maya writing is ideographic rather than phonetic, that its characters depict ideas rather than sounds, should perhaps be qualified by reference to some linguistic studies which have attempted translations of glyphs on the basis of possible phonetic elements. In 1940 the American linguist Benjamin Whorf (191) published a monograph which analyzed a number of glyphs in terms of the possible syllabic values of some of their elements, and in this manner translated a sentence from the Codex Tro-Cortesianus. Whorf felt, however, that there were also some ideographic elements in the writings, and that these were sometimes combined with phonetic elements which expressed the same concept, in a reduplication which emphasized the meaning of the glyph.

A Russian linguist, J. B. Knorozov (50), has recently pub-

458

lished a paper in which he states his belief that the glyphs consist of ideographic and phonetic elements and key-signs. In Knorozov's analysis, a given element of a glyph may have two different meanings, depending upon whether it is used ideographically or phonetically, and the key-sign acts as a determinative to indicate which meaning shall be taken. His paper gives illustrations and appended translations of 380 signs, words, and sentences which he claims to have translated, but the available published material is still too meager to permit a real evaluation of his work.

The information on which most studies of Maya calendrics and writing have been based is given by Landa. Other material on Maya inscriptions and their translations, which deal largely with calendric and astronomical information, may be found in Beyer (3), Morley (78, 79, 80, 82), and Thompson (168).

Teeple (154) discusses Maya astronomy; Willson (194), the astronomical material in the Codices; Guthe (34), the lunar count; and Thompson, the Maya solar year (158) and mathematical system (164).

References for the Books of Chilam Balam are given in the Note to chapter iv, and for the Annals of the Cakchiquels in the Note to chapter x. The Popul Vuh is available in a translation by Recinos (102).

Additional references for the Codices are given in the Note to chapter xi, and Von Hagen (186) describes more fully the manufacture of the bark paper on which they were written.

CHAPTER XIII

References dealing with Tikal and Uaxactun have been given in the Note to chapter iii; Copan, Quirigua, Coba, and Piedras Negras, in the Note to chapter iv; Chichen Itza and Mayapan, in the Note to chapter v.

The house mounds at Uaxactun are described more fully by Wauchope (188) and Ricketson and Ricketson (108). A description of a Maya community in western British Honduras is given by Willey, Bullard, and Glass (193). It should be noted, however, that the high population density evidenced by this site is atypical, and was no doubt due to the fact that the area sampled was an alluvial river bottom. This is far richer land than characterizes the Maya area as a whole, and is of a sort which would provide subsistence for a greater concentration of population.

E. H. Thompson (155) discusses the chultunes of the Puuc area, and Villa R. (182) the Coba-Yaxuna causeway.

Marquina (69) deals with pre-Spanish architecture throughout Mesoamerica, and Totten (173) with Maya architecture specifically; Proskouriakoff's album of Maya architecture (97) is illustrated with reconstruction drawings of the principal Maya sites based on archaeological evidence. Brainerd (8) traces the chronological and regional variations in the building techniques used in Maya corbeled vaults.

CHAPTER XIV

The most recent study which traces the development of Maya sculpture as shown on the stelae is that of Proskouriakoff (98). The time span during which stelae were carved is divided into Early and Late Periods, and the latter is divided into Formative, Ornate, Dynamic, and Decadent phases. The study analyzes the changing styles of representation of subject matter which remained consistently the same.

Some of the best illustrations of Maya sculpture are those of Stephens (151, 152), Catherwood (17), and Maudslay and Maudslay (73). These drawings of stelae and wall panels have seldom been equaled, and details are shown in them with such clarity and precision that they have been of great assistance in studies of Maya hieroglyphic writing. The illustrations in Stephens and Catherwood are now more than a century old, and those in Maudslay and Maudslay more than a half century, and in some cases they record details of carving which have subsequently become obscured.

Ruz' own accounts of the finding and excavation of the Palenque tomb are listed in the Bibliography (122, 124, 125, 126). A brief resumé of the work is given here.

In 1949, 23 steps were discovered and in 1950, 23 more, ending in a landing at a depth 15 meters below the top of the pyramid; in 1951, two narrow, horizontal air-shafts were cleared, which extended 8 meters through to the west side of the pyramid. From this landing a new stairway of 22 steps went toward the east, whereas the first flight went toward the west (Plate 27, p. 181). The foot of this second flight was blocked by a wall of stone, at the bottom of which was found a masonry box containing three clay plates, three shells, eleven pieces of jade, and one pearl. The clearing of this wall revealed a great triangular vertical stone slab, with a crude grave at the base of it which contained five male skeletons and one female.

This slab formed the entry to a room 6.6 meters high by 9 meters long, to which four steps descended from the entrance. The width of the room varies from 1.8 meters at the entry to 3.9 meters at its widest point. Because of the exceptional height of the vault, it was strengthened by five cross-pieces of stone. The floor of the room is 24 meters below the top of the pyramid, and 2 meters below the ground level.

The walls are decorated with stucco bas-reliefs (Plate 100c, p. 413), showing a procession of nine magnificently dressed priests with headdresses of quetzal plumes. The center of the crypt is occupied by a monolithic sarcophagus 1 meter high, 2.1 meters wide, and 3 meters long, which rests on six stone supports; the four at the corners are ornamented by carved human figures. A slab 3.8 meters long by 2.2 meters wide by .25 meter thick serves as a cover to the sarcophagus. The sides of this slab carry fifty-four carved hieroglyphs, thirty of which give a date of approximately A.D. 700. The entire top of the slab is beautifully sculptured (Plate 100, *b* and *d*). It shows the semireclining figure of a man, resting on a great mask; his gaze is fixed on a cruciform motif which rises above him. On the arms of the cross crawls a two-headed serpent, from whose mouths emerge small figures; the arms themselves end in stylized serpent heads. The slab is circled by a band which is decorated largely with astronomical glyphs. Some slate pendants and fragments of a jade mosaic were found on top of the slab, and two beautiful stucco heads (Plate 98, *b* and *c*, p. 411) under the sarcophagus.

In November 1952, this slab was lifted, revealing a smooth stone slab which fitted exactly into the opening of the sarcophagus. Removal of this inner cover disclosed a male human skeleton, lying on its back (Plate 99*a*, p. 412). Around the head were found hair ornaments, jade earplugs, and the fragments of a jade mosaic mask. The breast was covered with a sort of breastplate made of various kinds of beads; the arms were adorned with bracelets, and there was a ring on each finger. Two jade idols were also found (Plate 98*a*), one at the feet and the other at the level of the pelvis.

The fact that the tomb is found below the level of the ground on which the pyramid rests, and the great size and weight of the sarcophagus, indicate that the body had been buried before the pyramid was erected. This pyramid and temple are thus essentially a funerary monument, a tribute to the particularly sacred character of the personage buried there. Needless to say, however, this interpretation cannot be extended to include all Maya pyramids, for intensive archaeological investigation has shown that constructions of this nature are exceedingly rare in Mesoamerica.

Rivet (110) has excellent illustrations on the Palenque tomb, as well as on Maya art and architecture in general. His book includes color plates of all the Bonampak murals.

CHAPTER XV

Some descriptions of the ceramics from various Maya sites may often be found in the general reports on the sites, but Longyear's study (57) deals exclusively with the ceramics of Copan. Brainerd's report on the archaeological ceramics of Yucatan (9) is based upon ceramic sequences from a number of sites in that region. This more comprehensive survey will no doubt aid in establishing a clearer relative chronology for the sites involved, and show the relationship of this chronology to that of the Peten. It may also indicate the amount of contact not only between the various sites in Yucatan, but also between Yucatan and the Peten.

CHAPTER XVI

Guatemalan textiles are discussed by Osborne (89), and the weaving techniques of the Lacandon Maya, which seem to be similar to aboriginal techniques, by Tozzer (174). A number of the text figures in Proskouriakoff (98) show the great elaboration in the clothing, headdresses, and ornaments depicted on the stelae, and Barrera Vásquez' study (2) discusses Maya featherwork.

The Bonampak murals are illustrated in color by Villagra (185) and Ruppert, Thompson, and Proskouriakoff (120), and the frescoes from the Temple of the Warriors are shown in Morris, Charlot, and Morris (87).

The metalwork recovered from the Cenote of Sacrifice at Chichen Itza is extensively analyzed by Lothrop (59), who doubts the authenticity of some of the pieces illustrated in this chapter. He feels there is reason to believe that the objects shown in Figure 55 (a, b, d, e, f) and all of the objects in Figure 56 are forgeries.

Discussions and illustrations of Maya art may be found in Covarrubias (22), Joyce (44), Keleman (45), Spinden (142), and Toscano (172).

Music among the Maya was little more than an adjunct to the dance, and musical instruments were mainly of percussion type. Thompson (169) gives some discussion of music among the ancient Maya, while Tozzer (174) discusses that of the modern Lacandon. Vaillant's study of the Aztecs (181) highlights their music and instruments. The musicians of the Bonampak murals are treated in Ruppert, Thompson, and Proskouriakoff (120).

CHAPTER XVII

A full discussion of the theories of cultural evolution outlined in this chapter may be found in V. Gordon Childe's *Man Makes Himself* and *Social Evolution*, and in Julian Steward's *Theory of Culture Change*.

It is generally conceded that true urbanization did not exist during the Classic stage, in that there were no cities comprising many acres of closely packed dwellings. However, although this formal criterion of urbanization is lacking, the Maya may have had a kind of "dispersed urbanism." It is possible that surrounding a center like Tikal, for example, for several miles in all directions, there were numerous small hamlets which were more or less semi-continuous. This would have meant a fairly dense population, even though the spacing and arrangement were not those of a true city. The Maya achievements must surely have resulted from being able to draw upon the efforts of a great many people, and even with foot transportation this was probably possible over a fairly wide area.

Recent archaeological work by Gordon Willey (192) in the Belize Valley in western British Honduras has shown a kind of settlement pattern previously unknown in the Maya area during the Classic stage. The Belize Valley settlements, located on river terraces or on hill slopes, are house-mound clusters, ranging from a dozen or so mounds to more than three hundred. In most clusters there are usually one or more larger mounds which quite possibly were pyramid bases for small temples or platforms for palace-like buildings.

Domestic refuse from the flanks of the house mounds included polychrome and figure-painted ware, and vessels with elaborately carved designs. Fine pottery was found in association with burials, and one Late Classic burial was accompanied by a fine jade gorget and several objects of polished stone. One of these, a monolithic axe, bore a rather inexpertly rendered Ahau glyph.

These discoveries would seem to indicate that, in this area at least, the gulf between rural village and ceremonial center was not so great as it was earlier believed to have been. The village dwellers apparently possessed some of the finer material objects, participated in a rather widely distributed religious and ritual life, and at least knew about and valued the intellectual attainments of the great ceremonial centers, even though they may not have understood them fully.

This might suggest an eventual modification of the picture of a Classic-stage society dominated by a relatively few great centers, to which the outlying areas were merely a kind of rural backwater.

A description of the radiocarbon technique and lists of dates which it has yielded for various parts of the world may be found in Libby (55). Johnson (42) and Wauchope (190) discuss the implications of the revised dates for reconstructions of New World culture history.

The intricacies of the correlation problem are analyzed by Beyer (4), Kidder and Thompson (49), Palacios (92), and Teeple (153). The Spinden (145) and Thompson (156, 161) studies show the differences in interpretation of the available evidence which have led to the formulation of these competing correlations.

BIBLIOGRAPHY

Ancona, Eligio

(1)   1889. *Historia de Yucatán.* 2d ed. 4 vols. Barcelona.

Barrera Vásquez, Alfredo

(2)   1939. "Algunos datos acerca del arte plumaria entre los mayas," *Cuadernos Mayas No. 1.* Mérida.

Beyer, Hermann

(3)   1930. "The Analysis of the Maya Hieroglyphs," *Internat. Arch. Ethnog.,* Bd. 31, S. 1–20. Leyden.

(4)   1935. "On the Correlation between Maya and Christian Chronology," *Maya Research,* Vol. II, No. 1, pp. 64–72. New York.

(5)   1937. "Studies on the Inscriptions at Chichen Itza," *Contributions to American Archaeology,* Vol. IV, No. 21; Carnegie Institution of Washington Publication No. 483, 1937, pp. 37–175, pls. 1–14. Washington, D.C.

Biologia Centrali-Americana

(6)   1889–1902. *Biologia Centrali-Americana; or, Contributions to the Knowledge of the Fauna and Flora of Mexico and Central America.* Edited by E. DuCane Godman and Osbert Salvin. 61 secs. London.

Botany of the Maya Area

(7)   1936. *Botany of the Maya Area: Miscellaneous Papers.* Carnegie Institution of Washington Publication No. 461. Washington, D.C.

Brainerd, George W.

(8)   1954. *The Maya Civilization.* Southwest Museum. Los Angeles.

(9)   *The Archaeological Ceramics of Yucatan.* Manuscript in press. University of California, Anthropological Records. Berkeley.

Brinton, D. G.

(10)   1882. *The Maya Chronicles.* Brinton's Library of Aboriginal American Literature, No. 1. Philadelphia.

(11)   1885. *The Annals of the Cakchiquels. The Original Text, with a Translation, Notes, and Introduction.* Brinton's Library of Aboriginal American Literature, No. 6. Philadelphia.

Bullard, William R., Jr.

(12)   1952. "Residential Property Walls at Mayapan," *Current Reports,* Carnegie Institution of Washington, Department of Archaeology, No. 3. Washington, D.C.

467

(13)   1953. "Property Walls at Mayapan," *Carnegie Institution of Washington Year Book*, No. 52, pp. 258–64. Washington, D.C.

CARNEGIE INSTITUTION OF WASHINGTON

(14)   1929. *The Art of the Maya*. Carnegie Institution of Washington News Service Bulletin, Vol. I, No. 36, March 17. Washington, D.C.

CARRILLO Y ANCONA, CRESCENCIO

(15)   1937. *Historia antigua de Yucatán*. Mérida.

CASO, ALFONSO

(16)   1937. "The Religion of the Aztecs," *Revista Mexicana de Estudios Antropológicos*, Vol. III, No. 1. Mexico.

CATHERWOOD, F.

(17)   1844. *Views of Ancient Monuments in Central America, Chiapas, and Yucatan*. New York.

Civilization of Ancient America

(18)   1951. *The Civilization of Ancient America*. Sol Tax, editor. Chicago.

Codex Dresdensis

(19)   1880. *Die Maya-Handschrift der Königlichen Bibliothek zu Dresden*; herausgegeben von Prof. Dr. E. Förstemann. Leipzig.

Codex Peresianus

(20)   1887. *Manuscrit hiératique des anciens Indiens de l'Amérique Centrale conservé à la Bibliothèque Nationale de Paris, avec une introduction par Léon de Rosny*. Publié en couleurs. 2d ed. Paris.

Codex Tro-Cortesianus

(21)   1892. *Códice Maya denominado Cortesiano que se conserva en el Museo Arqueológico Nacional* (Madrid). Reproducción fotocromolitográfica ordenada en la misma forma que el original hecha y publicada bajo la dirección de D. Juan de Dios de la Rada y Delgado y D. Jerónimo López de Ayala y del Hierro. Madrid. To this should be added the plates reproducing the Codex Troanus taken from Abbé C. E. Brasseur de Bourbourg's Manuscrit. Troano, Paris, 1869–70. These two codices are parts of one original.

COVARRUBIAS, MIGUEL

(22)   1954. *The Eagle, the Jaguar, and the Serpent: Indian Art of the Americas* Knopf. New York.

DÍAZ DEL CASTILLO, BERNAL

(23)   1956. *The Discovery and Conquest of Mexico*. Farrar, Strauss and Cudahy. New York.

Diccionario de Motul

(24)   1929. *Diccionario de Motul, Maya Español*. Atribuido a Fray Antonio de

Ciudad Real y *Arte de Lengua Maya* por Fray Juan Coronel. Edición hecha por Juan Martínez Hernández. Mérida.

FERNANDEZ, MIGUEL ANGEL, AND BERLIN, HEINRICH

(25) 1954. "Drawings of Glyphs of Structure XVIII, Palenque," *Notes on Middle American Archaeology and Ethnology*, No. 119. Carnegie Institution of Washington. Washington, D.C.

FOLLETT, P. H. F.

(26) 1932. "War and Weapons of the Maya." Middle American Research Series, Publication No. 4. *Middle American Papers*, Tulane University. New Orleans.

GANN, T. W. F.

(27) 1918. *The Maya Indians of Southern Yucatan and Northern British Honduras.* Bureau of American Ethnology, Smithsonian Institution, Bulletin 64. Washington, D.C.

(28) 1927. *Maya Cities. A Record of Exploration and Adventure in Middle America.* London.

GANN, T. W. F., AND THOMPSON, J. E. S.

(29) 1931. *The History of the Maya, from the Earliest Time to the Present Day.* New York.

GATES, WILLIAM

(30) 1937. *Yucatan before and after the Conquest, by Friar Diego de Landa, with Other Related Documents, Maps and Illustrations.* Translated, with notes. Maya Society Publication No. 20. Baltimore.

(31) 1938. *A Grammar of Maya.* Maya Society Publication No. 13. Baltimore.

GORDON, G. B.

(32) 1896. "Prehistoric Ruins of Copan, Honduras." A Preliminary Report of the Explorations by the Museum, 1891–95. *Memoirs of the Peabody Museum of American Archaeology and Ethnology*, Harvard University, Vol. 1, No. 1. Cambridge.

GRISCOM, LUDLOW

(33) 1932. "The Distribution of Bird-Life in Guatemala," *Bulletin of the American Museum of Natural History*, Vol. LXIV. New York.

GUTHE, C. E.

(34) 1932. "The Maya Lunar Count," *Science*, n.s., Vol. 75, No. 1941, pp. 271–77. Lancaster.

HERRERA, ANTONIO DE

(35) 1726–30. *Historia general de los hechos de los castellanos en las islas i tierra firme del mar oceano.* 5 vols. Madrid.

469

HESTER, JOSEPH A., JR.

(36) 1954. *Natural and Cultural Bases of Ancient Maya Subsistence Economy.* University of California, Los Angeles, Ph.D. dissertation.

HEWETT, E. L.

(37) 1911. "Two Seasons' Work in Guatemala," *Bulletin of the Archaeological Institute of America*, Vol. II, pp. 117–34. Norwood. (Reprinted under same title as *Paper No. 21, School of American Research*, Archaeological Institute of America, Santa Fe.)

(38) 1912. "The Excavations at Quirigua in 1912," *Bulletin of the Archaeological Institute of America*, Vol. III, pp. 163–71. Norwood. (Reprinted as "The Third Season's Work in Guatemala," *Paper No. 22, School of American Research*, Archaeological Institute of America, Santa Fe.)

(39) 1916. "Latest Work of the School of American Archaeology at Quirigua," *Holmes Anniversary Volume*, pp. 157–62. Washington, D.C.

HOLMES, W. H.

(40) 1895–97. *Archaeological Studies among the Ancient Cities of Mexico.* Part I, *Monuments of Yucatan*, pp. 1–138; Part II, *Monuments of Chiapas, Oaxaca and the Valley of Mexico*, pp. 138–338. *Anthropological Series*, Vol. I. Field Columbian Museum, Chicago.

HUNTINGTON, ELLSWORTH

(41) 1912. "The Peninsula of Yucatan," *Bulletin of the American Geographical Society*, Vol. XLIV, No. 11, pp. 801–22. Lancaster.

JOHNSON, FREDERICK

(42) 1955. "Reflections upon the Significance of Radiocarbon Dates," in *Radiocarbon Dating*. University of Chicago Press. Chicago.

JONES, MORRIS R.

(43) 1952. "Map of the Ruins of Mayapan, Yucatan, Mexico," *Current Reports*, Carnegie Institution of Washington, Department of Archaeology, No. 1. Washington, D.C.

JOYCE, THOMAS A.

(44) 1927. *Maya and Mexican Art.* London.

KELEMAN, PÁL

(45) 1943. *Medieval American Art.* 2 vols. New York.

KIDDER, A. V.

(46) 1937. "Notes on the Ruins of San Agustin Acasaguastlan, Guatemala," *Contributions to American Archaeology*, Vol. III, No. 15. Carnegie Institution of Washington Publication No. 456. Washington, D.C.

(47) 1947. *The Artifacts of Uaxactun, Guatemala.* Carnegie Institution of Washington Publication No. 576. Washington, D.C.

KIDDER, A. V., JENNINGS, J. D., AND SHOOK, E. M.

(48) 1946. *Excavations at Kaminaljuyú, Guatemala.* Carnegie Institution of Washington Publication No. 561. Washington, D.C.

KIDDER, A. V., AND THOMPSON, J. E. S.

(49) 1938. "The Correlation of Maya and Christian Chronology," *Co-operation in Research*, Carnegie Institution of Washington Publication No. 501, pp. 493–510. Washington, D.C.

KNOROZOV, JURIJ V.

(50) 1955. "The Writing of the Ancient Mayans: A Study of Deciphering," *Sovjetskaja Etnografija*, No. 1, Academy of Sciences of the Union of Soviet Socialist Republics.

LA FARGE, OLIVER

(51) 1947. *Santa Eulalia. The Religion of a Cuchumatan Indian Town.* Chicago.

LA FARGE, OLIVER, AND BYERS, DOUGLAS

(52) 1931. *The Year Bearer's People.* Middle American Research Series, Publication No. 3, Department of Middle American Research, Tulane University. New Orleans.

LANDA, DIEGO DE

(53) 1938. *Relación de las cosas de Yucatán.* Mérida.

LAS CASAS, BARTOLOMÉ DE

(54) 1909. "Apologética historia de las Indias," *Neuva Biblioteca de Autores Españoles. Historiadores de Indias.* Vol. I. Madrid.

LIBBY, WILLARD F.

(55) 1955. *Radiocarbon Dating.* University of Chicago Press. Chicago.

LIZANA, BERNARDO DE

(56) 1893. *Historia de Yucatán. Devocionario de Nuestra Señora de Izmal y conquista espiritual impresa en 1633.* 2d ed. Museo Nacional de México, Mexico.

LONGYEAR, J. M.

(57) 1952. *Copan Ceramics. A Study of Southeastern Maya Pottery.* Carnegie Institution of Washington Publication No. 597. Washington, D.C.

LOTHROP, S. K.

(58) 1924. *Tulum. An Archaeological Study of the East Coast of Yucatan.* Carnegie Institution of Washington Publication No. 335. Washington, D.C.

(59) 1952. *Metals from the Cenote of Sacrifice, Chichen Itza, Yucatan.* Cambridge.

LUNDELL, C. L.

(60) 1934. "The Agriculture of the Maya," *Southwest Review*, Vol. XIX, pp. 65–77. Dallas. Department of Botany and Herbarium, University of Michigan, Paper No. 445. Ann Arbor.

(61) 1937. *The Vegetation of Peten*. Carnegie Institution of Washington Publication No. 478. Washington, D.C.

McQUOWN, NORMAN A.

(62) 1956. "The Classification of the Maya Languages," *Intl. J. American Linguistics*, Vol. 22, pp. 191–95, July 1956.

Maize and the Maya

(63) 1938. *Maize and the Maya*. Carnegie Institution of Washington News Service Bulletin, Vol. IV, No. 26, pp. 217–24, May 8. Washington, D.C.

MAKEMSON, MAUD W.

(64) 1951. *The Book of the Jaguar Priest: a Translation of the Book of Chilam Balam of Tizimin, with Commentary*. Henry Schuman. New York.

MALER, TEOBERT

(65) 1901. "Researches in the Central Portion of the Usumatsintla Valley. Report of Explorations for the Museum, 1898–1900," *Memoirs of the Peabody Museum of American Archaeology and Ethnology*, Harvard University, Vol. II, No. 1, pp. 1–75. Cambridge.

(66) 1903. "Researches in the Central Portions of the Usumatsintla Valley. Reports of Explorations for the Museum," *Memoirs of the Peabody Museum of American Archaeology and Ethnology*, Harvard University, Vol. II, No. 2, pp. 77–208. Cambridge.

(67) 1911. "Explorations in the Department of Peten, Guatemala. Tikal. Report of Explorations for the Museum," *Memoirs of the Peabody Museum of American Archaeology and Ethnology*, Harvard University, Vol. V, No. 1, pp. 3–135. Cambridge.

MANGELSDORF, P. C., AND REEVES, R. G.

(68) 1945. "The Origin of Maize: Present Status of the Problem," *American Anthropologist*, Vol. XLVII, No. 2, pp. 235–43. Menasha, Wisconsin.

MARQUINA, I.

(69) 1951. *Arquitectura prehispánica*. Instituto Nacional de Antropología e Historia. Mexico.

MASON, J. A.

(70) 1931. "A Maya Carved Stone Lintel from Guatemala," *Univ. Mus. Bull.*, University of Pennsylvania, Vol. III, No. 1, pp. 5–7, pls. I–III. Philadelphia.

(71) 1932. "Excavations at Piedras Negras," *Univ. Mus. Bull.*, University of Pennsylvania, Vol. III, No. 6, pp. 178, 179. Philadelphia.

(72) 1935. "Preserving Ancient America's Finest Sculptures," *National Geo-*

graphic Magazine, Vol. LXVIII, No. 5, pp. 537–70, color plates I–VIII. Washington, D.C.

MAUDSLAY, A. P. AND A. C.

(73)   1899. *A Glimpse at Guatemala, and Some Notes on the Ancient Monoments of Central America.* London.

Maya and Their Neighbors, The

(74)   1940. *The Maya and Their Neighbors.* New York.

MEANS, P. A.

(75)   1917. "History of the Spanish Conquest of Yucatan and of the Itzas," *Papers of the Peabody Museum of American Archaeology and Ethnology*, Harvard University, Vol. VII. Cambridge.

Mexican and Central American Antiquities

(76)   1904. *Mexican and Central American Antiquities, Calendar Systems, and History.* Twenty-four papers by Eduard Seler, E. Förstemann, Paul Schellhas, Carl Sapper, and E. P. Dieseldorff, translated from the German under the supervision of Charles P. Bowditch. Bureau of American Ethnology, Smithsonian Institution, Bulletin 28. Washington, D.C.

MORLEY, S. G.

(77)   1911. "The Historical Value of the Books of Chilam Balam," *American Journal of Archaeology*, Archaeological Institute of America, 2d ser., Vol. XV, No. 2, pp. 195–214. Norwood.

(78)   1915. *An Introduction to the Study of the Maya Hieroglyphs.* Bureau of American Ethnology, Smithsonian Institution, Bulletin 57. Washington, D.C.

(79)   1920. *The Inscriptions at Copan.* Carnegie Institution of Washington Publication No. 219. Washington, D.C.

(80)   1925. "The Earliest Mayan Dates," *Congrès International des Américanistes, Compte-rendu de la XXIᵉ session*, Göteborg, 1924, Part 2, pp. 655–67. Göteborg Museum, Göteborg.

(81)   1935. *Guide Book to the Ruins of Quirigua.* Carnegie Institution of Washington Supplemental Publication No. 16. Washington, D.C.

(82)   1937–38. *The Inscriptions of Peten.* Carnegie Institution of Washington Publication No. 437. 5 vols. Washington, D.C.

(83)   1947. *The Ancient Maya.* 2d ed. Stanford University Press. Stanford, California.

(84)   1953. *La Civilización Maya.* Translation by Adrián Recinos. 2d ed. Fondo de Cultura Económica. Mexico.

MORLEY, S. G. AND FRANCES R.

(85)   1939. "The Age and Provenance of the Leyden Plate," *Contributions to American Anthropology and History*, Vol. V, No. 24; Carnegie Institution of Washington Publication No. 509. Washington, D.C.

473

Morris, Ann Axtell

(86)   1931. *Digging in Yucatan.* New York.

Morris, E. H., Charlot, Jean, and Morris, A. A.

(87)   1931. *The Temple of the Warriors at Chichen Itza, Yucatan.* Carnegie Institution of Washington Publication No. 406. Washington, D.C.

Murie, Adolph

(88)   1935. "Mammals from Guatemala and British Honduras," *University of Michigan, Museum of Zoology, Miscellaneous Publications,* No. 26, pp. 7–30. Ann Arbor.

Osborne, Lily de Jongh de

(89)   1935. *Guatemala Textiles.* New Orleans.

Page, John L.

(90)   1933. "Climate of the Yucatan Peninsula." See Shattuck, George C., 1933, *The Peninsula of Yucatan,* chapter 20.

(91)   1937–38. "The Climate of Peten, Guatemala." See Morley, S. G., 1937–38, *The Inscriptions of Peten,* Appendix 2.

Palacios, Enrique Juan

(92)   1932. *Maya-Christian Synchronology or Calendrical Correlation.* Middle American Research Series, Publication No. 4, pp. 147–80. *Middle American Papers,* Department of Middle American Research, Tulane University. New Orleans.

(93)   1933. *El calendario y los jeroglíficos cronográficos mayas.* Mexico.

Pearse, A. S., Creaser, E. P., and Hall, F. G.

(94)   1936. *The Cenotes of Yucatan. A Zoological and Hydrographic Survey.* Carnegie Institution of Washington Publication No. 457. Washington, D.C.

Pollock, H. E. D.

(95)   1937. "The Casa Redonda at Chichen Itza, Yucatan," *Contributions to American Archaeology,* Vol. III, No. 17; Carnegie Institution of Washington Publication No. 456, 1937, pp. 120–54, pls. 1–8. Washington, D.C.

(96)   1954. "Department of Archaeology," *Carnegie Institution of Washington Year Book* No. 53, pp. 263–67.

Proskouriakoff, T.

(97)   1946. *An Album of Maya Architecture.* Carnegie Institution of Washington Publication No. 558. Washington, D.C.

(98)   1950. *A Study of Classic Maya Sculpture.* Carnegie Institute of Washington Publication No. 593. Washington, D.C.

(99)   1954. "Mayapan, the Last Stronghold of a Civilization," *Archaeology,* Vol. 7, No. 2.

(100)   1955. "The Death of a Civilization," *Scientific American,* Vol. 192, No. 5.

474

RADIN, PAUL

(101) 1920. *The Sources and Authenticity of the Ancient Mexicans.* University of California Publications in American Archaeology and Ethnology, Vol. XVIII, No. 1. Berkeley.

RECINOS, ADRIÁN

(102) 1950. *Popol Vuh: The Sacred Book of the Ancient Quiché Maya.* English version by Sylvanus G. Morley and Delia Goetz. University of Oklahoma Press. Norman.

RECINOS, ADRIÁN, AND GOETZ, DELIA

(103) 1953. *The Annals of the Cakchiquels.* University of Oklahoma Press. Norman.

REDFIELD, MARGARET PARK

(104) 1937. "The Folk Literature of a Yucatecan Town," *Contributions to American Archaeology*, Vol. III, No. 13; Carnegie Institution of Washington Publication No. 456, 1937, pp. 1–50. Washington, D.C.

REDFIELD, ROBERT

(105) 1941. *The Folk Culture of Yucatan.* Chicago.

REDFIELD, ROBERT, AND VILLA R., ALFONSO

(106) 1934. *Chan Kom, a Maya Village.* Carnegie Institution of Washington Publication No. 448. Washington, D.C.

RICKETSON, O. G., JR.

(107) 1933. "The Culture of the Maya. I. Excavations at Uaxactun." Carnegie Institution of Washington Supplemental Publication No. 6, pp. 1–15. Washington, D.C.

RICKETSON, O. G., JR., AND E. B.

(108) 1937. *Uaxactun, Guatemala. Group E—1926–1931.* Carnegie Institution of Washington Publication No. 477. Washington, D.C.

RICKETSON, O. G., JR., AND KIDDER, A. V.

(109) 1930. "An Archaeological Reconnaissance by Air in Central America," *Geographical Review*, American Geographical Society, Vol. XX, No. 2, pp. 177–206. New York.

RIVET, PAUL

(110) 1954. *Cités maya.* 4th ed. A. Guillot. Paris.

ROYS, RALPH L.

(111) 1931. *The Ethno-Botany of the Maya.* Middle American Research Series, Publication No. 2. Department of Middle American Research, Tulane University. New Orleans.

(112) 1933. *The Book of Chilam Balam of Chumayel.* Carnegie Institution of Washington Publication No. 438. Washington, D.C.

· (113) 1940. "Personal Names of the Maya of Yucatan," *Contributions to American Anthropology and History*, Vol. VI, No. 31; Carnegie Institution of Washington Publication No. 523, 1940, pp. 31–48. Washington, D.C.

(114) 1943. *The Indian Background of Colonial Yucatan.* Carnegie Institution of Washington Publication No. 548. Washington, D.C.

RUPPERT, KARL

(115) 1931. "Temple of the Wall Panels, Chichen Itza," *Contributions to American Archaeology*, Vol. I, No. 3; Carnegie Institution of Washington Publication No. 403, 1931, pp. 117–40; pls. 1–18. Washington, D.C.

(116) 1935. *The Caracol at Chichen Itza, Yucatan, Mexico.* Carnegie Institution of Washington Publication No. 454. Washington, D.C.

(117) 1943. *The Mercado, Chichen Itza, Yucatan, Mexico.* Carnegie Institution of Washington Publication No. 546, Contribution 43. Washington, D.C.

RUPPERT, KARL, AND DENISON, J. H., JR.

(118) 1943. *Archaeological Reconnaissance in Campeche, Quintana Roo and Peten.* Carnegie Institution of Washington Publication No. 543. Washington, D.C.

RUPPERT, K., SHOOK, E. M., SMITH, A. L., AND SMITH, R. E.

(119) 1953–54. "Chichen Itza, Dzibiac, and Balam Canche, Yucatan." *Carnegie Institution of Washington Year Book*, No. 53, pp. 286–89. Washington, D.C.

RUPPERT, K., THOMPSON, J. E. S., AND PROSKOURIAKOFF, T.

(120) 1955. *Bonampak, Chiapas, Mexico.* Carnegie Institution of Washington Publication No. 602. Washington, D.C.

RUZ LHUILLIER, ALBERTO

(121) 1945. *Campeche en la arqueología maya.* Mexico.

(122) 1952. "Camara secreta del Templo de las Inscripciones," *Tlatoani*, Vol. I, Nos. 3–4.

(123) 1952. "Palenque, fuente inagotable de tesoros arqueológicos," *México de hoy*, Vol. IV, No. 48.

(124) 1952. "Estudio de la cripta del Templo de las Inscripciones en Palenque," *Tlatoani*, Vol. I, Nos. 5–6.

(125) 1953. "Suntuoso sepulcro en la cripta de Palenque," *México de hoy*, Vol. V, No. 55.

(126) 1954. "La pirámide-tumba de Palenque," *Cuadernos Americanos*, Vol. LXXIV, pp. 141–59.

(127) 1954. "Exploraciones en Palenque," *Thirtieth International Congress of Americanists*. London.

SAHAGÚN, BERNARDINO DE

(128) 1938. *Historia general de las cosas de Nueva España.* 5 vols. Mexico.

SAPPER, KARL

(129) 1896. "Sobre la geografía física y la geología de la Península de Yucatán," *Inst. Geol. Mex.*, No. 3. Mexico.

SATTERTHWAITE, LINTON, JR.

(130) 1936. "Notes on the Work of the Fourth and Fifth University Museum Expeditions to Piedras Negras, Peten, Guatemala," *Maya Research*, Vol. III, No. 1, pp. 74–93. New Orleans.

(131) 1936. "The Sixth Piedras Negras Expedition," *Univ. Mus. Bull.*, University of Pennsylvania, Vol. VI, No. 5, pp. 14, 18, pls. V–VII. Philadelphia.

(132) 1937. "Identification of Maya Temple Buildings at Piedras Negras," *Publications of the Philadelphia Anthropological Society*, Vol. I, pp. 161–77. Philadelphia.

SCHELLHAS, PAUL

(133) 1904. *Representation of Deities of the Maya Manuscripts.* 2d ed. Translated by Selma Wesselhoeft and A. M. Parker. *Papers of the Peabody Museum of American Archaeology and Ethnology*, Harvard University, Vol. IV, No. 1, pp. 1–47. Cambridge.

SCHMIDT, KARL P., AND ANDREWS, E. W.

(134) 1936. "Notes on Snakes from Yucatan," *Field Museum of Natural History, Zoological Series*, Vol. XX, No. 18, pp. 167–87. Chicago.

SCHOLES, FRANCE V., Y OTROS

(135) 1936. *Documentos para la historia de Yucatán. Tomo I. 1550–1561.* Mérida.

SHATTUCK, G. C., AND OTHERS

(136) 1933. *The Peninsula of Yucatan. Medical, Biological, Meteorological and Sociological Studies.* Carnegie Institution of Washington Publication No. 431. Washington, D.C.

SHOOK, E. M.

(137) 1954. *The Temple of Kukulcan at Mayapan.* Carnegie Institution of Washington, Current Reports No. 20. Washington, D.C.

SHOOK, E. M., AND IRVING, WILLIAM

(138) 1955. *Colonnaded Buildings at Mayapan.* Carnegie Institution of Washington, Current Reports No. 22. Washington, D.C.

SMITH, A. L.

(139) 1950. *Uaxactun, Guatemala: Excavations of 1931–37.* Carnegie Institution of Washington Publication No. 588. Washington, D.C.

SMITH, PHILIP E.

(140) 1955. *Excavations in Three Ceremonial Structures at Mayapan.* Carnegie Institution of Washington, Current Reports No. 21. Washington, D.C.

SMITH, ROBERT E.

(141) 1954. *Explorations on the Outskirts of Mayapan.* Carnegie Institution of Washington, Current Reports No. 18. Washington, D.C.

SPINDEN, H. J.

(142) 1913. "A Study of Maya Art," *Memoirs of the Peabody Museum of American Archaeology and Ethnology*, Harvard University, Vol. VI. Cambridge.

(143) 1917. *Ancient Civilization of Mexico and Central America.* American Museum of Natural History, Handbook Series, No. 3. New York.

(144) 1917. "The Origin and Distribution of Agriculture in America," *Proc. Internat. Cong. Americanists, 19th Sess.*, Washington 1915, pp. 269–76. Washington, D.C.

(145) 1924. "The Reduction of Mayan Dates," *Papers of the Peabody Museum of American Archaeology and Ethnology*, Harvard University, Vol. VI, No. 4. Cambridge.

(146) 1928. "In Quest of Ruined Cities," *Scientific American*, Vol. CXXXVIII, No. 2, pp. 108–11. New York.

STADELMAN, RAYMOND

(147) 1940. "Maize Cultivation in Northwestern Guatemala," *Contr. Amer. Anthropol. and Hist.*, Vol. VI, No. 33. Carnegie Institution of Washington Publication No. 523, pp. 83–264. Washington, D.C.

STANDLEY. PAUL C.

(148) 1930. "Flora of Yucatan," Field Museum of Natural History, Publication No. 279; *Botanical Series*, Vol. III, No. 3. Chicago.

STEGGERDA, MORRIS

(149) 1936. "A Physical and Physiological Description of Adult Maya Indians from Yucatan," *Measures of Men*; Middle American Research Publication No. 7. Department of Middle American Research, Tulane University. New Orleans.

(150) 1941. *Maya Indians of Yucatan.* Carnegie Institution of Washington Publication No. 531. Washington, D.C.

STEPHENS, JOHN L.

(151) 1841. *Incidents of Travel in Central America, Chiapas and Yucatan.* 2 vols. New York.

(152) 1843. *Incidents of Travel in Yucatan.* 2 vols. New York.

TEEPLE, J. E.

(153) 1926. "Maya Inscriptions: The Venus Calendar and Another Correlation," *American Anthropologist*, n.s., Vol. XXVIII, No. 2, pp. 402–8. Menasha, Wisconsin.

(154) 1931. "Maya Astronomy," *Contributions to American Archaeology*, Vol. I, No. 2; Carnegie Institution of Washington Publication No. 403, 1931, pp. 29–115. Washington, D.C.

THOMPSON, E. H.

(155)   1897. "The Chultunes of Labna," *Memoirs, Peabody Museum, Harvard University*, Vol. I, No. 3. Cambridge.

THOMPSON, J. ERIC S.

(156)   1927. "A Correlation of the Mayan and European Calendars," *Field Museum of Natural History Publication No. 241*, Anthropological Series, Vol. XVIII, No. 1. Chicago.

(157)   1927. *The Civilization of the Mayas.* Field Museum of Natural History, Anthropology Leaflet 25, 1st ed. Chicago.

(158)   1932. "The Solar Year of the Mayas at Quirigua, Guatemala," *Field Museum of Natural History, Anthropological Series*, Vol. XVII, No. 4. Chicago.

(159)   1933. *Mexico Before Cortez.* New York.

(160)   1934. "Sky Bearers, Colors and Directions in Maya and Mexican Religion," *Contributions to American Archaeology*, Vol. II, No. 10. Carnegie Institution of Washington Publication No. 436, pp. 209–42, pls. 1–5. Washington, D.C.

(161)   1935. "Maya Chronology: The Correlation Question," *Contributions to American Archaeology*, Vol. III, No. 14. Carnegie Institution of Washington Publication No. 456, pp. 51–82. Washington, D.C.

(162)   1939. *Excavations at San Jose, British Honduras.* Carnegie Institution of Washington Publication No. 506. Washington, D.C.

(163)   1939. "The Moon Goddess in Middle America: with Notes on Related Deities," *Contributions to American Anthropology and History*, Vol. V, No. 29. Carnegie Institution of Washington Publication No. 509, pp. 127–73. Washington, D.C.

(164)   1942. "Maya Arithmetic," *Contributions to American Anthropology and History*, Vol. VII, No. 36. Carnegie Institution of Washington Publication No. 528, pp. 37–62. Washington, D.C.

(165)   1943. "A Trial Survey of the Southern Maya Area," *American Antiquity*, Vol. IX, pp. 106–34.

(166)   1943. "Pitfalls and Stimuli in the Interpretation of History Through Loan Words," *Philological and Documentary Studies*, Vol. I, No. 2. Middle American Research Institute, Tulane University Publication No. 11, pp. 17–28. New Orleans.

(167)   1945. "A Survey of the Northern Maya Area," *American Antiquity*, Vol. XI, pp. 2–24.

(168)   1950. *Maya Hieroglyphic Writing. Introduction.* Carnegie Institution of Washington Publication No. 589. Washington, D.C.

(169)   1954. *The Rise and Fall of Maya Civilization.* University of Oklahoma Press. Norman, Oklahoma.

(170)   1954. *A Presumed Residence of Nobility at Mayapan.* Carnegie Institution of Washington. Current Reports No. 19. Washington, D.C.

479

THOMPSON, J. ERIC S., POLLOCK, H. E. D., AND CHARLOT, JEAN
(171)   1932. *A Preliminary Study of the Ruins of Coba, Quintana Roo, Mexico.* Carnegie Institution of Washington Publication No. 424. Washington, D.C.

TOSCANO, S.
(172)   1944. *Arte precolombino de México y de la América Central.* Universidad Nacional Autónoma de México. Mexico.

TOTTEN, G. O.
(173)   1926. *Maya Architecture.* Washington, D.C.

TOZZER, A. M.
(174)   1907. *A Comparative Study of the Maya and the Lacandones.* New York.
(175)   1911. "A Preliminary Study of the Prehistoric Ruins of Tikal, Guatemala; A Report of the Peabody Museum Expedition, 1909–1910," *Memoirs of the Peabody Museum of American Archaeology and Ethnology,* Harvard University, Vol. V, No. 2. Cambridge.
(176)   1912. "The Value of Ancient Mexican Manuscripts in the Study of the General Development of Writing," *Smithsonian Institution Annual Report,* 1911, pp. 493–506, pls. 1–5. Washington, D.C.
(177)   1921. "A Maya Grammar with Bibliography and Appraisement of the Works Noted," *Papers of the Peabody Museum of American Archaeology and Ethnology,* Harvard University, Vol. IX. Cambridge.
(178)   1941. "Landa's 'Relación de las cosas de Yucatán.'" *Papers of the Peabody Museum of American Archaeology and Ethnology,* Harvard University, Vol. XVIII. Cambridge.

TOZZER, A. M., AND ALLEN, G. M.
(179)   1910. "Animal Figures in the Maya Codices," *Papers of the Peabody Museum of American Archaeology and Ethnology,* Harvard University, Vol. IV, No. 3. Cambridge.

ULVING, TOR
(180)   1955. "A New Decipherment of the Maya Glyphs," *Ethnos* No. 2 and 3. Stockholm.

VAILLANT, GEORGE C.
(181)   1941. *The Aztecs of Mexico. Origin, Rise and Fall of the Aztec Nation.* Garden City, New York. (Also published in the Pelican series of "Penguin Books," 1950.)

VILLA R., ALFONSO
(182)   1934. "The Yaxuna-Cobá Causeway," *Contributions to American Archaeology,* Vol. II, No. 9; Carnegie Institution of Washington Publication No. 436, pp. 187–208, 1934, pls. 1–9. Washington, D.C.

VILLACORTA C., J. ANTONIO
(183) 1927. *Arqueología Guatemalteca.* Sociedad de Geografía e Historia de Guatemala. Guatemala.
(184) 1930. *Códices Mayas.* Sociedad de Geografía e Historia de Guatemala. Guatemala.

VILLAGRA, A.
(185) 1949. *Bonampak, la ciudad de los muros pintados.* Mexico.

VON HAGEN, V. W.
(186) 1944. *The Aztec and Maya Papermakers.* J. J. Augustin. New York.

WADELL, HAKON
(187) 1937–38. "Physical-Geological Features of Peten, Guatemala." See Morley, S. G., 1937–38, *The Inscriptions of Peten,* Appendix 1.

WAUCHOPE, ROBERT
(188) 1934. "House Mounds of Uaxactun, Guatemala," *Contributions to American Archaeology,* Vol. II, No. 7. Carnegie Institution of Washington Publication No. 436, 1934, pp. 107–71, pls. 1–9. Washington, D.C.
(189) 1938. *Modern Maya Houses.* Carnegie Institution of Washington Publication No. 502. Washington, D.C.
(190) 1954. "Implications of Radiocarbon Dates from Middle and South America," *Middle American Research Reports,* Vol. II, No. 2. Tulane University. New Orleans.

WHORF, BENJAMIN LEE
(191) 1956. "Decipherment of the Linguistic Portion of the Maya Hieroglyphs," in *Language, Thought, and Reality.* The Technology Press of Massachusetts Institute of Technology, John Wiley and Sons, New York, and Chapman and Hall, Ltd. London.

WILLEY, GORDON R.
(192) 1956. "The Structure of Ancient Maya Society: Evidence from the Southern Lowlands," *American Anthropologist,* Vol. 58, No. 5.

WILLEY, GORDON R., BULLARD, W. R., AND GLASS, J. B.
(193) 1955. "The Maya Community of Prehistoric Times," *Archaeology,* Vol. VIII, No. 1, pp. 18–25.

WILLSON, ROBERT W.
(194) 1924. "Astronomical Notes on the Maya Codices," *Papers of the Peabody Museum of American Archaeology and Ethnology,* Harvard University, Vol. VI, No. 3. Cambridge.

WISDOM, CHARLES
(195) 1940. *The Chorti Indians of Guatemala.* Chicago.

XIMÉNEZ, FRANCISCO
(196) 1929–31. *Historia de la provincia de San Vicente de Chiapa y Guatemala.* 3 vols. Sociedad de Geografía e Historia de Guatemala. Guatemala.

INDEX

A

Acalan, Province of, 106, 115–16, 118
Acanceh, 74, 268, 352
Acropolis at Copan, 276, 279
agriculture, 128–30, 132–42, 183, 433, 453–56; collapse of, 70, 71; development of, 129–30; origin of, 52, 128; tools of, 129, 136
Aguilar, Gerónimo de, 100–101, 103
Ah Canul, Province of, 107, 110–11
ah chembal uinicob, 149
ah cuch cabob, 154
Ah Dzun Xiu, 98
ah holpopob, 155
ah kulelob, 154
Ah Naum Pat, 104
Ah Puch, god of death, 190–91, 198, 200, 201, 206
ah tooc, 132
Ah Ziyah Xiu, 98
Ah Zupan Xiu, 98
ahau, 145
Ahaucan Mai, 155–56
ahkin, 157
ahkinob, 149
ahmen, 157
akalche, 9
Ake, 105
Alaminos, Anton de, 102
alautun, 237
Alcayaga, Jacobo de, 122
almehenob, 149, 154
Altar de Sacrificios, 65
Alvarado, Pedro de, 103, 109
andesite, 330, 331
Angkor Vat, 436
animals, 7, 11, 142, 406, 420; domestic, 32, 129, 133, 140, 422, 427
Annals of the Cakchiquels, 255, 457
archaeology of the Maya area, vii, 51, 59, 90, 94, 144, 185–86, 261–62, 279, 286–87, 299, 461, 464
architecture, 46, 47–48, 56, 59, 83–86, 94–95, 261–329, 427, 433, 452, 460; colonnades, 83, 286, 329; corbeled roof, 40–41, 56, 184, 310, 315–16, 460; development of, 74–77, 310, 315–16, 320–21; Puuc period, 79, 197, 293–94; Toltec influence on, 83–86, 88, 261, 267
Archives of the Indies, 115
arithmetic, 48, 237, 239–41, 244, 429, 459
art, 46, 55, 59, 82, 84–86, 143, 146, 306, 331, 388, 427, 433, 452; crafts, 380–423, 463; decadence in, 70, 86, 88, 91, 347, 422; motifs and symbols, 84, 324, 383–84; *see also* architecture; human figure in art; pottery; sculpture; wall paintings
Ascension Bay, 15, 102
astronomy, 132, 156, 276, 279, 428–29, 459; development of, 44, 55; knowledge of, 55, 244, 256–60, 429; observatories, 257–58, 286, 299–300
Atlantean figures, 84, 189–90, 347, 349
atole, 31, 177
Avendaño, Andres de, 120–23, 124
azote (bastinado), 34
Aztecs, 41, 85, 91, 102, 103, 115–16, 236, 422, 433, 453, 457, 458; military orders of, 84

B

Bacab, 188, 197, 214, 215, 217
Baker, M. Louise, 340
baktun, 63, 65, 237, 243
Balakbal, 63
Balboa, Vasco Nuñez de, 100
ball courts, 285–86

banqueta, 175–76
Bartolomé de las Casas, 423
basketry, 142, 384–85
batab, 149, 154–55
Becan, 270
Belize River, 9
Belize Valley, 464
Bell, Betty, v
Belma, 105
Bolontiku, see Nine Gods of the Lower
    World
Bonampak, 452; murals at, 57–58, 146,
    393, 427, 456, 462, 463
Brainerd, George W., v, 424, 425, 433
British Honduras, 3, 17, 91, 144, 459, 464
buildings, classification of, 321, 322–23
    (Table VIII); decoration of, 84–85,
    321, 324, 329; description of, 83–85,
    315–29; *see also* architecture; houses;
    temples
burial customs, 180, 182
burial offerings, 44, 393, 464

C

cabildo, 110, 111
cacao, 11, 158; *see also* Ek Chuah
Cakchiquel, 163, 230, 255
calabtun, 237
Calakmul, 268, 307–8, 332
calendar, 38, 46, 52, 55, 88, 183, 229–
    37; correction, 229–30, 244, 246, 256–
    57, 259–60, 429; day, 230–31, 429–
    30; month, 231, 234–35; year, 45,
    230–31, 234–36, 256–57, 459
Calendar Round, 231, 235–36
caluac, 82
Campeche, 3, 15, 17, 73, 74, 76, 89, 91,
    94, 101, 102, 107–9, 110–13, 124,
    144, 365, 372
Candelaria River, 9
Canek, 116, 118–21, 123–25, 148
cannibalism, 100, 208
Cape Catoche, 101
capes, 174, 395, 420, 423
capstones, painted, 399

captive figures, 159, 404
Caracol at Chichen Itza, 84, 286, 452
Carnegie Institution of Washington, vii–
    viii, 35, 94, 135, 139, 267, 279, 286,
    299, 387, 414, 415
caryatids, 84
Castillo at Chichen Itza, 210, 351, 410,
    415
Catherwood, F., vi–vii, 460
Cauich, 120
causeways, 158, 271, 294, 309–10, 460
ceiba, 194
Ceme, Eustaquio, 33
cenote, 15–16, 77, 89, 130, 264, 266, 287,
    449; *see also* Well of Sacrifice
ceramic periods, 48, 59, 74–75, 90–91,
    367–70, 372–74, 379; *see also* pottery
Ceremonial Bar, Double-Headed, 146
ceremonial centers, 46, 47, 52, 88–89,
    140, 261–68, 270, 373, 426, 464;
    abandonment of, 68, 70–71, 88–89,
    90–91, 97–99, 146, 148, 266, 438;
    classification of, 267–68, 269 (Table
    VIII), 270; decline of, 79, 438–39,
    451; *see also individual sites*
ceremonies, 132, 146, 157, 164, 191–94,
    196–97, 206, 208–21, 224, 250, 388,
    406, 428; *hetzmek*, 164; marriage,
    167–68; New Year's, 157, 213–16;
    ocna, 196–97; puberty, 157, 165–66
Cerro de las Mesas, 65
chac (priest), 157, 165, 208–9, 217, 219
Chac (rain god), 186, 195, 196–97, 201–
    2, 205, 206, 220, 226
Chac Mool, 84–85, 347, 349
Chacmultun, 399
Chakan, Province of, 111, 120–21, 123–
    26
Chakanputun, 270
Chaltuna, 7
Chama region, 393
Champoton, 101, 102, 106, 110
Chan Kom, 33
Charlot, Jean, 332, 336–37
Chauaca, Province of, 105, 107, 112
Chel, 97–98, 108, 148

Chenes region, 75–76, 79, 373–74
Chetumal, 106; Province of, 107, 112
Chiapa, 67
Chiapas, 3, 4, 7, 17, 67, 109, 162, 365, 416, 452
Chichen Itza, 68, 73, 80–91, 96, 107, 135, 137–39, 143–44, 180, 182, 185, 210–11, 266–67, 268, 270, 279, 285–87, 324, 329, 347, 349, 351, 365–66, 399, 406, 410, 415–16, 418, 452, abandonment of, 87, 90; description of, 80–81, 210; founding of, 80–81
Chilam Balam, Books of, 78, 83, 96, 254–55, 270, 451; of Chumayel, 78, 88, 97, 203, 255, 385, 451; of Mani, 78, 87, 255; of Tizimin, 97, 255, 451
chilan, 156, 208–9, 254
children, 159–60, 163–66, 211, 393
China, 432
Chinkultic, 65, 67
Chixoy Valley, 399
Chochkitam, 270
chocolate, 142, 177
Chontal, 115, 118
Chorti, 450
Christianity, 36–37, 111, 116, 118–21, 127, 186, 254–55
chronological system, Maya, 55, 183, 229–30, 241–49, 256–57, 429; starting point of, 241–43, 450
chronology, 59, 367–68, 451, 462; Maya and Christian, 256, 368, 443–48, 465
chultun, 89, 262, 264–65, 266, 460
Chunchintok, 268
Chuntuqui, 122, 123
cities, see ceremonial centers
civilization, Maya: appraisal of, 51, 263, 265, 339, 388, 424–41; decline of, 60, 68–71, 73, 96, 266, 379, 425, 430, 438–39, 444, 451; development of, 4, 16, 46–48, 51, 56, 57, 73–77, 451; origin of, 13, 40–41, 44–45, 51
Civiltuk, 268
clan organization, 161–62
Classic stage, 40, 57–60, 63, 65, 67–71,

73–78, 143–44, 225, 266, 425, 430, 436–38, 450, 464
clay modeling, 352, 365–66, 369; figurines, 369, 372
climate, 3, 4, 11, 69–70, 251, 449, 453–54
Coba, 65, 73, 95, 268, 270, 309–10, 451
Cochua, 112
Cockscomb Peak, 9
Cocom, 81–82, 91, 98–99, 148, 182
codices, 96, 197, 198, 210, 242, 249–54, 370, 385, 428–29; Bodley, 258; Dresdensis, 186, 188, 203, 249–51, 257, 259, 399, 458; Peresianus, 196, 202, 205, 212, 249–51, 254, 260, 399, 458; Perez, 132, 255; Tro-Cortesianus, 186, 191, 196, 201, 249–51, 399, 458
Cogolludo, 97
Cohuanacox, 114
col, 129
Colombia, 211, 416
Comalcalco, 316, 352
comales, 90, 369, 370
common people, 149, 158–59; life of, 31–36, 158, 163–69, 171–72, 174–80, 379, 404, 450, 452, 457
Conil, 105
copal, 332, 387; see also pom
Copan, 60, 63, 65, 67, 71, 180, 268, 306, 316, 330, 334, 339, 345, 368, 406, 415, 451, 462; abandonment of, 270; description of, 276, 279; stelae, 132, 206, 331, 340; temples, 206, 276, 340
Copan River, 279
copper objects, 211, 415–16, 420
Córdoba, see Hernández de Córdoba
corn, 128–30, 132–37, 263, 453–56; in Maya diet, 31, 175–77; origin of, 7, 128, 449, 456; yield, 137–40
cornfield, 128–30, 132–40, 178, 453–56; harvesting of, 136; location of, 129–30; size of, 130, 137; stages in making, 129–30, 132–37, 453–54; yield of, 137–40, 455–56

Cortez, Hernando, 68, 100, 103–4, 114–18, 251
cosmogony, *see under* religion
Costa Rica, 415, 416
cotton, 141, 380–81, 383, 455–56
Couoh, 110
Cozumel, Island of, 95, 102, 103, 104, 112, 157
cremation, 182
Cuauhtemoc, 114–16
Cuicuilco, 45
cultures, evolution of, 424–25, 430–36, 463–64
Cupules, 107, 112
customs, *see* common people, life of; ceremonies; dances

D

dances, 155, 193, 208, 209, 215–18, 221, 388
dansantes of Monte Alban, 45
d'Avila, Alonso, 104–6, 107, 109
death, 179–80, 182; symbols of, 115, 198, 200, 201, 202, 420
deities, *see* gods
Delgado, Diego, 119–20
Diaz del Castillo, Bernal, 103, 115
Dimick, John, 451
diseases, 88, 157, 214, 216; cures, 38, 178–79, 191; malaria, 70; smallpox, 97, 101; yellow fever, 70
Douglass, A. S., 368
drainage basin, 3, 7, 15
dress, 32, 85, 169–72, 174–75, 457, 463; of women, 172, 174; of rulers and priests, 165, 169, 174, 388, 393, 395, 420, 422–23; of warriors, 105, 169, 174
drinks, 31, 176–77, 217, 218, 221, 224
Durán, Bartolomé, 126
dyes, 142, 384, 387
Dzibikal, 108
Dzibilchaltun, 73
Dzilam, 73, 108–9

E

Eagles, military order of, 84
Early period of the Classic stage, 59–60
earthquakes, 69
Egypt, 432–33, 437, 449
Ek Chuah, 188, 200–201, 221
Ekab, Province of, 100, 104, 112
El Encanto, 65
El Meco, 105
El Palmar, 420
El Quiché, Department of, 4, 182
El Salvador, 56
El Tabasqueño, 268
embroidery, 32, 172, 383–84, 420
encomenderos, 112
Espiritu Santo Bay, 15
Etzna, 65, 67, 73, 75
ex, 169

F

family ties, 35–36, 163, 168
fasting, 191, 206, 218
fauna, *see* animals; jaguars; quetzal
Feathered Serpent in art, 84
featherwork, 169, 174–75, 217, 268, 388, 420, 422–2⅔, 463
Fine Orange pottery, 89–90, 91, 379
flint objects, 351, 420
flora, *see* plants; forests
Förstmann, Ernst, 242
foods, 11, 140–41, 154, 158, 176–77; *see also* corn; fruits; vegetables
forests, 11, 130, 132–33; height of, 9; materials yielded, 141–42, 333, 387
frescoes, *see* wall paintings
fruits, 11, 141–42, 267
Fuensalida, Bartolomé de, 118–19
Fuentes y Guzman, 422

G

García de Palacio, Diego, 306
Gates, William, 21
Gibbon, Edward, 227
Godoy, Lorenzo de, 110

gods, 132, 188–206, 224–26, 427–28, 458; corn, 197–98, 205, 345; creation, 188, 194–96, 427–28; death and destruction, 188, 190, 194, 198, 201–2, 420; moon, 202, 458; North Star, 200–201; rain, 186, 188, 195, 196–97, 202, 206, 210; suicides, 202–3; sun, 195, 202, 206; the heavens, 194–96; war, 188, 200, 201, 206; wind, 132, 197, 201–2, 214; see also patron gods

goldwork, 89, 101, 109, 175, 210–11, 279, 415–16, 418

González, Juan, 126

Goodman, J. T., 242

Goodman-Martínez Hernández-Thompson correlation, 443–48, 465

government, 57–58, 82, 88, 96, 143–46, 148–49, 425, 430, 431, 434, 436–38, 456–57; hereditary rule, 145

Grijalva, Juan de, 101–2, 103

Grijalva River, 103

Guatemala, 3, 4, 7, 17, 44, 144, 316, 383–84, 450, 452, 463; highlands of, 4, 7, 41, 44–45, 52, 56, 69, 80, 89, 128, 368, 369, 380, 414, 416, 420

Guerrero, Gonzalo de, 100–101, 106

H

haab, 231, 234–35, 429

hair, manner of wearing, 164, 169, 174

halach uinic, 144–46, 149, 154, 158, 174, 271

hammocks, 177–78

headdresses, 174–75, 388, 420, 423

head-variant numerals, 206, 237, 239

Healey, Giles, v, 388

hemp and henequen, 140, 141–42, 263

Hernández de Córdoba, Francisco, 101, 102

Herrera, Antonio de, 155, 172, 185

Hester, Joseph, v, 453–56

hetzmek, 164

Hieroglyphic Stairway, 276, 345

hieroglyphic writing, *see* writing

High Priest's Tomb at Chichen Itza, 180

history, Maya, 40, 87, 96, 242; epochs, 59; records of, 249–50, 254–55, 428–29; *see also* Classic stage; Postclassic stage; Preclassic stage; Spanish Conquest

Hochob, 268

Holactun, 73

Holmes, William H., 332

Holmul, 268, 393

Holmul River, 121

Hondo River, 9

Honduras, 3, 4, 7, 17, 44, 109, 114, 416

Honduras-Hibüeras, 109, 114

honey, 11, 177, 217, 219, 267

Hopelchen, 119

hotun, 63, 212, 307

houses, 142, 177–78, 261–62, 267, 310, 404, 464

Huastec area, 17, 20, 370

huipiles, 172

human figure in art, 56, 333–34, 339–40, 404, 406, 410

Hun Uitzil Chac Tutul Xiu, 148–49

Hunab Ku, 188, 194–95

Hunac Ceel, 82

I

Ichpaatun, 65, 73

ideographic writing, 227–28, 458–59

idolatry, 94, 118, 120, 185–86, 191, 225–26

idols, 118, 127, 157, 206, 212–16, 218–21, 225–26; making of, 219–20

Inca civilization, 433

incense, 192–93, 200, 211, 214, 217; burners, 91, 192, 374

Indus Valley, 449

Initial Series, 60, 229–30, 242–44, 246–47, 430; earliest date in, 73–74; latest date in, 68

insects, 11

introducing glyph, 243

irrigation, 45, 431, 433

Isla de Mujeres, 95, 101

Itza, 80–81, 86–87, 116, 117–21, 123–27

Itzamna, 188, 194–96, 197, 205, 214, 216, 220

Ixchel, 163, 195–96, 201, 202
Ixlu, 68
Ixtab, 202–3
Izamal, 82, 268, 270

J

jade, 268, 287, 406, 410, 414; deposits and sources of, 89, 414; hardness of, 414; objects, 174–75, 180, 211, 406, 410, 414, 461–62
jaguar, 254; in art, 84, 271, 276, 279, 286–87; in dress and ornament, 174, 406, 410; military order of, 84
Jaguar Stairway, 276, 279, 340
jaguar thrones, 347, 349
Jaina, Island of, 73, 365, 372
Jonuta, 365

K

Kabah, 76, 264, 265, 294, 299
k'abal, 373, 379
Kaminaljuyu, 79, 368, 406, 410, 414
kanlol, 179
katun, 63, 67–68, 237, 243, 247–49; ending, 211–12, 247; thirteen gods of the, 211–12; wheel, 247–48
Kidder, A. V., 71
kin, 237
kinchiltun, 237
King of Spain, 104, 145
Kinich Ahau, 195, 215, 216, 410
Knorozov, J. B., 458–59
Kukulcan, 80–81, 87, 88, 94, 185, 195, 201–2, 208, 217–18, 225, 285, 324
kuum, 175

L

Labna, 76, 264, 265
labor, see manpower
Lacandons, 162, 183, 192–93, 366, 380–81, 450, 457, 458, 463
Lacantun River, 4
Laguna de Términos, 102
lahuntun, 63, 212
Lake Amatitlan, 4, 7

Lake Atitlan, 7
Lake Bacalar, 15, 78, 118
Lake Izabal, 7, 117
Lake Peten Itza, 7, 81, 116, 117, 120
Landa, Bishop Diego de, vi, 86, 97, 178, 188, 225, 228, 247–49, 250, 258, 261, 267, 429, 450; on ceremonies and rites, 87, 165–68, 191–92, 193, 194, 210, 212, 215, 221; on Chichen Itza, 80–82; on Maya personality and customs, 24, 33, 36, 95, 134–35, 145, 159, 160, 172, 177, 178, 179–80, 182; on priesthood, 155–57
languages, Maya, 21, 51, 449–50; dialects of, 17–20; map of, 19 (Plate 7); see also Zuyua
lapidary art, 406, 410, 414
Late period of the Classic stage, 59–60, 63, 65
law, 31, 154–55, 159, 423
Leyden Plate, 51–52, 55, 242, 406, 451
lime, 13, 320; kilns, 320
limestone, 13, 15, 310, 315, 330–33; quarrying, 308, 332–33
lintels, 84, 271, 349, 351, 422
Lizana, Father, 77–78
Loche, 105
Long Count, see Initial Series
loom, Maya, 381–83

M

machete, 129–30
McQuown, Norman A., v, 449
maize, see corn
Mamantel River, 9
Mani, 98, 148–49, 217, 268; Province of, 107, 108, 111, 148
Manikin Scepter, 145–46
manpower, 58, 89, 139–40, 178, 263–65, 456; conscription of, 45, 47, 265–66, 434
manuscripts, native, vi, 78, 97, 179, 186, 249–55, 258–60, 370
Marina, 103
marriage, 161–62, 167–68; average age at, 24, 31, 167; taboos, 162, 167

mask panel, 294
mathematics, *see* arithmetic
matting, 384–86
Maudslay, Alfred P., vii, 242, 460
Maya area, 3–4, 434, 435–36; map of, 5;
    physiography of, 4, 7, 9, 13, 15, 16, 76,
    426, 449; river systems, 4, 9
Maya Mountains, 9, 116
Mayapan, 80–82, 90–91, 94–96, 148,
    266–67, 270; abandonment of, 90; con-
    federation, 91, 143–44; description, 91,
    94–95, 267; fall of, 96, 97–98, 217,
    452; founding of, 81–82, 87, 91
measurement, 130
mecates, 130
men, work of, 164, 177–78, 433
merchants, 200–201; *see also* trade
Mérida, 108, 111, 112, 117, 118, 119,
    120, 123, 124, 268, 270, 385
Mesoamerica, 44–46, 57, 79, 89, 128,
    136, 236, 352, 450, 458
Mesopotamia, 431–32, 437
metalwork, 415–20, 426, 463
Mexican invasion, 20–21, 73, 77, 79–91,
    94–96, 185–86, 225, 266, 418
Mexican mercenaries, 82, 91, 96
Mexico, 3, 56, 132, 210, 225, 249, 250,
    285, 365, 414, 415, 432, 453; Valley
    of, 44, 79, 94, 95, 211, 263, 416, 451,
    453
military orders, 84
milpa, *see* cornfield
Ministry of Public Education, Mexico, 286
Miró, José Ignacio, 251
Mirones, Francisco de, 119–20
mirrors, 414
Mixtec, 96, 250; art, 94, 404
Moan bird, 188, 200
Mochis, 105
modern Maya, 21–36, 164, 167–68, 169,
    172, 176–78, 183, 450, 458
monochrome pottery, 74, 77, 369, 372–74
Montejo, Francisco de, 102, 103–10, 251
Montejo, Francisco de, the Younger, 106–
    13; cousin of, 110–13
moon count, 244, 256–57

Moran, Father, 423
Morley, Sylvanus G., v
mosaics, 286–87, 414–15
Motagua River, 4
Motul, 148
murals, *see* wall paintings
music, 463
myths, 203, 242, 254–55; creation, 188–
    90, 242; culture, 195, 202; deluge,
    188–90; man, 188; the afterlife, 194,
    202–3

N

Naabon Cupul, 107
Naachtun, 334, 339
Nachan Can, 100
Nachi Cocom, 98, 228
nacom (priest), 156–57, 208
nacom (war chief), 154, 221
Nahuatl, 20, 21, 103
Nakum, 65, 307–8
name glyphs of the gods, 195–202, 204–5,
    243
names, personal, 161–62, 163, 164
Namux Chel, 108
Naranjo, 63, 65, 307–8
Nebaj vase, 399
New River, 9
Nicuesa, Diego de, 100
Nieto, Diego, 117
Nine Gods of the Lower World, 190–91,
    203–4, 216, 352; name glyphs, 229,
    243
Nito, 117
nobles, 149, 154, 174, 178, 180, 182, 457
Nohthub, 120
Nuestra Señora de los Remedios y San Pablo
    de los Itzaes, 127
numerical system, 239–41; *see also* arith-
    metic

O

Oaxaca, 44, 45, 91, 211, 416
ocna festival, 196–97
Old Woman Goddess, 188
Old World civilizations, 48, 430–32

Olid, Cristóbal de, 103, 114
Olmec culture, 45
Orbita, Juan de, 118–19
Ordaz, Diego de, 103
Otzmal massacre, 98–99
Oxkintok, 65, 73, 74–75, 316
Oxlahuntiku, see Thirteen Gods of the Upper World
Oxpemul, 67

P

painting, 250, 352, 385–88, 393, 395–97, 399, 403–6; brushes, 387; colors used in, 171, 306, 332, 370, 372, 385–87; *see also* wall paintings
Palace of the Masks, 294
Palenque, 60, 65, 67, 180, 270, 306, 321, 334, 349, 352, 368, 387–88; description of, 306; Palace group, 67, 203–4, 306, 352; Ruz discovery, 180, 306, 339, 352, 410–13, 460–62; Temple of the Cross, 67; Temple of the Inscriptions, 180, 306, 339, 352
Panama, 89, 211, 415, 416
paper, 250, 459
Paredes, Captain, 123–24
Pasión River, 4, 9
pati, 158, 169, 174, 380
patron gods: of numerals, 206, 240; of the *katuns*, 204–5, 211–12; of the lower world, 190–91, 203–4, 216, 229, 243, 352; of the upper world, 190, 203–4, 240; of the year-bearers, 213–16
Paxbolon, Pablo, 115
Paxbolon Acha, 115
Peabody Museum of Archaeology and Ethnology, vii, 148, 211
Pech, 148
people, Maya, 17–39; Asiatic origin, 24; birth rate, 24; census, modern, 17, 20; death rate, 24; diet, 31; intelligence, 39; marriage, 161–62; physical characteristics, 21, 23–24, 51, 163–64, 450; population, 262–64; psychological characteristics, 31–35

Peru, 45, 128, 369, 427, 432; conquest of 109
Peten, 3, 7, 9, 11, 40–41, 67, 144, 195, 368, 372, 454–55, 462; central, 7, 9, 11, 48, 51, 60, 67–68, 184, 307; climate of, 11, 55, 195; depopulation of, 69–71, 73; forests of, 11, 13, 333; soil of, 7, 9
phonetic writing, 227, 458–59
physical environment, *see* Maya area
pictographic writing, 227
pictun, 237
Piedras Negras, 60, 63, 65, 67, 70, 184–85, 186, 212, 270, 306–7, 334, 349, 368, 406, 414, 451; stelae, 334, 339, 420; Wall Panel, 67, 307, 339, 343, 420
Pizarro, Francisco, 109
plague, 97
planting stick, 129, 134
plants, 9, 11, 141–42, 449, 454–55; medicinal, 179
Plumbate pottery, 89
political organization, *see* government
polychrome pottery, 40–41, 60, 75, 370, 373–74, 393, 396, 399
pom, 11, 171, 192–93
Popol Vuh, 188, 255, 459
popolna, 155
population, 47, 57, 262–65, 426, 431, 435; centers of, 79, 261
Postclassic stage, 40, 79–91, 94–99, 143–44, 225, 228, 260
potter's wheel, 373, 379, 427
pottery, 56, 89–91, 367–79, 393–99, 404, 427, 462, 464; Chicanel, 315; Classic-stage, 370–74, 379; Florescent, 372–73, 379; Formative, 74, 369–70, 372; Las Charcas, 369; Miraflores, 369; origin of, 369, 373; Postclassic, 379; Puuc, 74, 79, 373–74; Regional, 372–73; Sacatepequez, 369; Tepeu, 74, 75, 370; Tzakol, 60, 74, 184, 370
pozole, 31, 176–77
ppentacob, 149, 159
Ppustunich, 268

Preclassic stage, 40, 51–52, 55–56, 450–51

priesthood, 45–46, 57, 87–88, 155–58, 178–79, 206, 208–9, 225–26, 393, 395, 428, 430, 431, 437, 461; as hereditary office, 155; development of, 183–84, 225; fall of, 71, 73, 146, 148, 186

prophecies, 118, 121, 156, 157, 211, 217, 250, 254

Proskouriakoff, Tatiana, 60

puberty, 165–66

Pueblo Indians, 367–68

Pusilha, 65, 330

puuc, 15

Puuc region, 75–77, 79, 88–89, 90, 264–66, 294, 324, 372, 373–74, 460

pyramids of Egypt, 47

pyramid-temples, 56, 75, 180, 271, 285, 306, 319, 349, 460–62

Q

Quen Santo, 68

quetzal, 7, 174, 351, 383, 420, 422–23

Quetzalcoatl, 80–81, 96, 185, 202

Quiche, 255, 422

Quintana Roo, 3, 15, 17, 68, 73

Quirigua, 63, 65, 67, 212, 308, 330, 332, 334, 345, 347, 420, 451; description of, 308; stelae, 206, 308, 345, 347; zoömorphs, 206, 308, 345

R

radiocarbon dating, 128, 443–44, 465

rainfall, 4, 11, 69–70, 134, 454–55

rebozo, 172

Red Jaguar Throne, 286–87

Redfield, Robert, 266

Relación de las cosas de Yucatán, see Landa

religion, 36–37, 87–88, 163, 183–226, 427–28, 431, 434, 437–38, 457; cosmogony, 188–91, 255, 427–28; dualism, 190–91; heaven and hell, 194, 202; rise and development, 57, 60, 87, 96, 183–86; *see also* ceremonies; gods

religious pilgrimages, 91, 98, 210–11, 287

repartimientos, 112, 155

reptiles, 11

Rio Bec, 75–76, 79, 270, 373–74

Rio Dulce, 7, 117

Rio Tabasco, 102, 103

river systems, 4, 7, 9

rubber, 214, 285

Ruz Lhuillier, Alberto, v, 180, 181, 352, 410, 414, 460; *see also* Palenque

S

Sacalum, 119–20

sacbeob, 158, 309–10

sacrifice, 185, 191–92, 201, 206, 208–11, 214–15, 220, 221, 287, 428; bloodletting, 185, 191–92, 214, 219, 388; human, 85, 87, 157, 159, 184–86, 191, 201, 208–11, 214, 225, 324, 388, 393, 428

sacrificial knife, 208–9

Sahagun, Father, 422

St. James of the Gentlemen of Guatemala, 117

Salamanca, 106

Salinas River, 4

San Angel, 352, 365

San Buenaventura, Father, 123

San Juan Teotihuacan, *see* Teotihuacan

San Luis Potosí, 17

San Pablo and San Pedro River, 102

San Pedro Mártir River, 9

sandals, 169, 171

Sandoval, Gonzalo de, 103

sandstone, 330; carving, 334

Santa Elena Poco Uinic, 67

Santa Rita Corozal, 90, 91, 96, 399, 404

Santa Rosa Xtampak, 73, 399

Santo Domingo Island, 100, 104

sapote, 141, 443

Sarstún River, 9

Satterthwaite, Linton, 451

savannas, 7, 9, 71

Sayil, 76, 264, 265

Schellhas, Paul, 194

sculpture, 57, 59–60, 84–86, 88, 89, 195, 267–68, 271, 306–7, 308, 321, 324, 329, 330–66, 452, 460; bas-relief, 67, 84–85, 306; clay, 352, 365–66; phases of, 60; stone, 271, 333–34, 339–40, 345, 347, 349, 427, 461; wood, 219, 271, 349, 351
Secondary Series, 230, 244, 246
Seibal, 65, 68, 334
serpent in art, 285, 324, 347, 349, 351, 404, 410
serrania, 15
Shook, E. M., 451
Short Count, 246–49
Sisia, 105
slateware, 75, 77, 373–74
slaves, 58, 149, 159–60, 437
social organization, 33, 34, 143–44, 178, 436, 456–57; clans, 161–62, 457; classes, 144–46, 149, 154–59, 174–75, 434
soil, 7, 9, 13, 15, 129, 135–36, 453–55
Sotuta, 98, 112, 148, 268
Spanish Conquest, 33, 91, 96, 97, 99, 186, 379; of Peten, 114–27; of Yucatan, 79–80, 97, 100–113, 453
Spanish language, 21
Spinden correlation, 443–44, 465
spinning, 380–81
spoils of war, 104, 107
standard bearers, 85, 347, 349
stars and constellations, 258–60
Steggerda, Morris, 31, 139
stelae, 63, 73, 132, 299, 307-9, 332–34, 339, 340, 345, 347, 385, 452; cult, 65, 67–68; frequency of, 66; distribution of, 64; oldest known, 52, 55, 59, 184, 299
Stephens, John L., vi–vii, 351, 460
Steward, Julian, 432–33, 435
stucco, 352, 461; masks, 56, 462; modeling, 321, 330, 352
suicides, 194; Ixchel, goddess of, 202–3
superstitions, 37–39, 179–80, 213, 216, 219, 320
Supplementary Series, 244, 430

T

Tabasco, 3, 17, 74, 89, 103, 109, 114–15, 161, 365, 372
taboos, 161–62
Tajin, 79
tattooing, 166, 171–72, 174, 372
Tayasal, 116, 117–21, 124–27, 148, 225–26
Tayasal-Flores, 68
Tazes, Province of, 112
Tecoh, 98, 148
Temple of the Jaguars, 351, 399, 404, 422
Temple of the Warriors, 349, 399, 404, 452, 457, 463
temples, 257–58, 263–64, 319–20; ground plans, 318–20; round, 84; *see also* pyramid-temples
Tenciz, 117
Tenochtitlan, 114–15, 236, 457
Tenosique, 115
Teotihuacan, 45, 47, 79, 263–64, 410
Testera, Fray Jacobo de, 109–10
Tetlepanquetzal, 114–15
textiles, 141, 211, 250, 380–81, 383–84, 423, 463
Thirteen Gods of the Upper World, 190, 203–4, 240
T'ho, *see* Mérida
Thompson, J. Eric S., 71
Tibolon, 98
Ticul, 149
Tikal, 52, 68, 122, 209–10, 262, 268, 333–34, 349, 351, 427, 451; description of, 271; Stela 4, 334; temples, 271
Tila, 67
Tipu, 119–21
Tlaloc figure in art, 84
Tlatilco, 44
Toltecs, 77, 79–91, 94–96, 266–67, 379, 439, 452
Tonina, 65, 67, 268, 308, 330, 334
tools, 129–30, 134, 330–31, 414, 426–27, 434
tortillas, 90, 175–77
totemism, 162
Tozzer, Alfred M., 20

trade, 76, 89, 161, 374, 416, 426, 431;
in slaves, 159, 161
travel, modes of, 46, 89, 96, 122, 123–24,
399, 404, 426, 427
tree rings, dating by, 70, 367–68
Tro y Ortolano, Juan de, 251
tropical growth, 69, 70
Trujillo, 107
Tuchicaan, 111
Tula, 80, 83, 85, 88
Tulum, 73, 90, 95, 96, 102, 193, 316,
399, 404, 452
tun, 237
tupiles, 155
Tupp Kak ceremony, 220
turquoise, sources of, 89; used in mosaics,
286–87, 415
Tutul Xiu, *see* Xius
Tuxtla Statuette, 48, 450
Tzeltal, 162
Tzibanche, 65, 68, 73; Temple VII, 351
Tzimin Chac, 118
Tzocchen, 270
tzolkin, 163, 230–31, 234–35, 243, 429
tzompantli (skull rack), 84, 324, 329

U

u kahlay katunob, 255
Uaxactun, 48, 63, 67, 68, 184, 212, 261–
62, 299–300, 306, 315, 316, 333, 365–
66, 368, 387, 393, 410, 427, 451, 459;
description of, 299–300, 306; Stela 9,
52, 55, 242, 299; temples, 56, 180,
299–300, 315, 387
uinal, 237
Ulua, 161
Ulua River, 106
University of Pennsylvania, 340, 451
Uolantum, 63
Ursua, Martin de, 120, 121, 123–27
Usumacinta River, 4
Usumacinta Valley, 40, 65, 144, 306, 316
Uxmal, 76, 88, 91, 143–44, 148–49, 264,
265, 268, 270, 293–94, 349, 351, 427;
abandonment of, 148; description of,

293–94; House of the Magician, 293–
94, 347; Nunnery Quadrangle, 293;
Palace of the Governor, 149, 293, 294;
stelae, 347
Uxul, 65

V

Valdivia, 100, 101
vase painting, 370, 393–95, 399
Vásquez, Alfredo Barrera, 21
vegetables, 134–35, 140–42, 267; *see also*
corn
Velásquez, Diego de, 101, 104
Venus (planet), 230, 258–60, 276, 429
Veracruz, 17, 44, 79, 80, 89–90, 91, 109
Villagutierre Soto-Mayor, 97
volcanoes, 4, 7
vulture in art, 84

W

wall paintings, 91, 94, 208–9, 300, 306,
385, 387–88, 393, 399, 403–4
warfare, 45, 58, 70, 102, 105, 123–26,
154, 404, 418
warriors, 154, 194, 195, 221, 404
water, sources of, 15, 77, 89, 264–65, 460
weapons, 84, 85, 94, 105, 124–25, 146,
383, 419
weather forecasting, 57
weaving, 268, 380–81, 383–84, 463; *see
also* textiles
Well of Sacrifice at Chichen Itza, 98, 185,
210–11, 287
Wells, H. G., 227
Whorf, Benjamin, 458
Willey, Gordon R., v, 464
women, 163, 166–68, 194, 215, 379, 393;
work of, 90, 166–67, 175–77, 381
wood, kinds of, 9, 13, 141–42, 219, 250,
333; carving, 219, 330, 349, 351
writing, 46, 88, 156, 195–96, 227–30,
249–51, 253, 254–55, 428–29, 458–
59; development of, 51, 55; earliest,
51–52, 183, 195, 330; ideographic,
227–28; phonetic, 227; pictographic,
227

X

xamach, 175–76
Xaman Ek, 200, 201, 206
Xamanha, 105, 106
Xamantun, 68
Xculoc, 422
Xelha, 104, 105, 106
Xicalanco, 103, 106
Xiu, Francisco Montejo, 149
Xiu, Nemesio, 149
xiuhmolpilli, 236
Xius, 98–99, 107, 108, 110–11, 148–49
Xochicalco, 79
Xultun, 65, 68, 347, 349

Y

Yaxchilan, 60, 65, 67, 122, 270, 306–7, 334, 340, 388; lintels, 67, 206, 340; Stela 11, 146; temples, 203, 307
Yaxha, 65
Yaxuna, 74, 309–10
year, *see* calendar, year; *tzolkin*; *haab*
year-bearers, 234–36, 253–54
Yucatan, 17, 58, 195, 251, 264, 372ff, 420; agriculture in, 129–30, 132–40, 453–56; Classic sites in, 73ff; nomadic peoples in, 52; physical characteristics of, 3–4, 7, 9, 11, 13, 15–16; Postclassic era and sites in, 79–80, 94–96, 143ff, 266; Preclassic remains in, 41, 45; pre-Conquest disintegration of, 97–99; Spanish conquest of, 100–113; stelae in, 65, 67–68; trees and plants of, 141–42, 387
Yum Cimil, 200
Yum Kaax, 198

Z

zacan, 175–77
Zacualpa, 368
Zaculeu, 368
Zama, 102
zero, Maya conception of, 237, 240, 429
Ziyancaan Bakhalal, 78
zodiac, 260
zoömorphs, 308
Zubiaur, Pedro de, 123–24
Zucthok, 123
Zuyua, language of, 88

LIST OF TABLES

PAGE

I. Classification and Distribution of People in the Maya Linguistic Stock 18

II. Average Heights, Cephalic Indices, and Some Weights for Males and Females of Certain Maya Tribes, Plains and Pueblo Indians, American Whites, and Negroes 22

III. The Principal Epochs of Maya History 42

IV. Surely Dated Monuments and Buildings in Yucatan, Northern Campeche, and Quintana Roo, Mexico 72

V. A Summary of the Leading Events of Maya History for Fourteen Centuries—A.D. 317–1717 92

VI. List of Ceremonies, Their Objectives, and Corresponding Patron Gods and Sacred Dances Celebrated During the Year, According to Bishop Landa 222

VII. Classification of the Centers of the Maya Civilization According to Their Supposed Degrees of Relative Importance in Ancient Times 269

VIII. Classification of Maya Buildings and Other Constructions According to Their Probable Uses 322

IX. Selected Ceramic Sequences from the Maya Area 371

X. The Correlation of Maya and Christian Chronologies According to the Goodman-Martinez Hernandez-Thompson Correlation Formula 445

495

LIST OF FIGURES

PAGE

1.—Diagram showing length of time the cities of the Classic
stage erected dated monuments   64

2.—Diagram showing frequency of dated monuments during the
Classic stage   66

3.—Death of the Aztec Emperor, Cuauhtemoc, in the Province
of Acalan in 1525, according to the Mapa de Tepechpan. . .   116

4.—The "sundial" composed of Stelae 10 and 12, Copan, Hon-
duras   133

5.—Planting corn with the planting stick. Page 36, Codex Tro-
Cortesianus   134

6.—Classic and Postclassic ceremonial insignia, and weapons. . .   147

7.—Examples of Maya breechclouts, or *ex*, from the monuments
of the Classic stage   170

8.—Maya sandals, or *xanab*   171

9.—Destruction of the world by water. Page 74, Codex Dres-
densis   189

10.—The rain god nourishes a tree; the death god uproots it. Page
60, Codex Tro-Cortesianus   190

11.—Bloodletting rite. Page 95, Codex Tro-Cortesianus   192

12.—Name glyphs of the Nine Gods of the Lower World   204

13.—Name glyphs of the patron gods of the nineteen Maya months   205

14.—Sacrificial knife from the Well of Sacrifice, Chichen Itza,
Yucatan, Mexico   209

15.—Graffitti from Temple II at Tikal, Peten, Guatemala, show-
ing arrow-shooting ceremony   210

496

16.—Ceremony celebrating the end of the 20-year period, called
Katun 7 Ahau, perhaps A.D. 1323–42. Page 6, Codex Peresianus 213

17.—Woman on stilts. Page 36, Codex Tro-Cortesianus 215

18.—Glyphs for the twenty Maya days 232

19.—Glyphs for the nineteen Maya months 233

20.—Diagram showing the enmeshing of the 365-day civil year
with the 260-day sacred year 234

21.—Aztec glyphs for the *xiuhmol pilli* or 52-year period 236

22.—Glyphs for the nine known Maya time periods 238

23.—Glyphs for 0 and the numbers 1 to 19 inclusive 239

24.—Examples of Maya positional mathematics 241

25.—Examples of an Initial and a Supplementary Series: east side
of Stela E, Quirigua 245

26.—Period-ending date: Katun 16 ending on 2 Ahau 13 Tzec,
corresponding to the Initial Series 9.16.0.0.0 2 Ahau 13
Tzec 246

27.—Katun wheel. After Bishop Landa 248

28.—Design showing the snaring of a deer. Page 45, Codex Tro-
Cortesianus 252

29.—Three signs of the Maya zodiac: the scorpion, the turtle, and
the rattlesnake. Page 24, Codex Peresianus 253

30.—Representations of astronomical observatories in the Mexican
codices 258

31.—Part of a wooden door lintel from Temple IV, Tikal, Peten,
Guatemala. Now in the British Museum, London 275

32.—Plan of the Caracol, Chichen Itza, Yucatan, Mexico, showing its use as an astronomical observatory 287

33.—Diagram of the astronomical observatory at Group E, Uaxactun, Peten, Guatemala, for determining the dates of the solstices and equinoxes 300

34.—Cross-sections of Maya corbeled vaults 317

35.—Maya ground plans 318

36.—Maya stone chisels 331

37.—Initial Series introducing glyph on Stela 2, Copan, Honduras 331

38.—Quarry at Mitla, Oaxaca, Mexico. After Holmes 332

39.—Location of throne in Palace J-6, Piedras Negras 345

40.—Front view of Stela 10, Xultun 346

41.—Front view of Stela 7, Uxmal 348

42.—Design on carved wooden lintel, Temple of the Jaguars, Chichen Itza 350

43.—Example of Fine Orange ware from the Postclassic 375

44.—Classic and Postclassic textiles from the monuments, wall paintings, and pottery 381

45.—The goddess Ixchel weaving. Page 79, Codex Tro-Cortesianus 383

46.—Classic and Postclassic baskets from the monuments, wall paintings, and pottery 384

47.—Mat patterns shown on the backs of Postclassic monuments 386

48.—Sketch of the burial place of a high priest or principal lord in Structure A-I, Uaxactun, Peten, Guatemala 395

49.—Polychrome plate from tomb in Structure A-I, Uaxactun, Peten 396

50.—Polychrome plate from tomb in Structure A-I, Uaxactun, Peten 397

51.—Polychrome plate from tomb in Structure A-I, Uaxactun, Peten 397

52.—Painted capstone from Temple of the Owl, Chichen Itza... 401

53.—Painted capstone from tomb, Chichen Itza 403

54.—Detail from wall painting of a battle, Temple of the Jaguars, Chichen Itza 405

55.—Examples of metalwork from Copan, Honduras, and from Chichen Itza, Yucatan 416

56.—Gold and copper objects from the Well of Sacrifice, Chichen Itza, Yucatan 418

57.—Central designs of three gold disks in repoussé technique from the Well of Sacrifice, Chichen Itza, Yucatan 419

LIST OF PLATES

PAGE

The Young Corn God, Copan, Honduras *Frontispiece facing* iii

1.—Physiographic Map of the Maya Area 5
2.—Views of the Southern Highlands 6
   a) Cuchumatanes Mountains, Guatemala
   b) Volcán de Agua, Guatemala, with Antigua in the foreground
3.—Views of the Southern Lowlands 8
   a) Usumacinta River near Yaxchilan, Chiapas
   b) Rain forest from the Acropolis at Uaxactun, Guatemala
4.—Views of the Southern Lowlands 10
   a) Central savanna, Guatemala
   b) Lake Peten Itza and the island town of Flores, Guatemala
5.—Views of the Southern and Northern Lowlands 12
   a) Rain forest, Guatemala
   b) Low forest and bush of northern Yucatan
6.—Views of the Northern Lowlands 14
   a) Sierra or low range of hills, northern Yucatan
   b) *Cenote* or natural cavern, Valladolid, northern Yucatan
7.—Linguistic Map of the Maya Area 19
8.—Lacandon Maya, Chiapas 25
9.—Lacandon Maya, Chiapas 26
10.—Yucatan Maya, Tixcacal Group, Quintana Roo 27
11.—Yucatan Maya, Chichen Itza, and Quiche Maya, Guatemala 28
12.—Yucatan Maya, Quintana Roo, and Huasteca Maya, San Luis Potosi 29

499

13.—Tzotzil Maya, Chiapas   30

14.—Early Monuments   49
    a) Tuxtla Statuette, San Andres Tuxtla, Veracruz
    b) Stela 1, El Baul, Guatemala
    c) Stela C, Tres Zapotes, Veracruz; back view

15.—The Leyden Plate   50

16.—Stela 9, Uaxactun   53

17.—Pyramids E-VII and E-VII-sub, Uaxactun   54

18.—Sculptures of the Classic Stage   61
    a) Lintel 1, Oxkintok, Yucatan
    b) Stela 11 (back), Yaxchilan, Chiapas
    c) Stela 12 (front), Piedras Negras, Guatemala

19.—Archaeological Map of the Maya Area   62

20.—Lacandon Felling a Tree   131

21.—Ancient Map of the Province of Mani, Yucatan   150

22.—Genealogical Tree of the Xiu Family of Mani, the Former
    Ruling House of Uxmal   151

23.—The Present Head of the Xiu Family and His Oldest Son,
    Ticul, Yucatan   152
    a) Don Nemesio Xiu
    b) Don Dionisio Xiu

24.—Residences of the Heads of the Xiu Family under the Native
    Maya, Spain, and Mexico   153
    a) Palace of the Governor, Uxmal, Yucatan; the Xiu as
        Maya rulers
    b) House of Francisco de Montejo Xiu, Mani, Yucatan;
        the Xiu as Spanish nobles
    c) House of Don Nemesio Xiu, Ticul, Yucatan; the Xiu as
        Mexican corn farmers

25.—Battle Scene from a Wall Painting in the Temple of the
    Warriors, Chichen Itza   160

26.—Huipiles, or Dresses of Maya Women from Guatemala and
    from Quintana Roo and Yucatan   173
    a) Huipil from Comalapa, Guatemala
    b) Huipil from San Pedro Sacatepaquez, Guatemala
    c) Huipil from Tixcacal, Quintana Roo
    d) Huipil from Mérida, Yucatan

27.—Cross Section of the Ruz Tomb   181

28.—Scenes of Human Sacrifice as Represented on the Monuments, Codices, and Wall-Paintings 187

29.—Principal Deities of the Maya Pantheon as Represented in the Codices 199

30.—Head-Variant Numerals and Lacandon at the Ruins of Yaxchilan 207

31.—Paintings of Cities of the Classic Stage by Carlos Vierra... 272
    a) Tikal, Guatemala
    b) Copan, Honduras
    c) Quirigua, Guatemala

32.—Map of the Central Section of Tikal 273

33.—Sculptures of the Classic Stage 274
    a) Wooden lintel, Temple IV, Tikal
    b) Sanctuary tablet, Temple of the Cross, Palenque

34.—Map of the Central Section of Copan 277

35.—Views of Copan 278
    a) Jaguar Stairway, East Court, the Acropolis
    b) Figure from the Jaguar Stairway
    c) Hieroglyphic Stairway, Temple 26

36.—Section of the Acropolis at Copan, Exposed by the Copan River 280

37.—Air Views of Classic-Stage Sites 281
    a) Copan
    b) Coba, Quintana Roo

38.—Air Views of Yucatecan Sites 282
    a) Chichen Itza
    b) Uxmal

39.—Map of the Central Section of Chichen Itza 283

40.—Views of Chichen Itza 284
    a) Temple of the Warriors, showing Northwest Colonnade in foreground
    b) Temple of the Warriors, showing feathered-serpent columns

41.—Views of Chichen Itza 288
    a) Ball court
    b) Temple of the Jaguars, south end of east wall of ball court

42.—Views of Chichen Itza 289

a) *Caracol* or astronomical observatory
b) The Sacred *Cenote* or Well of Sacrifice
43.—Turquoise Mosaic Disk 290
    a) Turquoise mosaic disk found in the Temple of the Chac
       Mool, inside the pyramid of the Temple of the Warriors
    b) Limestone box in which the disk was found
44.—Views of Chichen Itza 291
    a) The Castillo or principal temple
    b) Dance platform in front of the Castillo
45.—Paintings of Classic and Postclassic-Stage Cities, by Carlos
    Vierra 292
    a) Palenque (Classic Stage)
    b) Chichen Itza (Postclassic Stage)
    c) Uxmal (Late Classic Stage)
46.—Views of Uxmal 295
    a) The Nunnery Quadrangle, looking north
    b) South wing of the Nunnery Quadrangle; Palace of the
       Governor in the background
47.—Views of Uxmal 296
    a) East wing of the Nunnery Quadrangle
    b) West wing of the Nunnery Quadrangle
48.—House of the Magician, Uxmal 297
49.—Map of the Central Section of Uxmal 298
50.—Drawing of a Wall Painting in Structure B-XIII, Uaxactun 301
51.—Views of Uxmal, and Altar from Tikal 302
52.—Restorations of Classic-Stage Cities 303
    a) General view of Piedras Negras
    b) Model of Temples II, III, IV, at Tikal
53.—Stela 10 (Front), Seibal, Peten 304
54.—Sculptures of the Classic Stage 305
    a) Stela 12 (T-26), Tonina, Chiapas
    b) Stela E, Quirigua, Guatemala
    c) Stela 40, Piedras Negras, Guatemala, showing the corn
       god
55.—Stone Causeway Connecting Coba, Quintana Roo, and Yax-
    una, Yucatan 311
    a) Side of causeway at highest point
    b) Stone roller, found on top of the causeway

56.—Views of Kabah, Yucatan 312
   a) Palace of the Masks, the principal building
   b) The arch

57.—Maya Thatch and Sapling House 313
   a) Maya house, Hacienda Tanlum, Yucatan
   b) Reproduction of Maya house in stone as façade decoration. South wing of the Nunnery Quadrangle, Uxmal

58.—Stucco Masks, Pyramid E-VII-sub, Uaxactun 314
   a) Human type   *b*) Serpentine type

59.—Classic-Stage Façades 325
   a) The Labyrinth (Structure 19), Yaxchilan, Chiapas
   b) Temple of the Five Stories (Structure 10), Tikal

60.—Late Classic-Stage Façades, Puuc Period 326
   a) Corner mask panel from the House of the Magician, Uxmal
   b) Mask panel at top of west stairway, House of the Magician, Uxmal
   c) The Church, Nunnery group, Chichen Itza

61.—Postclassic-Stage Façades, Mexican Period 327
   a) Tzompantli, or Place of the Skulls, Chichen Itza
   b) Colonnade, interior of the Market, Chichen Itza

62.—Making a Limekiln at Chichen Itza 328
   a) Before burning
   b) After burning

63.—Monuments of the Early Period of the Classic Stage 335
   a) Stela 4, Tikal
   b) Stela 26, Uaxactun
   c) Stela 5, Uaxactun
   d) Stela 2, Tikal

64.—Four Steps in the Making of a Maya Monument, after the Original Drawings by Jean Charlot 336

65.—Four Steps in the Making of a Maya Monument, after the Original Drawings by Jean Charlot 337

66.—Four Sculptures with Identical Designs, Executed Over a Period of 153 Years at Piedras Negras 338
   a) Stela 25, erected A.D. 608
   b) Stela 6, erected A.D. 687
   c) Stela 11, erected A.D. 731
   d) Stela 14, erected A.D. 761

67.—Sculptures of the Early and Late Periods of the Classic Stage   341
   a) Stela 27, Yaxchilan, erected A.D. 514
   b) Stela 25, Naranjo, Guatemala, erected A.D. 615
   c) Stela 21, Naachtun, Guatemala, erected A.D. 687
   d) Stela P, Copan, erected A.D. 623

68.—Sculptures of the Classic Stage   342
   a) Stela H, Copan, erected A.D. 782
   b) Stela A, Copan, erected A.D. 731

69.—Wall Panel No. 3, Temple O-13, Piedras Negras   343
   a) Wall Panel, as found
   b) Pen-and-ink restoration by M. Louise Baker

70.—Throne and Model of a Temple   344
   a) Throne in Palace J6, Piedras Negras
   b) Model of Temple IV, Tikal

71.—Sculptured Lintels, Yaxchilan   353
   a) Lintel 25, from Structure 23
   b) Lintel 24, from Structure 23

72.—Sculptures of the Classic Stage   354
   a) Stela F, Quirigua
   b) Stela D, Quirigua
   c) Zoömorph P, Quirigua

73.—Sculptures of the Postclassic Stage at Chichen Itza, and at
   Uxmal   355
   a) Chac Mool
   b) Anthropomorphic support for a banner
   c) Red Jaguar Throne
   d) Atlantean figure altar support
   e) Support for a banner
   f) Altar in the so-called cemetery

74.—Sculptures of the Postclassic Stage at Chichen Itza and Uxmal   356
   a) Seated figure, Northwest Colonnade, Chichen Itza
   b) Same figure, profile
   c) Head emerging from the mouth of a serpent, House of
      the Magician, Uxmal
   d) Same head, profile

75.—Sculptures of the Postclassic Stage   357
   a) Door jamb, Structure 2C6, Kabah, Yucatan
   b) Door jamb, Structure 2C6, Kabah

c) Door jamb, Structure 2, Xculoc, Campeche
d) Door jamb, Structure 2, Xculoc

76.—Quarrying Operations (Classic Stage) 358
    a) Quarry stumps on base of Stela J, Quirigua
    b) Two partially quarried shafts, Calakmul, Campeche

77.—Stuccowork from Palenque 359
    (*a*) and (*b*) House D of the Palace Group, west façade

78.—Stuccowork from Comalcalco, Tabasco 360
    a) Figures on wall of tomb as restored
    b) Figures on wall of same tomb as found

79.—Stuccowork from Acanceh, Yucatan 361
    a) Figure of squirrel
    b) Figures of bat, eagle (?), jaguar (?), and serpent

80.—Uaxactun Ceramics, Mamom Phase 362
    a) Archaic clay head, "black dirt" stratum
    b) Another example of the same type
    c) Archaic female torso, "black dirt" stratum
    d) Other examples of the same type

81.—Clay Modeling from the Classic and Postclassic Stages among the Lacondon 363
    a) Effigy pipe, Temple of the Warriors, Chichen Itza
    b) Head from incense burner, Maypan
    c) Figurine made from an ancient mold, found near the Rio Chixoy, Chiapas
    d) Modern Lacandon incense burner, Chiapas

82.—Clay Figurines from the Island of Jaina, Campeche 364

83.—Slateware, Puuc Period, from Northern Yucatan 376
    a) Excavated fragment, Uxmal
    b) Bowl from Dzan
    c) Jar, provenance unknown
    d) Engraved vase found near Ticul

84.—Plumbate Ware, Mexican Period, from Northern Yucatan 377

85.—Late Decadent Wares, Period of Disintegration 378
    a) Coarse red ware tripod bowls, northern Yucatan
    b) Incense burner found near Chichen Itza

86.—Spinning and Weaving among the Lacandon Maya, Chiapas 382

87.—The Temple of the Murals at Bonampak 389
    a) Doorways of Rooms 1, 2, and 3

b) Floor plan, showing thickness of walls and comparative size of dais and floor space

88.—Interior of Room 2, Temple of the Murals, Bonampak.... 390
    a) A view from the back, toward the entrance
    b) Upper mural of the front wall

89.—Sacrificial Figures from the Mural of Room 2 391

90.—Attendants in the Sacrificial Ceremony 392

91.—Classic-Stage Polychrome Vase Presenting an Initial Series Date, Uaxactun 394

92.—Classic-Stage Polychrome Vases from the Chixoy Valley, Guatemala 398
    a) The Chama vase
    b) The Ratinlinxul vase

93.—Polychrome Vases from the Classic Stage and from the Postclassic Stage 400
    a) The Nebaj vase, Chixoy Valley, Guatemala
    b) Vase from northern Yucatan

94.—Wall Painting of a Fishing Village from the Temple of the Warriors, Chichen Itza 402

95.—Carved Jades (Classic Stage) 407
    a) Early Period pendant, Copan
    b) Pendant, Kaminaljuyu
    c) Pendant of Piedras Negras style
    d) Profile view
    e) Pendant, Piedras Negras
    f) Profile view

96.—Carved Jades (Classic Stage) 408
    a) Plaque showing Maya ruler
    b) Statuette from Temple A-XVIII, Uaxactun
    c) Profile

97.—Carved Jades (Postclassic Stage) 409
    a) Carved head and necklace from cache lying on the Red Jaguar Throne, Chichen Itza
    b) Head from cache under Castillo Stairway, Chichen Itza
    c) Figure from same cache

98.—Objects from the Ruz Tomb, Palenque 411
    a) Jade figurine

b) Stucco mask

c) Stucco mask of Classic-type profile

99.—Sarcophagus Found in the Ruz Tomb, Palenque   412
    a) The interior
    b) Detail of relief on the outer surface

100.—Interior of the Crypt, Temple of the Inscription, Palenque   413
    a) Entry
    b) Stucco figures on wall
    c) View toward entry steps
    d) View from steps

101.—Postclassic-Stage Goldwork. Well of Sacrifice, Chichen Itza   417
    a) Pendant
    b) Bell
    c) Three portions of mask

102.—Eccentric Chipped Flints (Classic Stage)   421
    a) Chipped flint from El Palmar, Campeche, like one held
        by figure on vase from Uaxactun
    b) Chipped flints from El Palmar
    c) Flint blades, Quirigua
    d) Flint ornament from a ceremonial staff, El Palmar
    e) Flint ornament from a ceremonial staff, Quirigua